PARENTING IS

TAILS FROM THE LITTERBOX

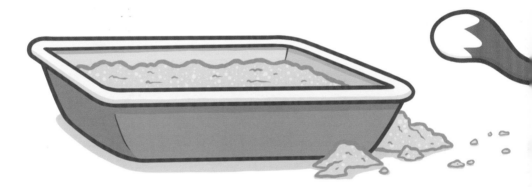

chesca Hause

Andrews McMeel
PUBLISHING®

TO MY MUSES, VICTOR, CASPER & J.
I COULD NEVER BE THIS FUNNY WITHOUT YOU ALL.

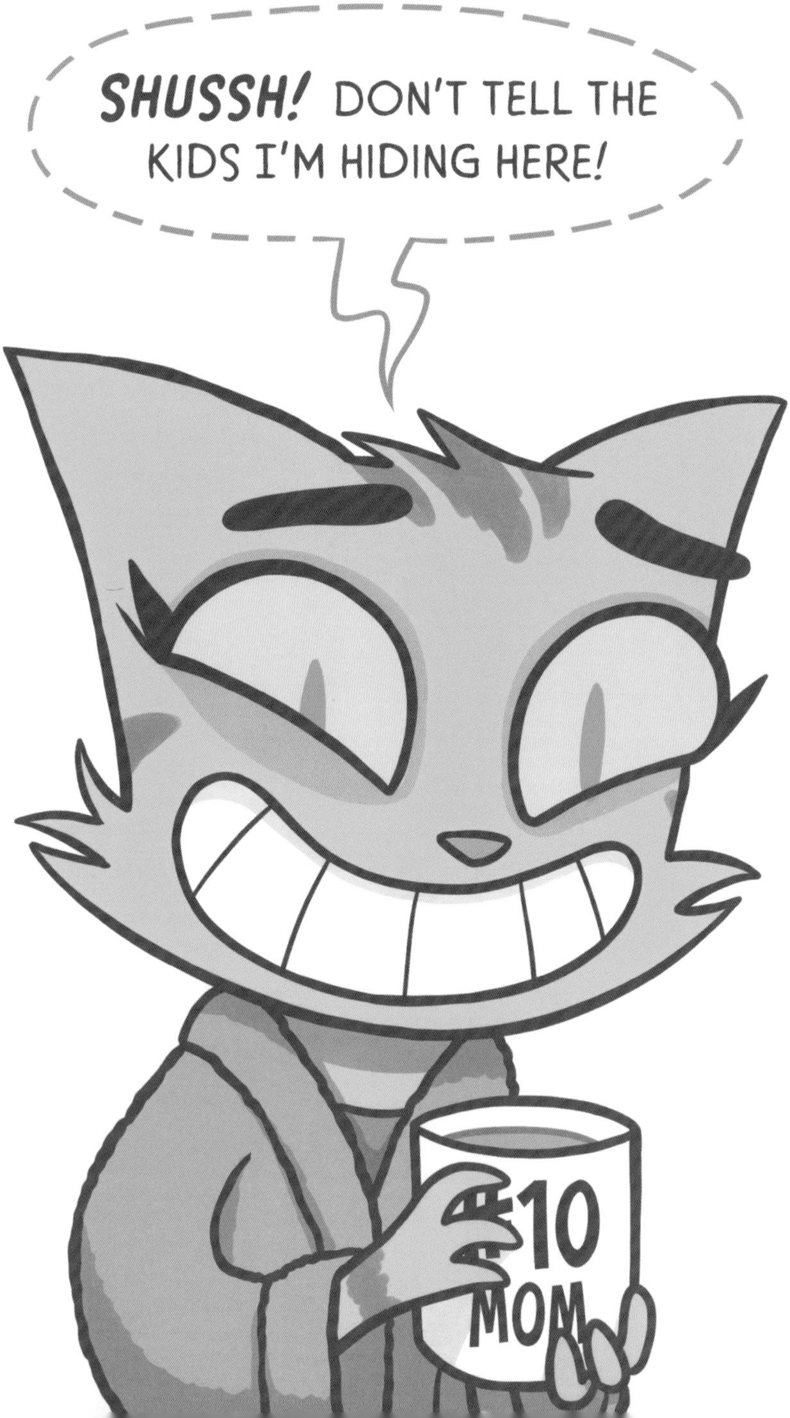
SHUSSH! DON'T TELL THE KIDS I'M HIDING HERE!
#10 MOM

CHAPTERS

INTRODUCTION

EVER SINCE I WAS LITTLE, I HAVE LOVED TO DRAW CARTOON ANIMALS. I'M NOT SURE WHY I AVOIDED HUMANS. PERHAPS I FOUND THEIR HAIR AND NOSES TOO HARD TO ILLUSTRATE, OR MAYBE THE COLORS AND SHAPES OF ANIMALS WERE JUST MORE FUN? FOR WHATEVER REASON, TALKING CARTOON ANIMALS HAVE ALWAYS BEEN A BIG DEAL IN MY LIFE.

THAT FIRST STEP INTO MOTHERHOOD WAS A DOOZY FOR ME, AND I WANTED TO USE MY ART TO CHEER UP OTHER MOMS OUT THERE WHO COULD BE STRUGGLING TOO. IT WASN'T UNTIL MY SECOND SON WAS ONE THAT I HAD MY EUREKA MOMENT.

WE WERE WATCHING *DANIEL TIGER'S NEIGHBORHOOD* FOR THE UMPTEENTH TIME. I FOUND MYSELF DAYDREAMING THAT MAYBE *THIS* TIME THINGS MIGHT NOT GO SO PERFECTLY FOR THE TIGER FAMILY—DANIEL MIGHT FLIP OUT AND POOP HIMSELF ON TROLLEY, OR MOM TIGER MIGHT DROP AN F-BOMB IN FRONT OF KING FRIDAY. I WANTED TO SEE *THAT* SHOW! THAT'S WHEN IT HIT ME. I COULDN'T MAKE A SHOW, BUT I COULD MAKE A COMIC STRIP! I BURST IN ON MY HUSBAND IN THE BATH AND ANNOUNCED, "I'M GOING TO MAKE A *DANIEL TIGER* PARODY COMIC!"

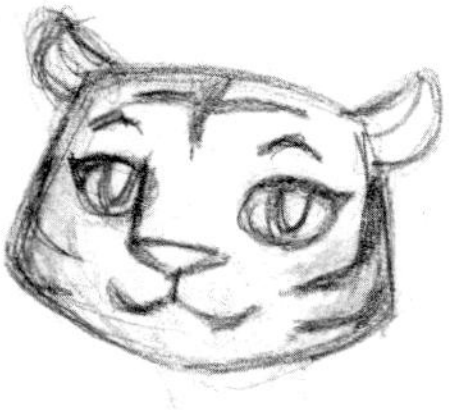 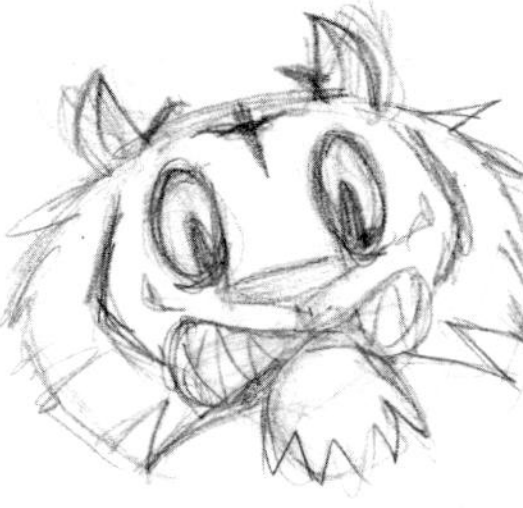 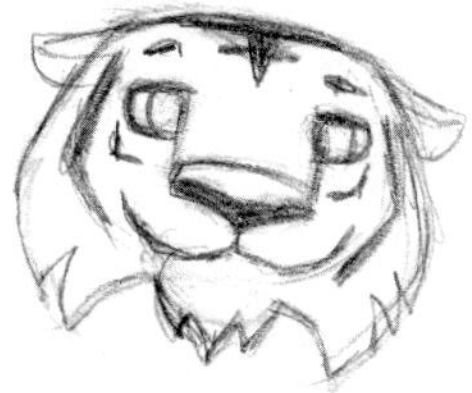

I SPENT THE NEXT MONTH FIGURING OUT THE CHARACTERS AND THE FIRST FEW STRIPS. I DESIGNED MY TIGER FAMILY, COMPLETE WITH BABY SISTER, TO PARODY THE SHOW. I SHOWED THE DESIGNS TO MY HUSBAND J, AND HE GAVE ME TWO BRILLIANT PIECES OF ADVICE: "WRITE WHAT YOU KNOW" AND "CATS ARE MORE FUN THAN TIGERS." INSPIRED, I MOVED AWAY FROM THE PARODY CONCEPT AND TOWARD RECOUNTING OUR OWN FAMILY'S (MIS)ADVENTURES AS CATS!

LUCKILY FOR ME, I AM A HABITUAL NOTETAKER AND LIST MAKER, PARTICULARLY UNDER PRESSURE. I WROTE DOWN *EVERYTHING* MY KIDS DID—THE GOOD, THE BAD, AND THE BIZARRE! IT WAS THE MOST BASIC KIND OF WAR JOURNAL, BUT READING BACK THROUGH THE FEVER DREAM OF MOTHERHOOD BROUGHT ME SUCH AN ODD JOY THAT I KEPT IT GOING FOR FOUR YEARS. IT PROVED TO BE A GOLDMINE OF COMIC MATERIAL! ON MAY 9TH, 2018, I POSTED THE FIRST-EVER *LITTERBOX COMIC*, BASED ON A TREATISE ON CAR PENISES MY OLDEST HAD DELIVERED WHILE BRUSHING HIS TEETH A YEAR PRIOR.

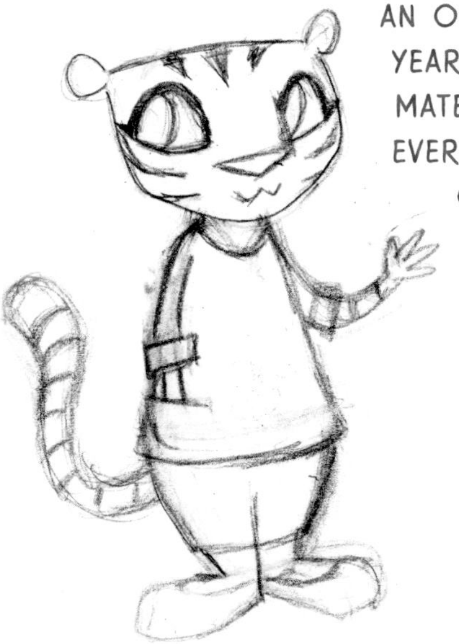

FRAN

ANIMAL: GINGER CAT

AGE: 38

STAR SIGN: PISCES

OCCUPATION: TECH SUPPORT CUSTOMER SERVICE (TELLING OLD PEOPLE TO TURN IT OFF AND ON AGAIN)

HOBBIES: SELF-PUBLISHING THE CULT SCI-FI HORROR SERIES *BLOOD GALAXY*, GAMING, COLLECTIBLES

LIKES: SUGAR, HORROR MOVIES, SEEING HER BOYS GETTING ALONG

DISLIKES: MESS, WEIRD FOOD

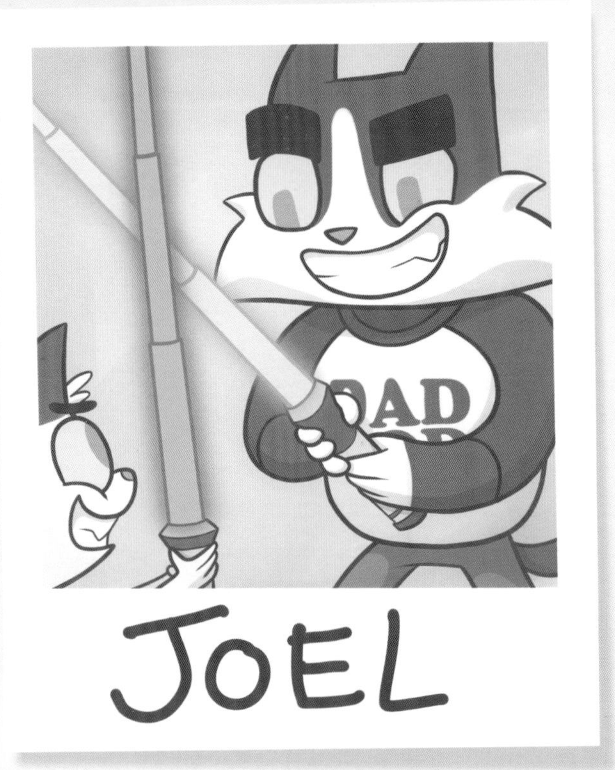
DAD
JOEL

ANIMAL: TUXEDO CAT

AGE: 36

STAR SIGN: GEMINI

OCCUPATION: INHERITED A SPACE IN A STRIP MALL, WHICH FUNCTIONS AS THE BASE FOR A ROTATING ASSORTMENT OF WHIMSICAL BUSINESS IDEAS

HOBBIES: PLAYS IN A COVER BAND WITH FRIENDS, GAMING, COLLECTIBLES, COOKING, A GROWING LIST OF CRAFT PROJECTS

LIKES: ROCK AND METAL, FANCY FOOD, WINDING UP THE KIDS WITH HIS DAD ANTICS

DISLIKES: FRAN BEING SAD, CHICKEN ON PIZZA

COOPER

ANIMAL: B&W CAT

AGE: 3

STAR SIGN: CAPRICORN

OCCUPATION: BEING ADORABLE

HOBBIES: CHASING MICE, CLIMBING TREES, EATING THINGS HE SHOULDN'T, ASKING WHEN CHRISTMAS IS

LIKES: BEING PICKED UP

DISLIKES: BEING PICKED UP

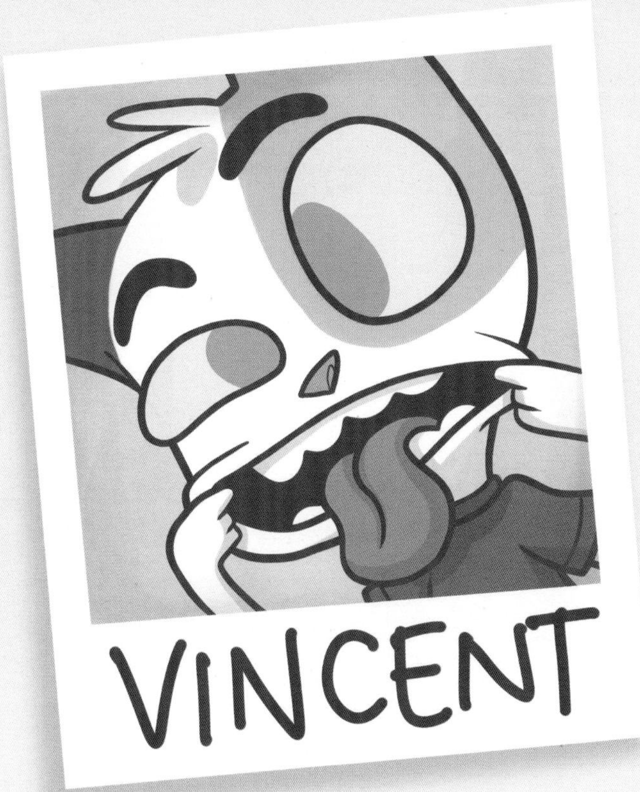
VINCENT

ANIMAL: CALICO CAT

AGE: 6

STAR SIGN: LEO

OCCUPATION: TROUBLE

HOBBIES: GAMING, DRAWING CREEPY THINGS, STARTING A PROJECT AND THEN RAGE-QUITTING

LIKES: MINECRAFT, MINECRAFT, MINECRAFT

DISLIKES: BOREDOM!

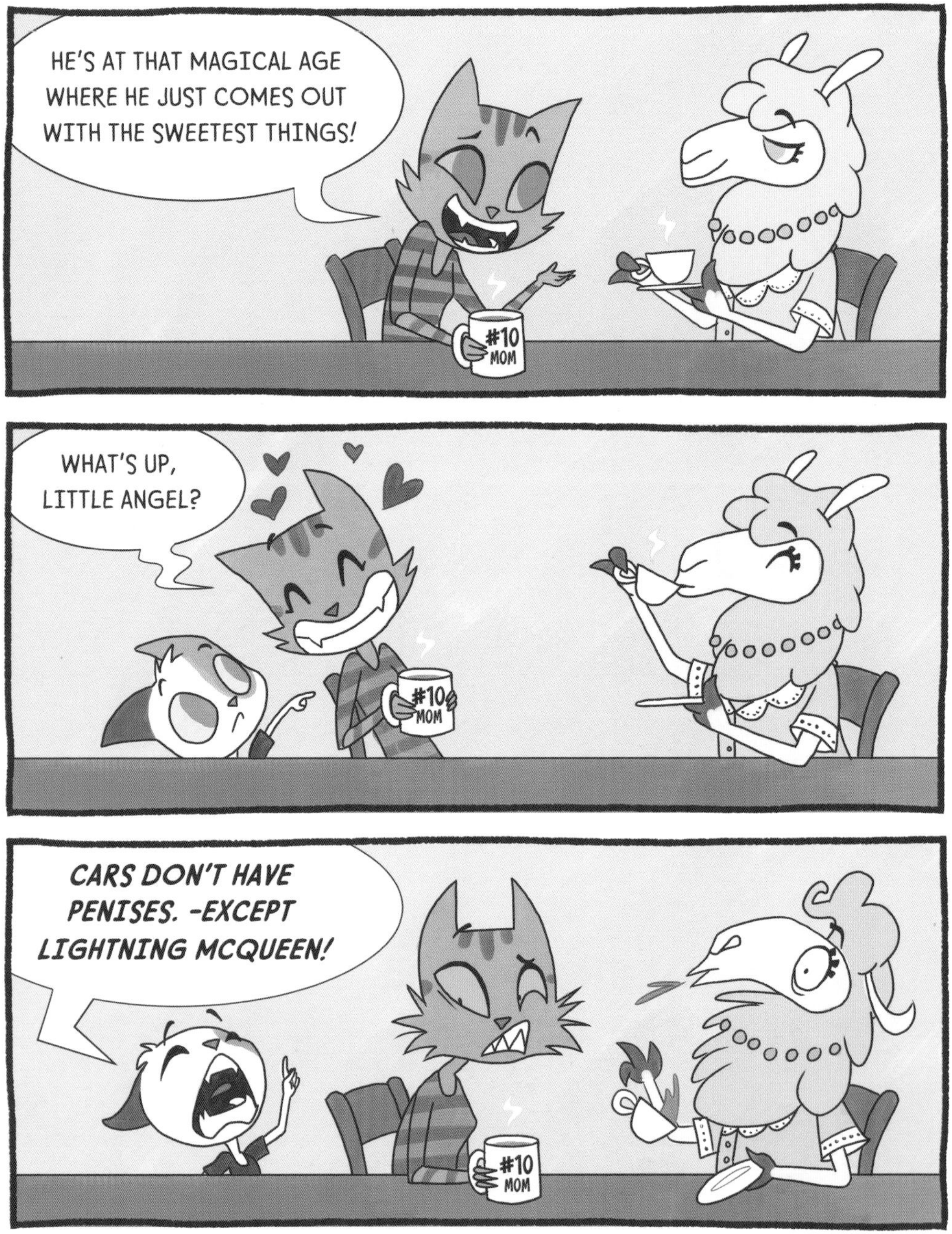
HE'S AT THAT MAGICAL AGE WHERE HE JUST COMES OUT WITH THE SWEETEST THINGS!
#10 MOM
WHAT'S UP, LITTLE ANGEL?
#10 MOM
CARS DON'T HAVE PENISES. -EXCEPT LIGHTNING MCQUEEN!
#10 MOM

FLIPPER INSTRUCTIONS

EVERY CHAPTER TITLE IS A...

Flipper!

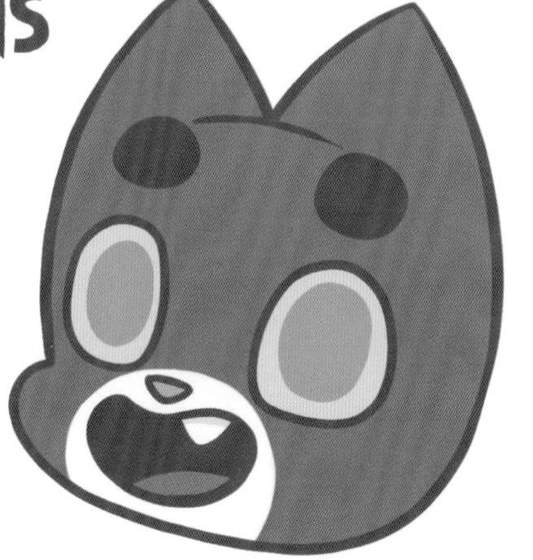

(NAMED BY MY YOUNGEST)

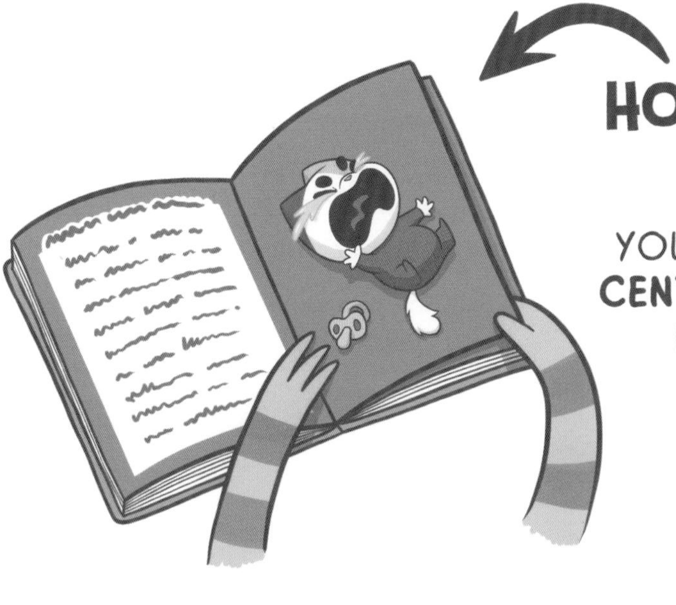

HOLD THE BOOK LIKE THIS!

YOUR **LEFT HAND** IN THE **CENTER** AND YOUR **RIGHT HAND** HOLDING A **SINGLE PAGE**.

KEEP THE BOOK **STEADY** WITH YOUR LEFT HAND AND **FLIP** BETWEEN THE TWO PAGES WITH YOUR RIGHT HAND UNTIL THEY

ANIMATE!

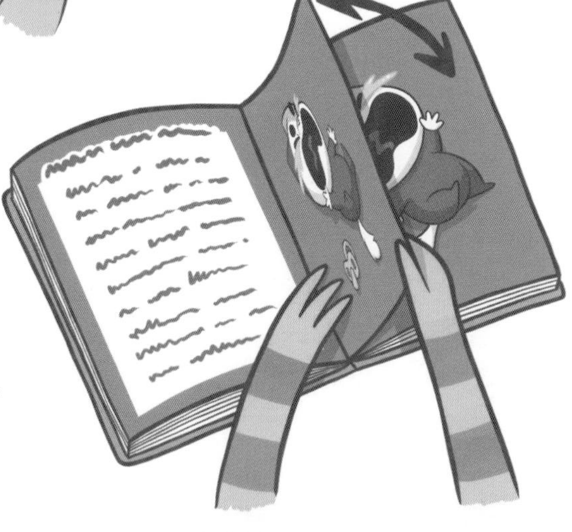

PARENTING LEVEL 1

I'VE NEVER BEEN A FAN OF BABIES. PETS? YES! ALL ABOUT PETS! BUT BABIES? I SPENT MOST OF MY LIFE AVOIDING THEM AS BEST I COULD. I'D PULL A FUNNY FACE AT ONE OCCASIONALLY, BUT THAT WAS THE EXTENT OF MY MATERNAL IMPULSES. IT WASN'T UNTIL I HIT 30 THAT I FELT AN URGE TO PLAY THE LIFE STAGE KNOWN AS "CHILDREN."

I WAS BASICALLY A BIG KID MYSELF. WE WOULD HAVE LOADS IN COMMON! BEFORE CHILDREN, THOUGH, COMES *BABIES.*

I THOUGHT WHEN I HELD MY SON FOR THE FIRST TIME, MY MOTHERING CIRCUITS (MOTHERBOARD?) WOULD SUDDENLY FIRE UP, BUT IT TURNS OUT IT DOESN'T ALWAYS WORK THAT WAY. I LOVED HIM, OF COURSE, BUT I DID NOT LOVE MY NEW LIFE. MY SON FELT THE SAME WAY. HE WAS NOT HAPPY ABOUT BEING A BABY AND HE MADE HIS DISAPPOINTMENTS ABOUT THE WORLD KNOWN—LOUDLY.

WHEN IT FELT LIKE THE COLIC WOULD NEVER END AND WE WOULD NEVER KNOW SLEEP AGAIN, MY HUSBAND STUCK A NOTE ABOVE THE CHANGING TABLE THAT READ: *WE'LL GET THROUGH THIS. THIS ISN'T HOW WE DIE.* SOMETIMES GALLOWS HUMOR IS ALL YOU'VE GOT. SOMETIMES IT'S ALL YOU NEED.

AND, FOR THE RECORD, HE WAS RIGHT!

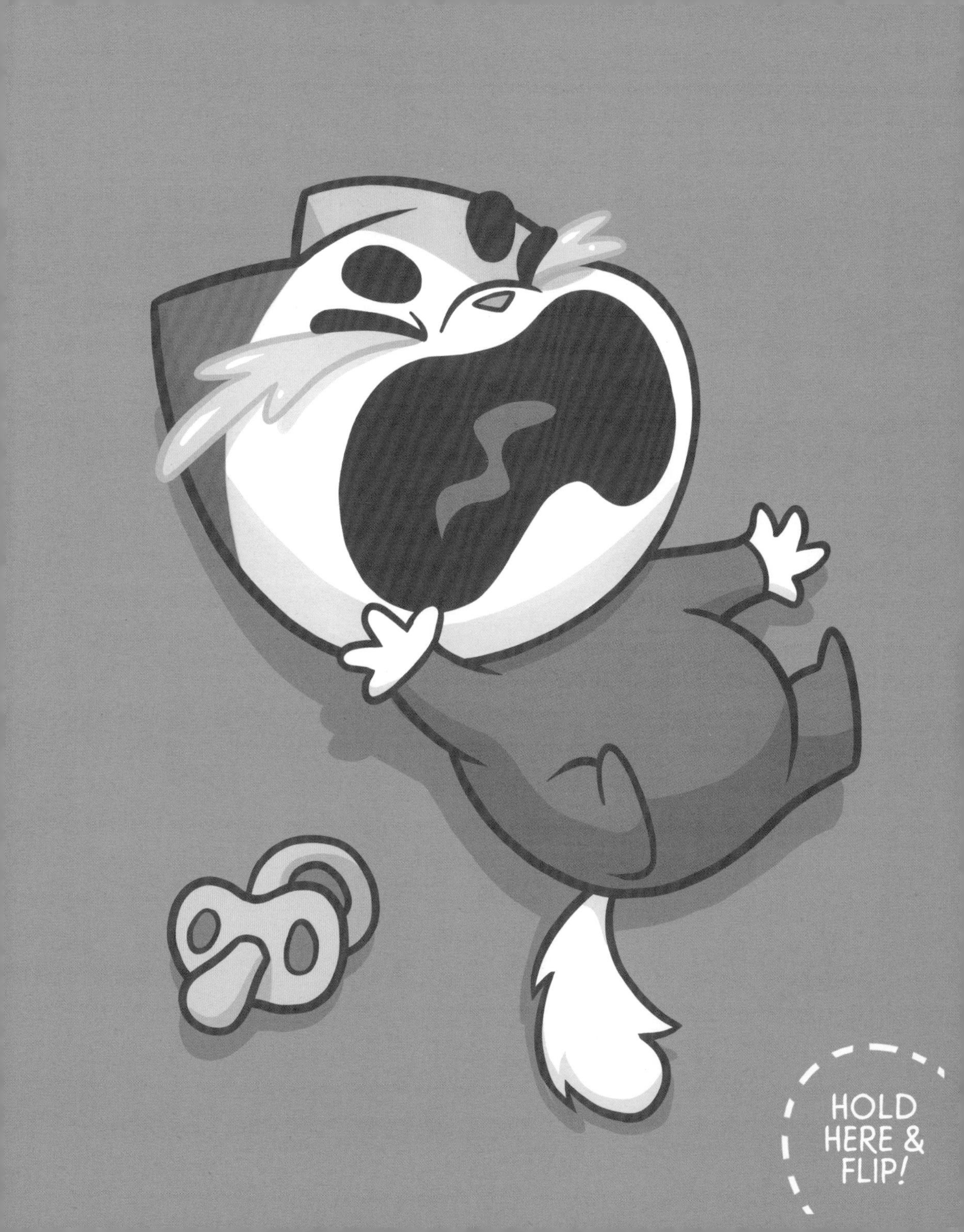
HOLD
HERE &
FLIP!

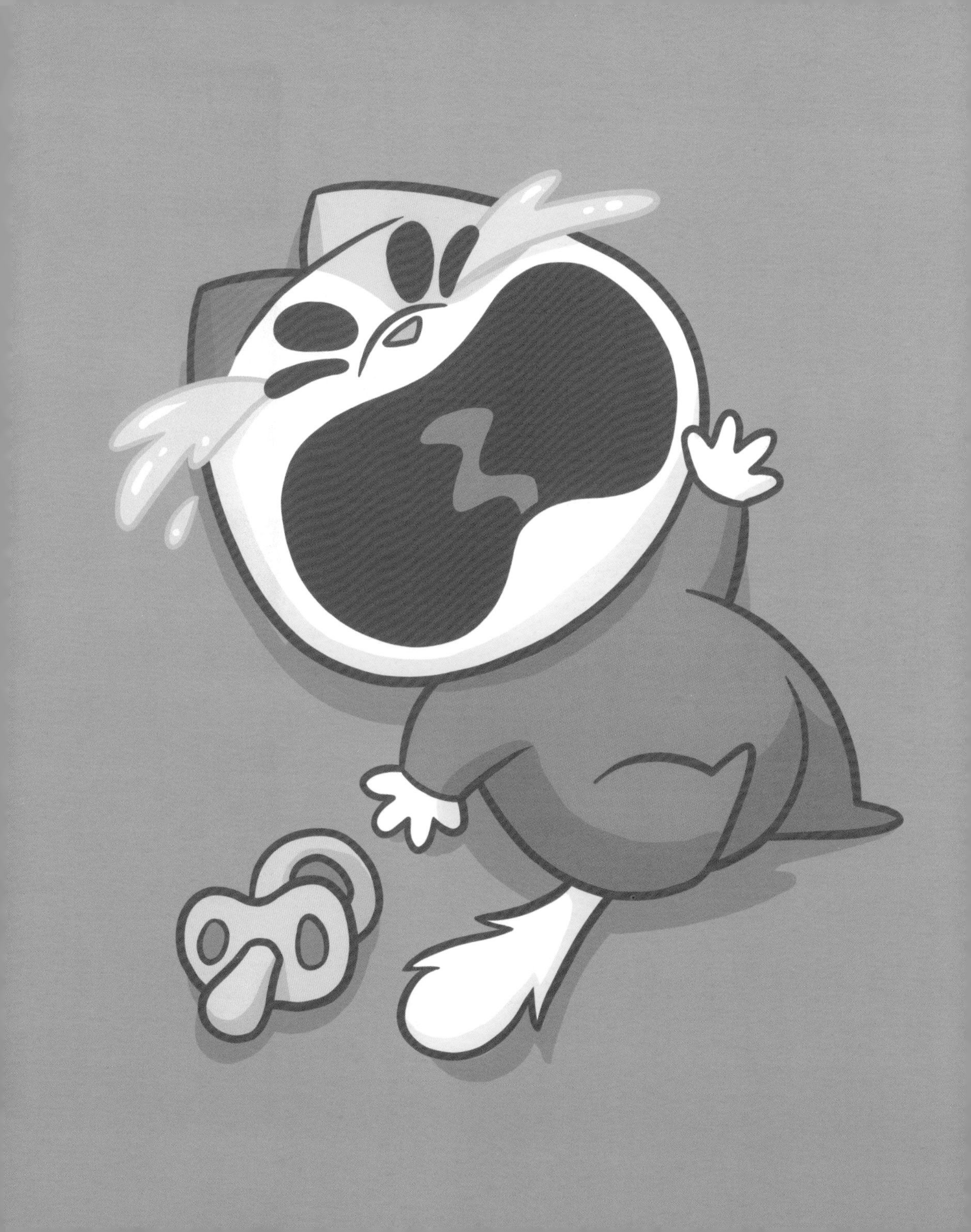

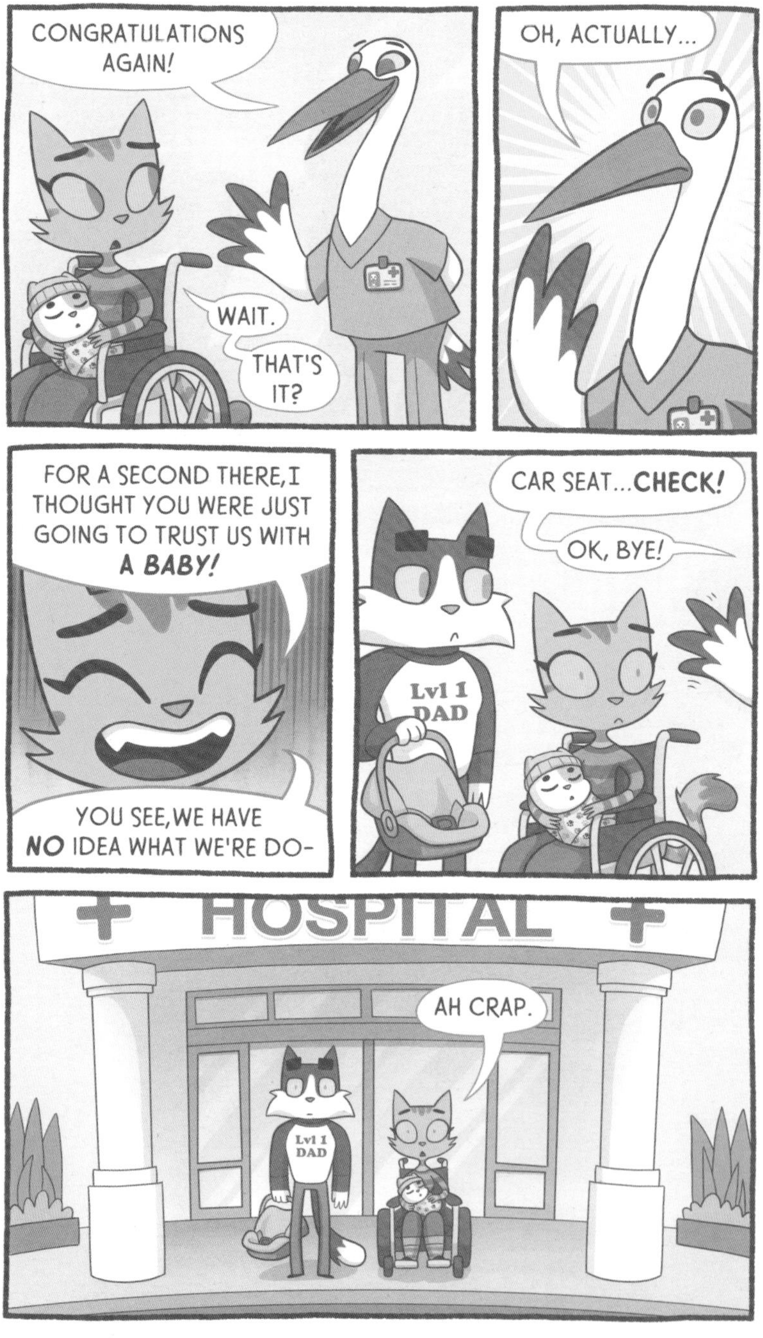
CONGRATULATIONS AGAIN!
WAIT.
THAT'S IT?
OH, ACTUALLY...
FOR A SECOND THERE, I THOUGHT YOU WERE JUST GOING TO TRUST US WITH A BABY!
YOU SEE, WE HAVE NO IDEA WHAT WE'RE DO-
CAR SEAT...CHECK!
OK, BYE!
Lvl 1 DAD
HOSPITAL
AH CRAP.
Lvl 1 DAD

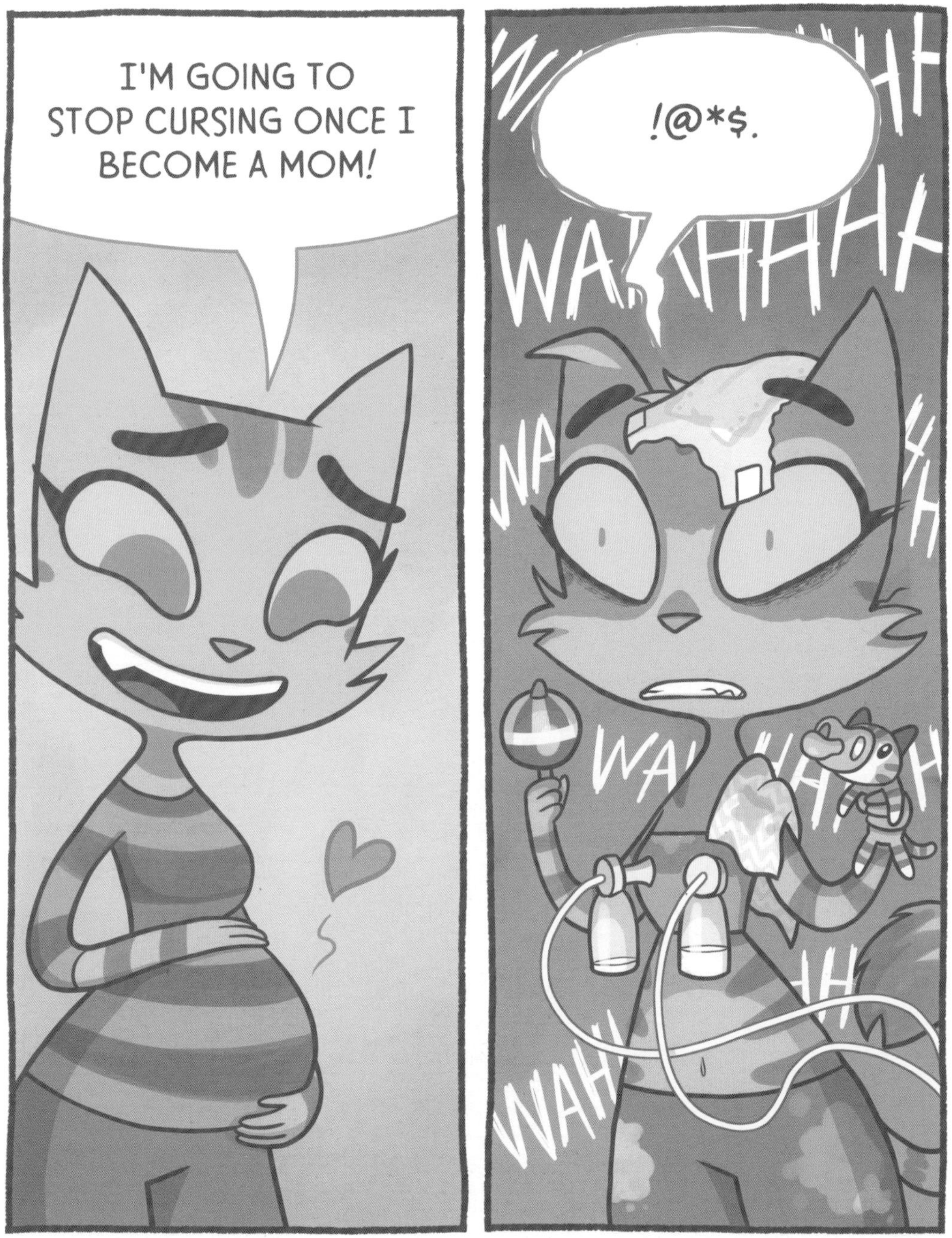
I'M GOING TO STOP CURSING ONCE I BECOME A MOM!
!@*$.
WAHHHHH
WA
WAH
WAH

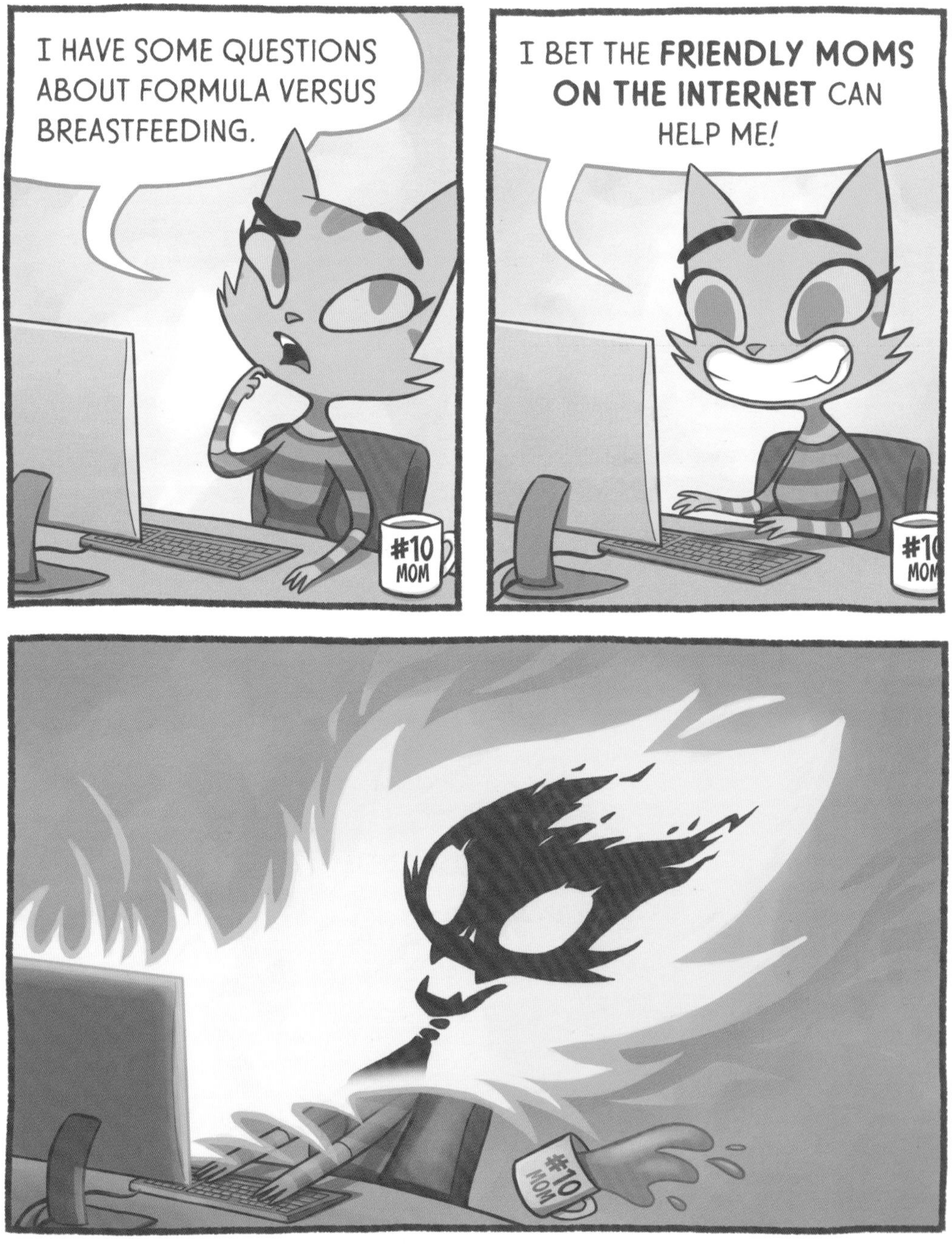
I HAVE SOME QUESTIONS ABOUT FORMULA VERSUS BREASTFEEDING.
#10 MOM
I BET THE **FRIENDLY MOMS ON THE INTERNET** CAN HELP ME!
#10 MOM
#10 MOM

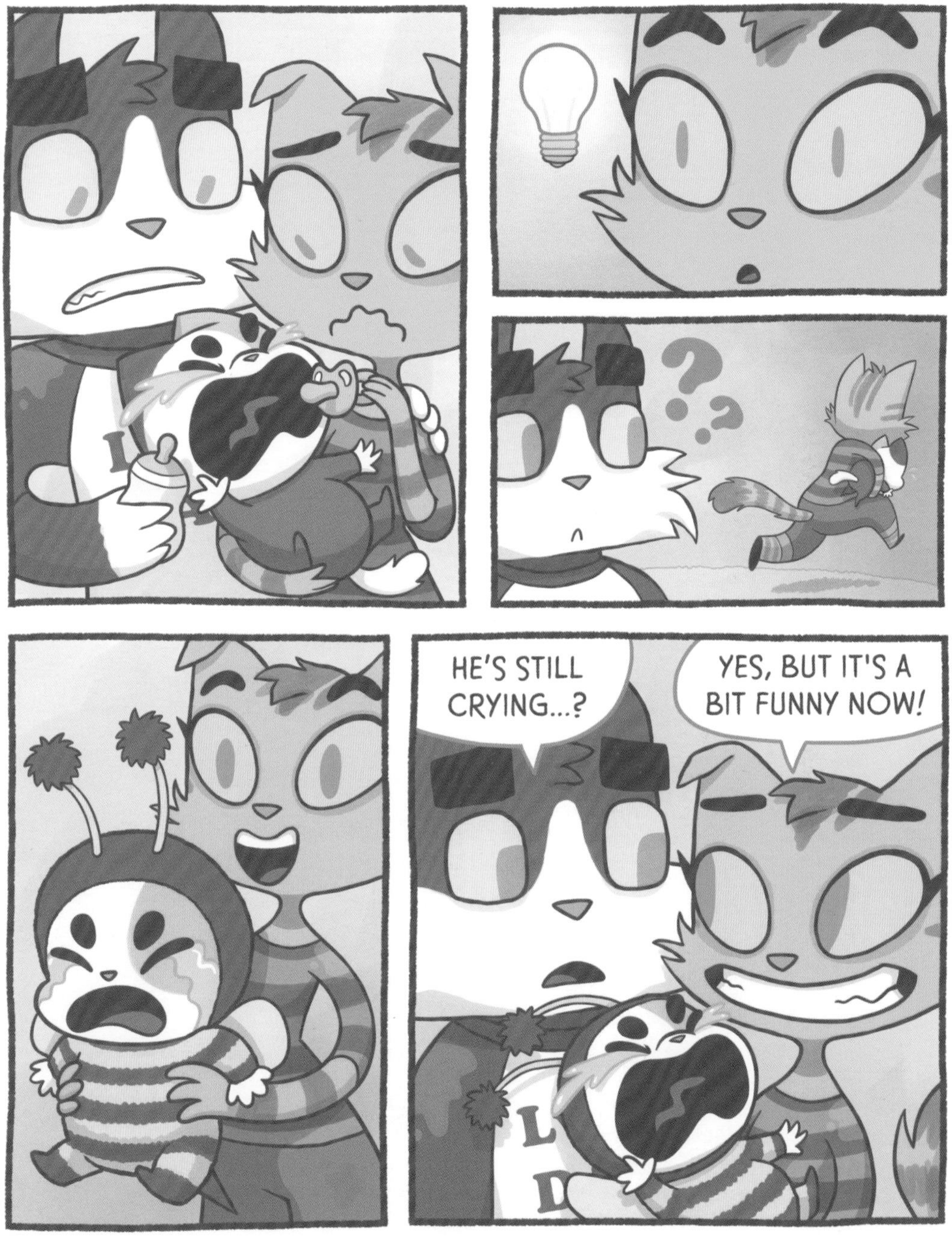
HE'S STILL CRYING...?
YES, BUT IT'S A BIT FUNNY NOW!

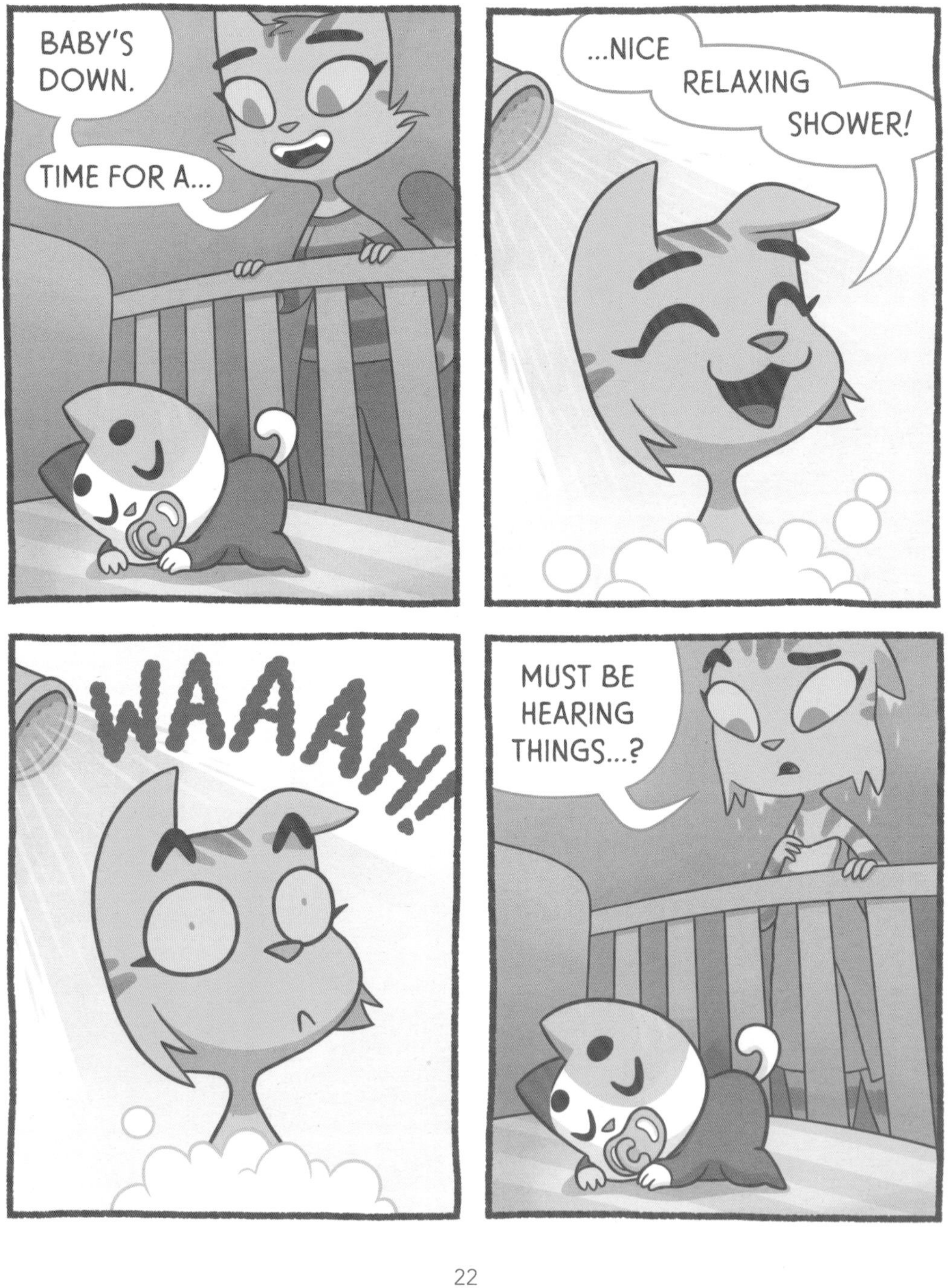
BABY'S DOWN.
TIME FOR A...
...NICE RELAXING SHOWER!
WAAAH!!
MUST BE HEARING THINGS...?

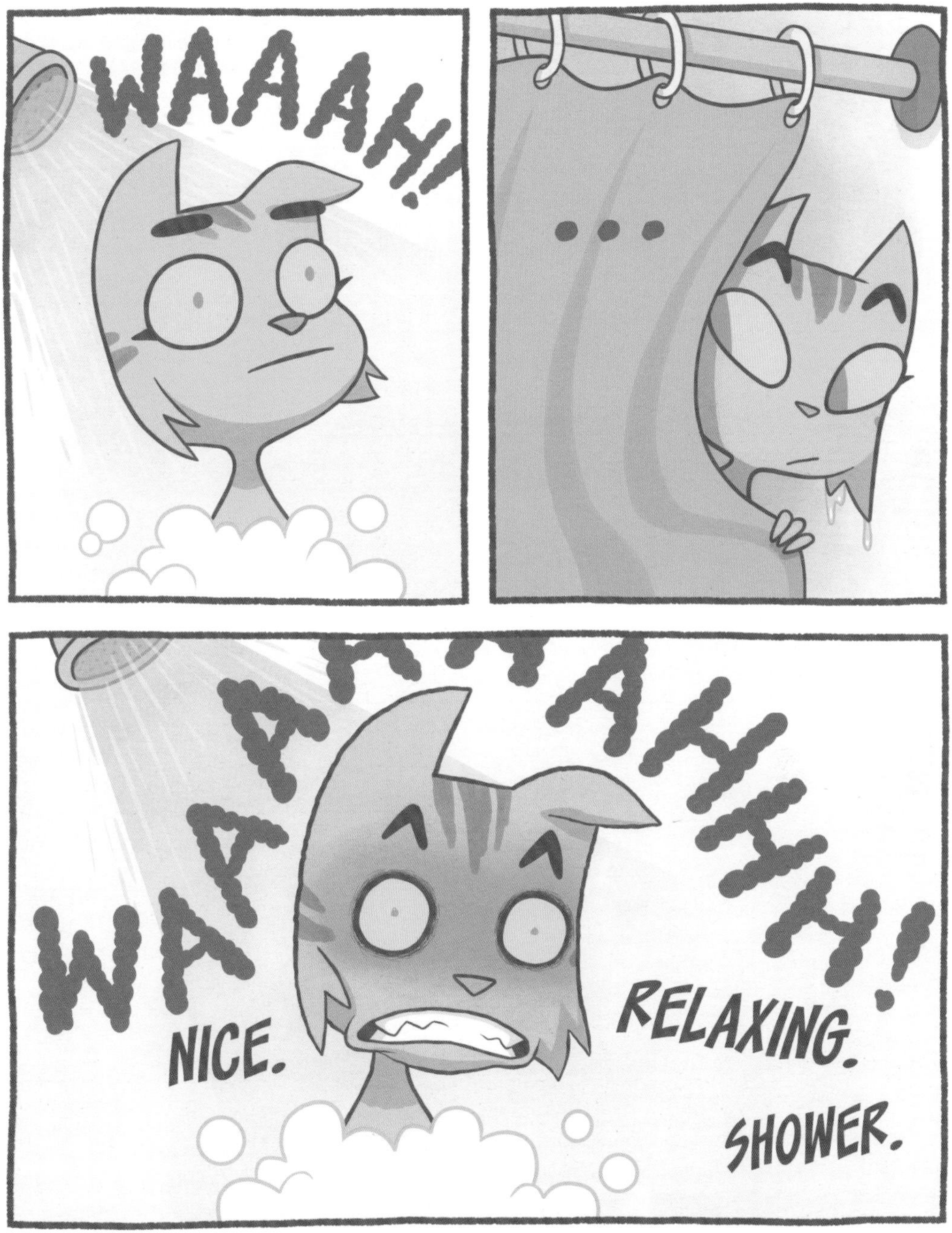
WAAAH!!
...
WAAAAAAHHHH!
NICE.
RELAXING.
SHOWER.

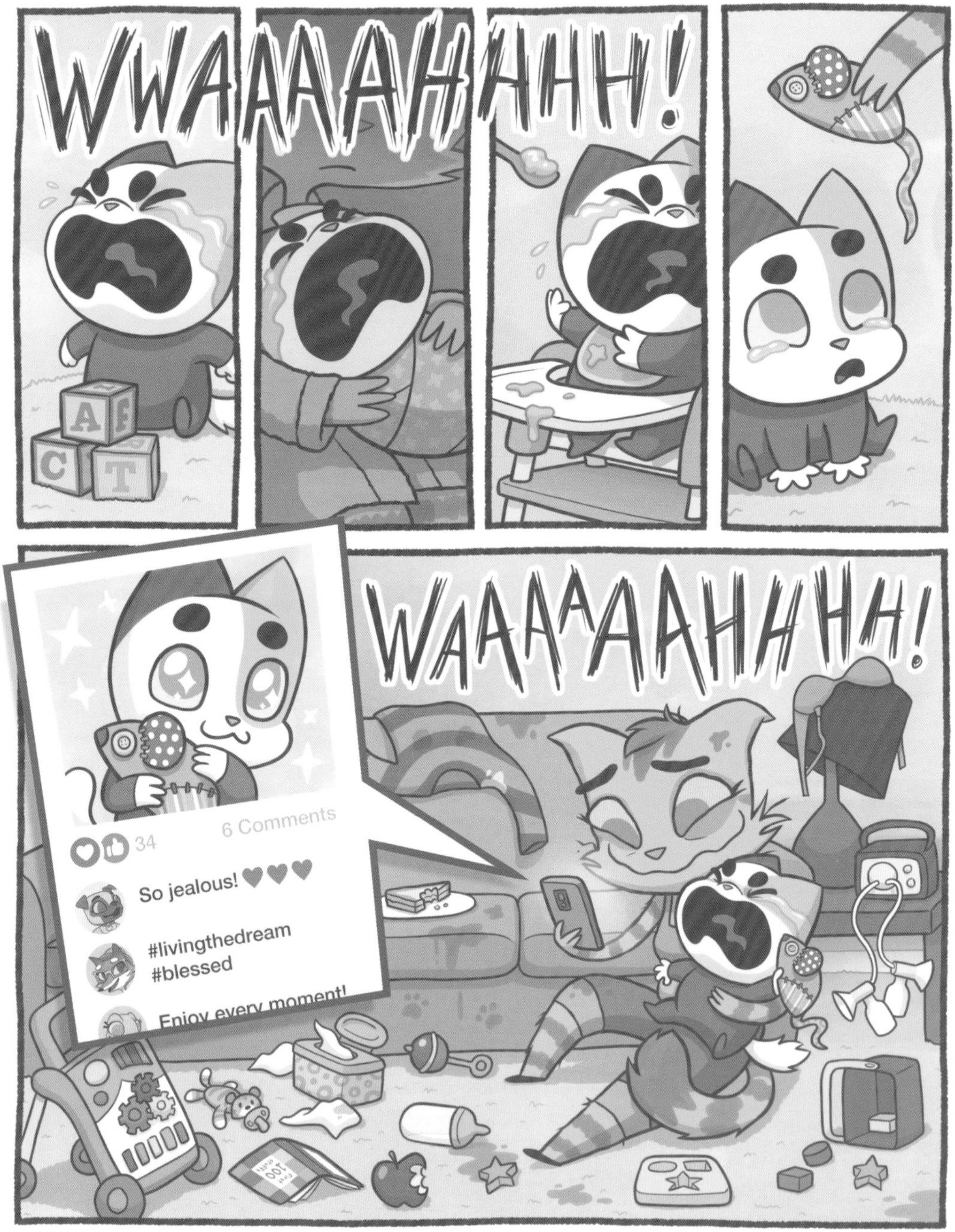
WWAAAAHHHH!
6 Comments
34
So jealous!
#livingthedream
#blessed
Enjoy every moment!
WAAAAAHHHH!

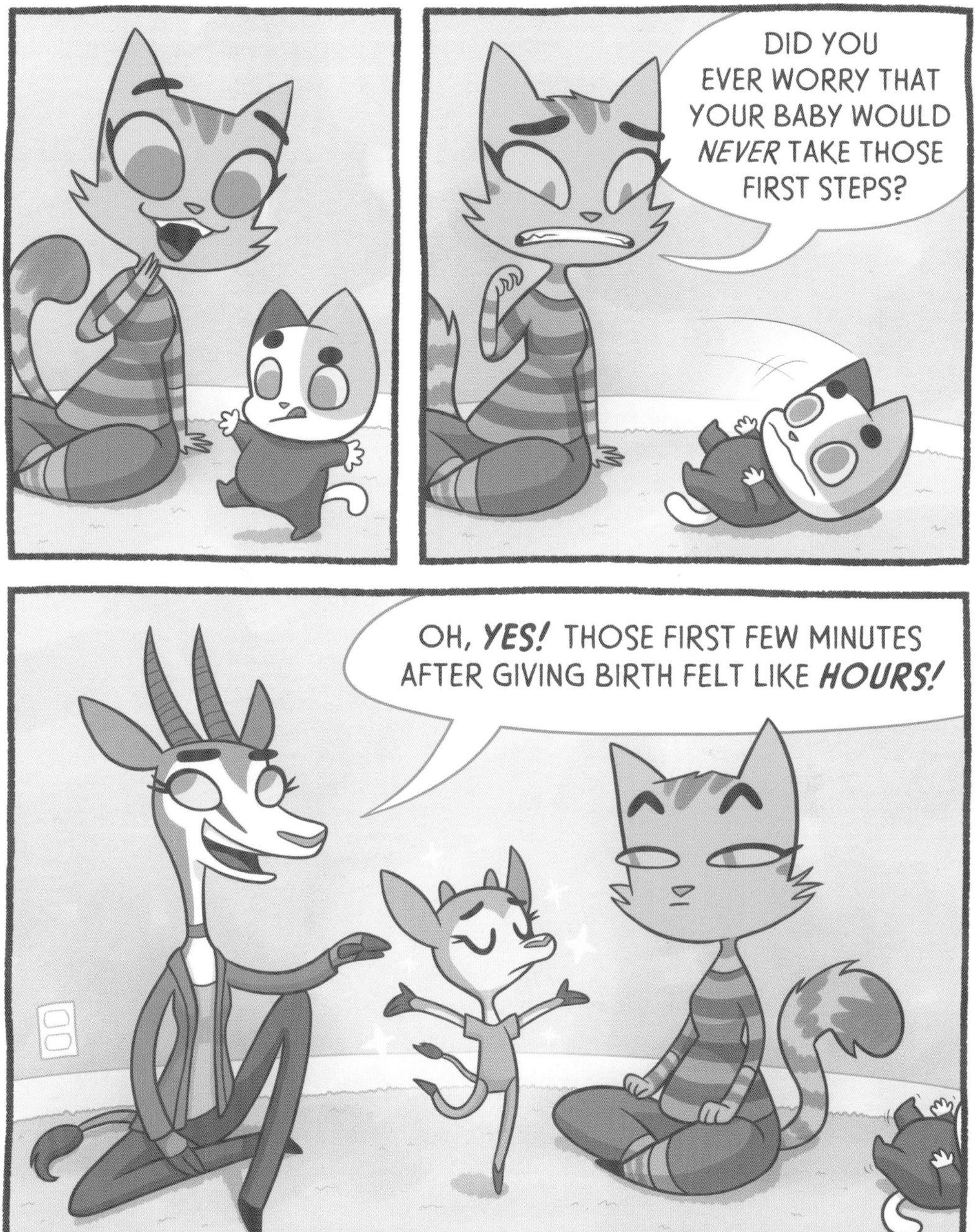
DID YOU EVER WORRY THAT YOUR BABY WOULD *NEVER* TAKE THOSE FIRST STEPS?
OH, ***YES!*** THOSE FIRST FEW MINUTES AFTER GIVING BIRTH FELT LIKE ***HOURS!***

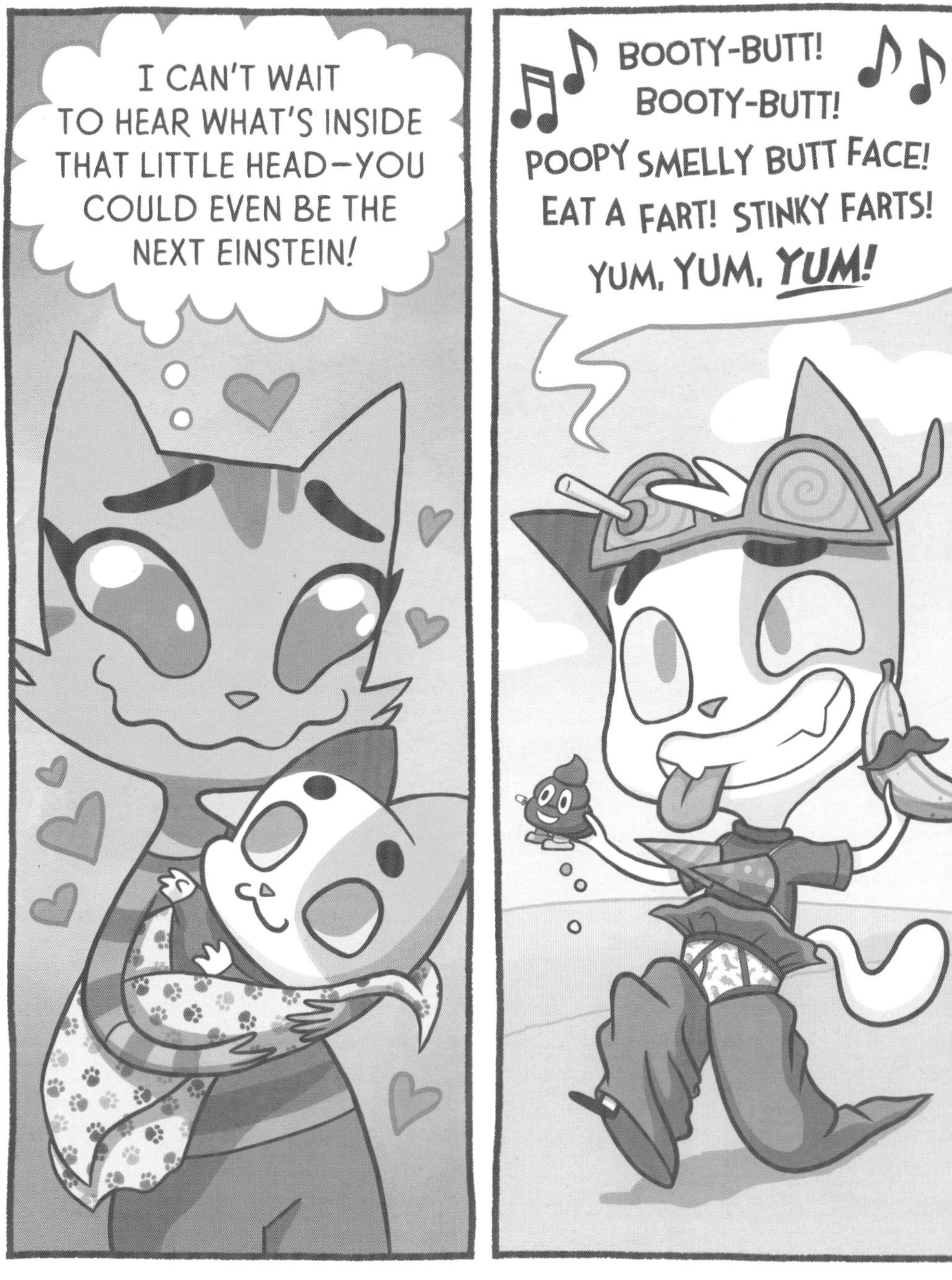
I CAN'T WAIT TO HEAR WHAT'S INSIDE THAT LITTLE HEAD—YOU COULD EVEN BE THE NEXT EINSTEIN!
BOOTY-BUTT! BOOTY-BUTT! POOPY SMELLY BUTT FACE! EAT A FART! STINKY FARTS! YUM, YUM, YUM!

BABY BINGO

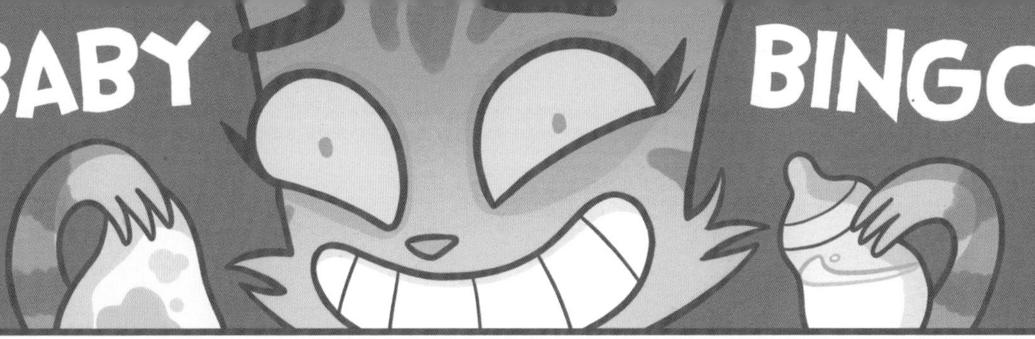

BLOW OUT	UGLY-CRIED AT SOMETHING SAPPY	SURVIVED A SLEEP REGRESSION	BECAME OVERLY INVESTED IN KIDS TV SHOW	GOT STUCK UNDER SLEEPING BABY AND SERIOUSLY CONSIDERED PEEING YOURSELF
GRINNED AT JUDGY STRANGER	CRAWLED OUT OF SLEEPING BABY'S ROOM	IMPRESSED BY POOP	CHANGED FROM DAY PJ'S TO NIGHT PJ'S	FORGOT HOW TO WORD REAL GOOD
MEMORIZED ALL BABY BOOKS	HEARD PHANTOM CRIES	**FREE SPACE** (THAT SOUNDS NICE)	DID SOMETHING YOU SWORE YOU'D NEVER DO AS A PARENT	IS IT AM OR PM?!
DREW EYEBROWS ON BABY	TOOK A MONTHLY PHOTO A MONTH LATE	DISCOVERED ORIGIN OF "THE SMELL"	PEED, POOPED, AND PUKED ON -GOTTA CATCH 'EM ALL!	SMELT YOURSELF TO FIGURE OUT WHEN YOU SHOWERED
UNDERSTOOD WHY SOME ANIMALS EAT THEIR YOUNG	BATH POOP	GOOGLED ALL THE THINGS!	REHEATED COFFEE +2 TIMES	BOUGHT GADGET THAT WILL SOLVE EVERYTHING!

#10 MOM

I SPENT A LOT OF MY FIRST PREGNANCY IN THE BATH, NODDING ALONG TO POSITIVE PARENTING BOOKS. I WAS GOING TO BE A *COOL* MOM, YOU SEE. WELL, IT'S LIKE MIKE TYSON SAYS, "EVERYBODY'S GOT A PLAN UNTIL THEY TAKE A DIAPER TO THE FACE." . . . I'M PARAPHRASING A LITTLE.

OUR OLDEST WAS WHAT PEOPLE GENEROUSLY CALL "SPIRITED." HE HAD HIS OWN IDEAS ABOUT HOW THE WORLD SHOULD WORK, AND MY ASPIRATIONS OF BEING A CHILLED-OUT MOM WERE ALMOST IMMEDIATELY "YEETED," AS THE KIDS SAY. MY NEW PARENTING STYLE IS BEST DESCRIBED AS THAT MEME OF THE LADY WITH EQUATIONS ALL AROUND HER HEAD: PART ACTUARY, PART HOSTAGE NEGOTIATOR. DO I LET THEM HAVE CANDY, OR WILL IT ROT ALL THEIR TEETH OUT? DOES IT MATTER, IF THEY'RE GETTING NEW TEETH ANYWAY? DO I INTERVENE, OR DO I LET HIM TOUCH THE STOVE AND LEARN A VALUABLE LESSON? HOW MUCH BURN OINTMENT IS TOO MUCH BURN OINTMENT? WHAT HAPPENS IF THEY EAT THE BURN OINTMENT? WHAT IS THE NUMBER FOR POISON CONTROL?

THE QUESTIONS ARE ENDLESS AND OFTEN HAVE NO CORRECT ANSWER. AS OVERWHELMING AS IT CAN BE, IT IS PRETTY GOOD COMIC MATERIAL . . .

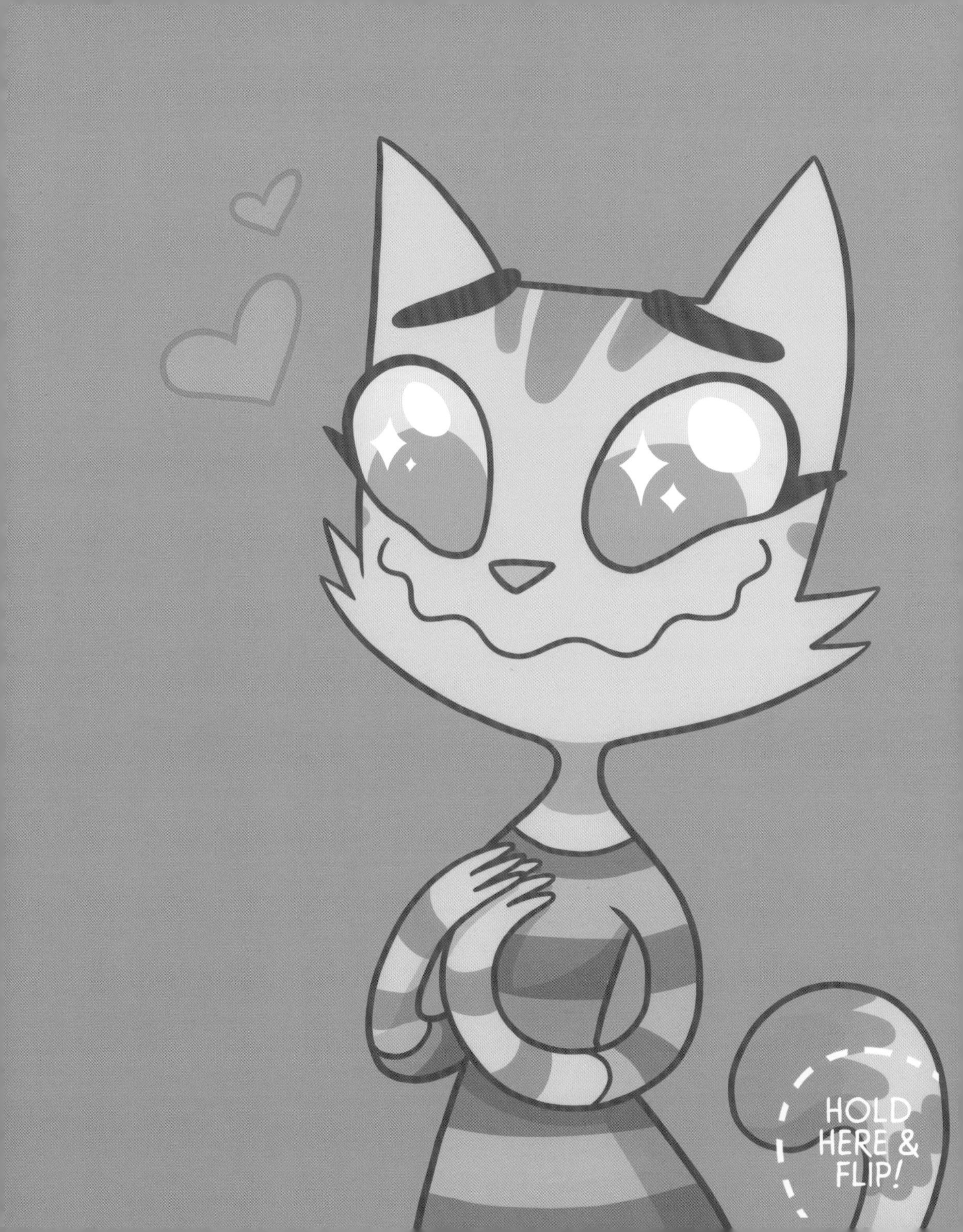
HOLD
HERE &
FLIP!

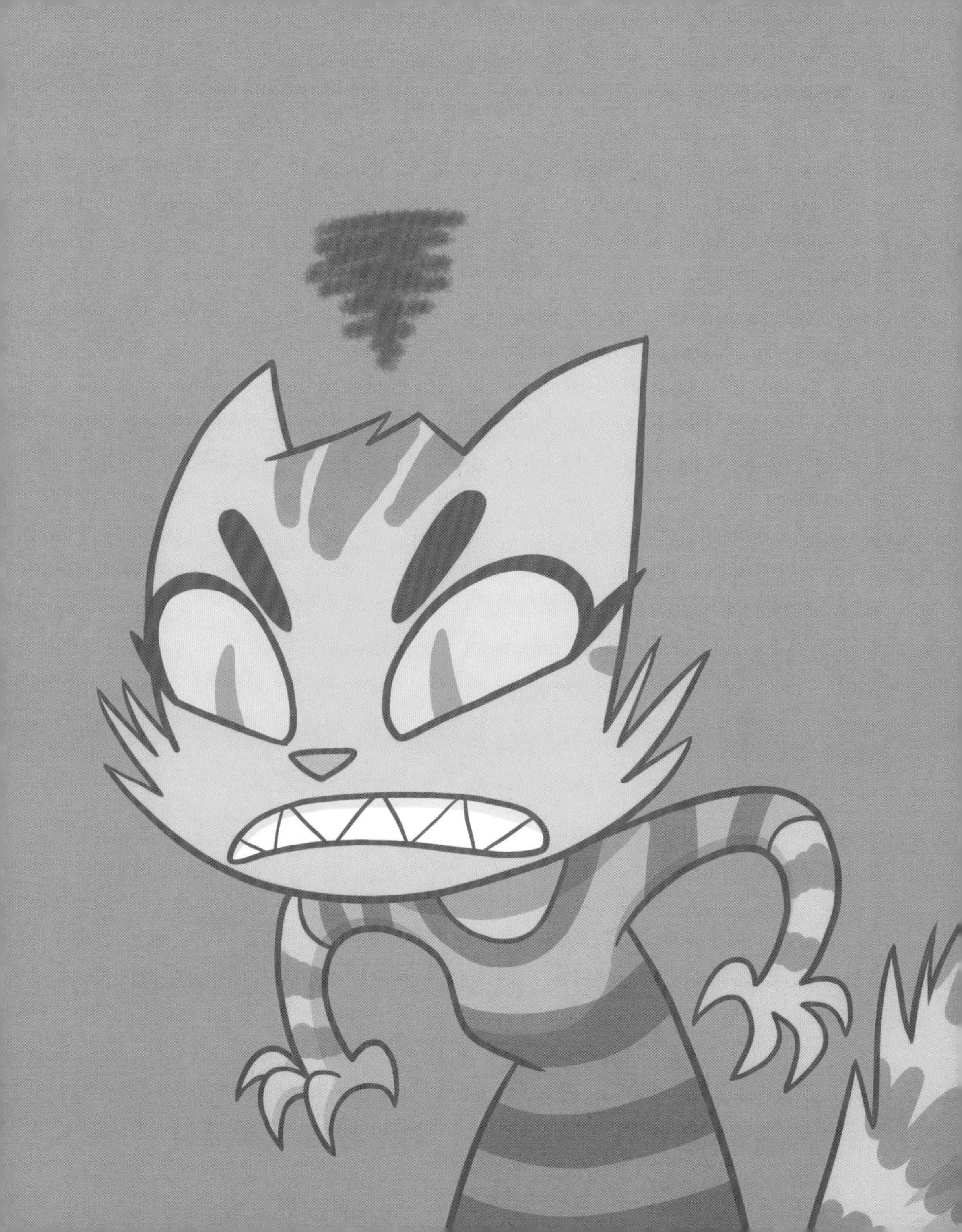

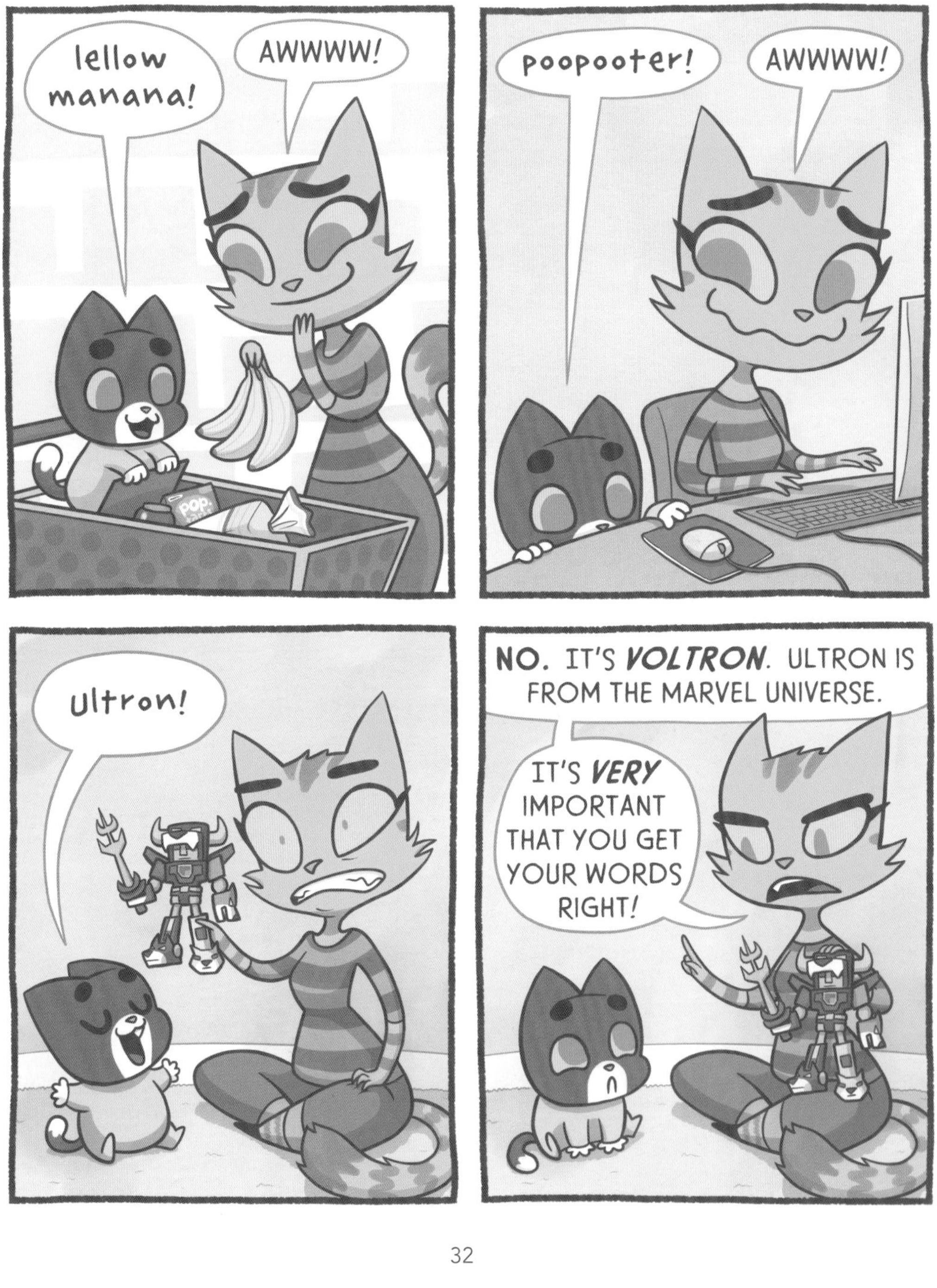
lellow manana!
AWWWW!
poopooter!
AWWWW!
Ultron!
NO. IT'S VOLTRON. ULTRON IS FROM THE MARVEL UNIVERSE.
IT'S VERY IMPORTANT THAT YOU GET YOUR WORDS RIGHT!
POP

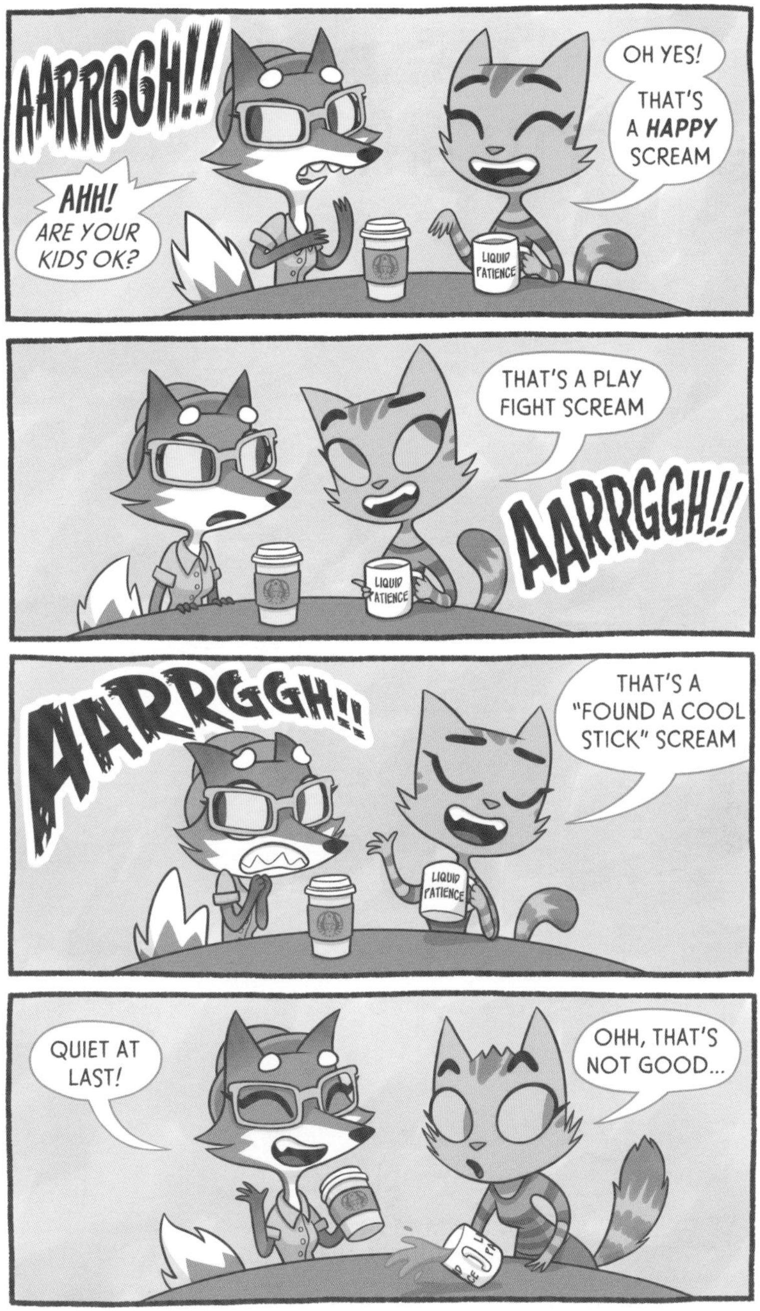
AARRGGH!!
AHH! ARE YOUR KIDS OK?
OH YES!
THAT'S A **HAPPY** SCREAM
LIQUID PATIENCE
THAT'S A PLAY FIGHT SCREAM
AARRGGH!!
AARRGGH!!
THAT'S A "FOUND A COOL STICK" SCREAM
QUIET AT LAST!
OHH, THAT'S NOT GOOD...

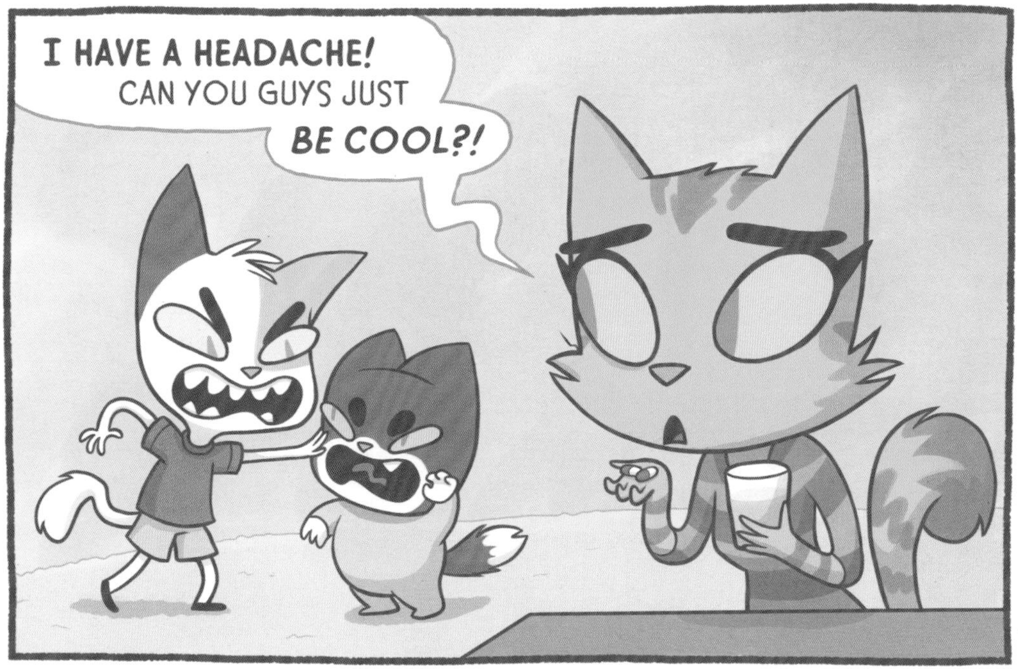
I HAVE A HEADACHE!
CAN YOU GUYS JUST
BE COOL?!

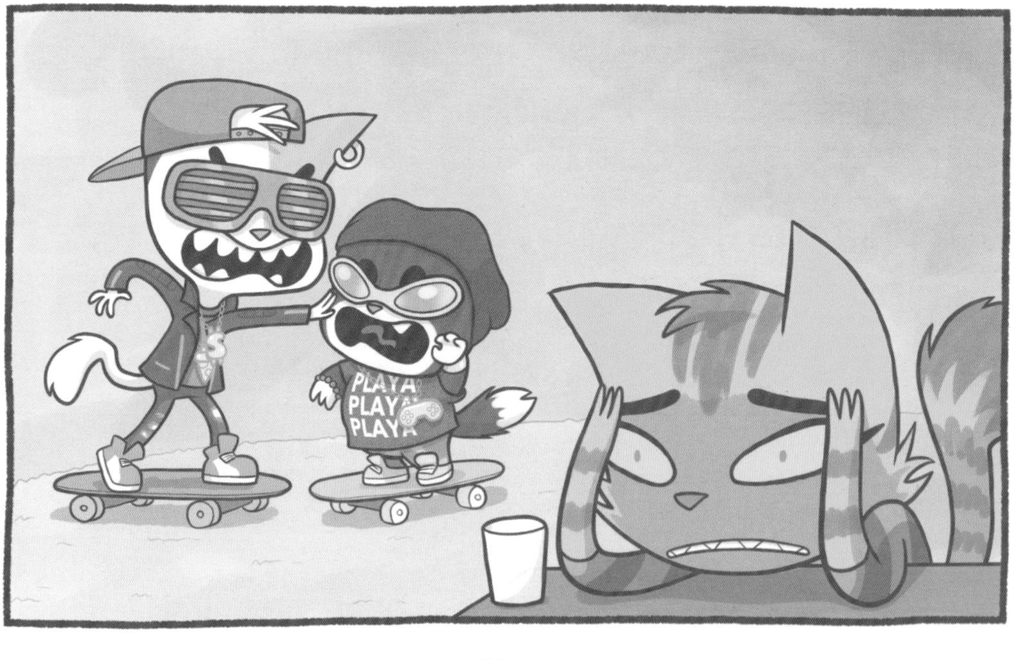
PLAYA
PLAYA
PLAYA

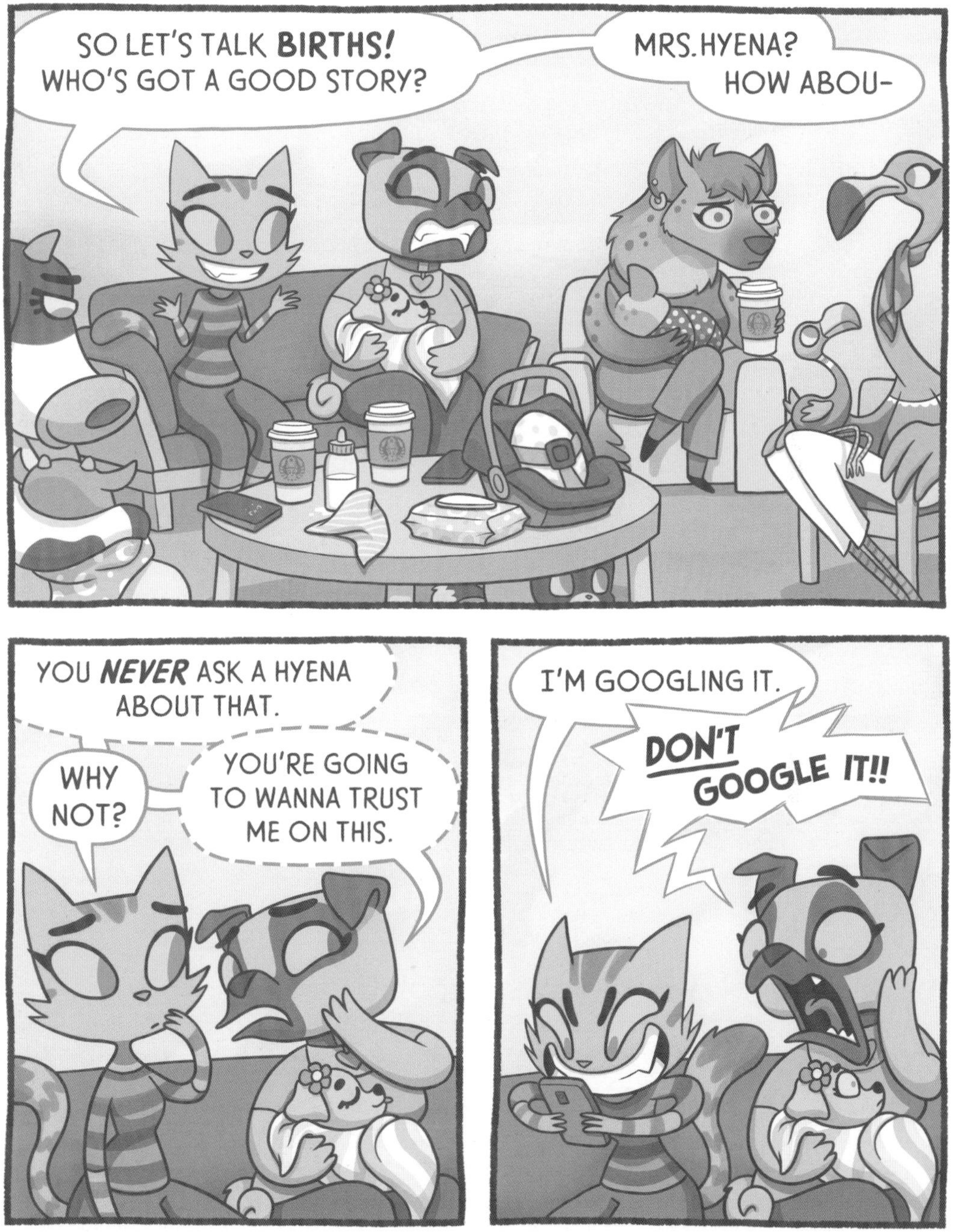
SO LET'S TALK **BIRTHS!** WHO'S GOT A GOOD STORY?
MRS.HYENA? HOW ABOU-
YOU ***NEVER*** ASK A HYENA ABOUT THAT.
WHY NOT?
YOU'RE GOING TO WANNA TRUST ME ON THIS.
I'M GOOGLING IT.
DON'T GOOGLE IT!!

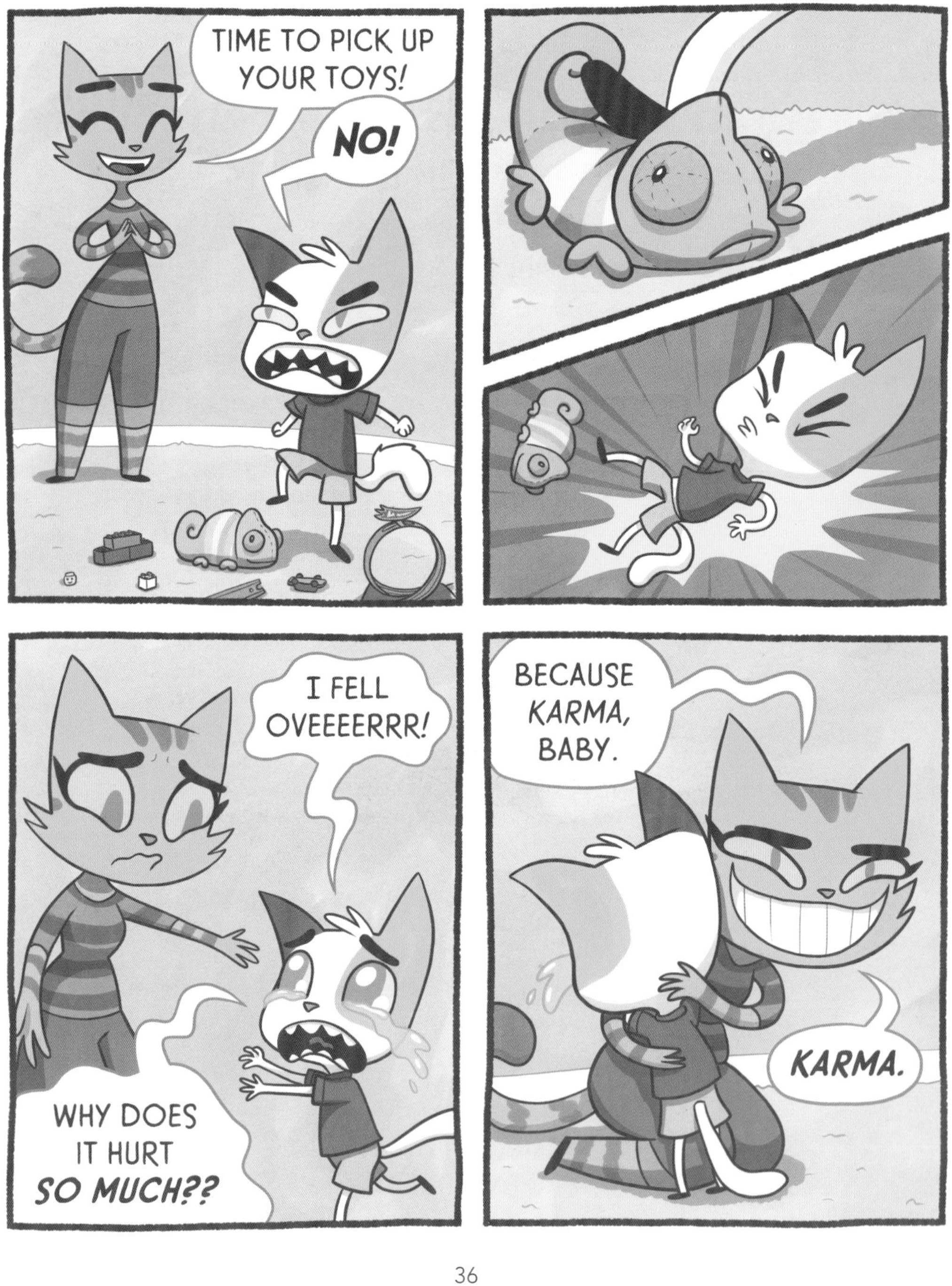
TIME TO PICK UP YOUR TOYS!
NO!
I FELL OVEEEERRR!
WHY DOES IT HURT SO MUCH??
BECAUSE KARMA, BABY.
KARMA.

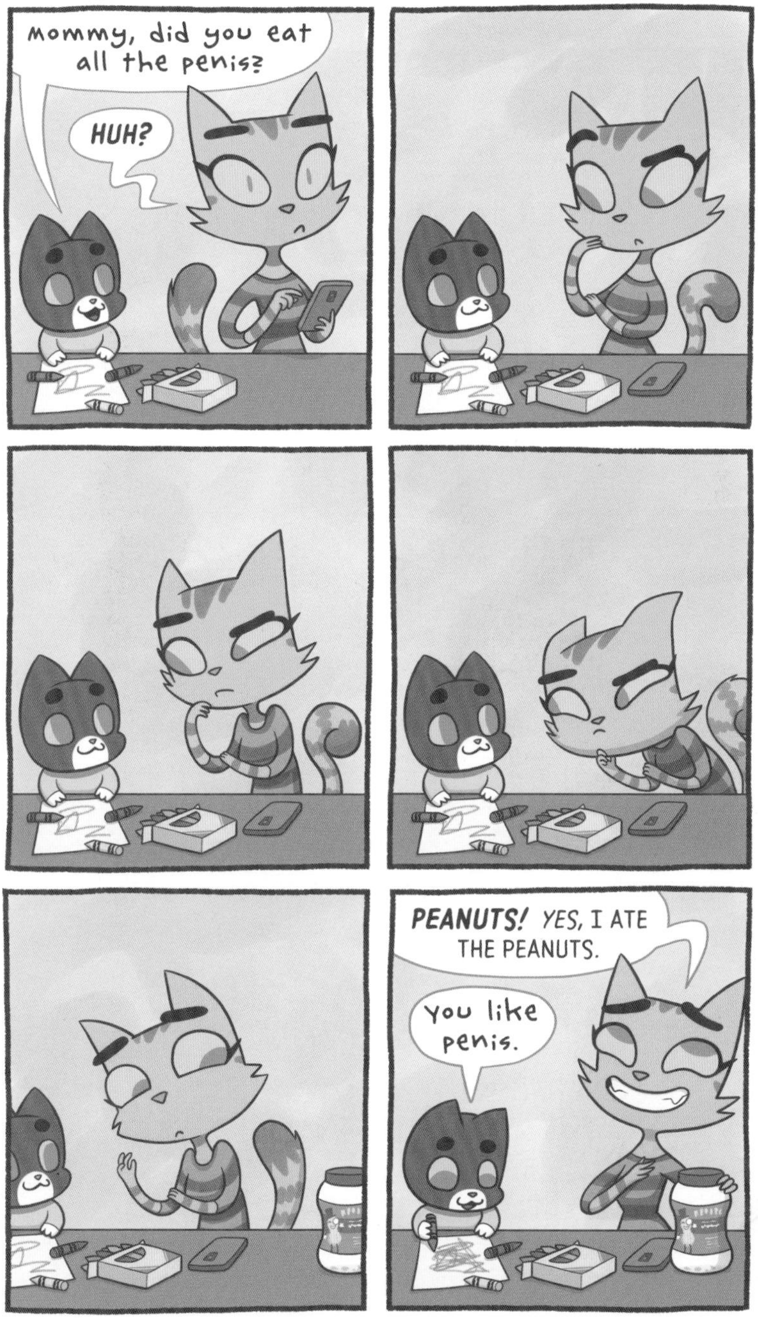
mommy, did you eat all the penis?
HUH?
PEANUTS! YES, I ATE THE PEANUTS.
You like penis.

BASED ON A TWEET BY @BUNANDLEGGINGS

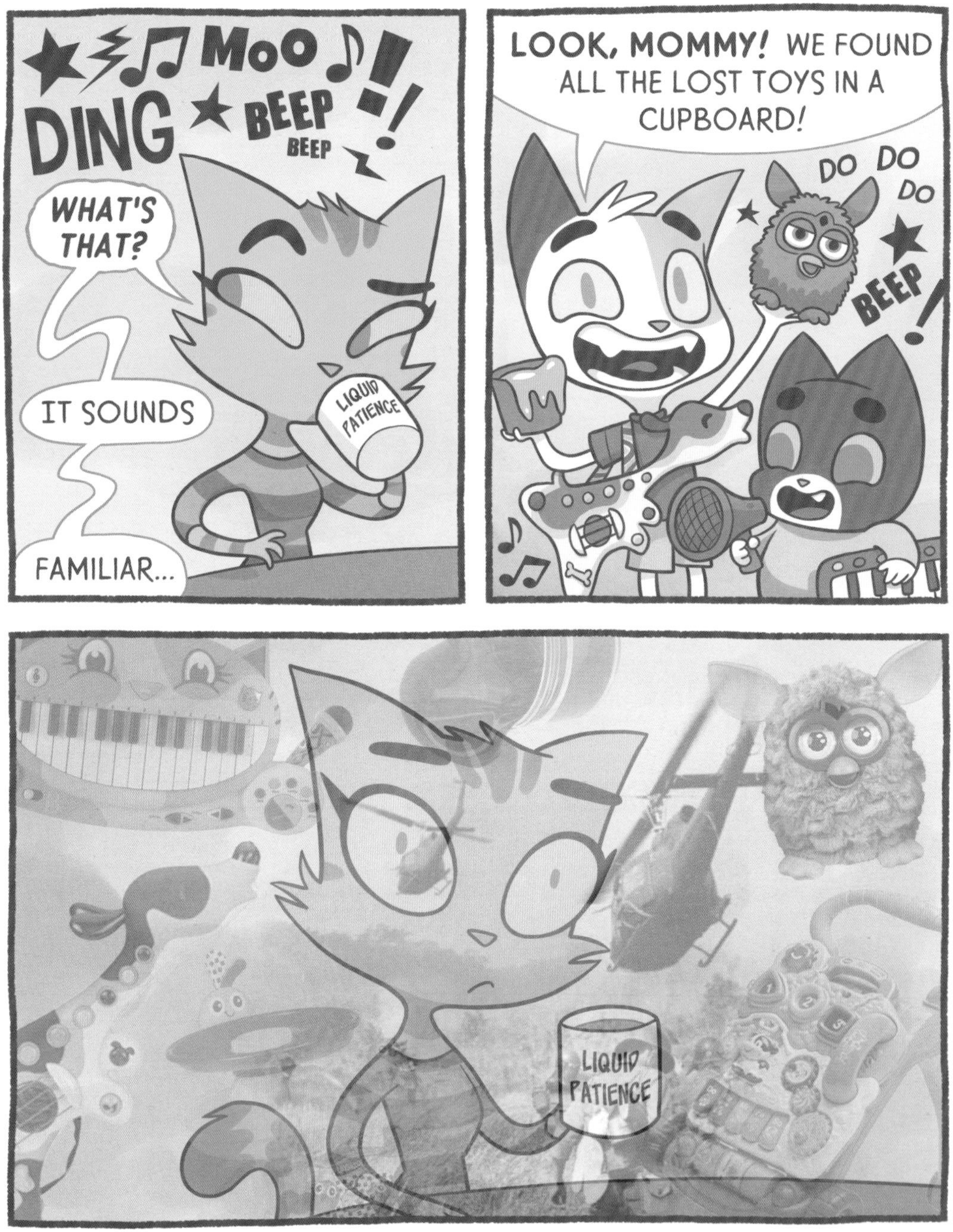
MOO
DING
BEEP
BEEP
WHAT'S THAT?
IT SOUNDS
FAMILIAR...
LIQUID PATIENCE
LOOK, MOMMY! WE FOUND ALL THE LOST TOYS IN A CUPBOARD!
DO DO DO
BEEP
LIQUID PATIENCE

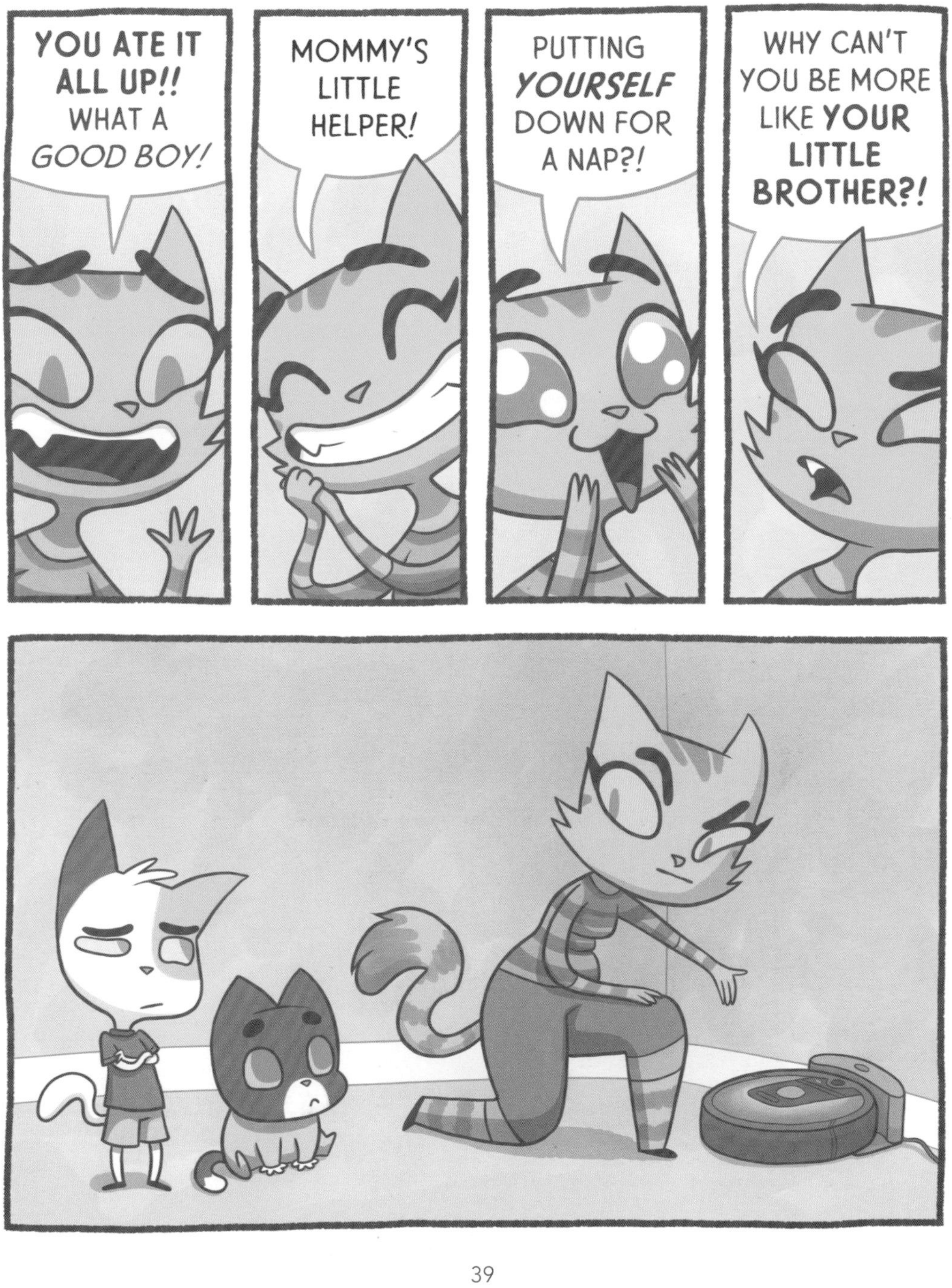
YOU ATE IT ALL UP!! WHAT A GOOD BOY!
MOMMY'S LITTLE HELPER!
PUTTING YOURSELF DOWN FOR A NAP?!
WHY CAN'T YOU BE MORE LIKE YOUR LITTLE BROTHER?!

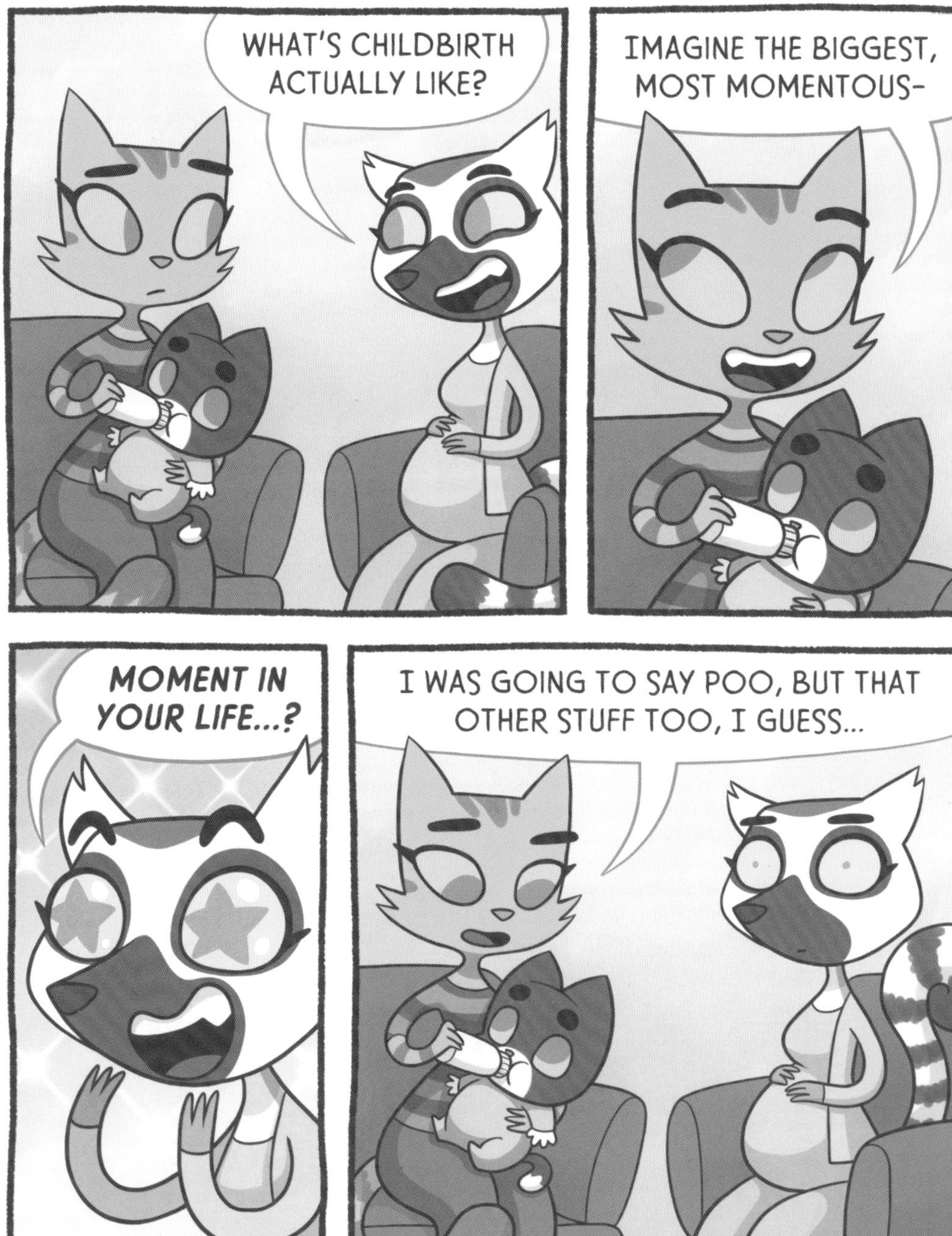
WHAT'S CHILDBIRTH ACTUALLY LIKE?
IMAGINE THE BIGGEST, MOST MOMENTOUS-
MOMENT IN YOUR LIFE...?
I WAS GOING TO SAY POO, BUT THAT OTHER STUFF TOO, I GUESS...

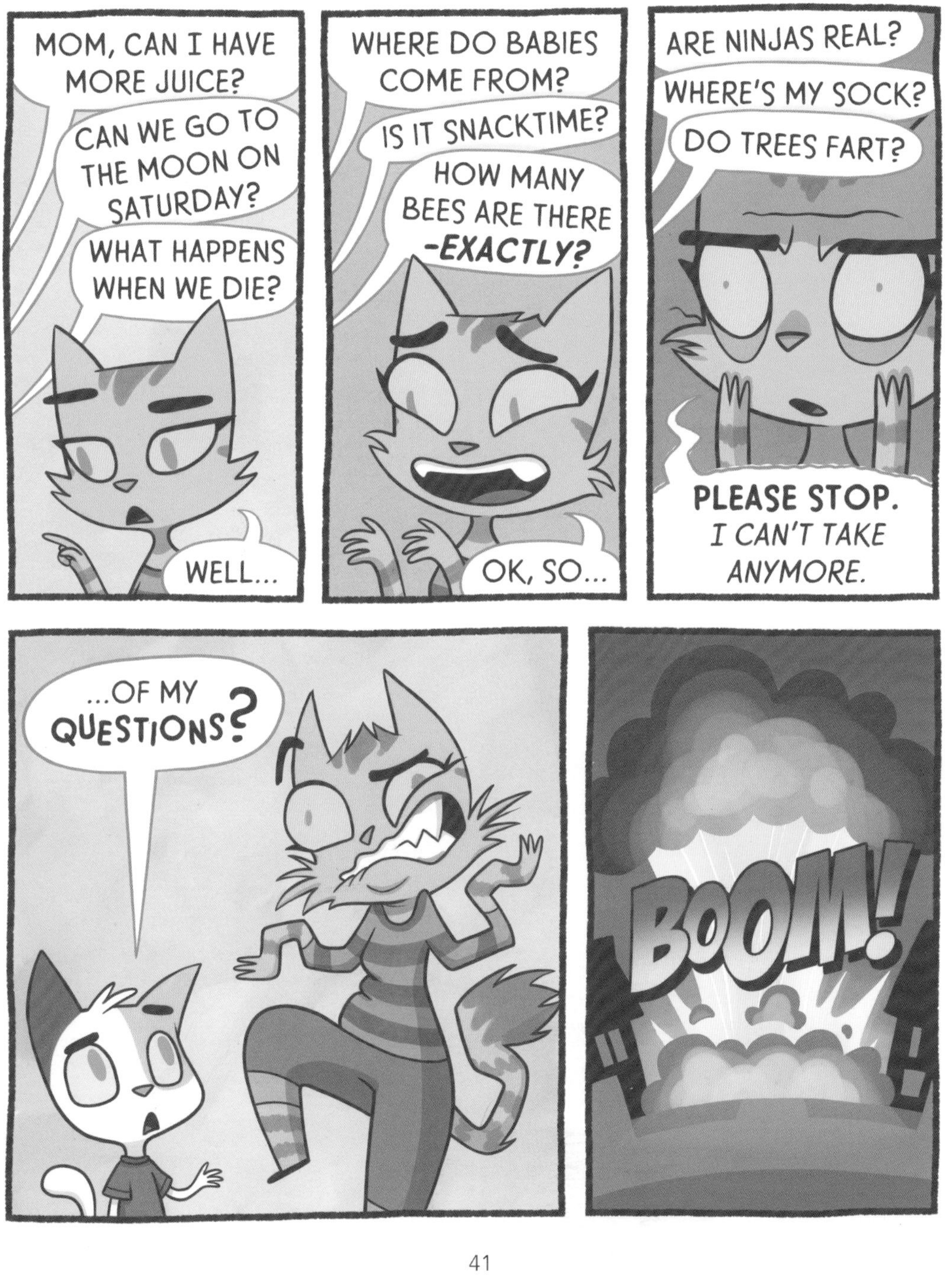
MOM, CAN I HAVE MORE JUICE?
CAN WE GO TO THE MOON ON SATURDAY?
WHAT HAPPENS WHEN WE DIE?
WELL...
WHERE DO BABIES COME FROM?
IS IT SNACKTIME?
HOW MANY BEES ARE THERE -EXACTLY?
OK, SO...
ARE NINJAS REAL?
WHERE'S MY SOCK?
DO TREES FART?
PLEASE STOP. I CAN'T TAKE ANYMORE.
...OF MY QUESTIONS?
BOOM!

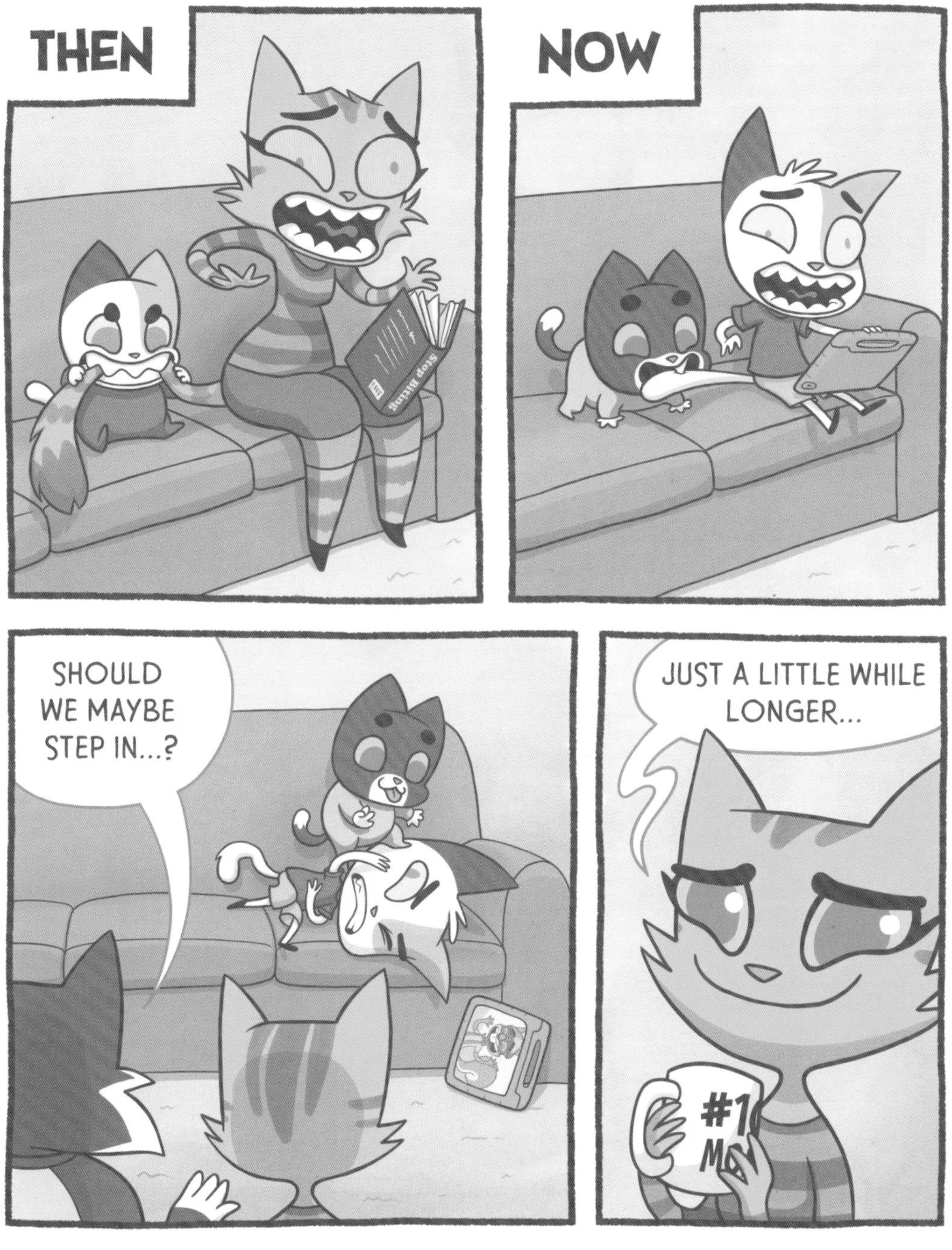
THEN
Stop Biting
NOW
SHOULD WE MAYBE STEP IN...?
JUST A LITTLE WHILE LONGER...
#1

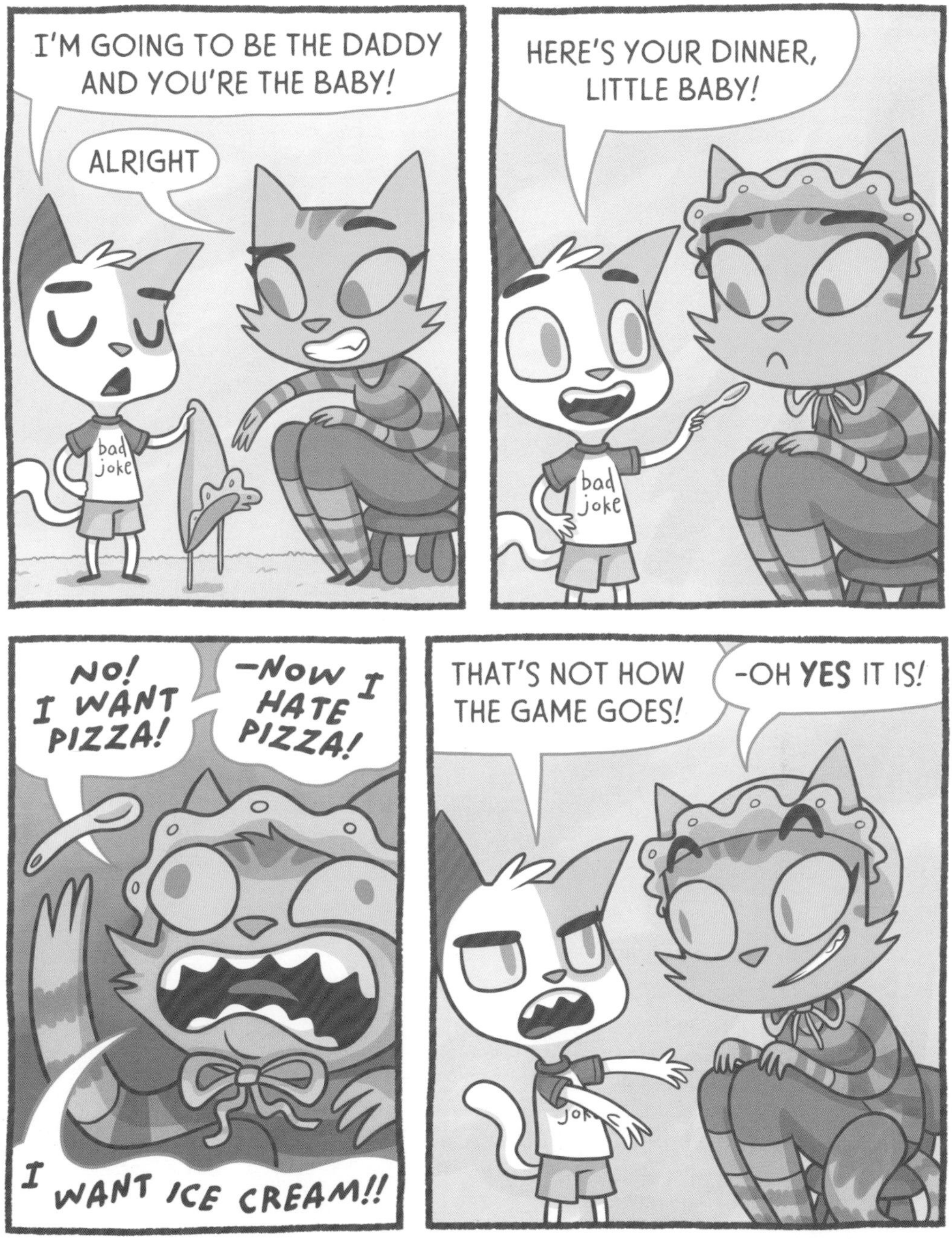
I'M GOING TO BE THE DADDY AND YOU'RE THE BABY!
ALRIGHT
bad joke
HERE'S YOUR DINNER, LITTLE BABY!
bad joke
NO! I WANT PIZZA!
-NOW I HATE PIZZA!
I WANT ICE CREAM!!
THAT'S NOT HOW THE GAME GOES!
-OH **YES** IT IS!

DAD BOD

DADS HAVE SUPERNATURAL POWERS. I'LL BE NAGGING THE KIDS, TRYING TO GET THEM TO DO THIS OR THAT WHILE THEY COMPLETELY IGNORE ME. THEN ALONG COMES J AND CASTS *BOOMING DAD VOICE*. THE KIDS' DEAFNESS IS MAGICALLY CURED AND WHATEVER I'VE BEEN TRYING TO DO FOR HOURS IS DONE!

HIS TELEPORTATION SKILLS COME IN HANDY TOO! WHEN THE KIDS ARE (SOMETIMES LITERALLY) BOUNCING OFF THE WALLS, J WILL SWOOP IN AND SPIRIT THEM AWAY TO SOMEWHERE FUN THAT ISN'T HERE AND LEAVE ME TO ENJOY THE SWEET, MERCIFUL PEACE.

DADS' AGGRO-MANAGEMENT ABILITIES ARE ALSO SECOND TO NONE WHEN THE LITTLES ARE ON THE WARPATH. BE IT PRETENDING HE'S FORGOTTEN THEIR NAMES OR POWER-BOMBING THEM ONTO THE BED, NO ONE CAN MAKE THE KIDS LAUGH LIKE THEIR DAD! THEIR GIGGLES ARE MUSIC TO MY EARS, AND I CAN'T HELP BUT BEAM AT MY KNIGHT IN SHINING BATHROBE.

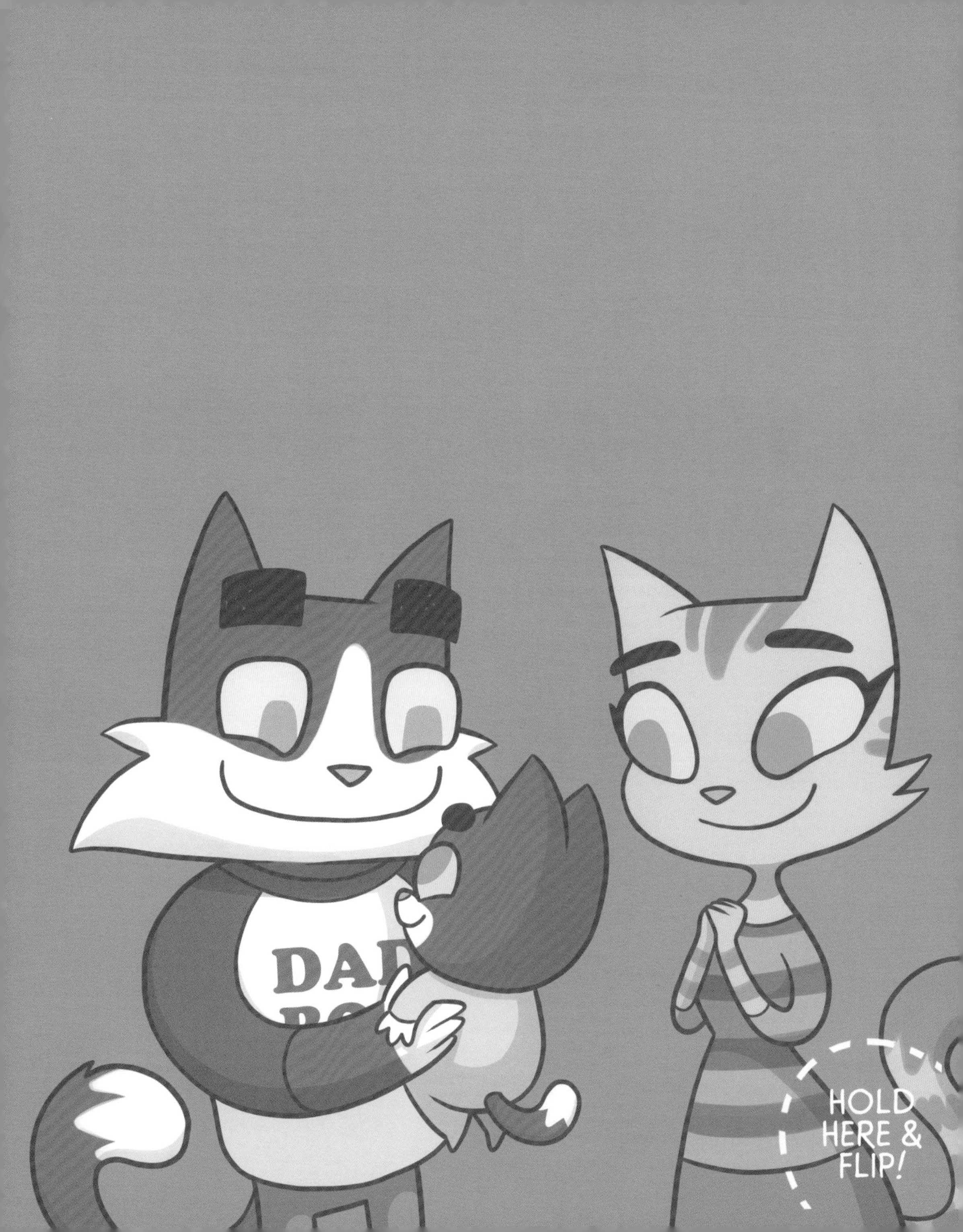
HOLD HERE & FLIP!

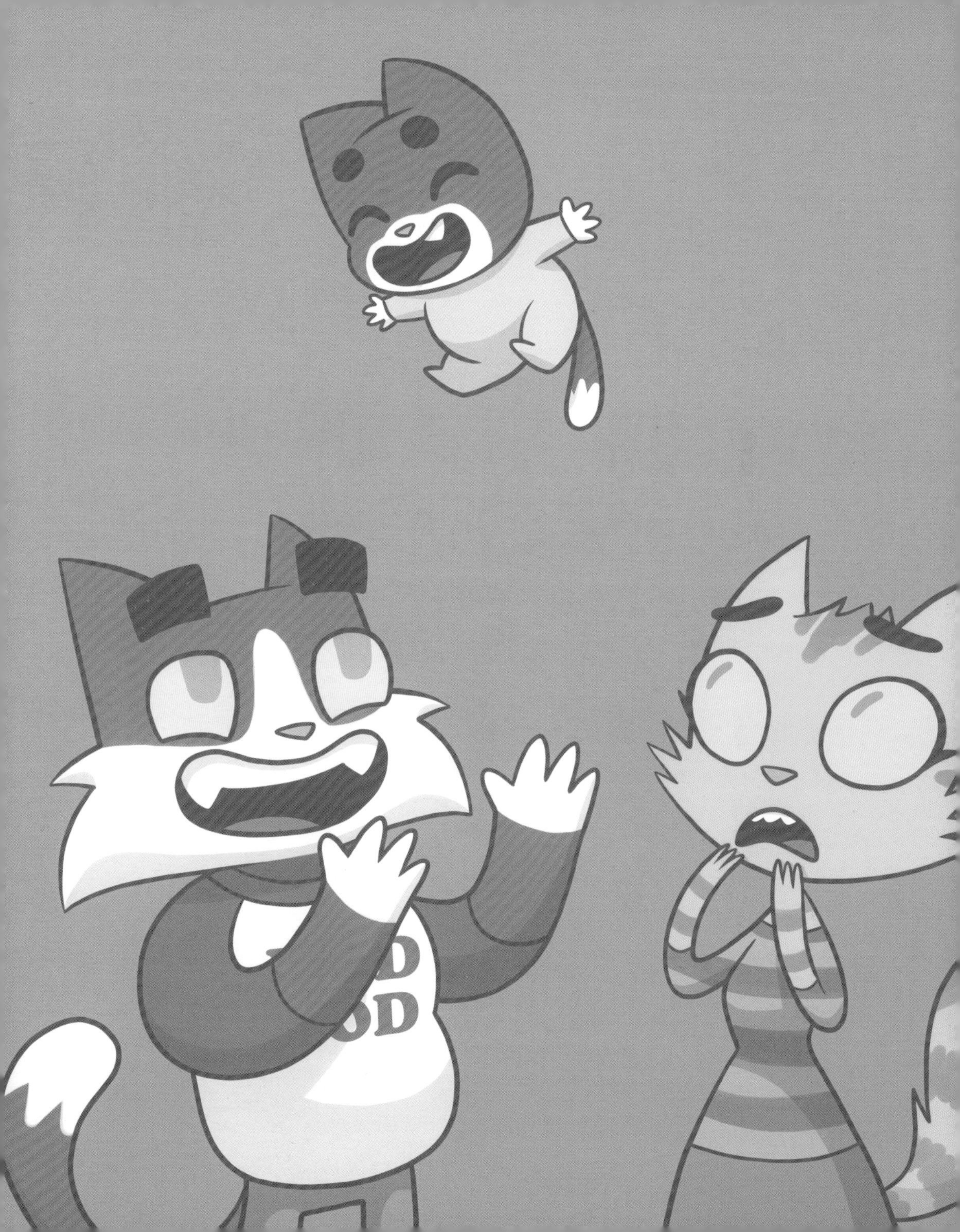

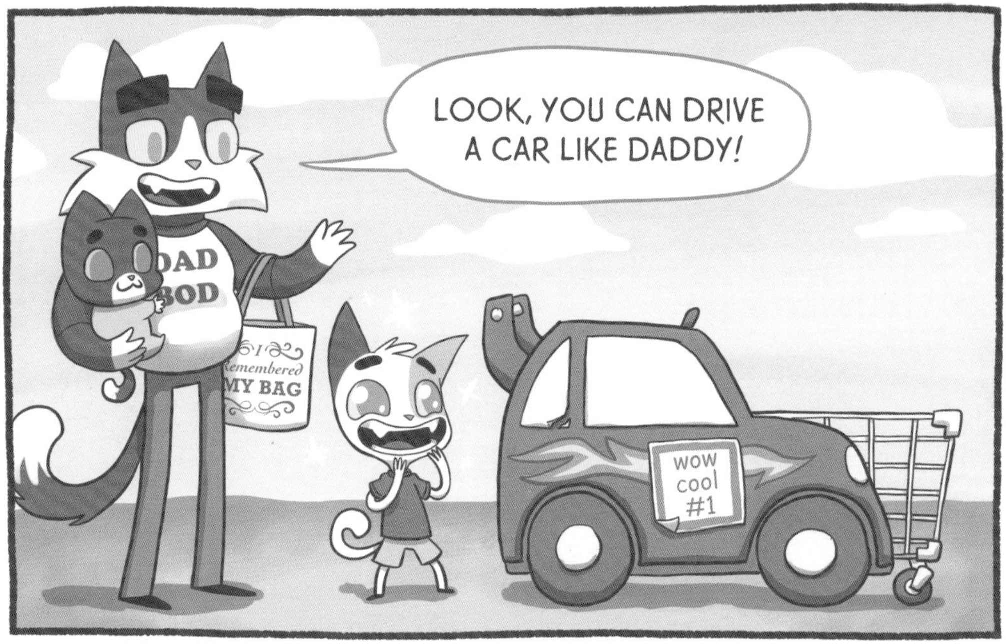
LOOK, YOU CAN DRIVE A CAR LIKE DADDY!
DAD BOD
I Remembered MY BAG
WOW cool #1

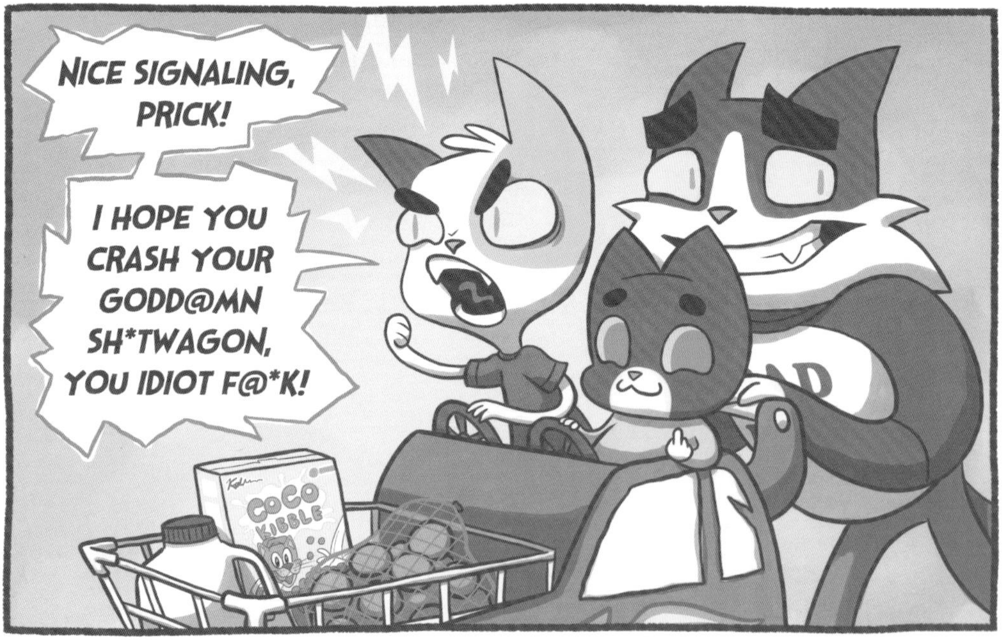
NICE SIGNALING, PRICK!
I HOPE YOU CRASH YOUR GODD@MN SH*TWAGON, YOU IDIOT F@*K!
COCO KIBBLE

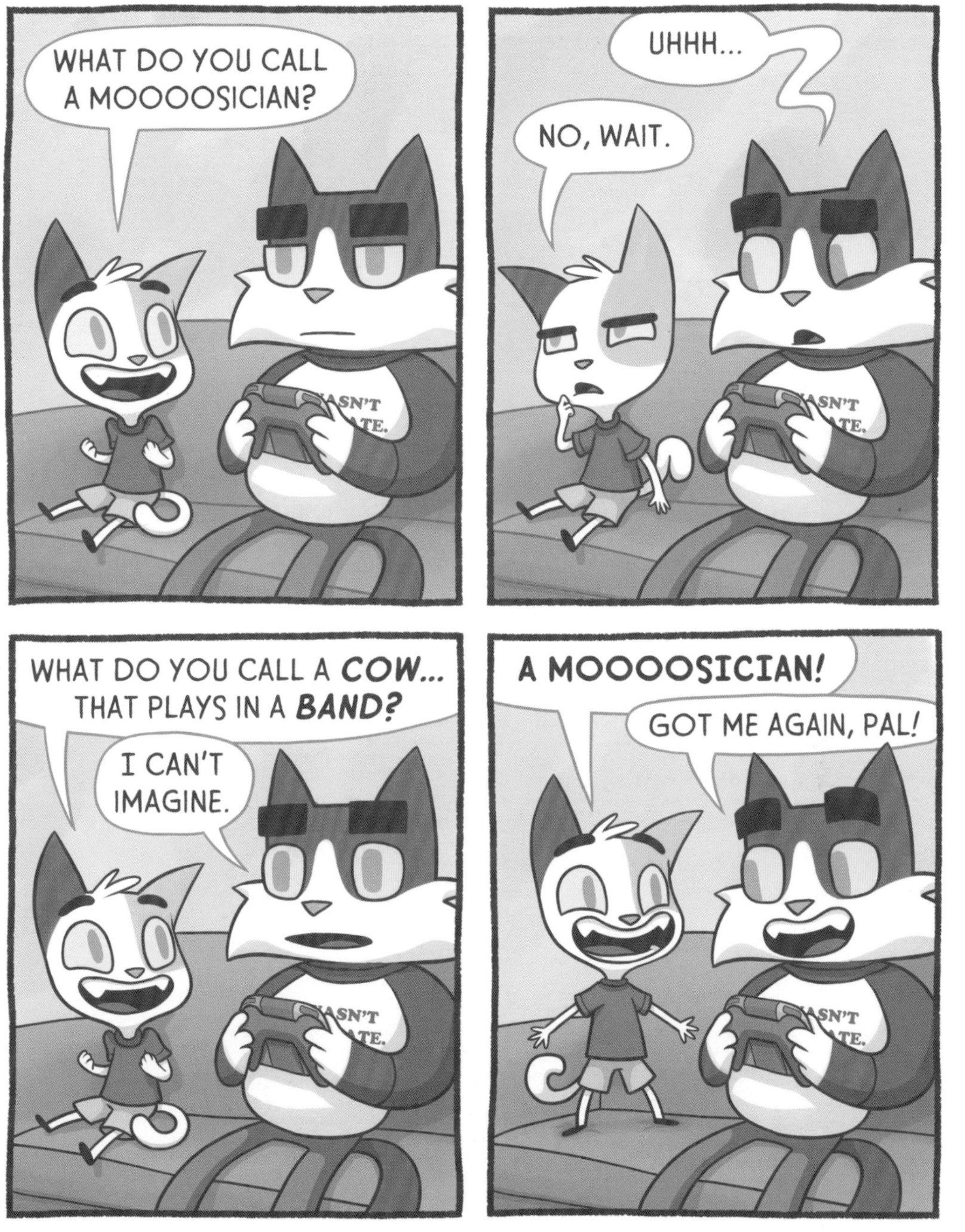
WHAT DO YOU CALL A MOOOOSICIAN?
UHHH...
NO, WAIT.
WHAT DO YOU CALL A ***COW...*** THAT PLAYS IN A ***BAND?***
I CAN'T IMAGINE.
A MOOOOSICIAN!
GOT ME AGAIN, PAL!

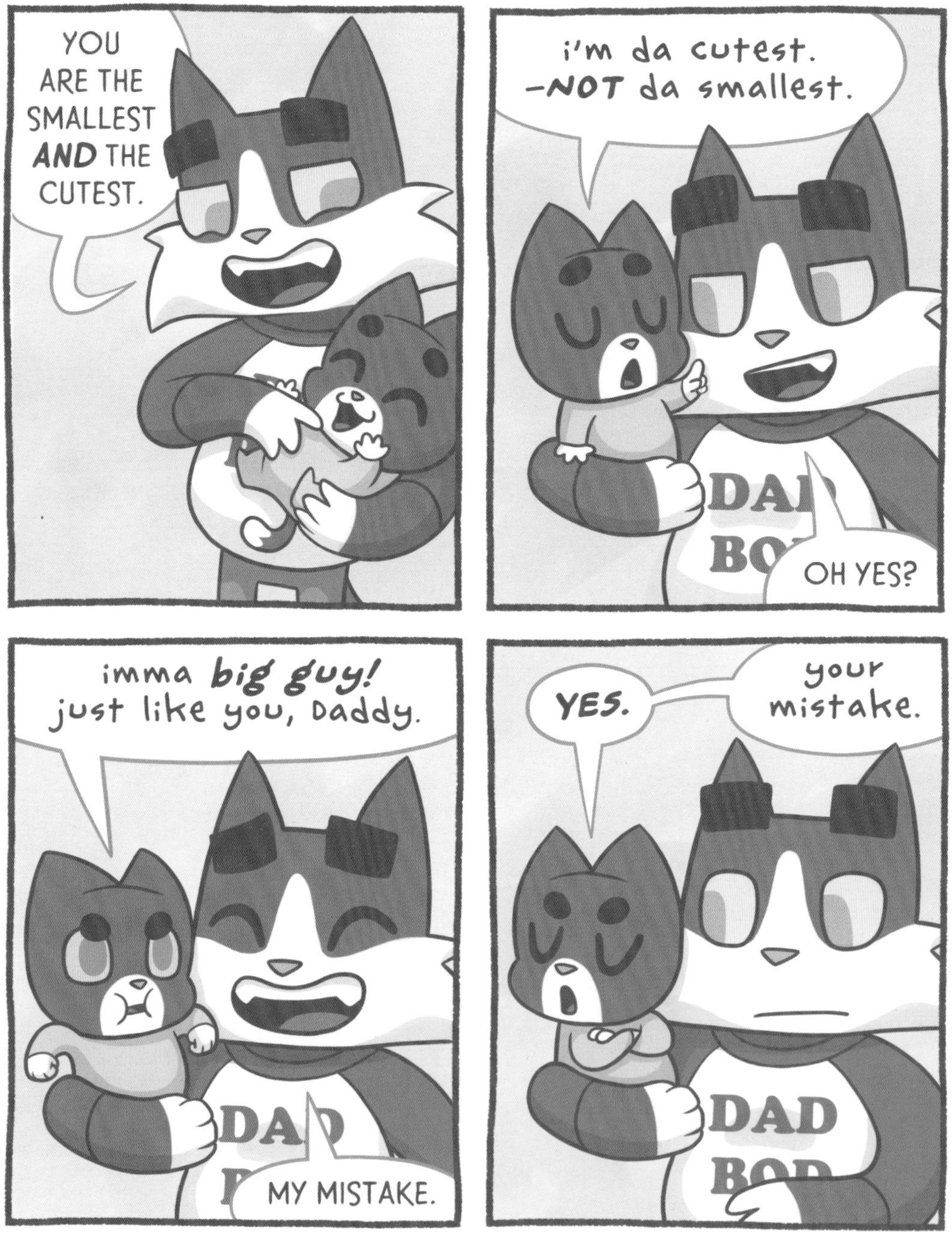
YOU ARE THE SMALLEST **AND** THE CUTEST.
i'm da cutest. –**NOT** da smallest.
OH YES?
imma **big guy!** just like you, Daddy.
MY MISTAKE.
YES.
your mistake.
DAD

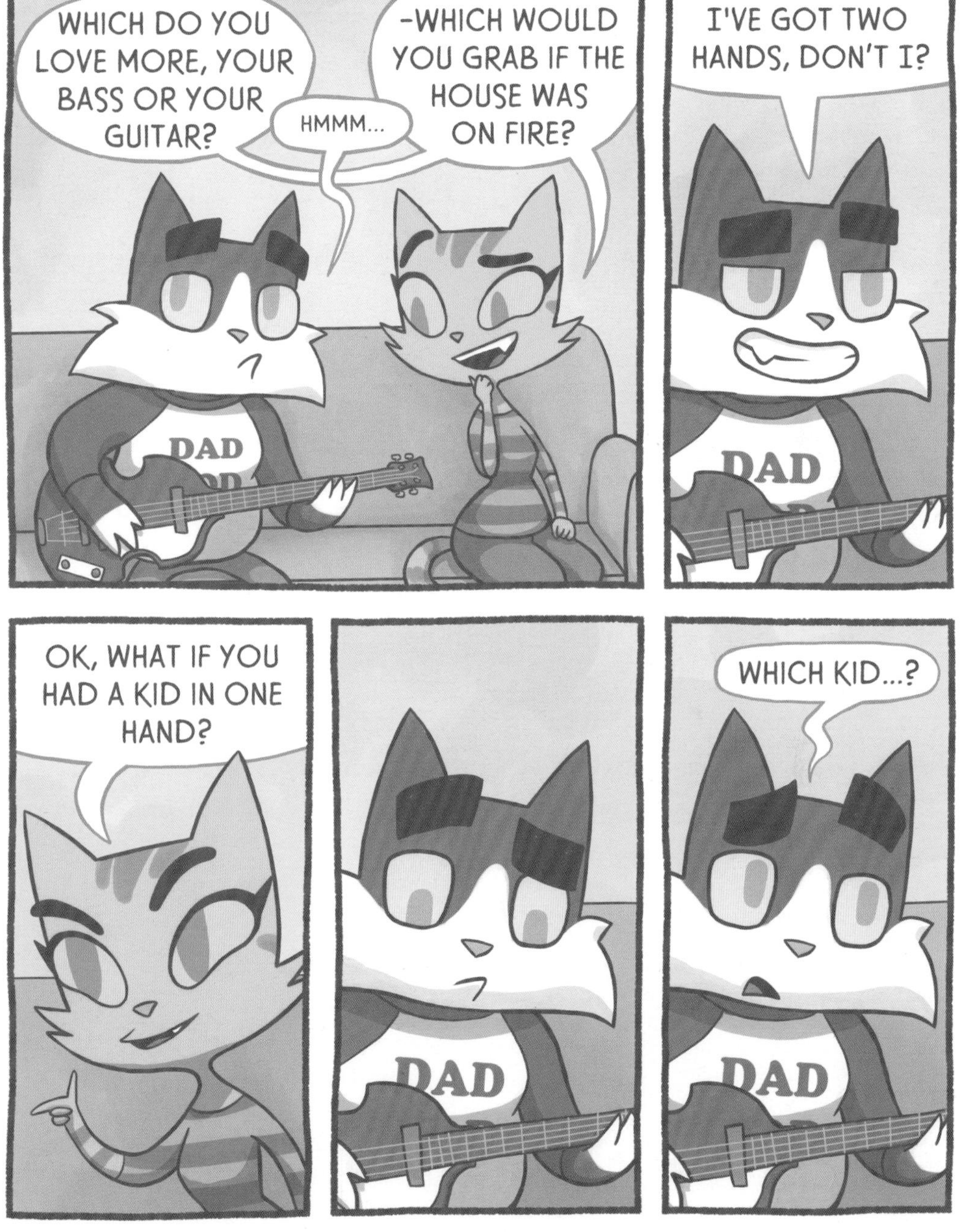
WHICH DO YOU LOVE MORE, YOUR BASS OR YOUR GUITAR?
HMMM...
-WHICH WOULD YOU GRAB IF THE HOUSE WAS ON FIRE?
DAD
I'VE GOT TWO HANDS, DON'T I?
DAD
OK, WHAT IF YOU HAD A KID IN ONE HAND?
DAD
WHICH KID...?
DAD

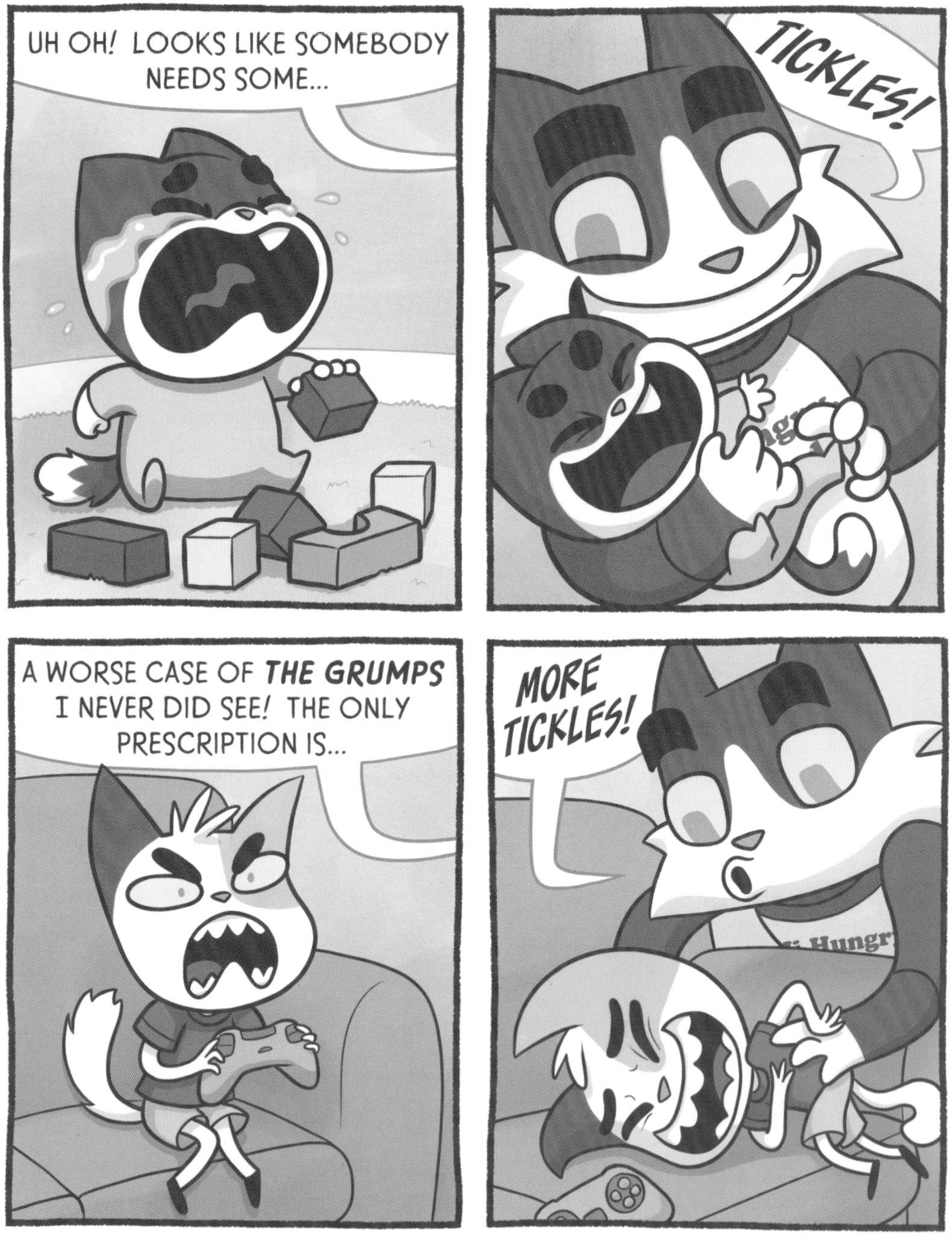
UH OH! LOOKS LIKE SOMEBODY NEEDS SOME...
TICKLES!
A WORSE CASE OF **THE GRUMPS** I NEVER DID SEE! THE ONLY PRESCRIPTION IS...
MORE TICKLES!

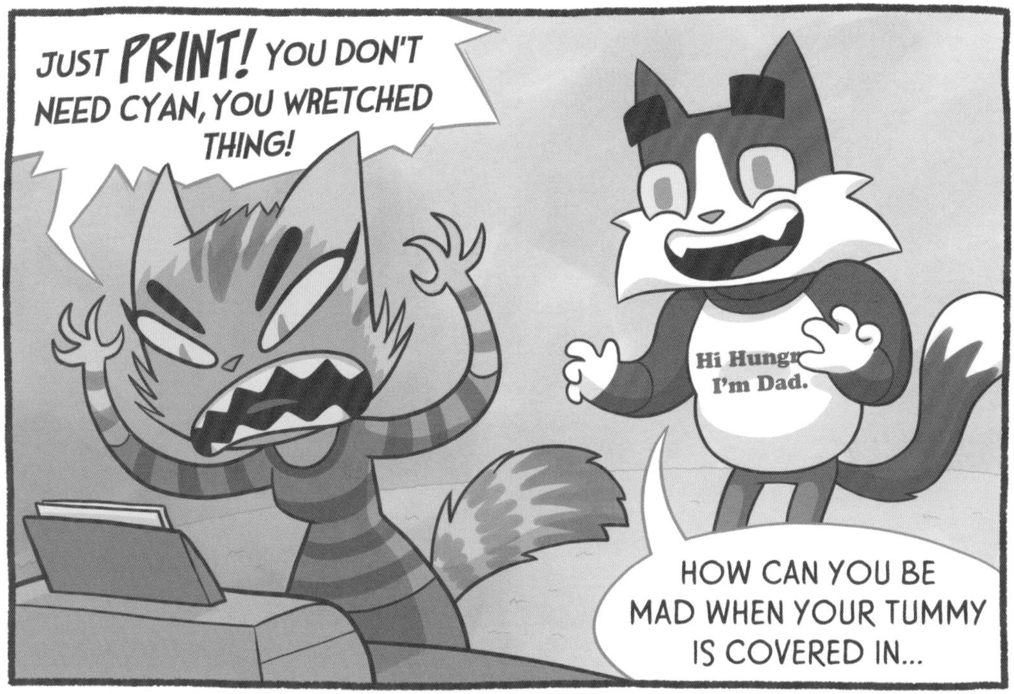
JUST PRINT! YOU DON'T NEED CYAN, YOU WRETCHED THING!
Hi Hungr I'm Dad.
HOW CAN YOU BE MAD WHEN YOUR TUMMY IS COVERED IN...

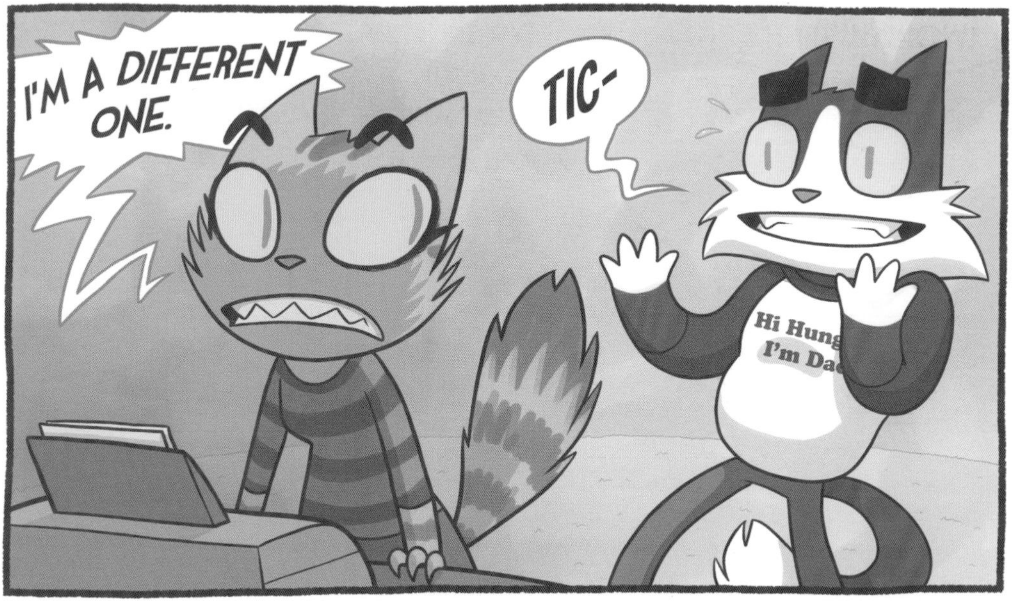
I'M A DIFFERENT ONE.
TIC-
Hi Hung I'm Dad

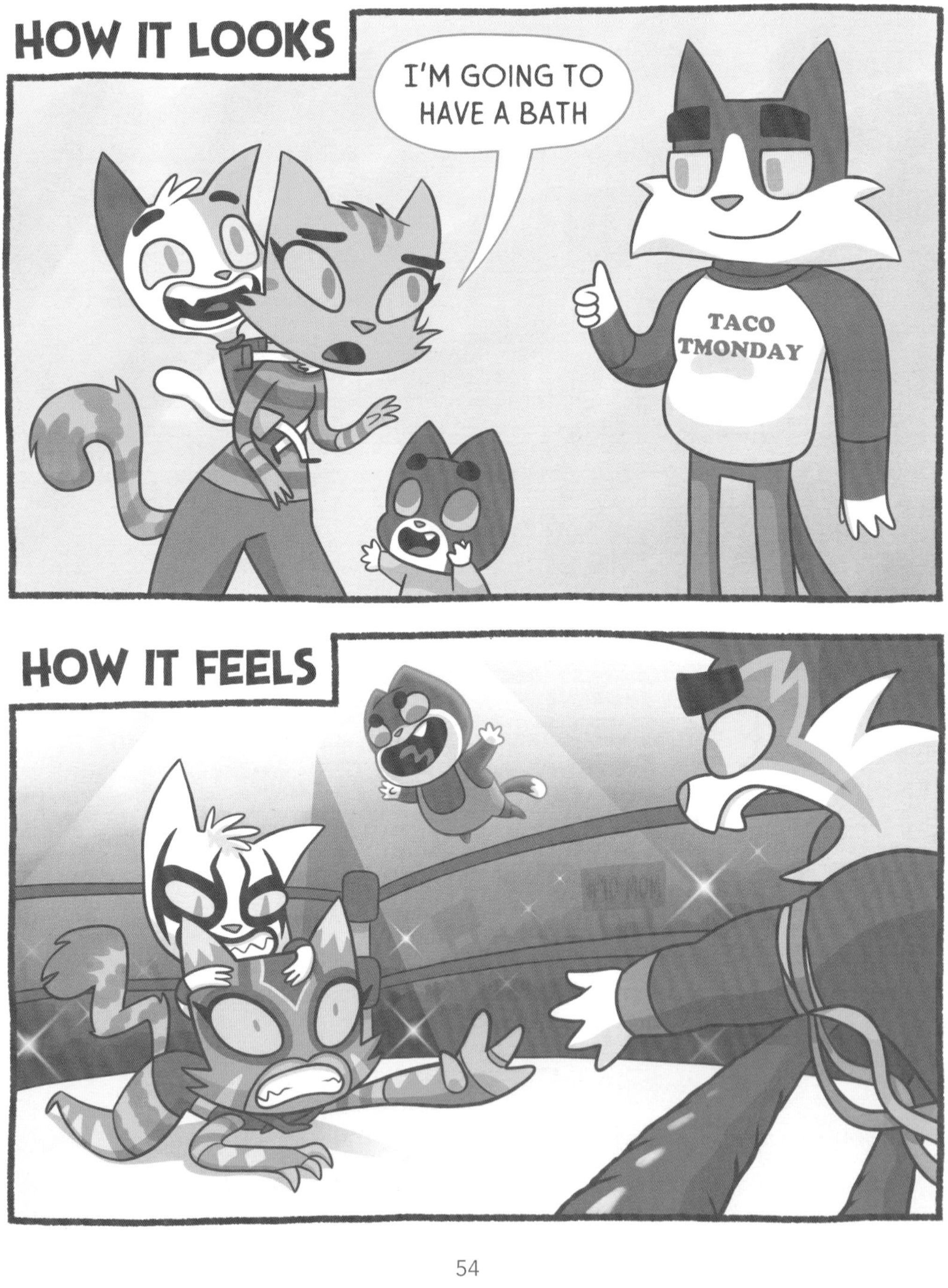
HOW IT LOOKS
I'M GOING TO HAVE A BATH
TACO TMONDAY
HOW IT FEELS

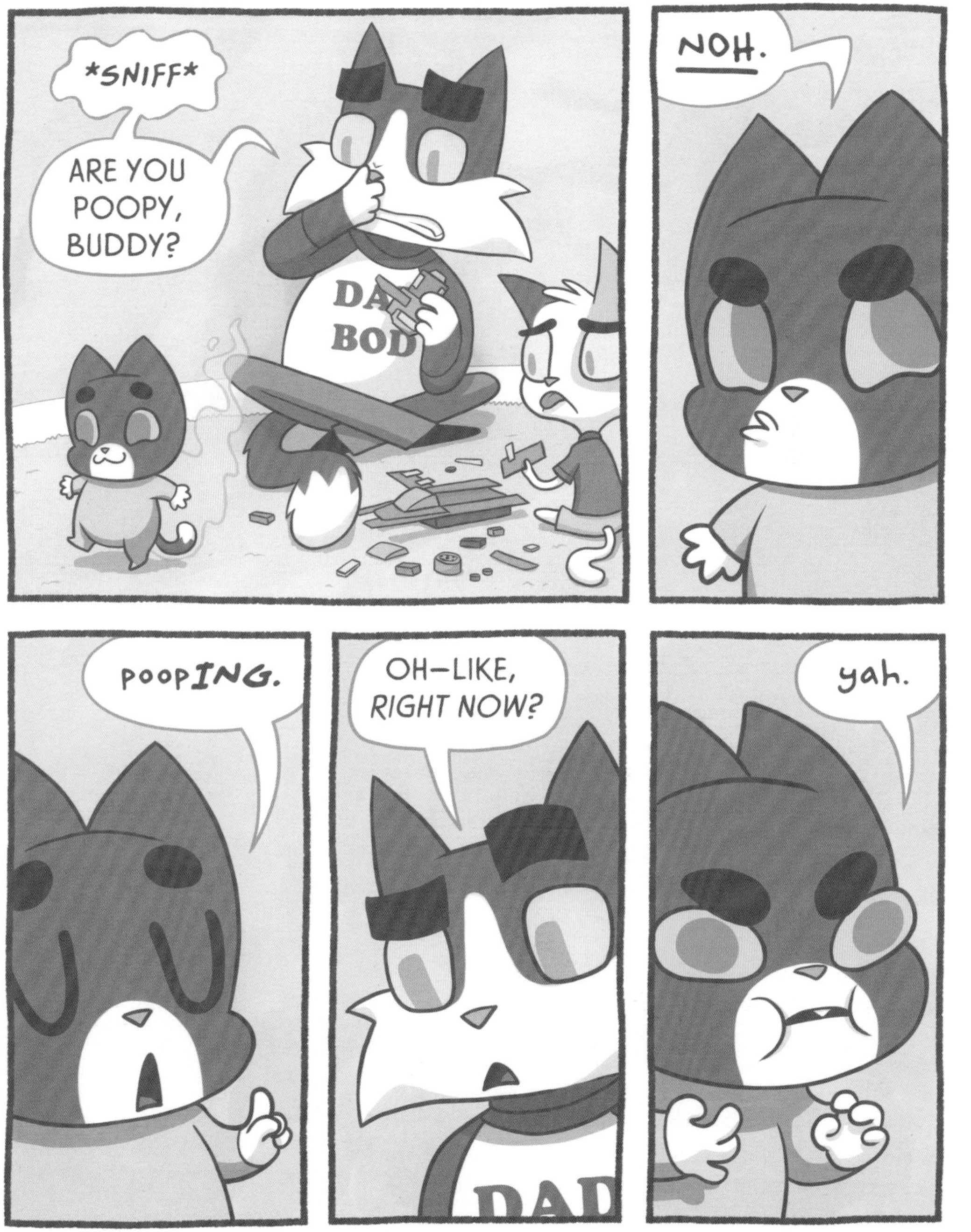
SNIFF
ARE YOU POOPY, BUDDY?
DAD BOD
NOH.
poopING.
OH—LIKE, RIGHT NOW?
DAD
yah.

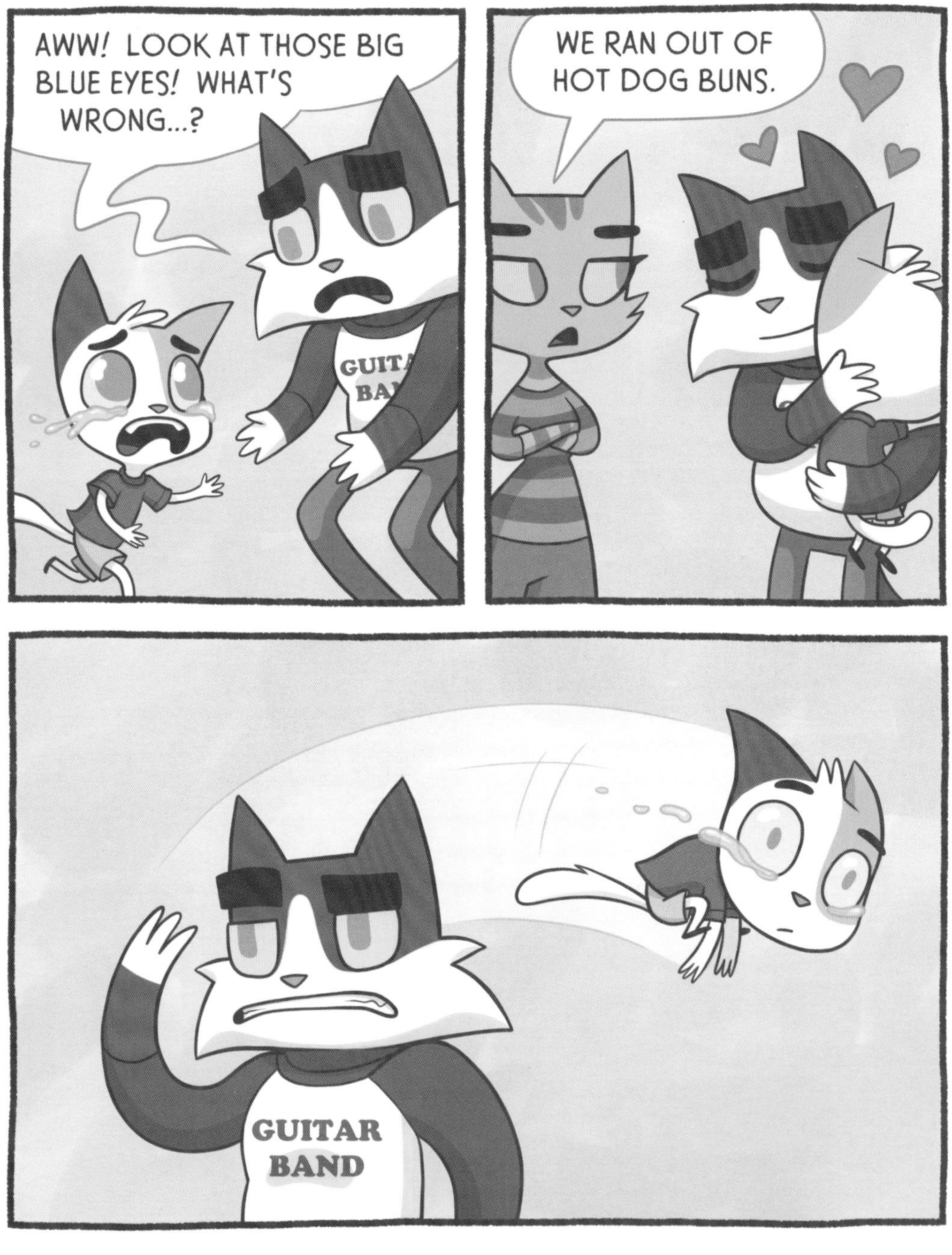
AWW! LOOK AT THOSE BIG BLUE EYES! WHAT'S WRONG...?
WE RAN OUT OF HOT DOG BUNS.
GUITAR BAND

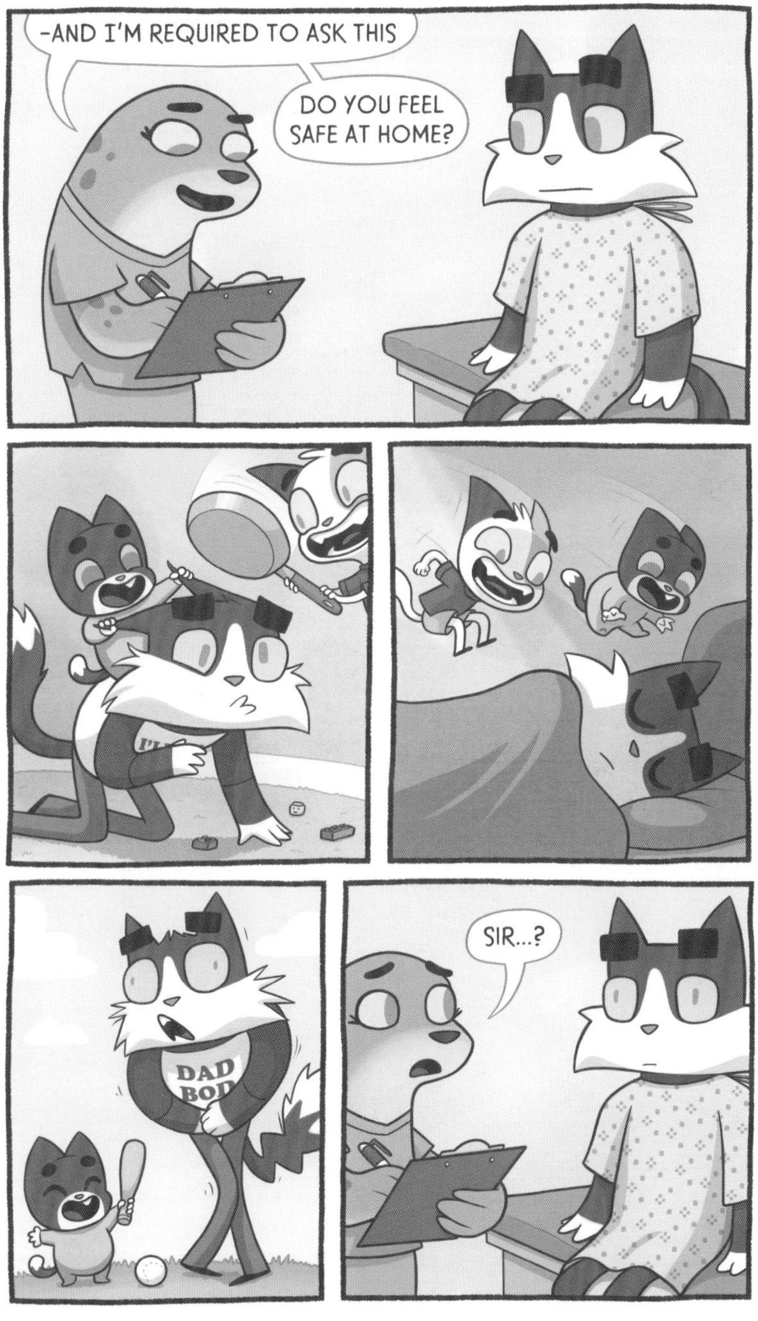
-AND I'M REQUIRED TO ASK THIS
DO YOU FEEL SAFE AT HOME?
DAD BOD
SIR...?

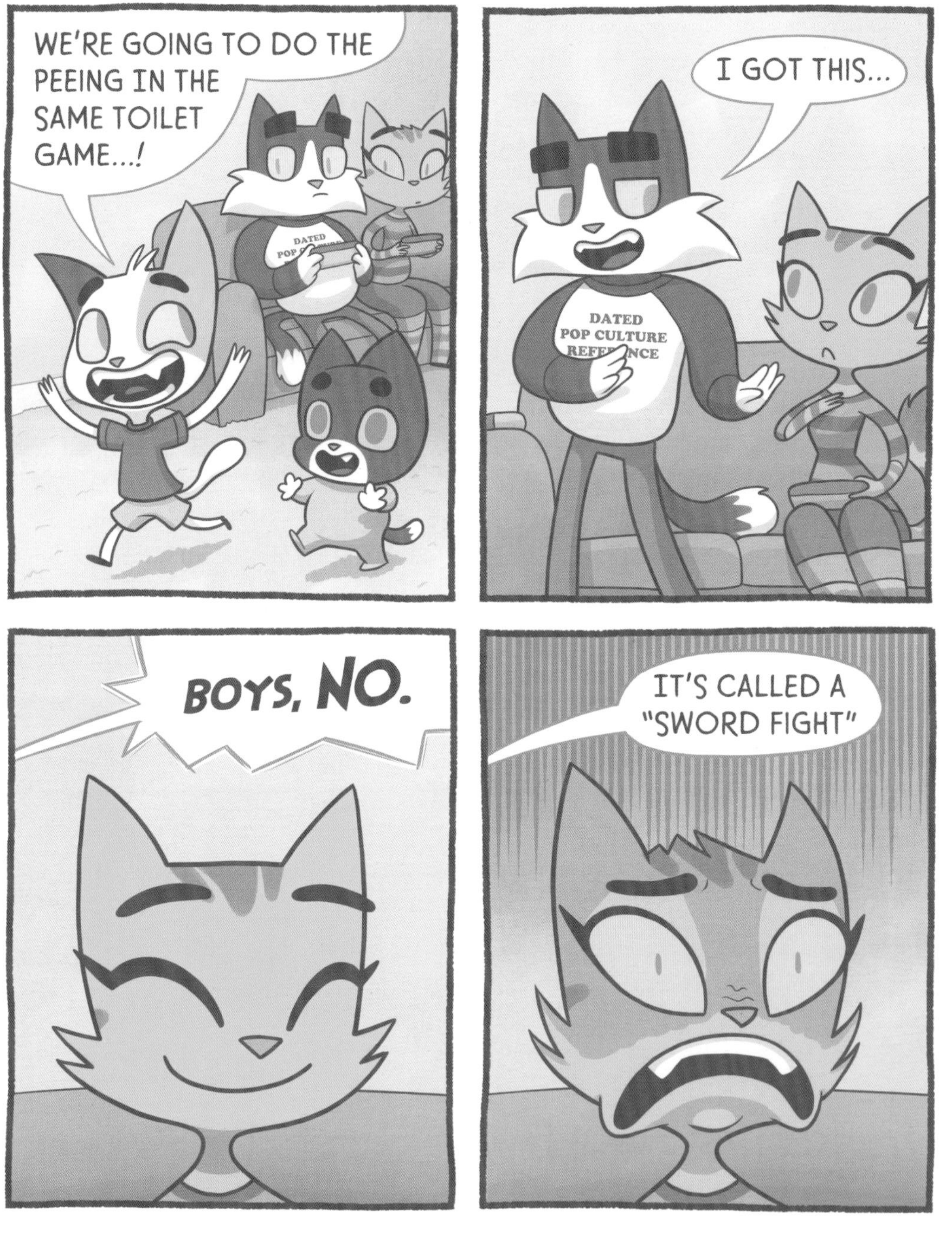
WE'RE GOING TO DO THE PEEING IN THE SAME TOILET GAME...!
DATED
I GOT THIS...
DATED
POP CULTURE
BOYS, NO.
IT'S CALLED A "SWORD FIGHT"

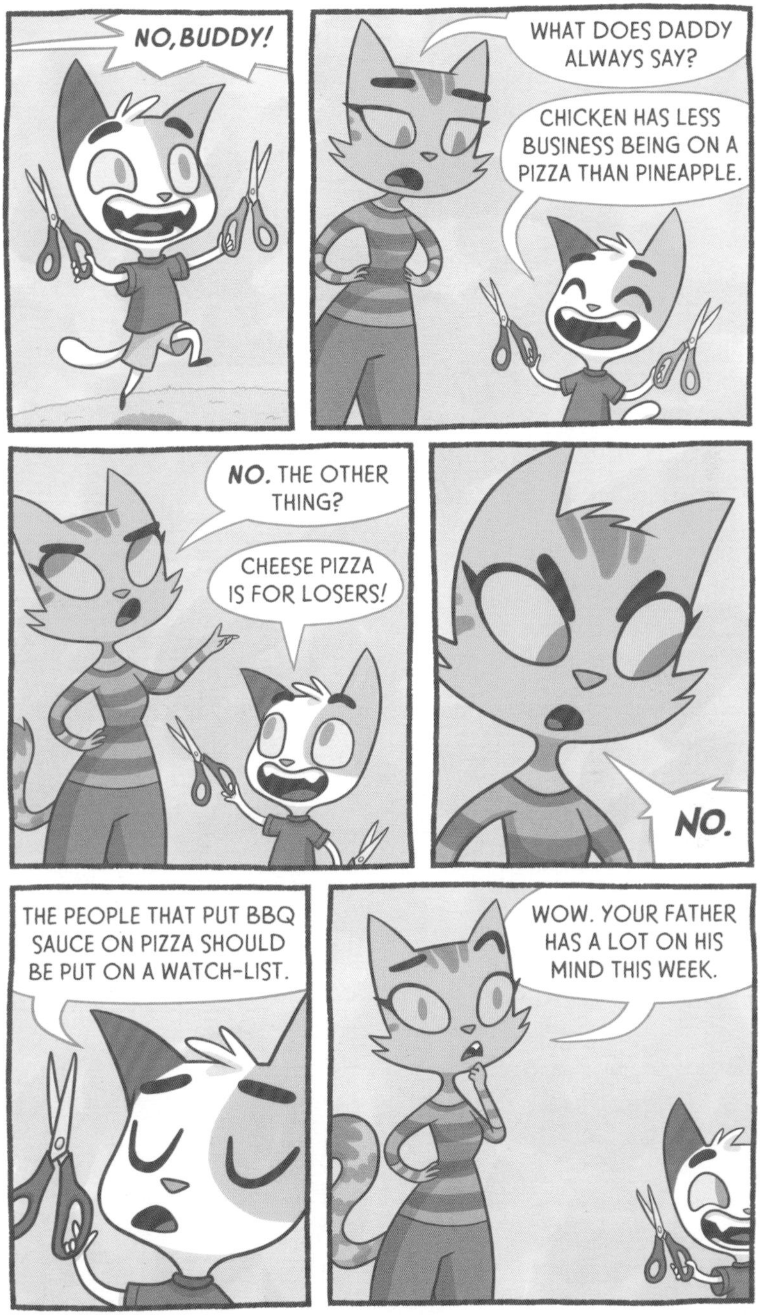
NO, BUDDY!
WHAT DOES DADDY ALWAYS SAY?
CHICKEN HAS LESS BUSINESS BEING ON A PIZZA THAN PINEAPPLE.
NO. THE OTHER THING?
CHEESE PIZZA IS FOR LOSERS!
NO.
THE PEOPLE THAT PUT BBQ SAUCE ON PIZZA SHOULD BE PUT ON A WATCH-LIST.
WOW. YOUR FATHER HAS A LOT ON HIS MIND THIS WEEK.

FEEDING TIME

I WAS A FUSSY EATER, SO REALLY, I DESERVE EVERYTHING I GET! I DIDN'T THINK MY KID WAS PICKY AT FIRST. AS A BABY, HE'D EAT WHATEVER DISGUSTING MUSH I OFFERED HIM, BUT THEN THE TODDLER YEARS ARRIVED AND HIS NEWFOUND VIEWS ON MUSH KNOCKED ME OFF MY SMUG PEDESTAL.

THE REAL VICTIM IS MY HUSBAND. HE IS AN EXCELLENT COOK BUT, UNFORTUNATELY, IS SADDLED WITH A FAMILY THAT WOULD HAPPILY EXIST ON CHEETO SANDWICHES AND HALLOWEEN CANDY. SOME DAYS WE RISE TO THE CHALLENGE, BUT OTHER DAYS IT'S DINO NUGGETS WITH A SIDE OF SANITY.

WE FOUGHT WITH OUR OLDEST ABOUT TRYING CHICKEN BURGERS FOR THE LONGEST TIME. THEY HAD EVERYTHING HE ALREADY ENJOYED, JUST IN A DIFFERENT CONFIGURATION. AFTER MONTHS OF PAINFULLY SLOW PROGRESS, HE FINALLY ATE ONE. HE LIKED IT SO MUCH, THAT WAS ALL HE WOULD EAT FOR WEEKS! THEN HE HATED THEM AGAIN, THEN HE LOVED THEM AGAIN . . . I CAN FEEL MY HAIR GOING GRAY JUST WRITING THIS.

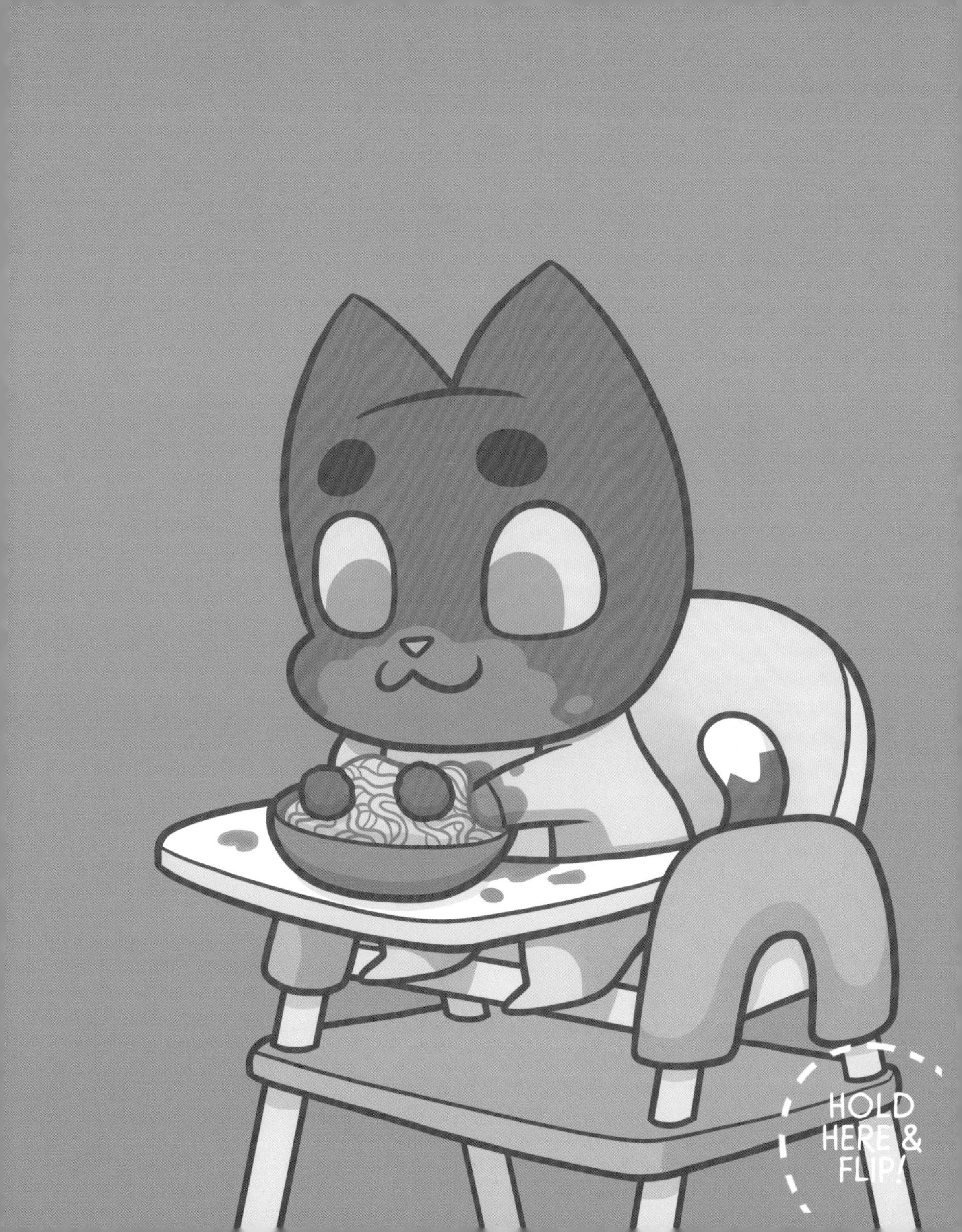
HOLD
HERE &
FLIP!

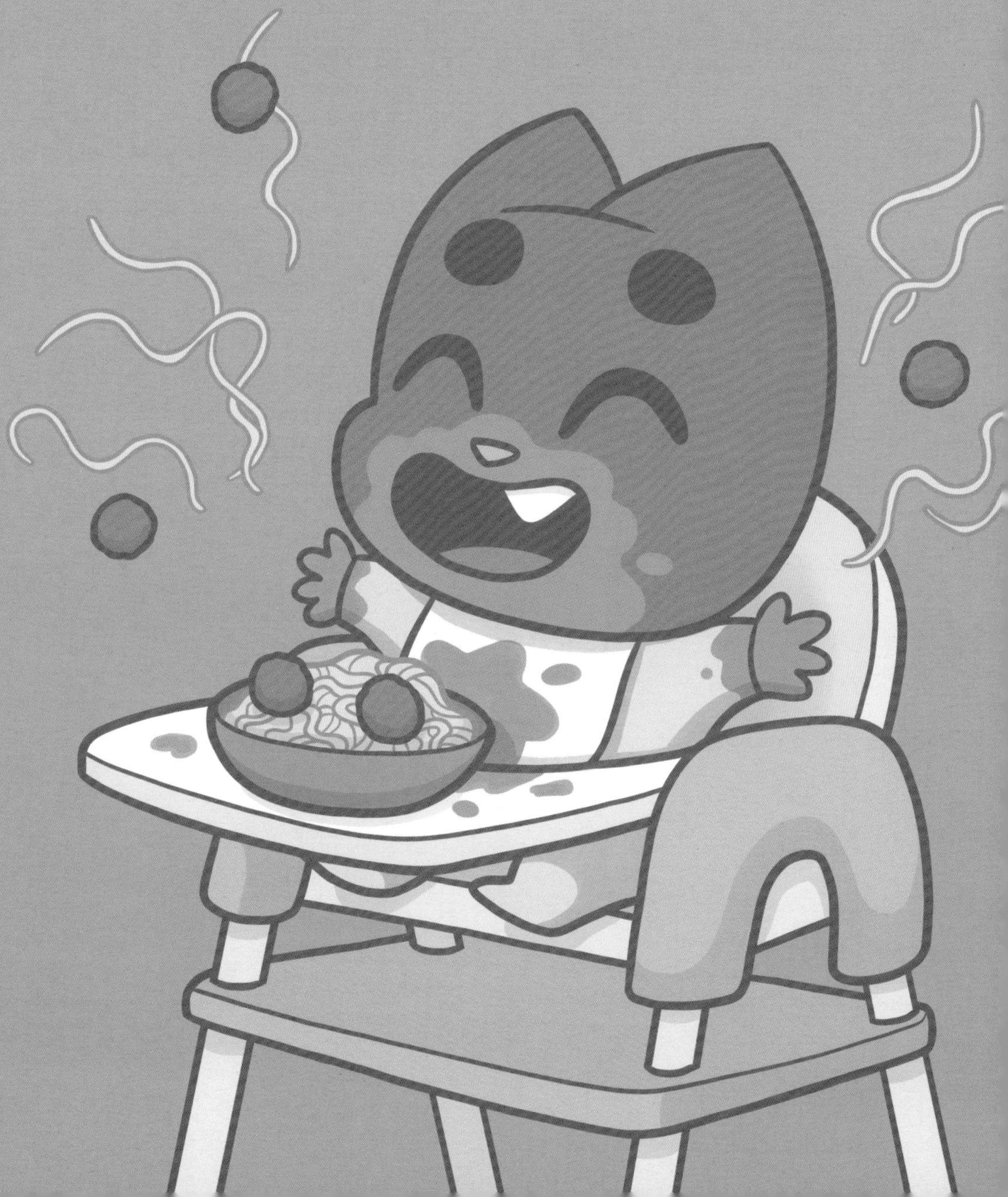

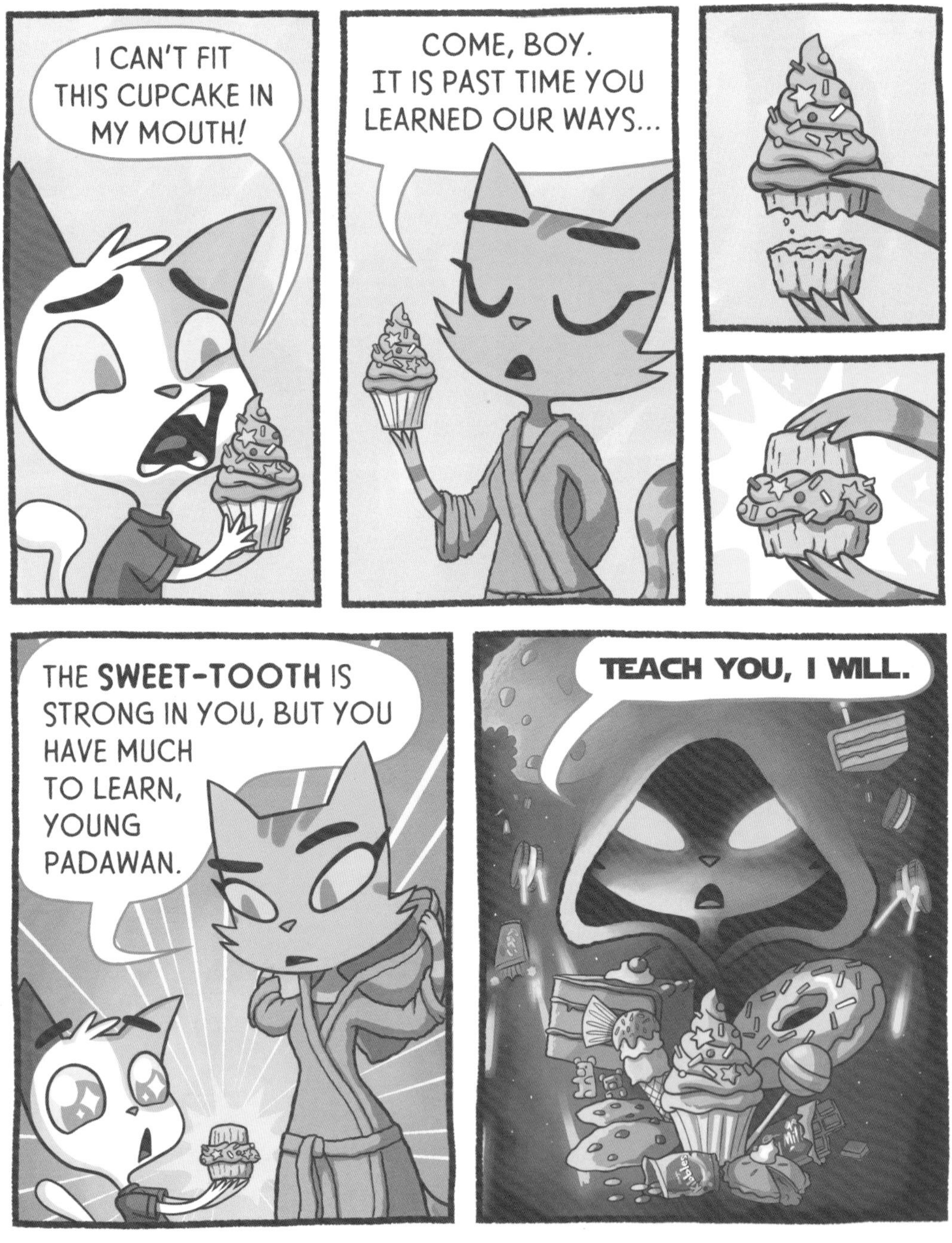
I CAN'T FIT THIS CUPCAKE IN MY MOUTH!
COME, BOY. IT IS PAST TIME YOU LEARNED OUR WAYS...
THE **SWEET-TOOTH** IS STRONG IN YOU, BUT YOU HAVE MUCH TO LEARN, YOUNG PADAWAN.
TEACH YOU, I WILL.

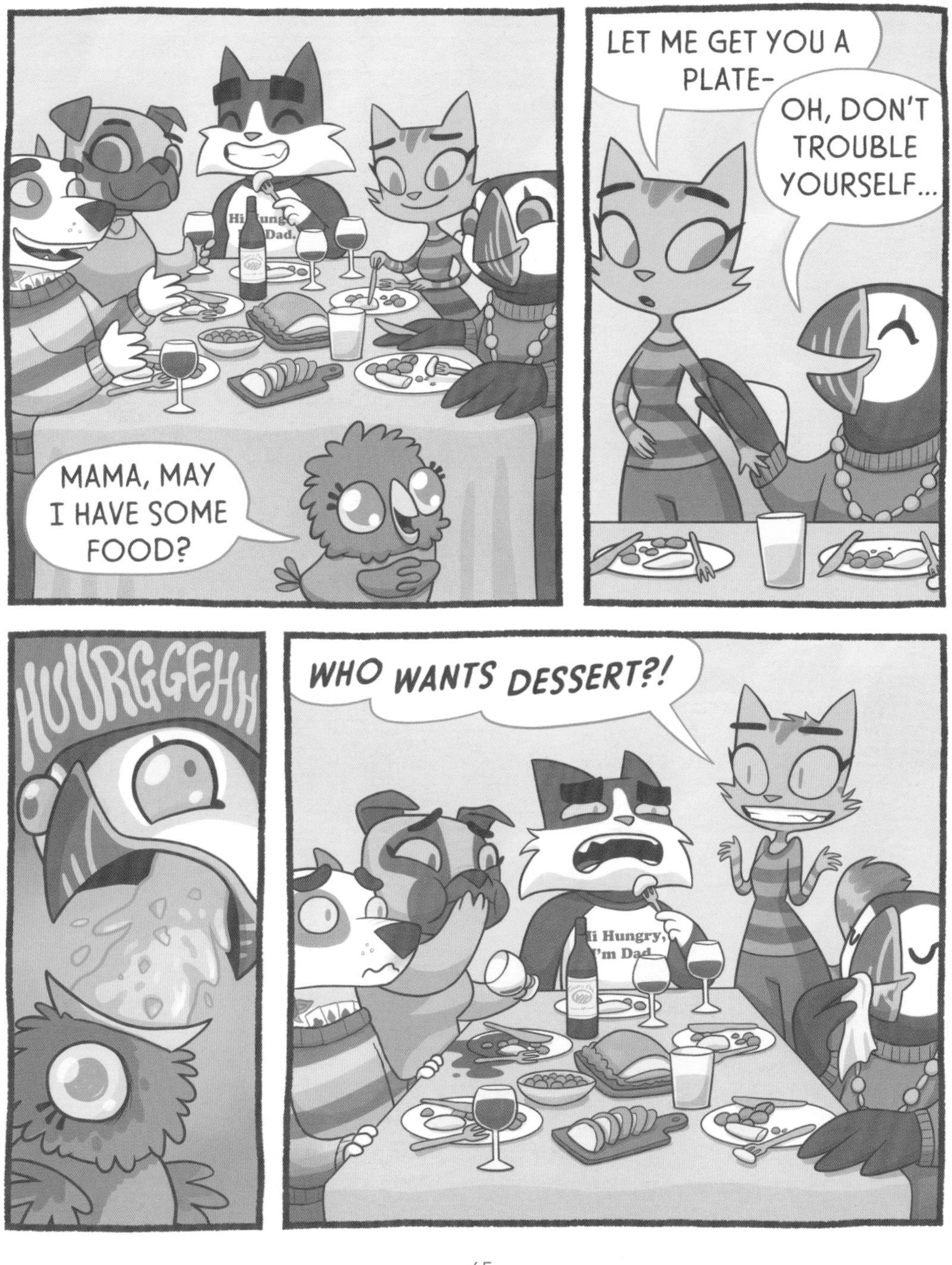
MAMA, MAY I HAVE SOME FOOD?
LET ME GET YOU A PLATE-
OH, DON'T TROUBLE YOURSELF...
HUURGGEHH
WHO WANTS DESSERT?!
Hi Hungry, I'm Dad.

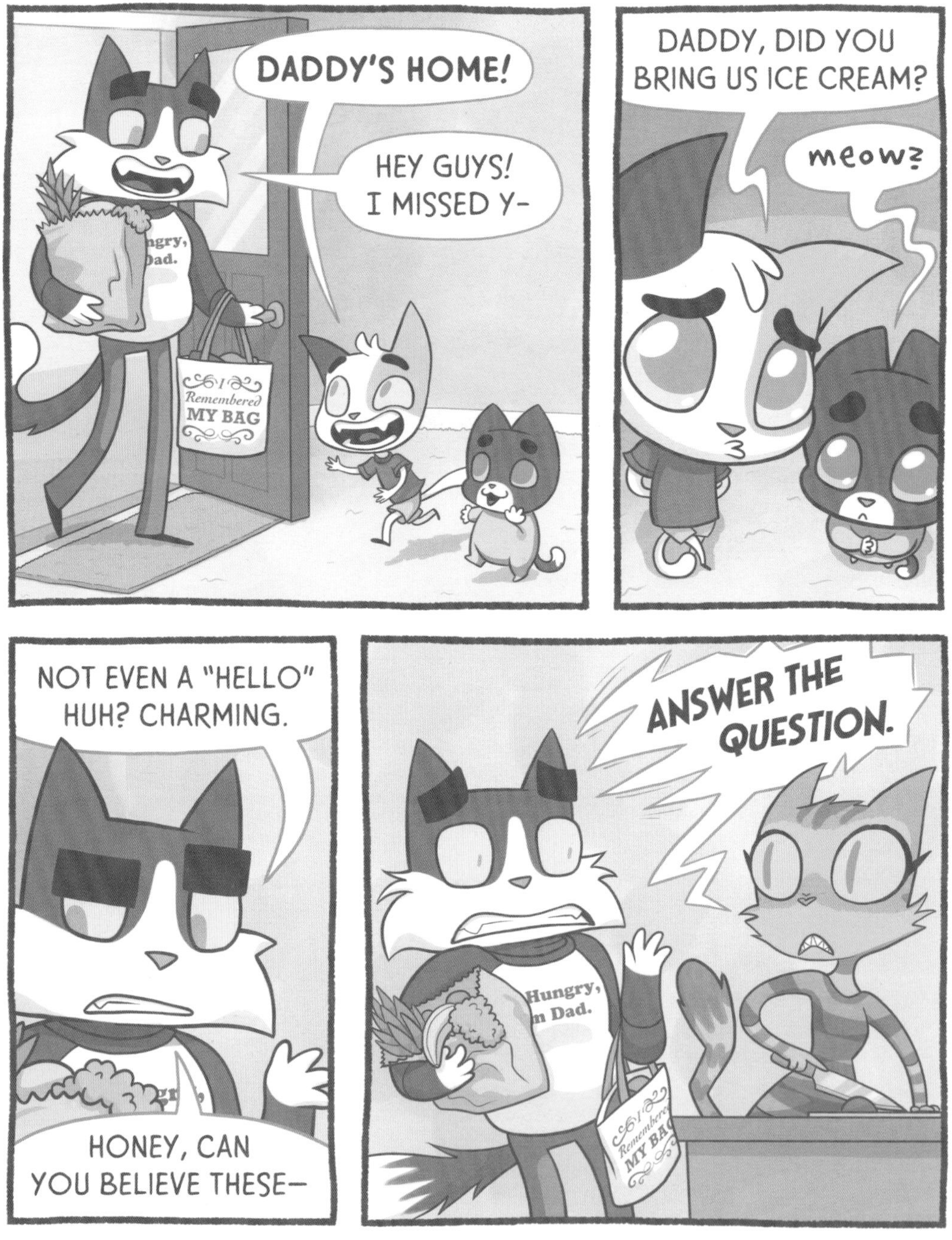
DADDY'S HOME!
HEY GUYS! I MISSED Y-
Hungry, Dad.
I Remembered MY BAG
DADDY, DID YOU BRING US ICE CREAM?
meow?
NOT EVEN A "HELLO" HUH? CHARMING.
HONEY, CAN YOU BELIEVE THESE—
ANSWER THE QUESTION.
Hungry, Dad.
I Remembered MY BAG

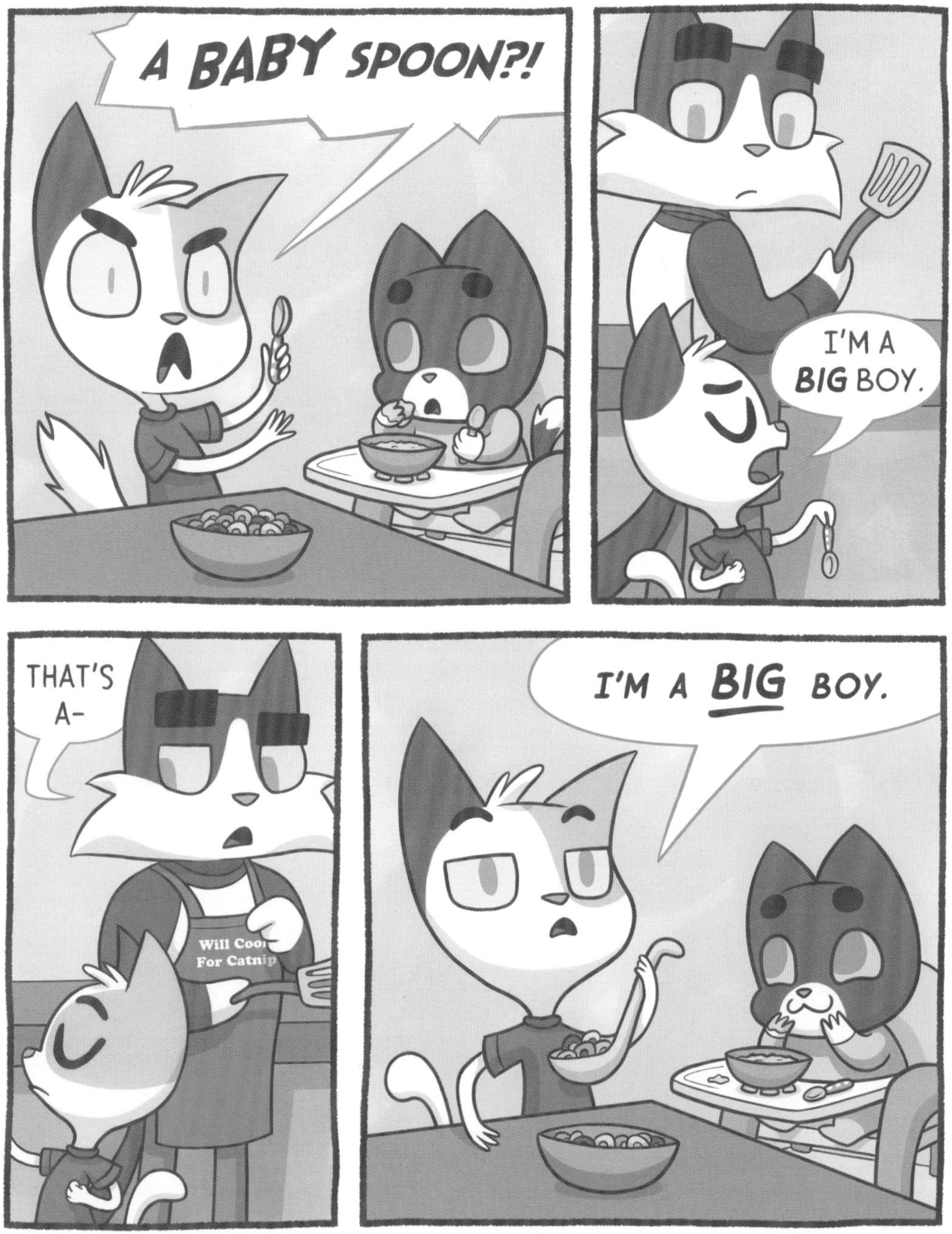
A BABY SPOON?!
I'M A BIG BOY.
THAT'S A-
Will Cook For Catnip
I'M A BIG BOY.

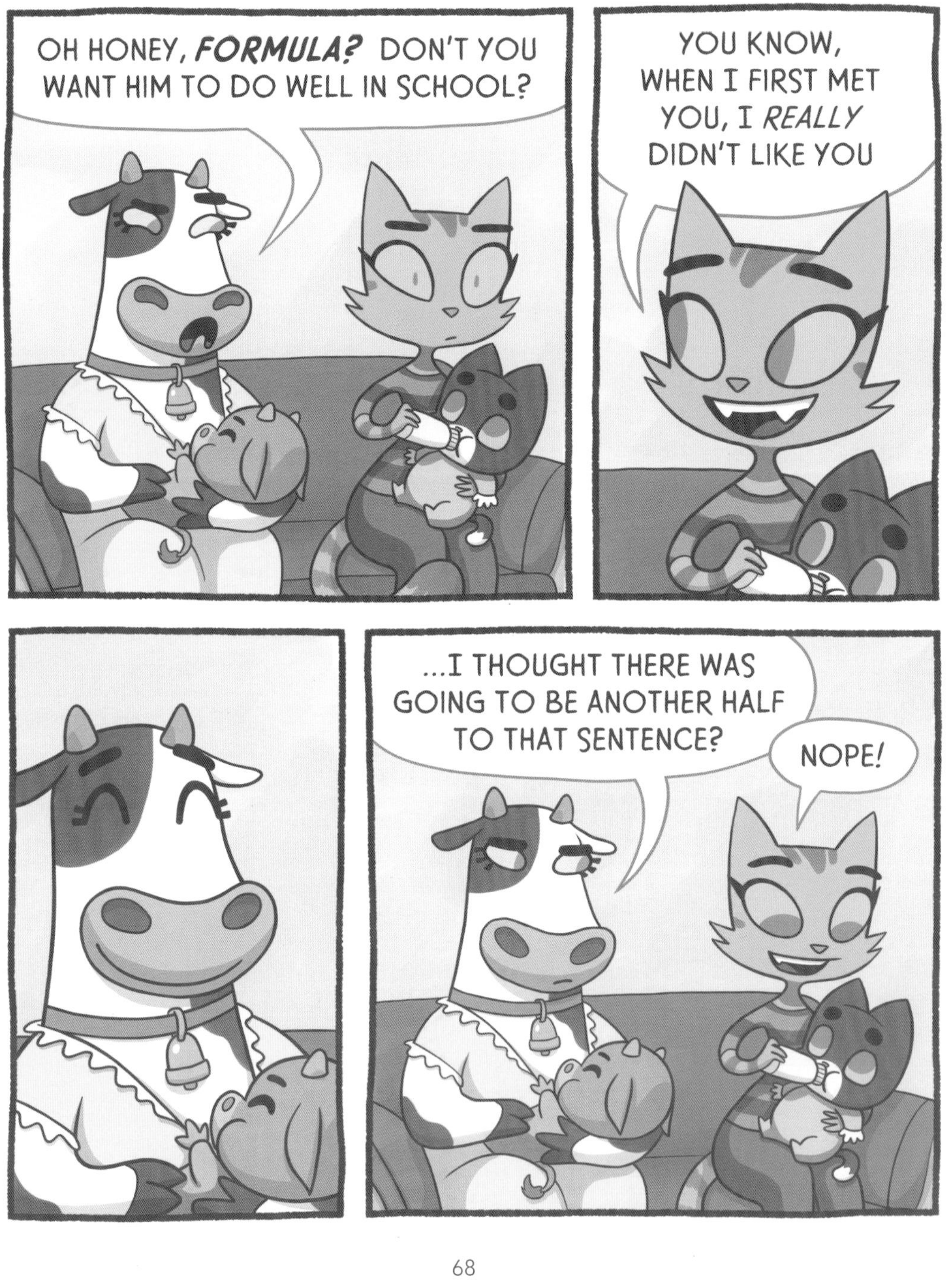
OH HONEY, ***FORMULA?*** DON'T YOU WANT HIM TO DO WELL IN SCHOOL?
YOU KNOW, WHEN I FIRST MET YOU, I *REALLY* DIDN'T LIKE YOU
...I THOUGHT THERE WAS GOING TO BE ANOTHER HALF TO THAT SENTENCE?
NOPE!

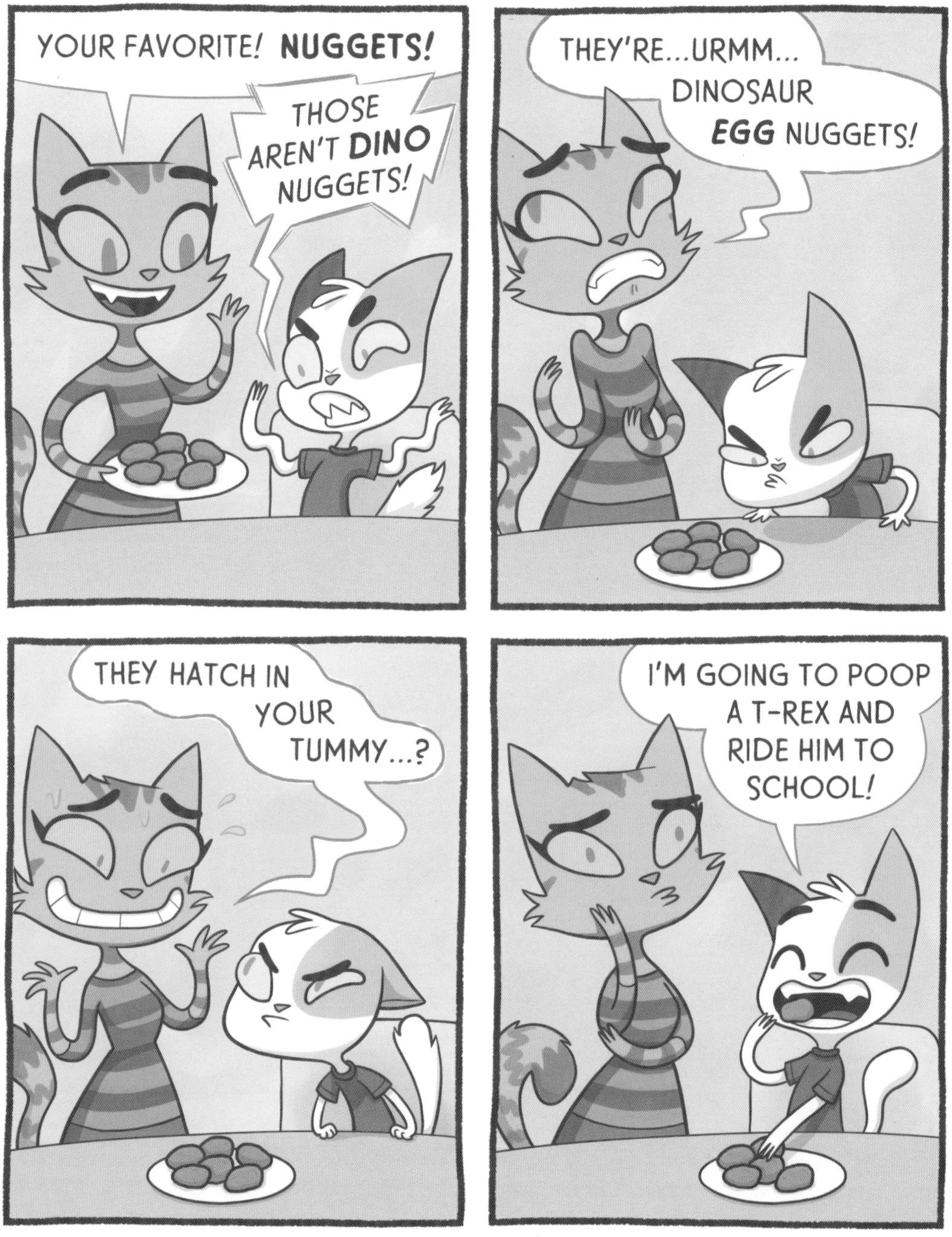
YOUR FAVORITE! **NUGGETS!**
THOSE AREN'T **DINO** NUGGETS!
THEY'RE...URMM... DINOSAUR **EGG** NUGGETS!
THEY HATCH IN YOUR TUMMY...?
I'M GOING TO POOP A T-REX AND RIDE HIM TO SCHOOL!

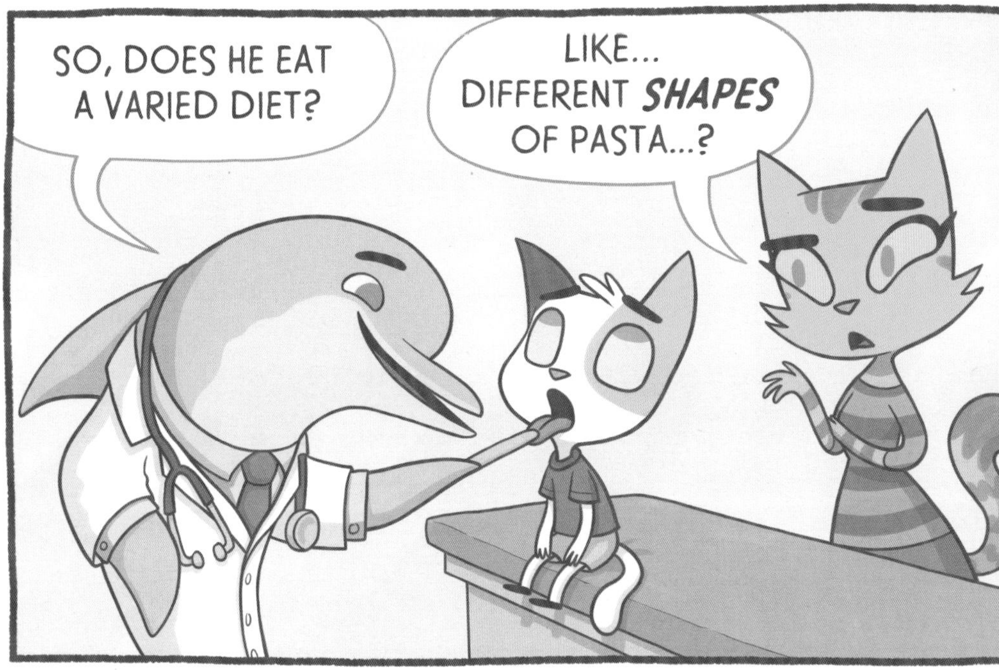
SO, DOES HE EAT A VARIED DIET?
LIKE... DIFFERENT **SHAPES** OF PASTA...?

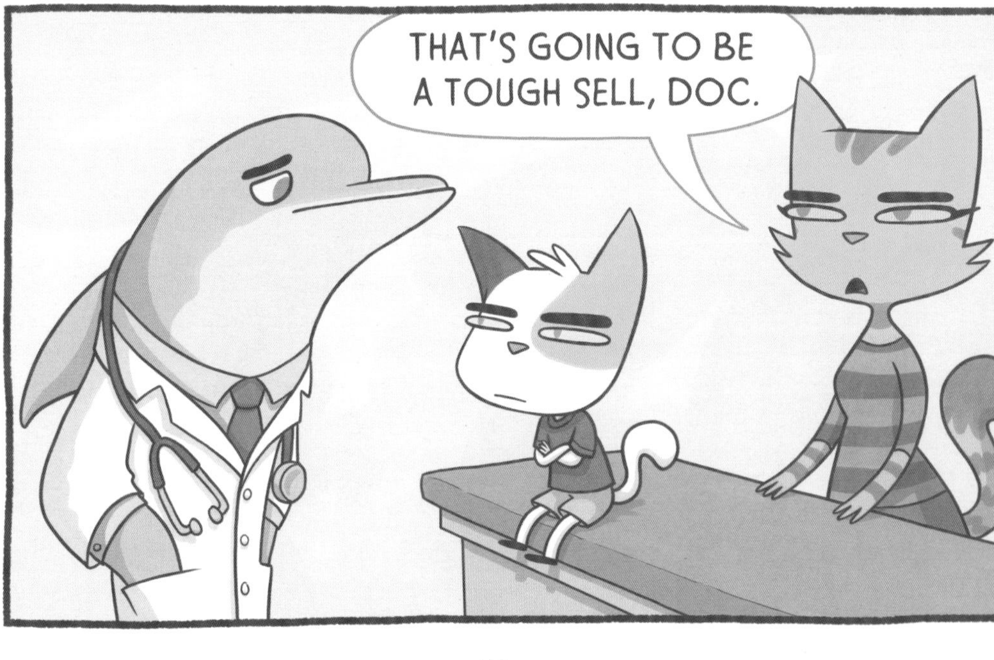
THAT'S GOING TO BE A TOUGH SELL, DOC.

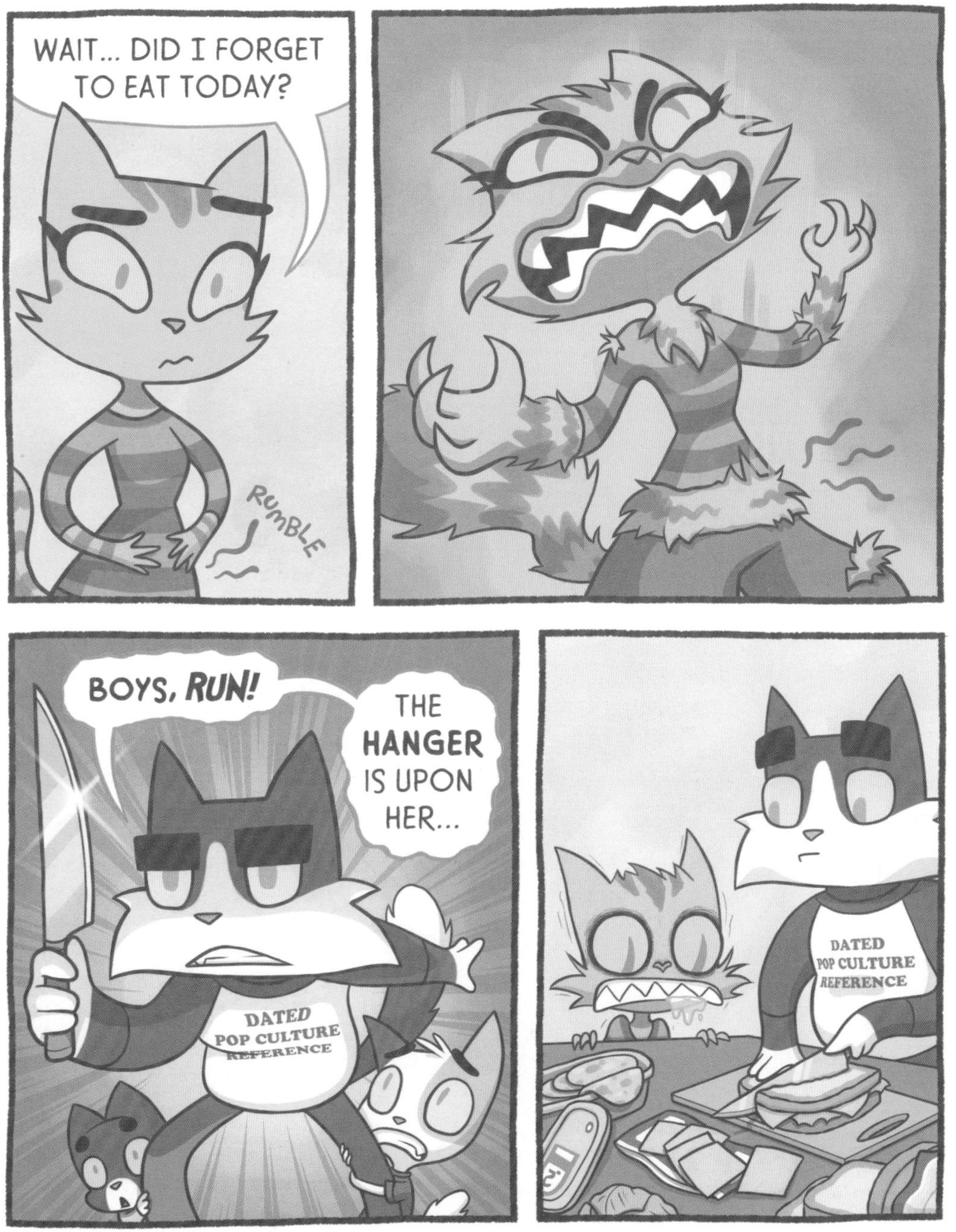
WAIT... DID I FORGET TO EAT TODAY?
RUMBLE
BOYS, RUN!
THE HANGER IS UPON HER...
DATED POP CULTURE REFERENCE
DATED POP CULTURE REFERENCE

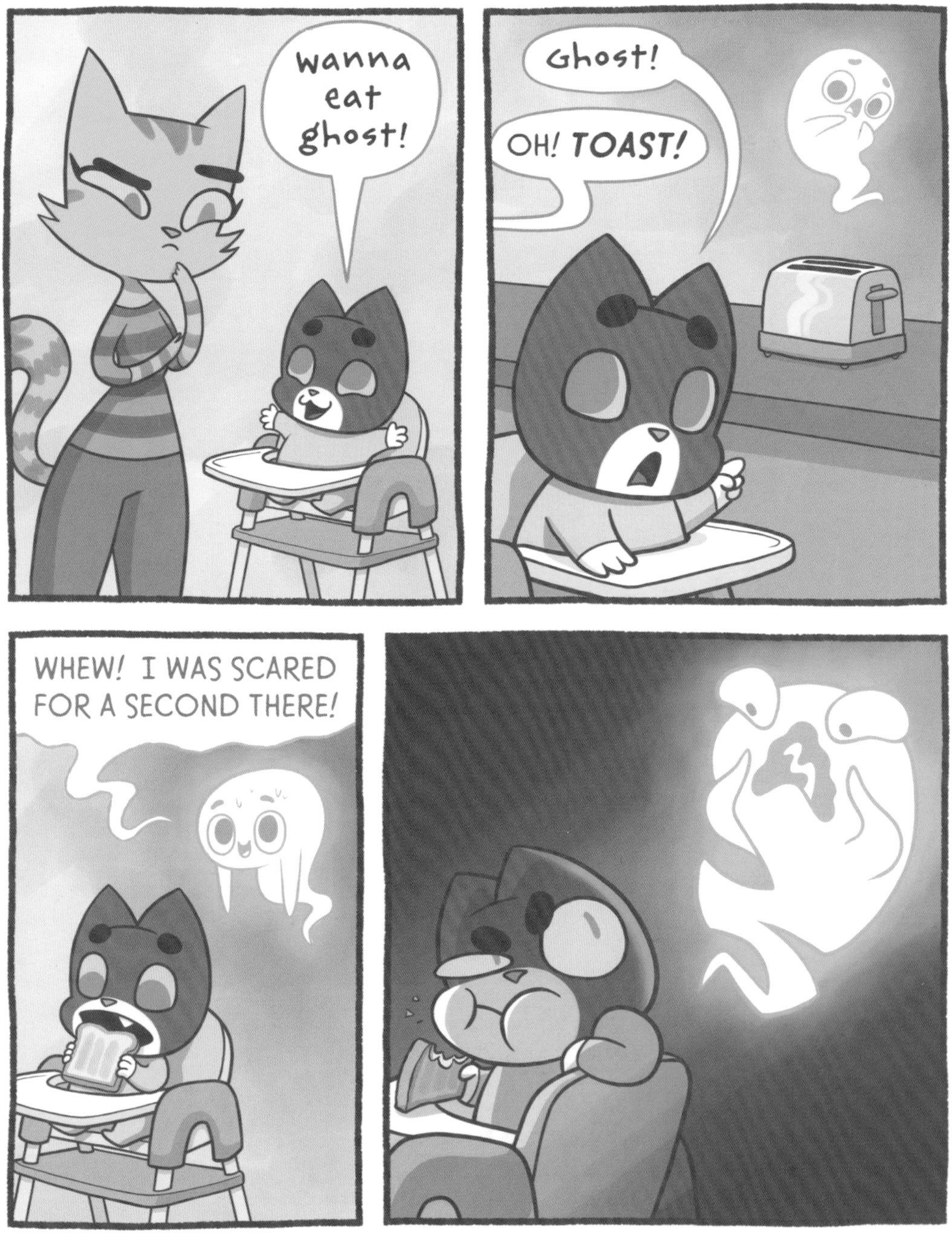
wanna eat ghost!
Ghost!
OH! TOAST!
WHEW! I WAS SCARED FOR A SECOND THERE!

BASED ON A TWEET BY @HOMEWITHPEANUT

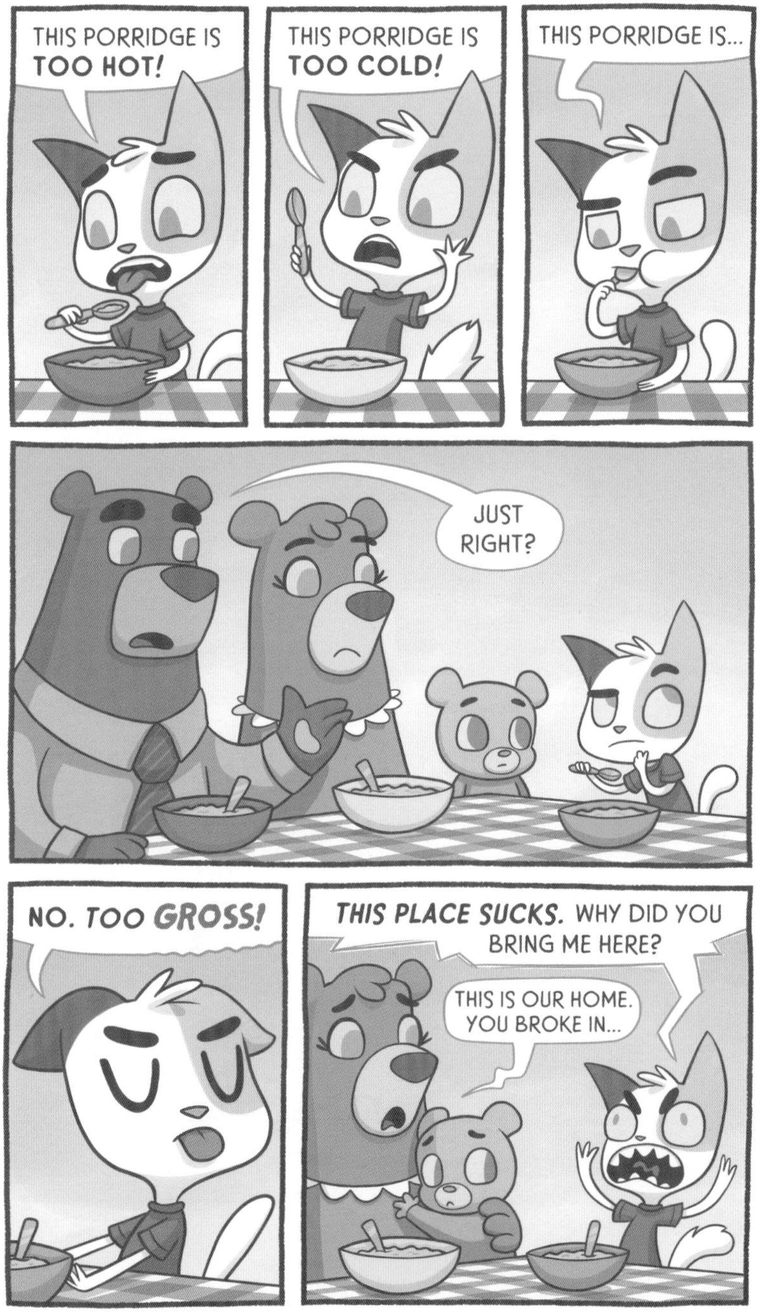
THIS PORRIDGE IS **TOO HOT!**
THIS PORRIDGE IS **TOO COLD!**
THIS PORRIDGE IS...
JUST RIGHT?
NO. *TOO* **GROSS!**
THIS PLACE SUCKS. WHY DID YOU BRING ME HERE?
THIS IS OUR HOME. YOU BROKE IN...

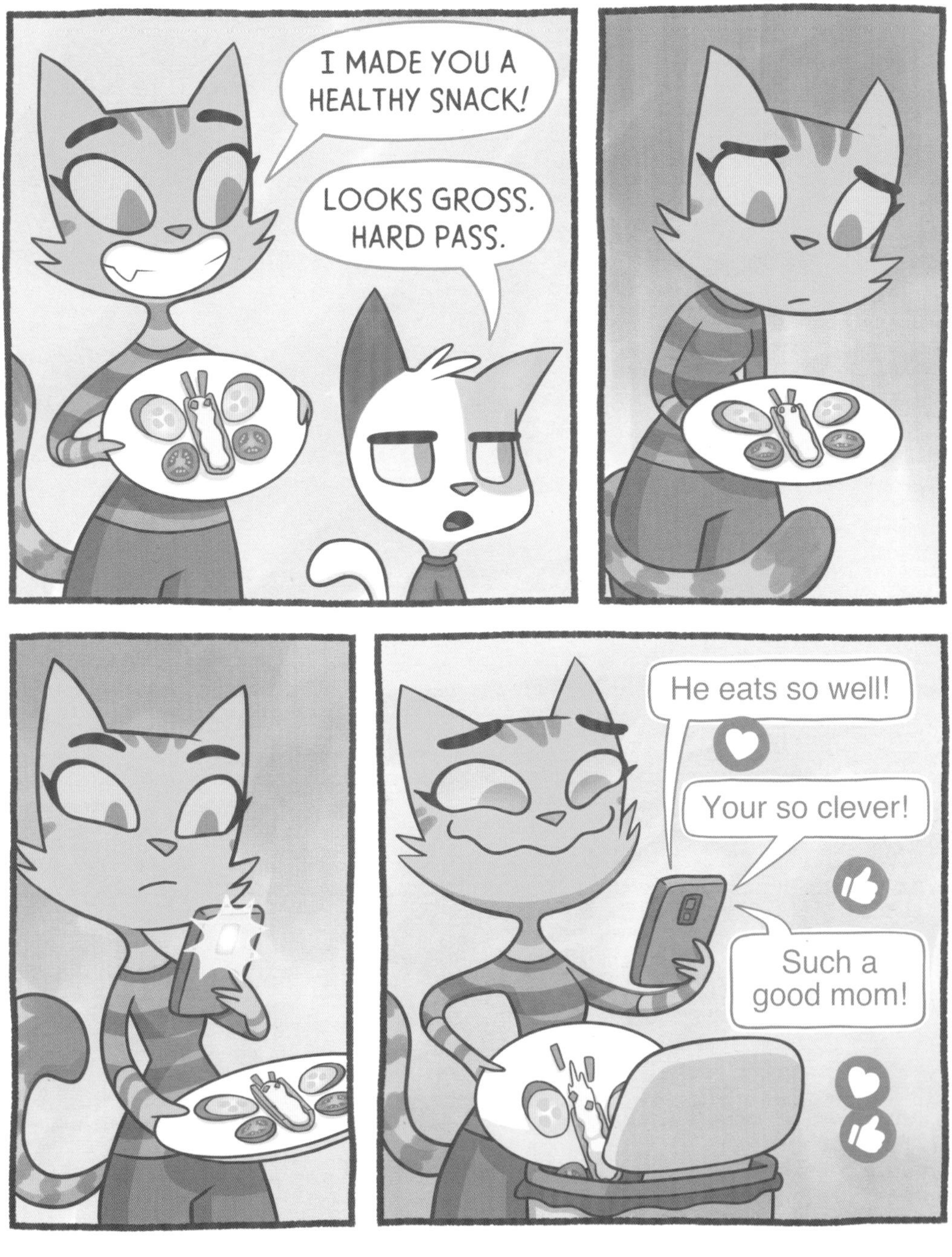
I MADE YOU A HEALTHY SNACK!
LOOKS GROSS. HARD PASS.
He eats so well!
Your so clever!
Such a good mom!

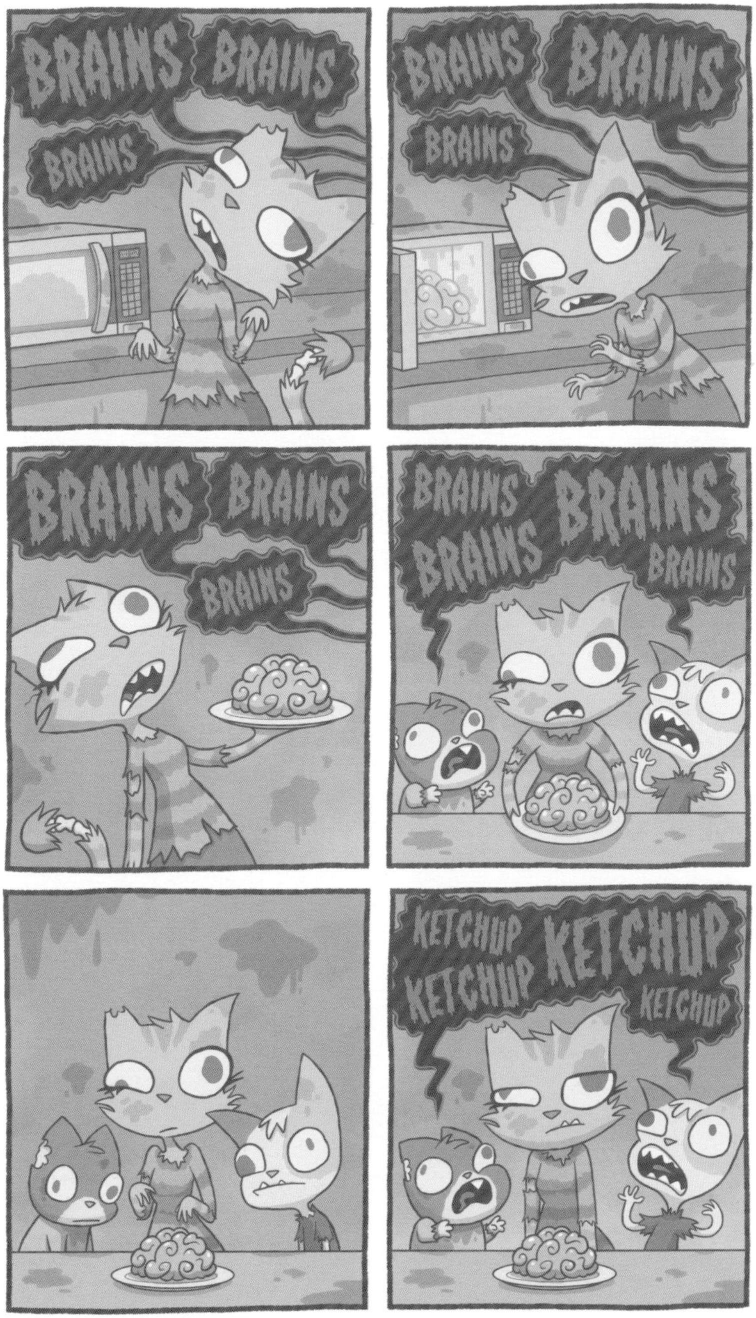
BRAINS
BRAINS
BRAINS
BRAINS
BRAINS
BRAINS
BRAINS
BRAINS
BRAINS
BRAINS
BRAINS
BRAINS
BRAINS
KETCHUP
KETCHUP
KETCHUP
KETCHUP

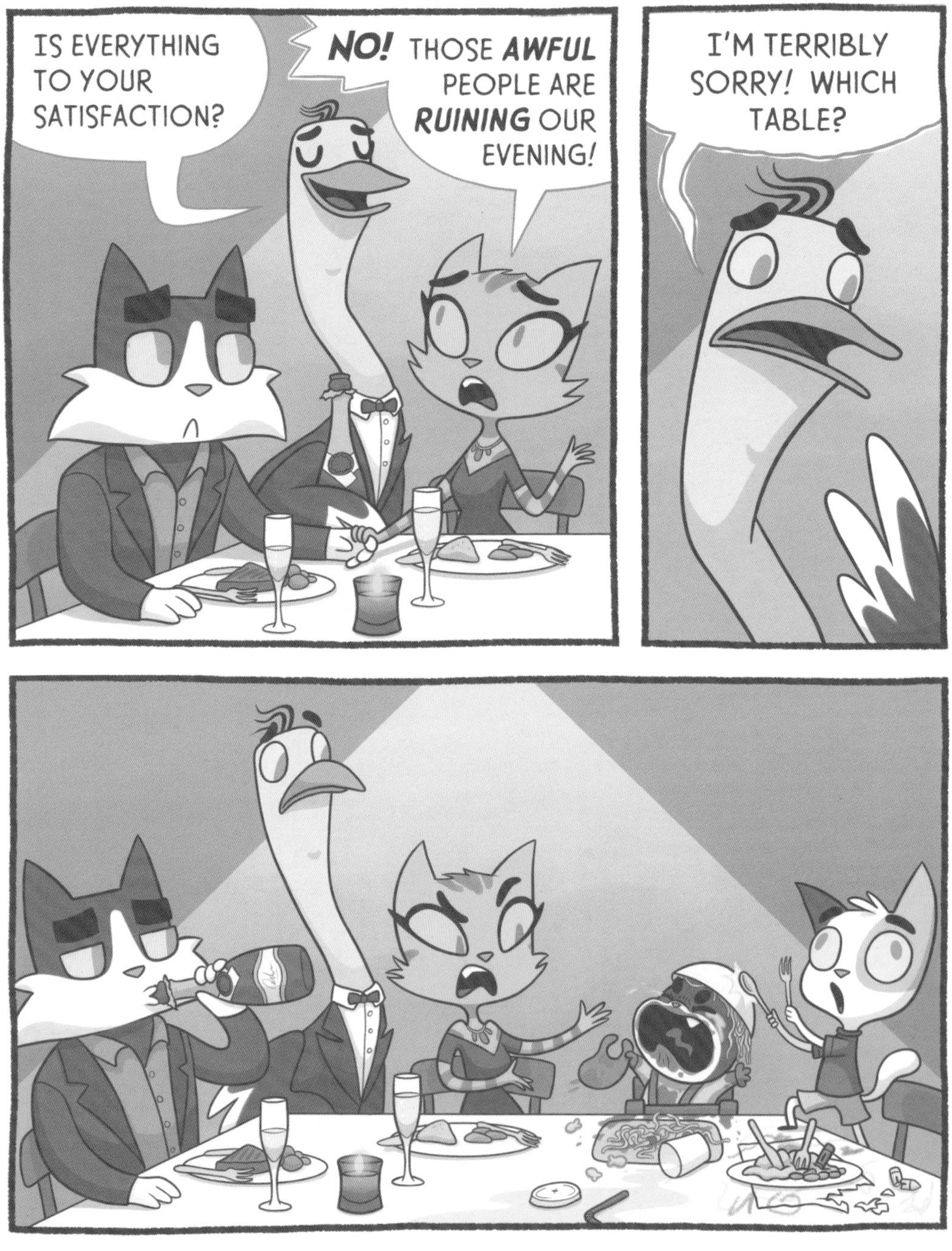
IS EVERYTHING TO YOUR SATISFACTION?
NO! THOSE AWFUL PEOPLE ARE RUINING OUR EVENING!
I'M TERRIBLY SORRY! WHICH TABLE?

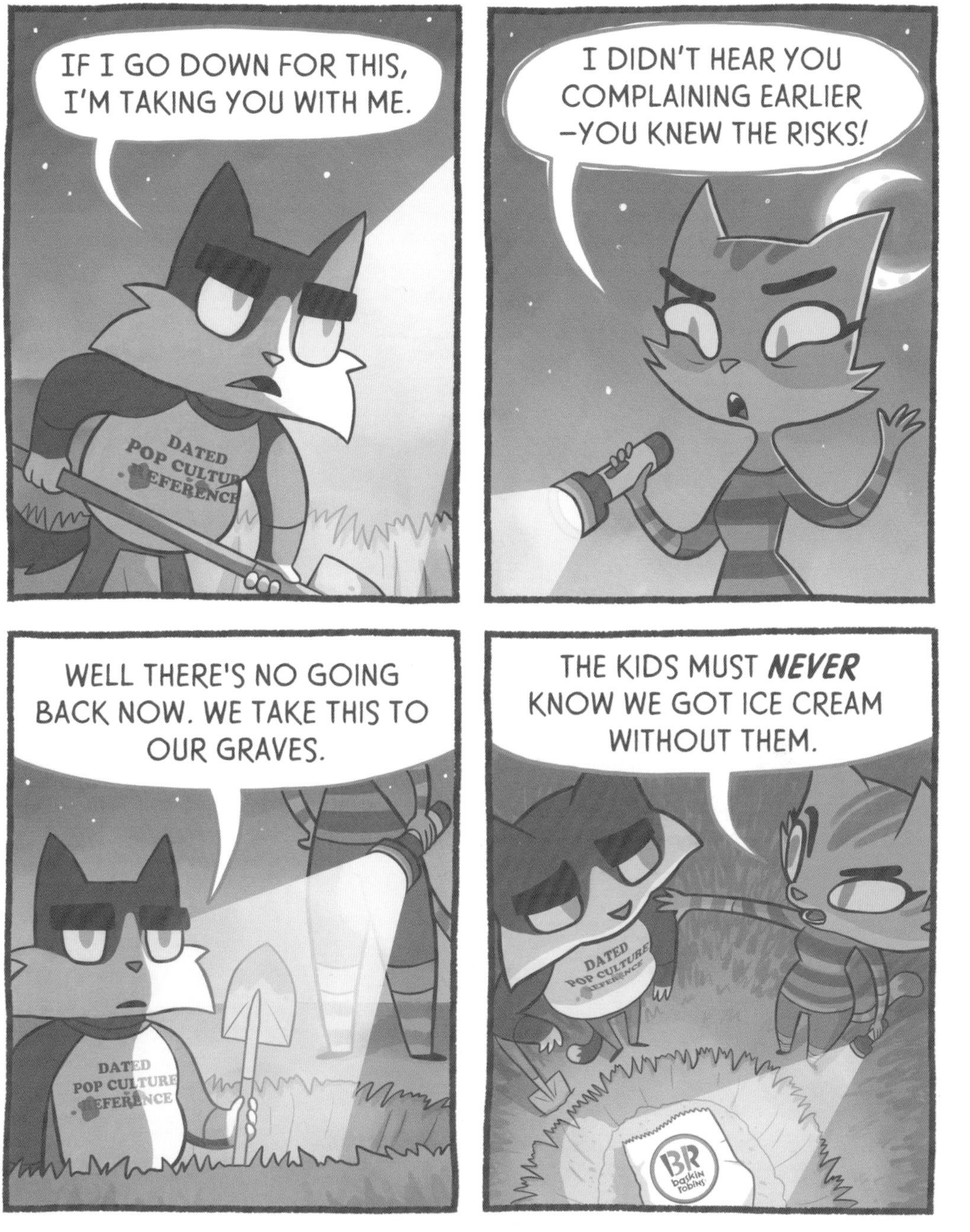
IF I GO DOWN FOR THIS, I'M TAKING YOU WITH ME.
I DIDN'T HEAR YOU COMPLAINING EARLIER —YOU KNEW THE RISKS!
WELL THERE'S NO GOING BACK NOW. WE TAKE THIS TO OUR GRAVES.
THE KIDS MUST ***NEVER*** KNOW WE GOT ICE CREAM WITHOUT THEM.

VENTURING OUT

OUR OLDEST WAS PERFECTLY HAPPY OUT AND ABOUT, SO LONG AS WE WERE MOVING. LIKE THE BUS IN *SPEED*, IF THE SHOPPING CART DROPPED BELOW A CERTAIN VELOCITY, HE WOULD EXPLODE. WE GOT INTO A GOOD SYSTEM OF ONE OF US GRABBING THE GROCERIES (FAST!) WHILE THE OTHER DID CIRCUITS AROUND THE SHOP. THIS WORKED FINE WHEN WE WERE TOGETHER, BUT SHOPPING SOLO WAS A NIGHTMARE VERSION OF *SUPERMARKET SWEEP*. I'D DO A DRIVE-BY OF AN AISLE AND GRAB WHAT I COULD. IF I COULDN'T GRAB MY CEREAL, THEN—*SHRUG*—STILL BETTER THAN THE ALTERNATIVE*!*

THINGS WERE VERY DIFFERENT WITH OUR SECOND GUY. HE WOULD PERCH IN THE BABY BASKET THING AND SMILE AT PEOPLE AND SING LITTLE SONGS ABOUT THE GROCERIES. PASSERSBY WOULD COMPLIMENT ME ON MY WELL-BEHAVED CHILD, AND AS MY EYES GLAZED OVER FROM THE FLASHBACKS, 2014-ME WOULD GROWL, *"I EARNED THIS! I DID MY TIME!"*

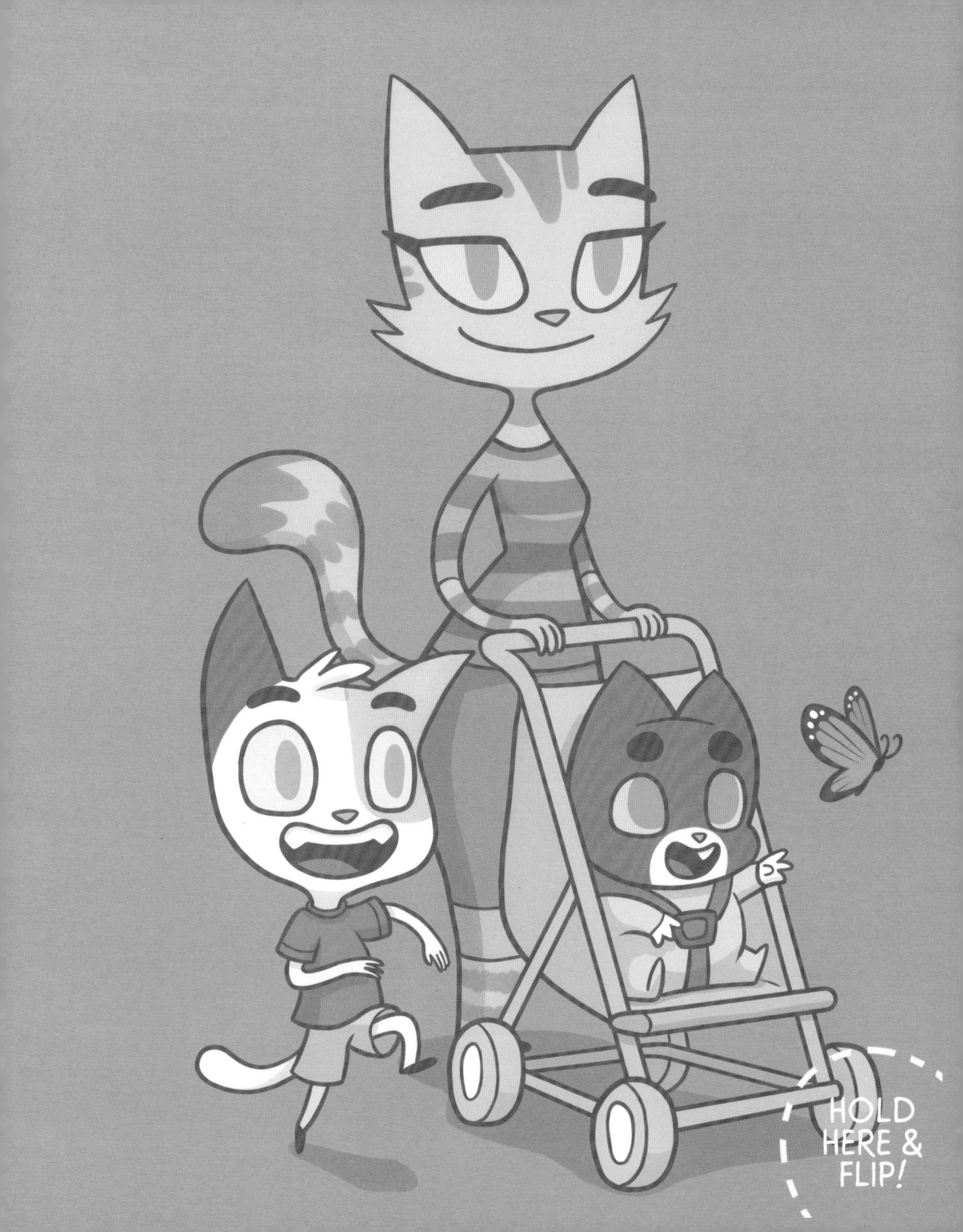
HOLD
HERE &
FLIP!

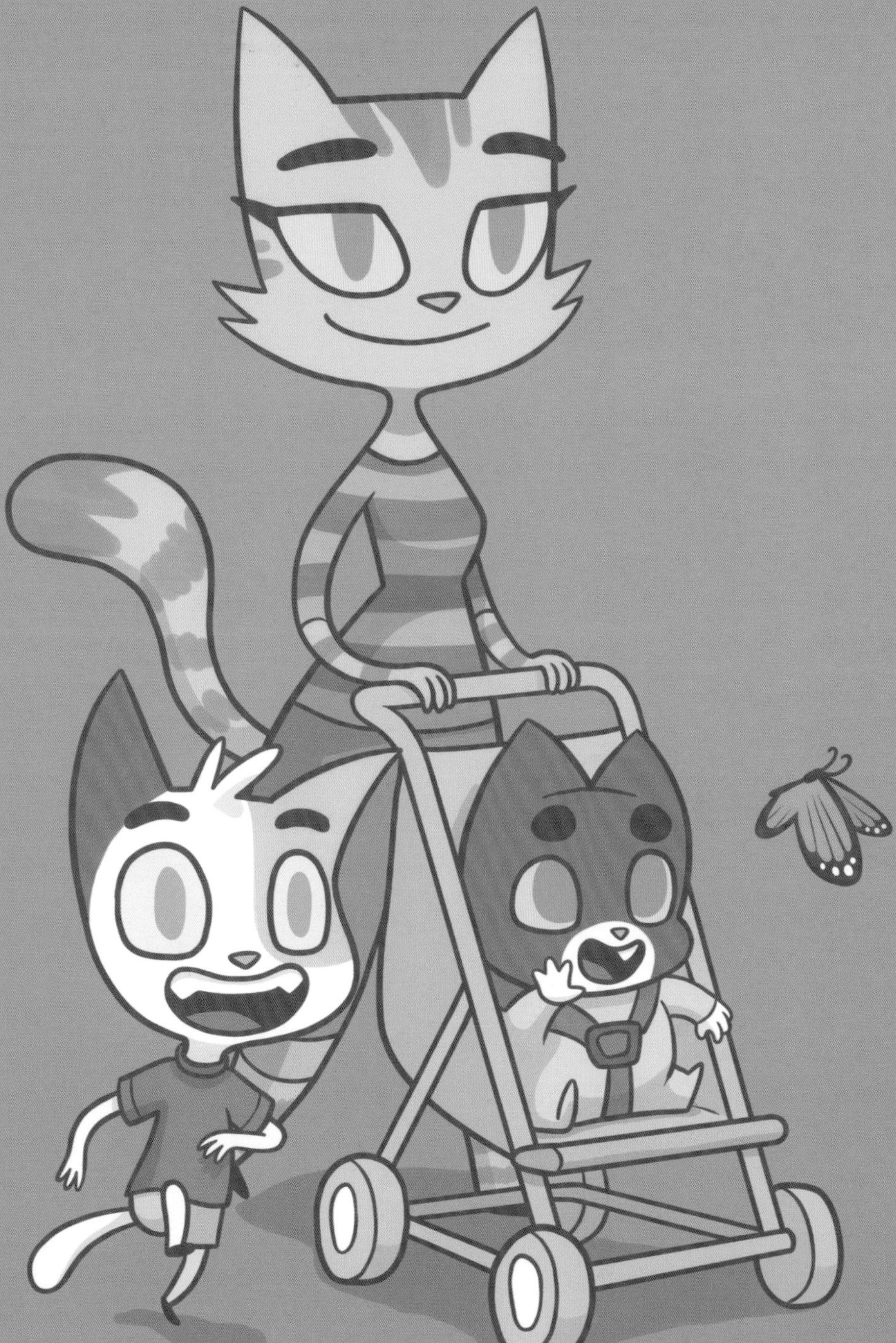

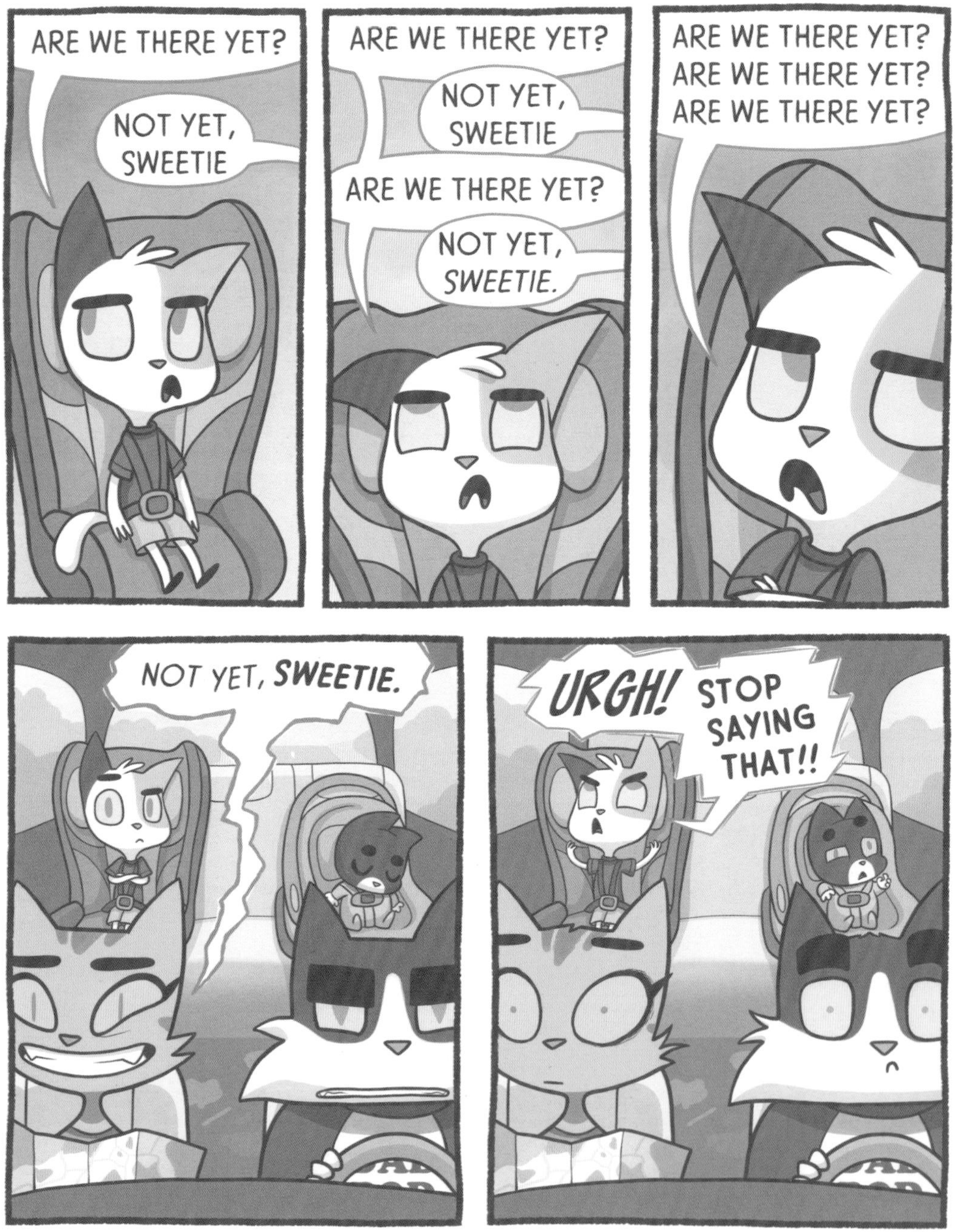
ARE WE THERE YET?
NOT YET, SWEETIE
ARE WE THERE YET?
NOT YET, SWEETIE
ARE WE THERE YET?
NOT YET, SWEETIE.
ARE WE THERE YET? ARE WE THERE YET? ARE WE THERE YET?
NOT YET, SWEETIE.
URGH!
STOP SAYING THAT!!

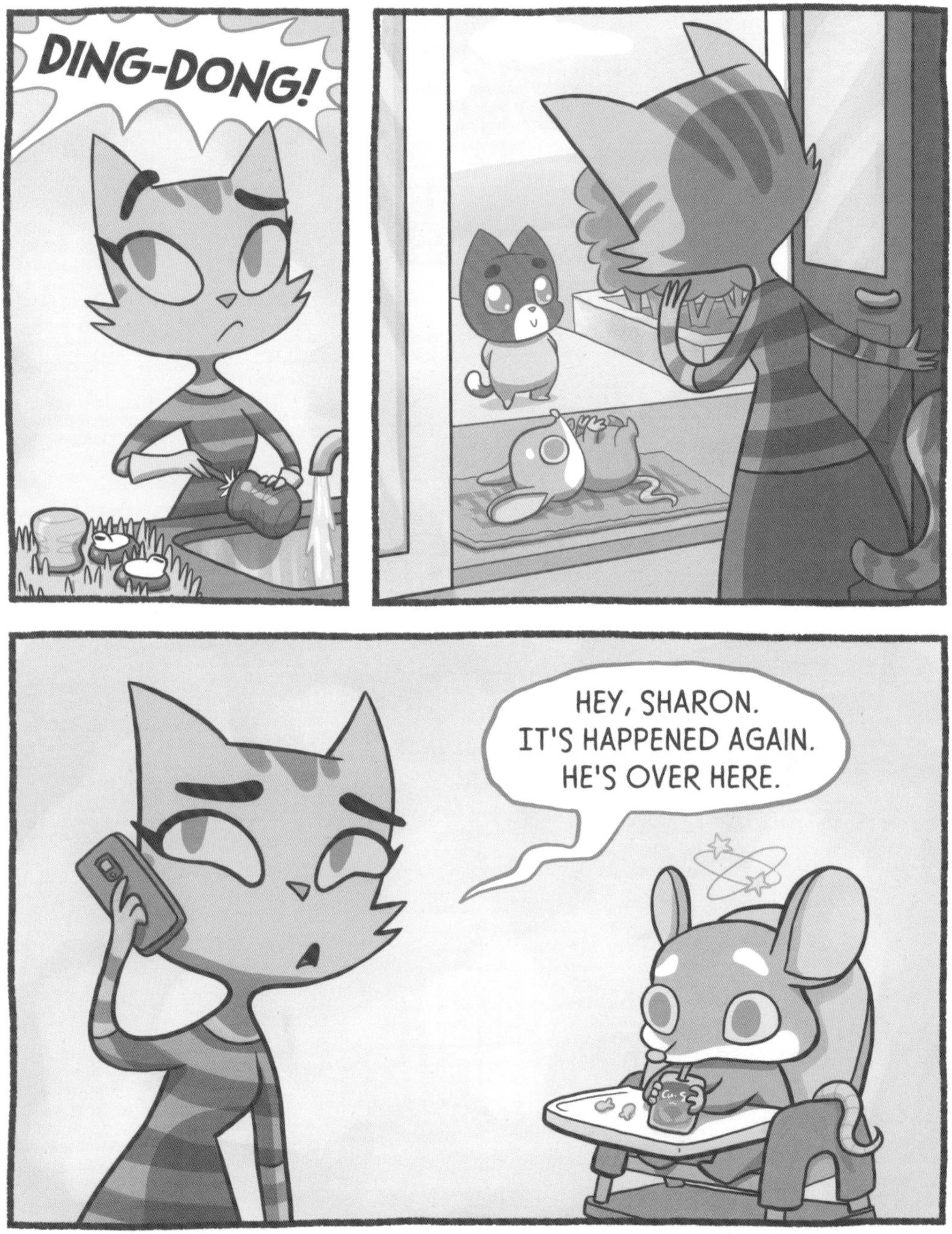
DING-DONG!
HEY, SHARON. IT'S HAPPENED AGAIN. HE'S OVER HERE.

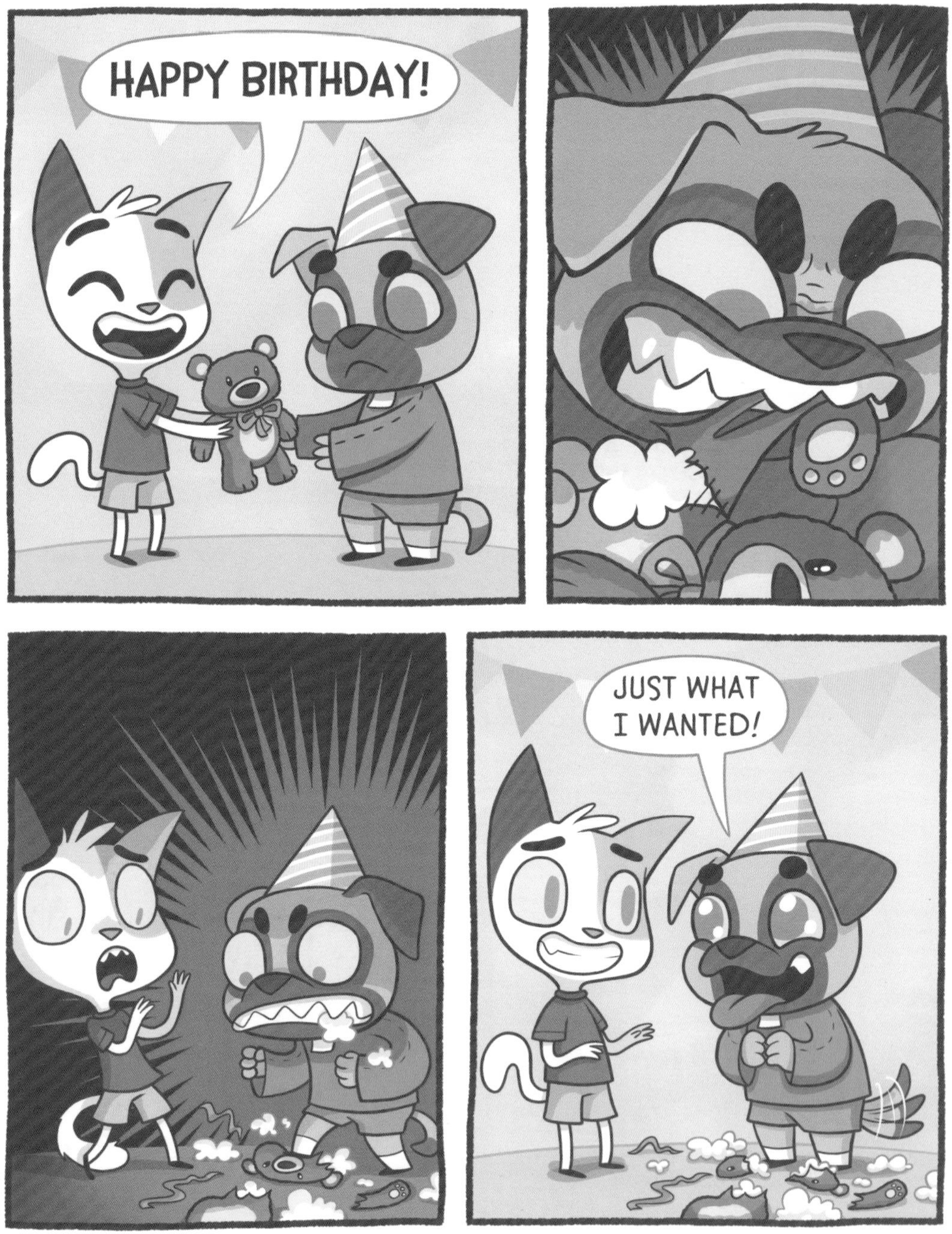
HAPPY BIRTHDAY!
JUST WHAT I WANTED!

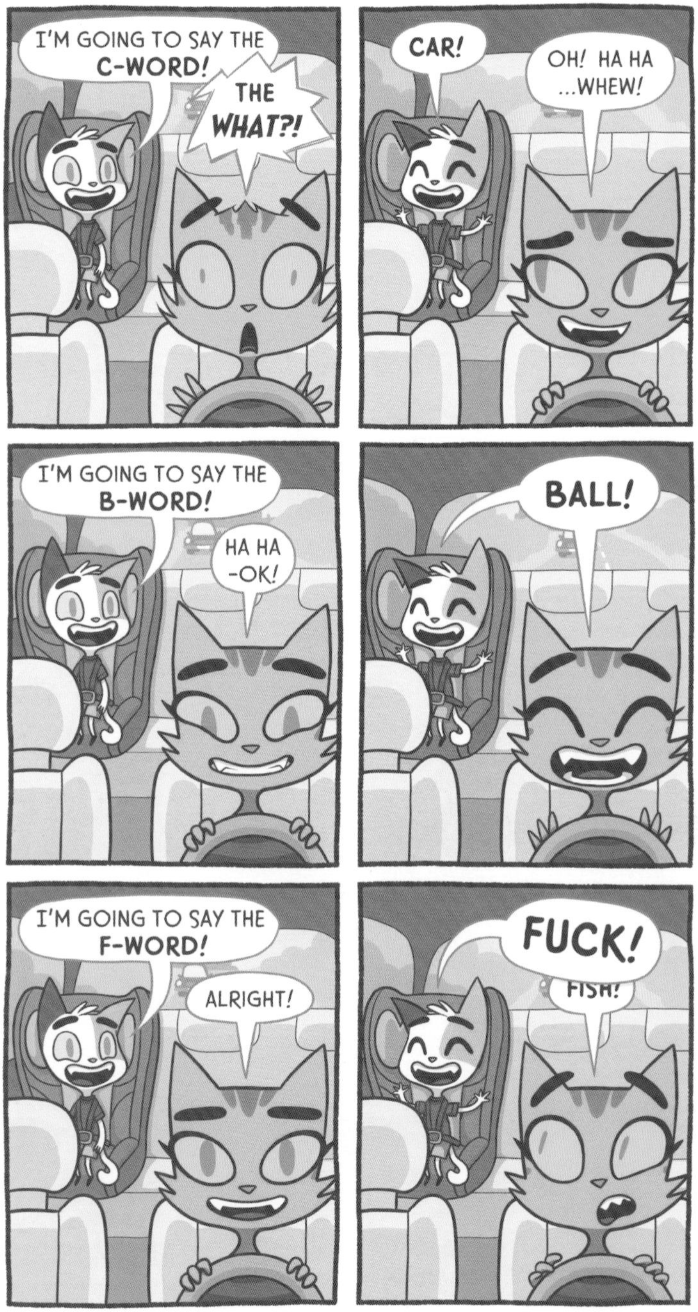
I'M GOING TO SAY THE C-WORD!
THE WHAT?!
CAR!
OH! HA HA ...WHEW!
I'M GOING TO SAY THE B-WORD!
HA HA -OK!
BALL!
I'M GOING TO SAY THE F-WORD!
ALRIGHT!
FUCK!
FISH!

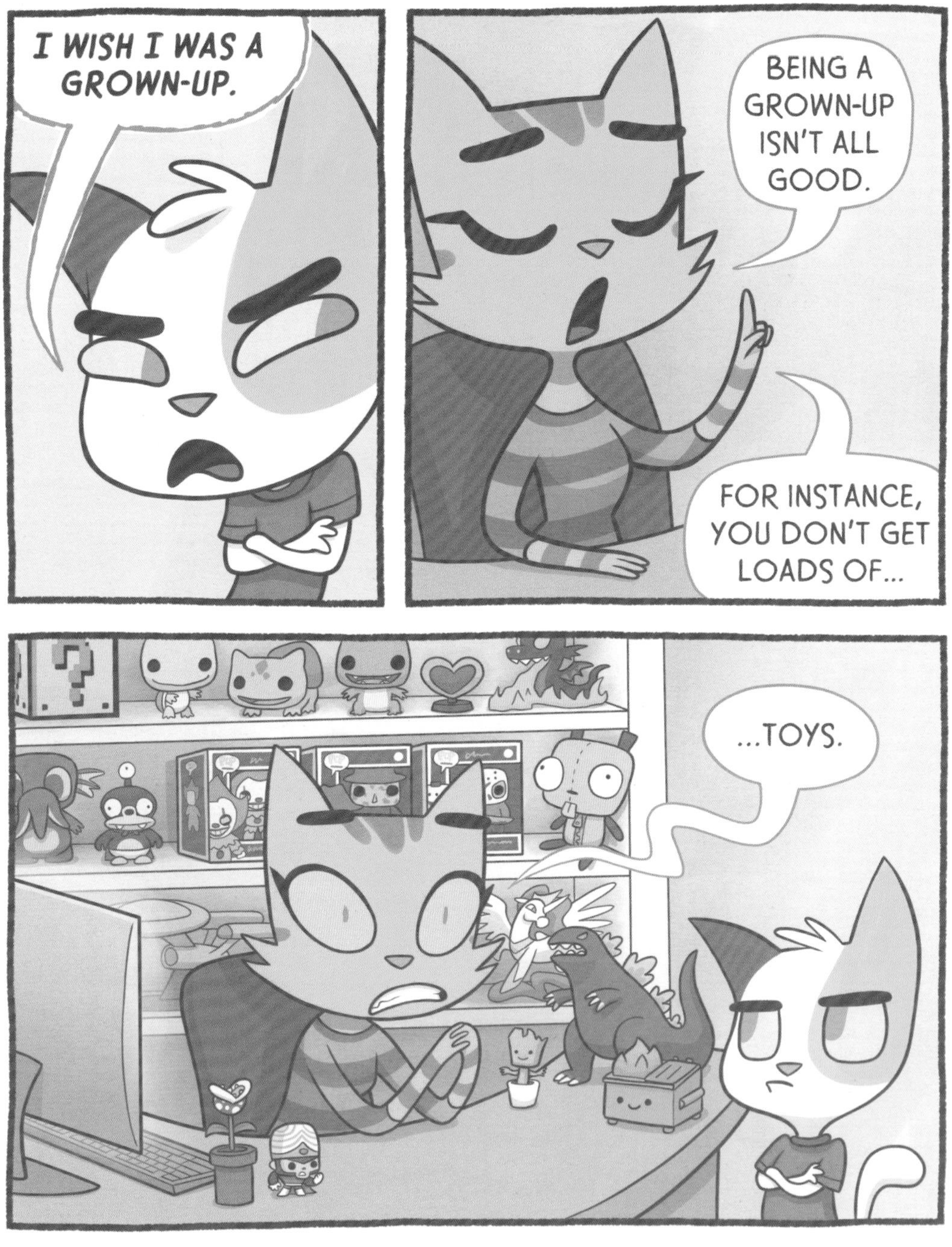
I WISH I WAS A GROWN-UP.
BEING A GROWN-UP ISN'T ALL GOOD.
FOR INSTANCE, YOU DON'T GET LOADS OF...
...TOYS.

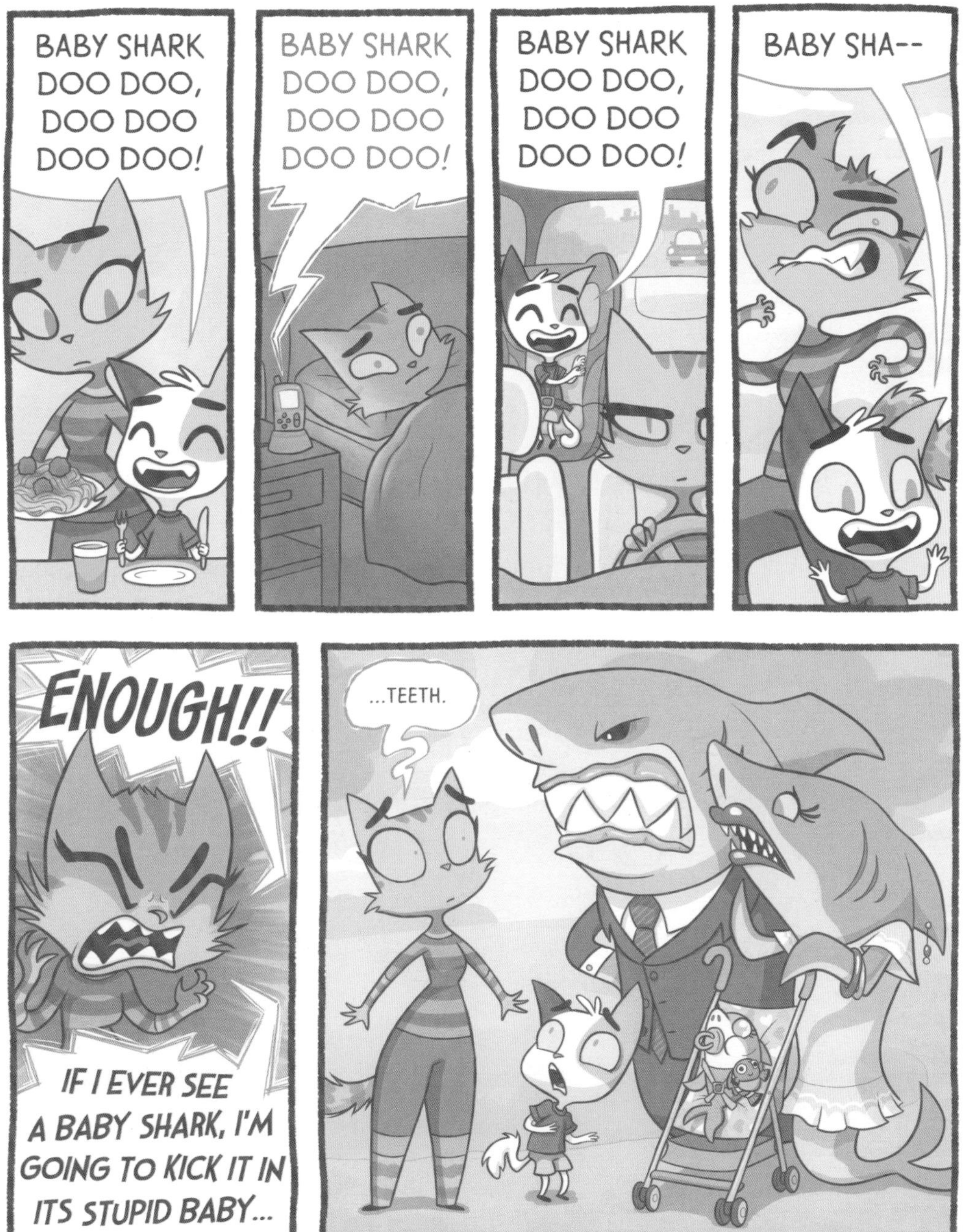
BABY SHARK DOO DOO, DOO DOO DOO DOO!
BABY SHARK DOO DOO, DOO DOO DOO DOO!
BABY SHARK DOO DOO, DOO DOO DOO DOO!
BABY SHA--
ENOUGH!!
IF I EVER SEE A BABY SHARK, I'M GOING TO KICK IT IN ITS STUPID BABY...
...TEETH.

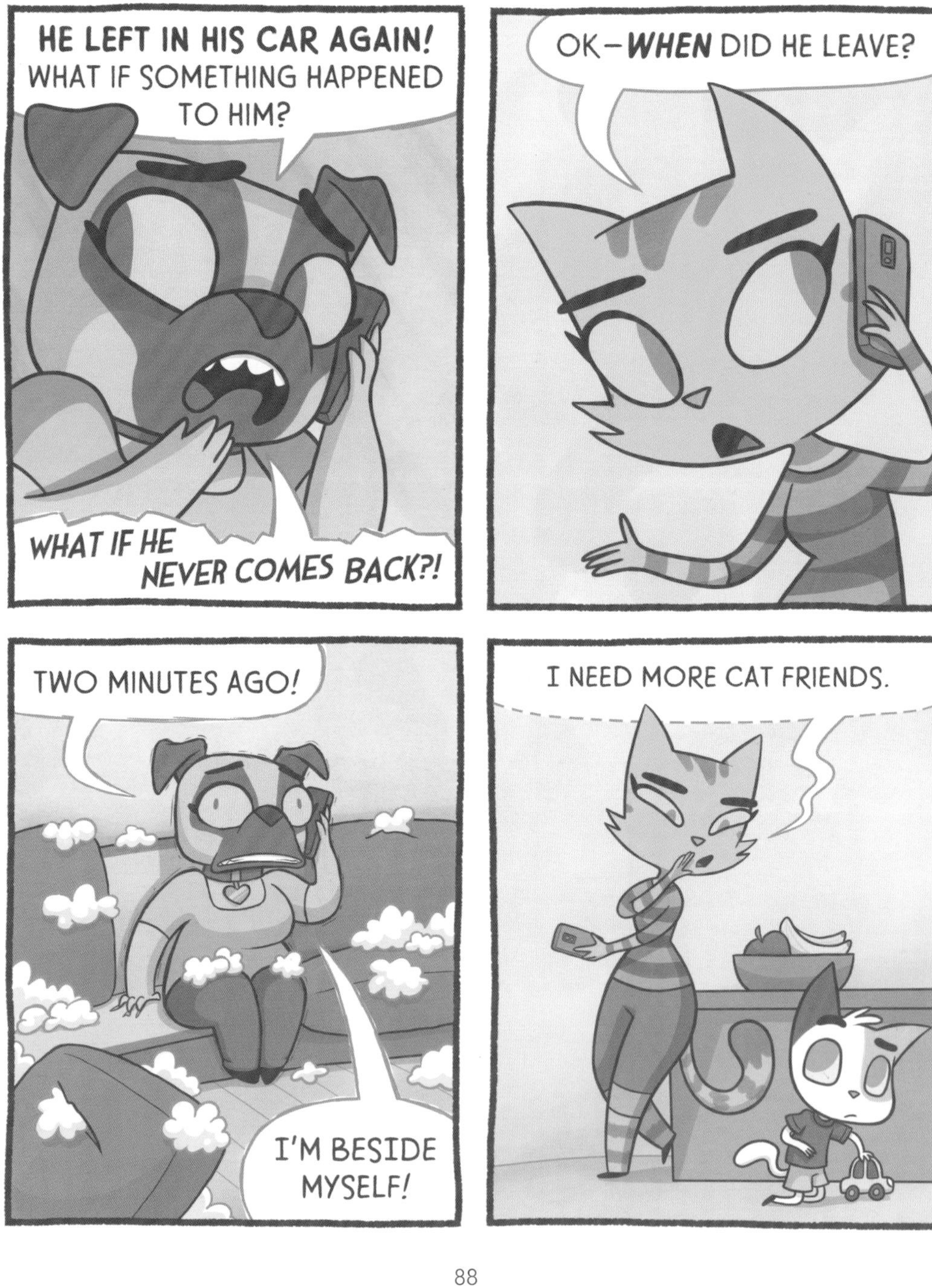

HE LEFT IN HIS CAR AGAIN!
WHAT IF SOMETHING HAPPENED TO HIM?
WHAT IF HE NEVER COMES BACK?!
OK—***WHEN*** DID HE LEAVE?
TWO MINUTES AGO!
I'M BESIDE MYSELF!
I NEED MORE CAT FRIENDS.

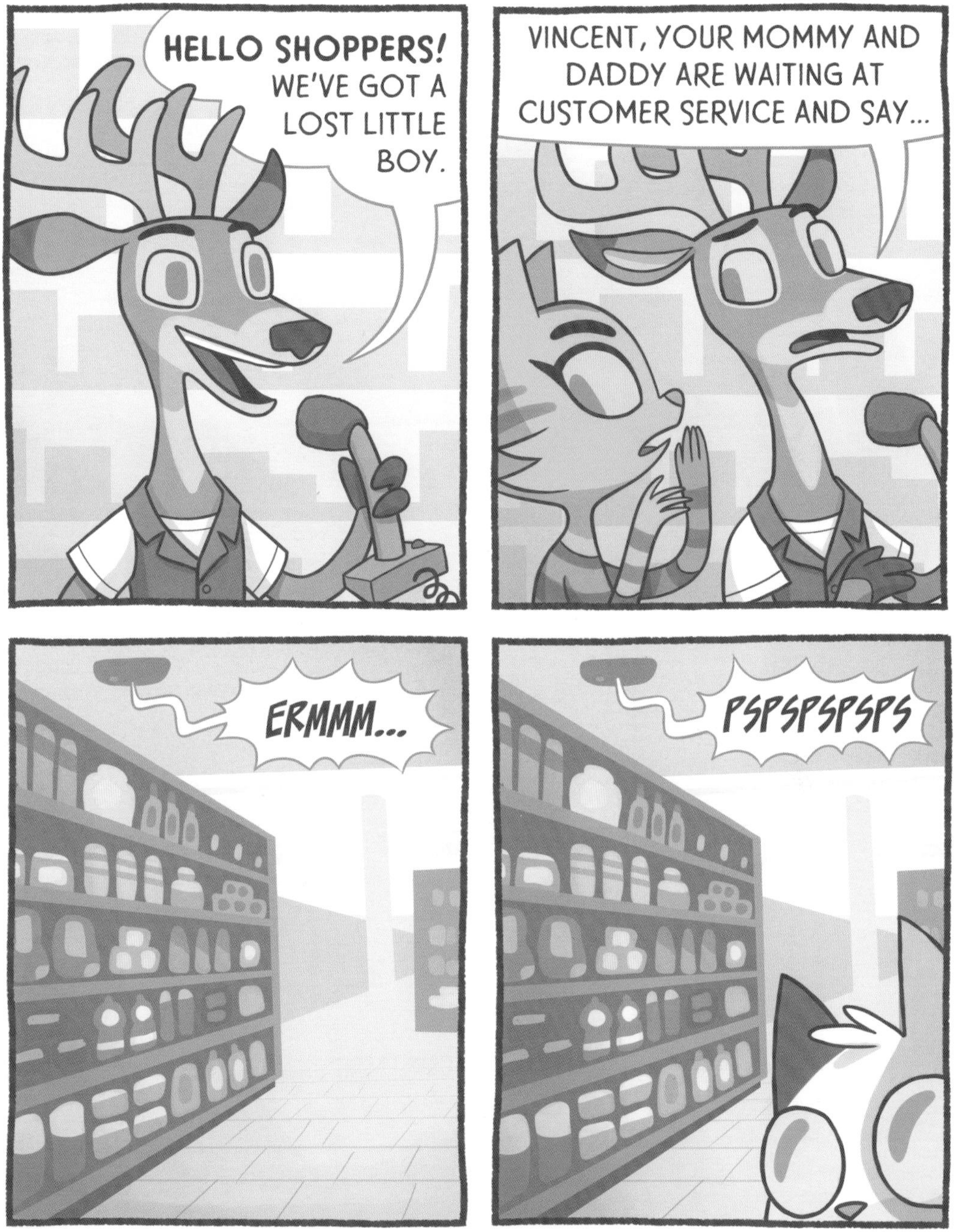
HELLO SHOPPERS! WE'VE GOT A LOST LITTLE BOY.
VINCENT, YOUR MOMMY AND DADDY ARE WAITING AT CUSTOMER SERVICE AND SAY...
ERMMM...
PSPSPSPSPS

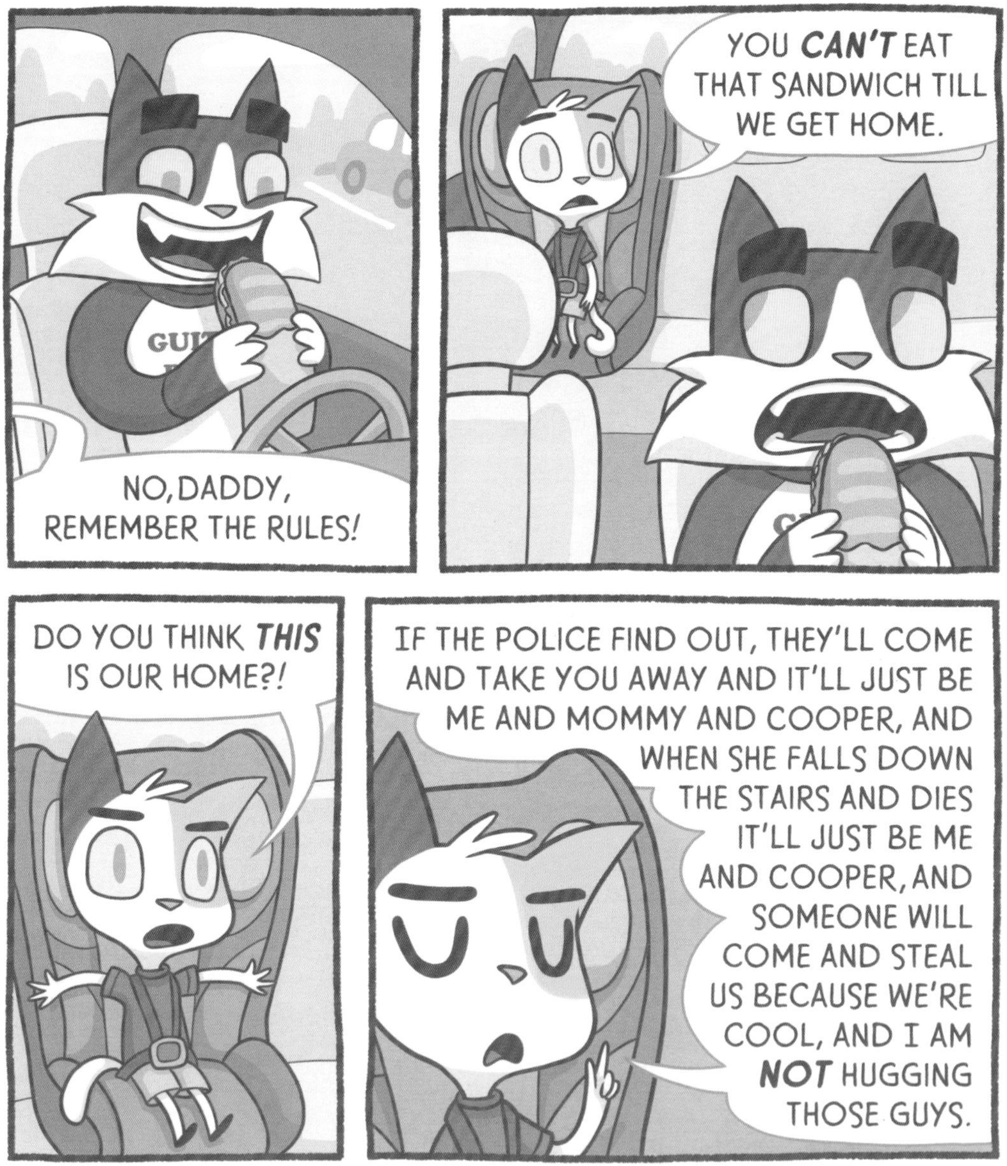
NO, DADDY, REMEMBER THE RULES!
YOU **CAN'T** EAT THAT SANDWICH TILL WE GET HOME.
DO YOU THINK **THIS** IS OUR HOME?!
IF THE POLICE FIND OUT, THEY'LL COME AND TAKE YOU AWAY AND IT'LL JUST BE ME AND MOMMY AND COOPER, AND WHEN SHE FALLS DOWN THE STAIRS AND DIES IT'LL JUST BE ME AND COOPER, AND SOMEONE WILL COME AND STEAL US BECAUSE WE'RE COOL, AND I AM **NOT** HUGGING THOSE GUYS.

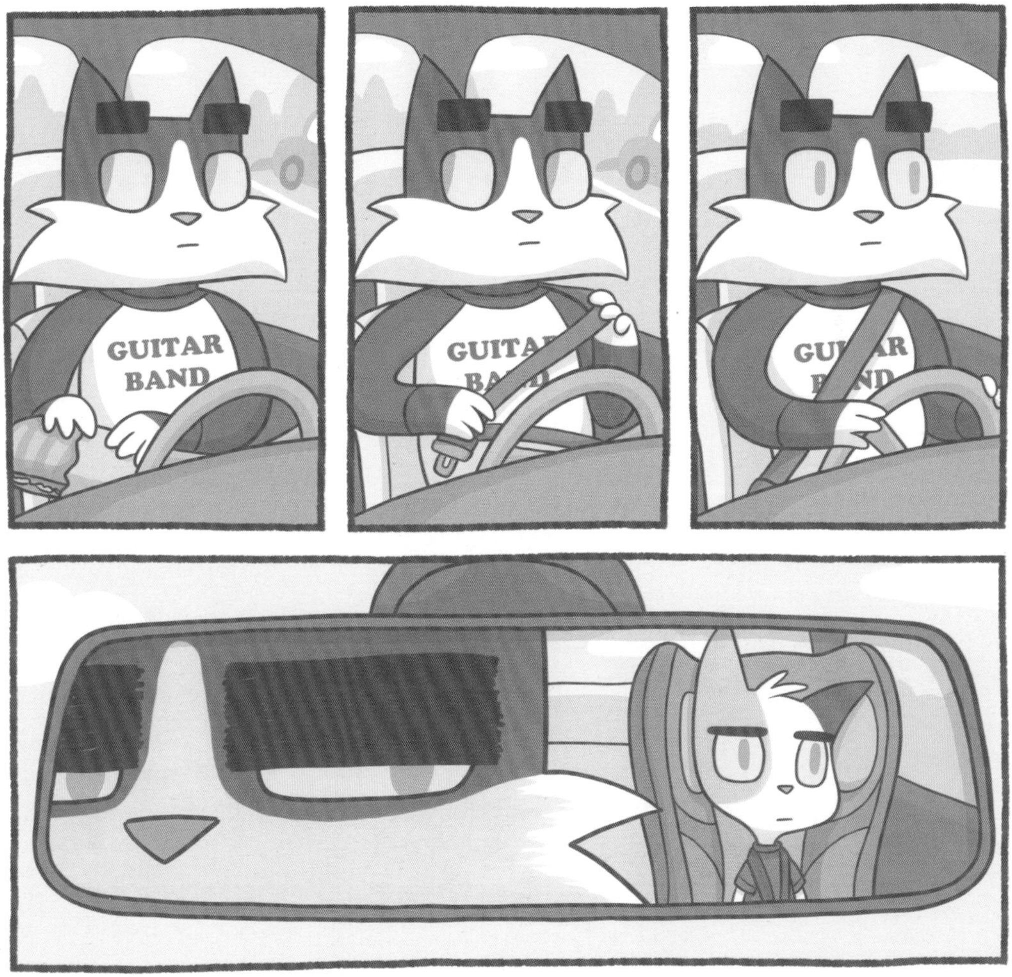
GUITAR
BAND

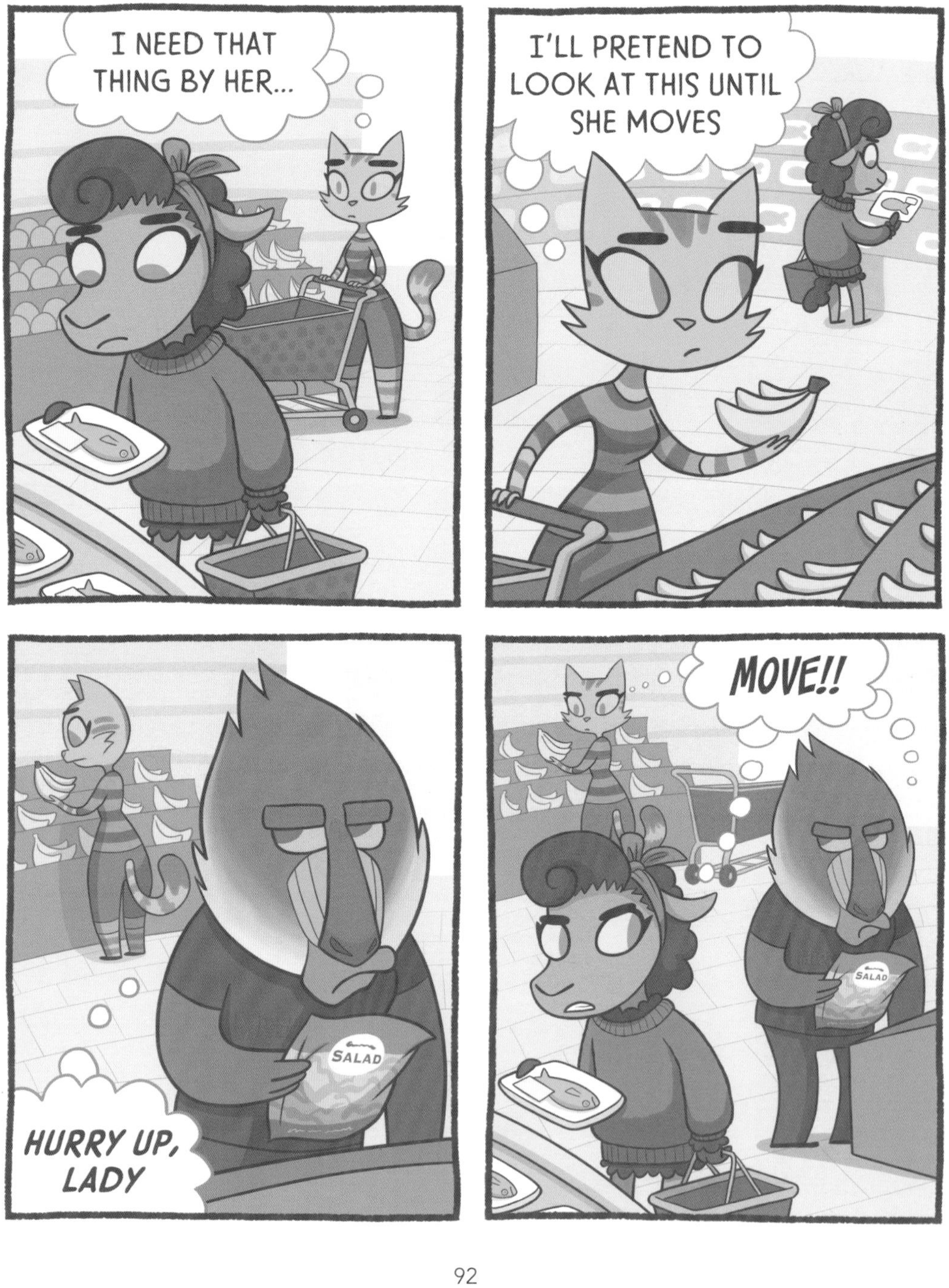
I NEED THAT THING BY HER...
I'LL PRETEND TO LOOK AT THIS UNTIL SHE MOVES
SALAD
HURRY UP, LADY
MOVE!!
SALAD

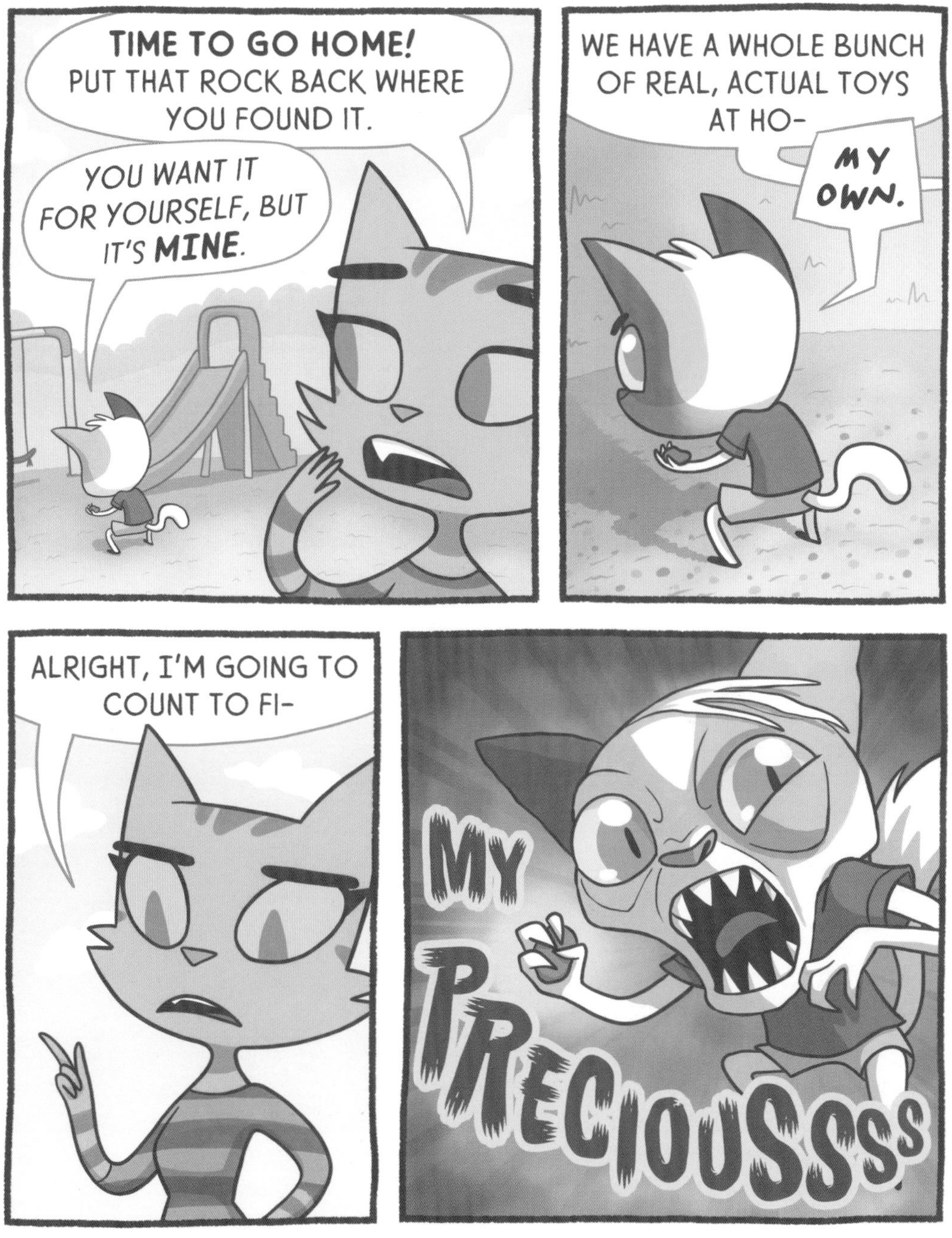
TIME TO GO HOME! PUT THAT ROCK BACK WHERE YOU FOUND IT.
YOU WANT IT FOR YOURSELF, BUT IT'S MINE.
WE HAVE A WHOLE BUNCH OF REAL, ACTUAL TOYS AT HO-
MY OWN.
ALRIGHT, I'M GOING TO COUNT TO FI-
MY PRECIOUSSSS

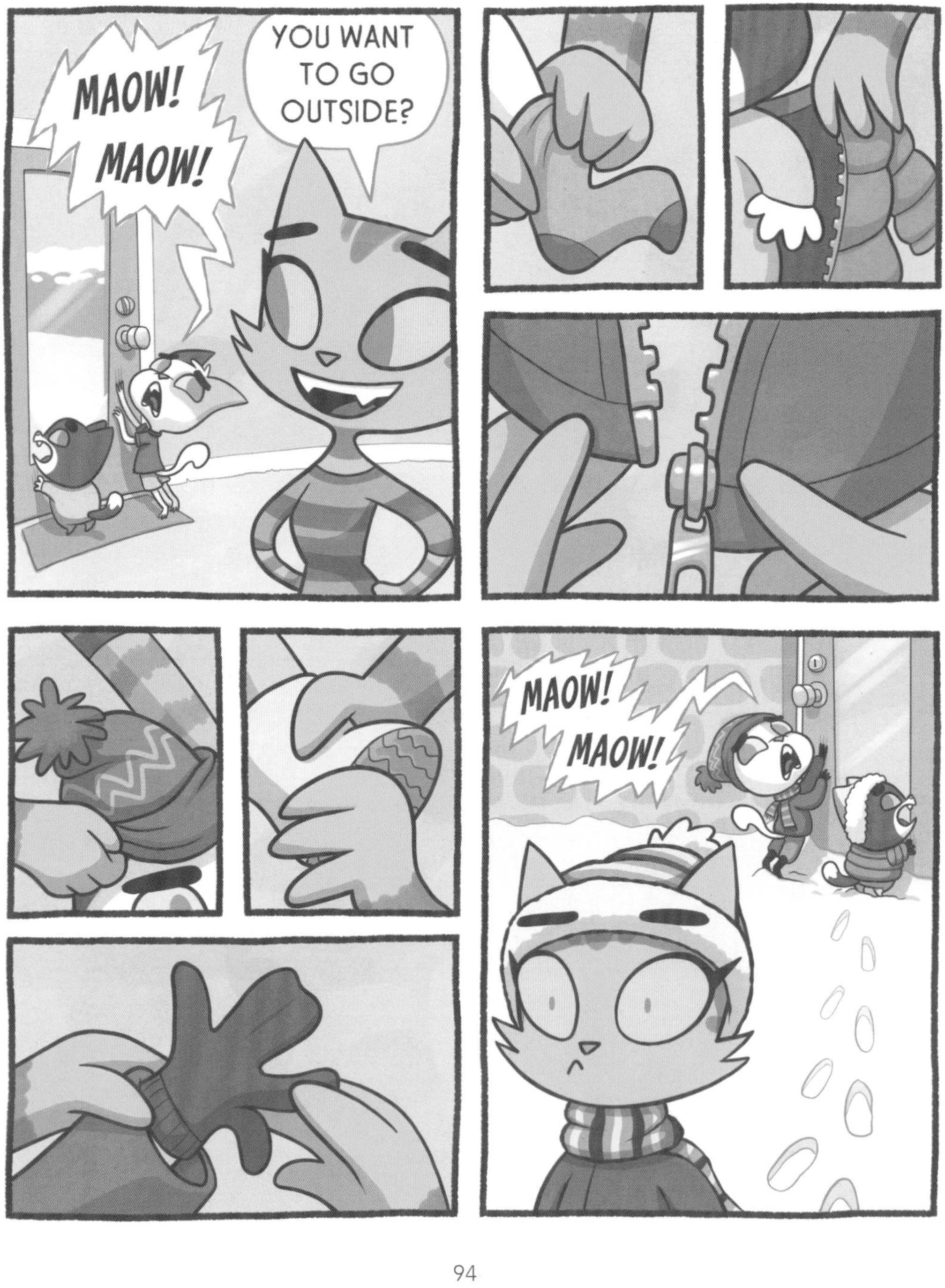
MAOW!
MAOW!
YOU WANT TO GO OUTSIDE?
MAOW!
MAOW!

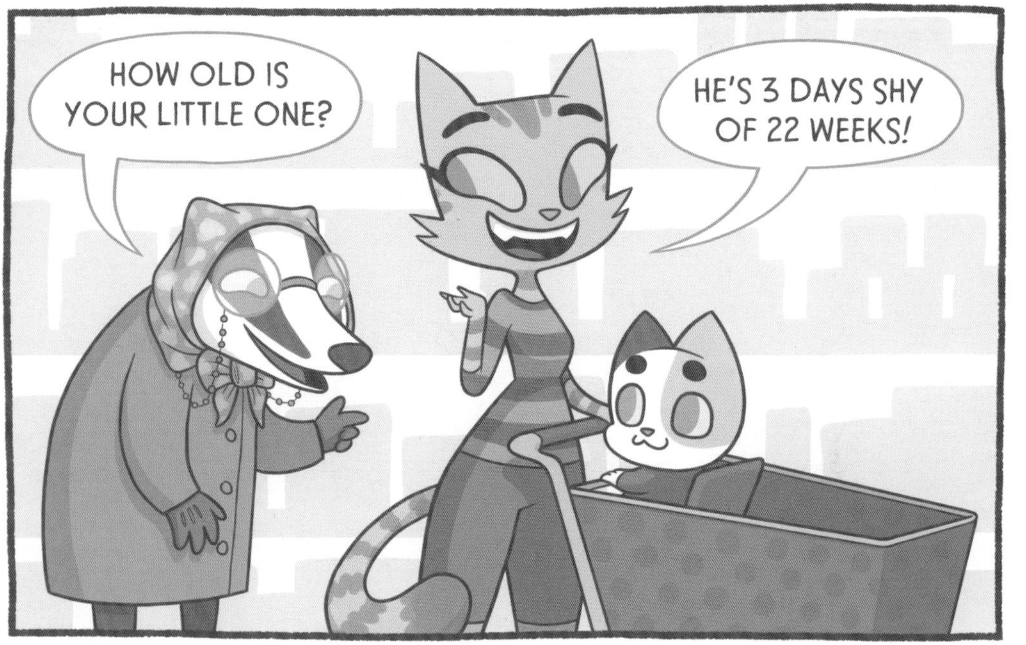
HOW OLD IS YOUR LITTLE ONE?
HE'S 3 DAYS SHY OF 22 WEEKS!

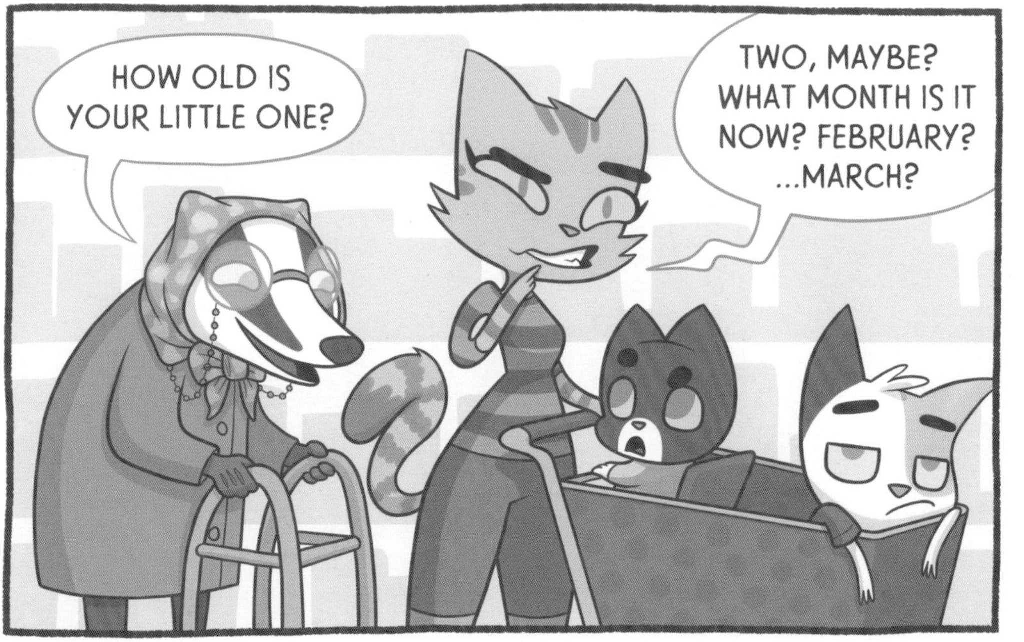
HOW OLD IS YOUR LITTLE ONE?
TWO, MAYBE? WHAT MONTH IS IT NOW? FEBRUARY? ...MARCH?

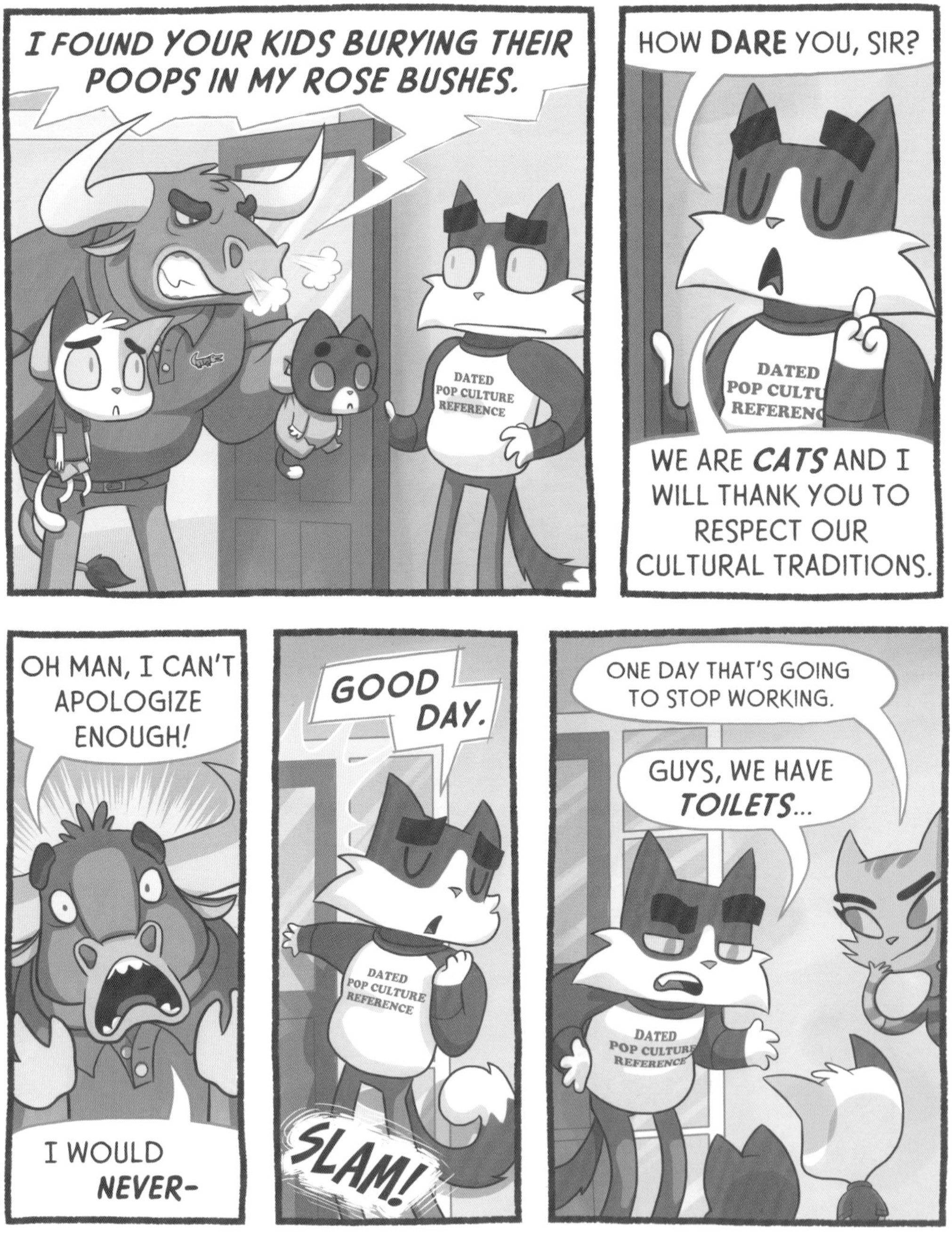
I FOUND YOUR KIDS BURYING THEIR POOPS IN MY ROSE BUSHES.
DATED POP CULTURE REFERENCE
HOW DARE YOU, SIR?
WE ARE CATS AND I WILL THANK YOU TO RESPECT OUR CULTURAL TRADITIONS.
OH MAN, I CAN'T APOLOGIZE ENOUGH!
I WOULD NEVER-
GOOD DAY.
DATED POP CULTURE REFERENCE
SLAM!
ONE DAY THAT'S GOING TO STOP WORKING.
GUYS, WE HAVE TOILETS...
DATED POP CULTURE REFERENCE

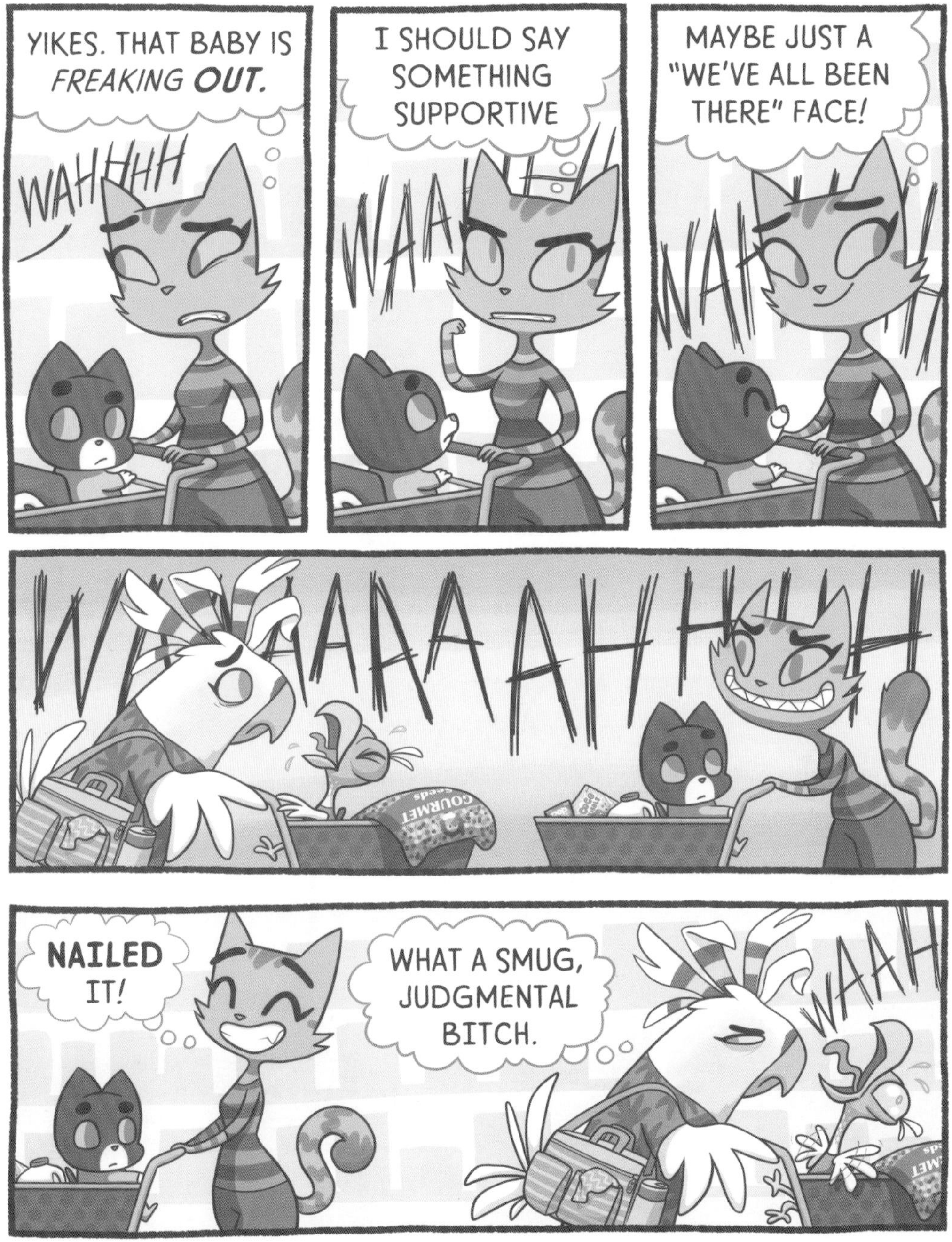
YIKES. THAT BABY IS FREAKING OUT.
WAHHHH
I SHOULD SAY SOMETHING SUPPORTIVE
MAYBE JUST A "WE'VE ALL BEEN THERE" FACE!
WAAAAAAAHHHHH
GOURMET
Seeds
NAILED IT!
WHAT A SMUG, JUDGMENTAL BITCH.
WAAH

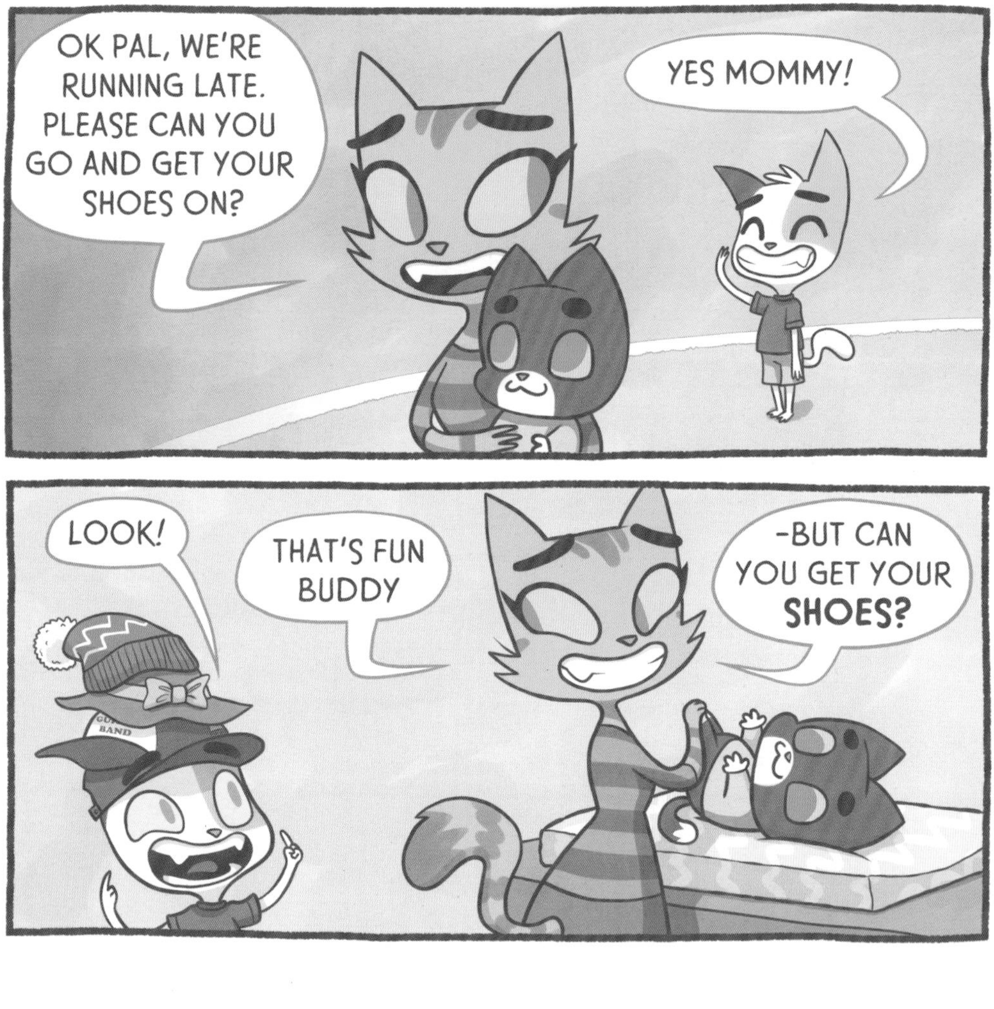
OK PAL, WE'RE RUNNING LATE. PLEASE CAN YOU GO AND GET YOUR SHOES ON?
YES MOMMY!
LOOK!
THAT'S FUN BUDDY
-BUT CAN YOU GET YOUR **SHOES?**

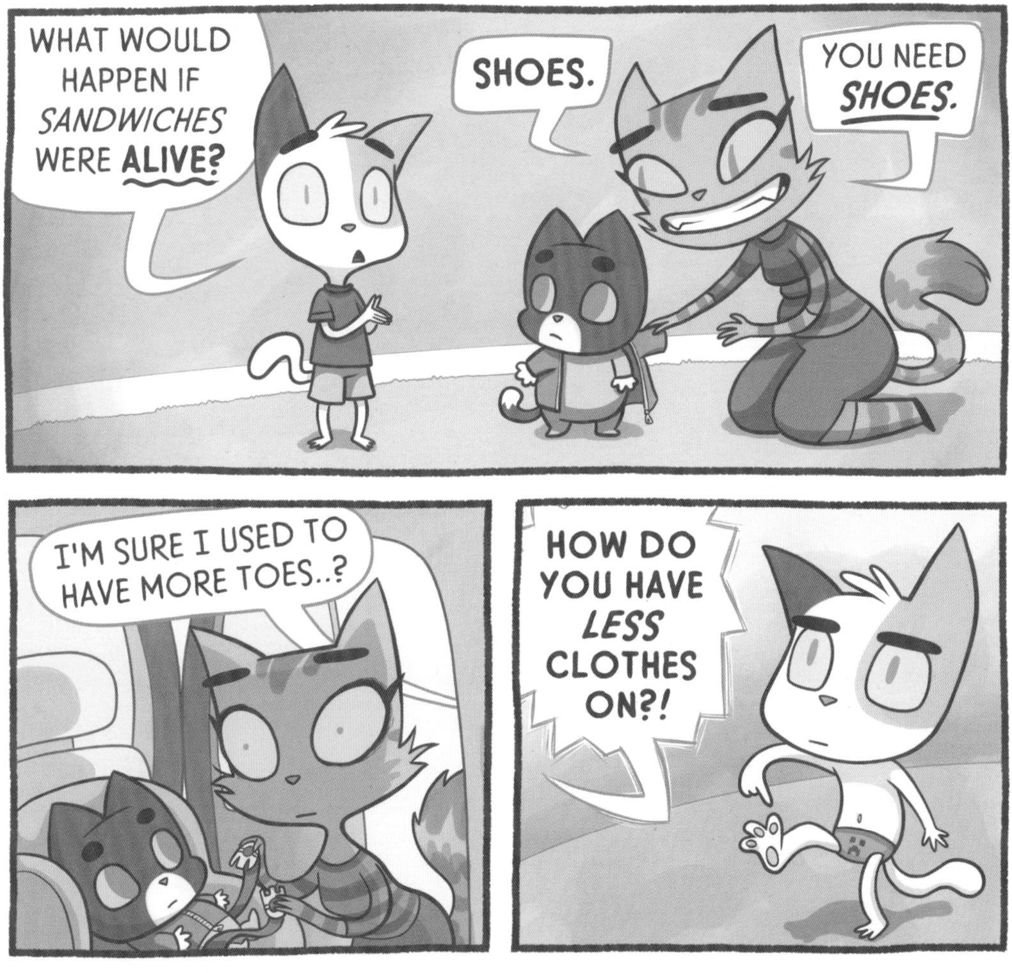
WHAT WOULD HAPPEN IF SANDWICHES WERE ALIVE?
SHOES.
YOU NEED SHOES.
I'M SURE I USED TO HAVE MORE TOES..?
HOW DO YOU HAVE LESS CLOTHES ON?!

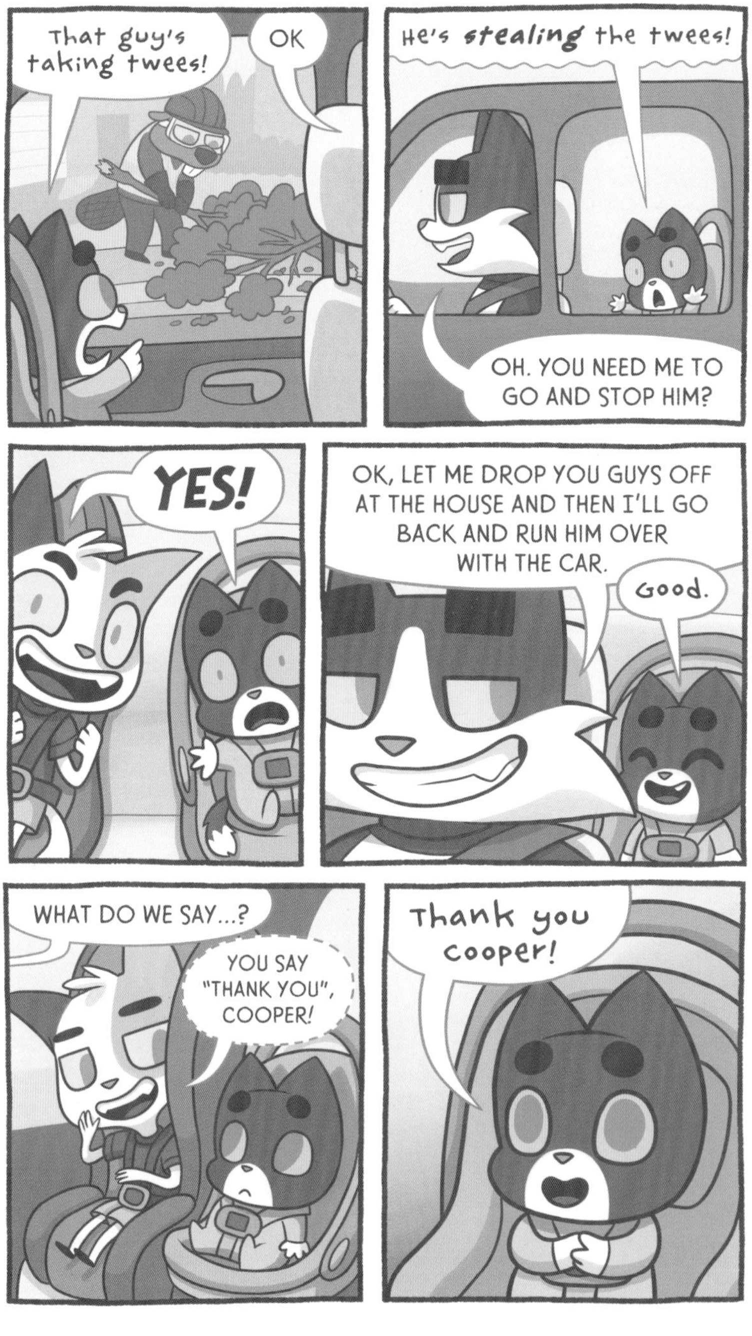
That guy's taking twees!
OK
He's **stealing** the twees!
OH. YOU NEED ME TO GO AND STOP HIM?
YES!
OK, LET ME DROP YOU GUYS OFF AT THE HOUSE AND THEN I'LL GO BACK AND RUN HIM OVER WITH THE CAR.
Good.
WHAT DO WE SAY...?
YOU SAY "THANK YOU", COOPER!
Thank you cooper!

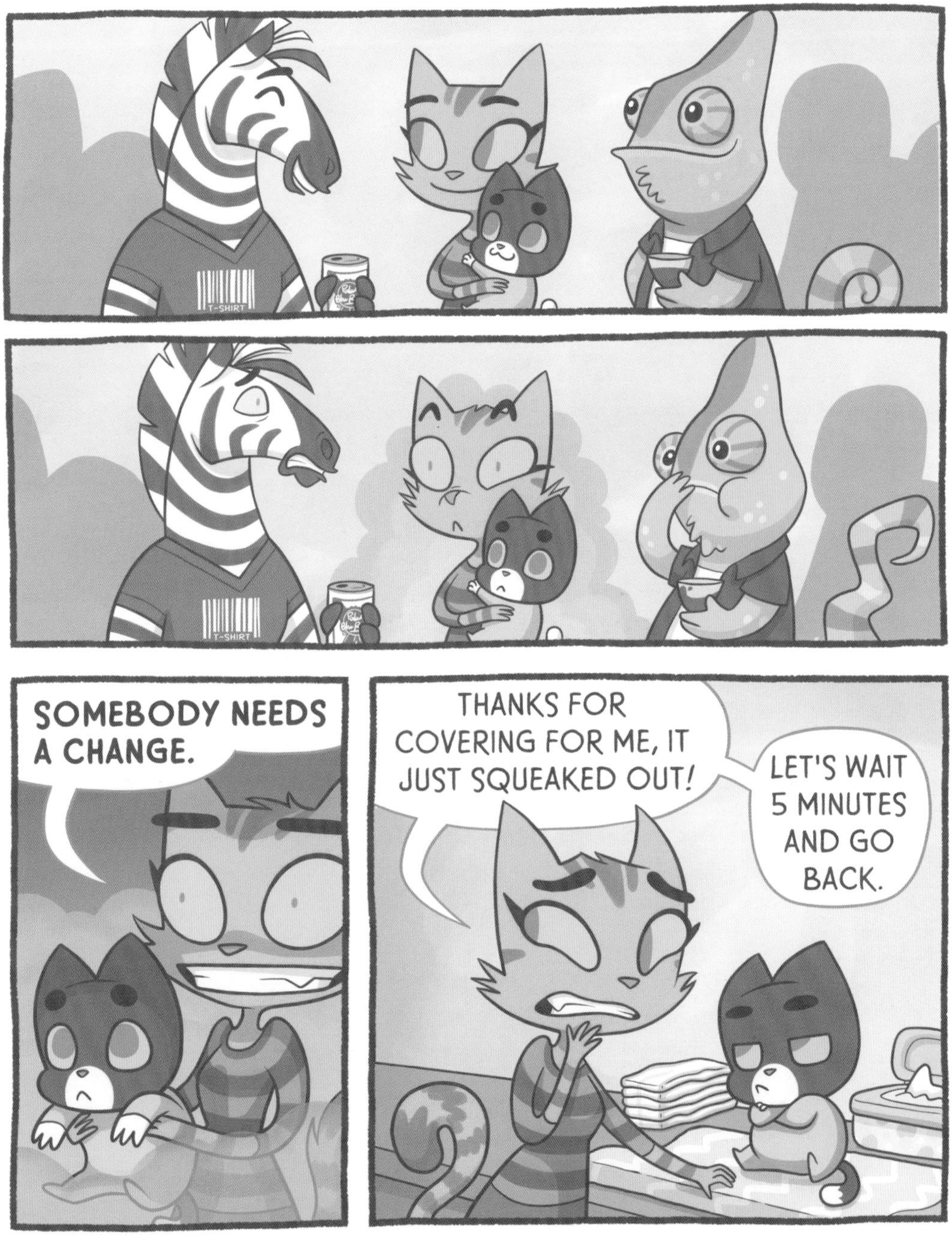
T-SHIRT
T-SHIRT
SOMEBODY NEEDS A CHANGE.
THANKS FOR COVERING FOR ME, IT JUST SQUEAKED OUT!
LET'S WAIT 5 MINUTES AND GO BACK.

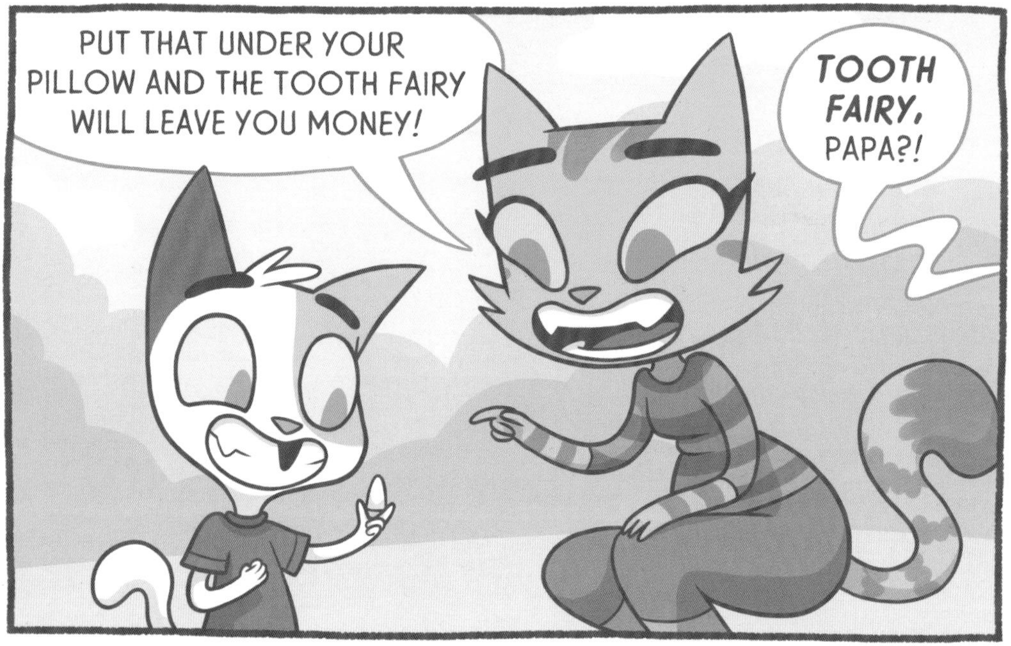
PUT THAT UNDER YOUR PILLOW AND THE TOOTH FAIRY WILL LEAVE YOU MONEY!
TOOTH FAIRY, PAPA?!

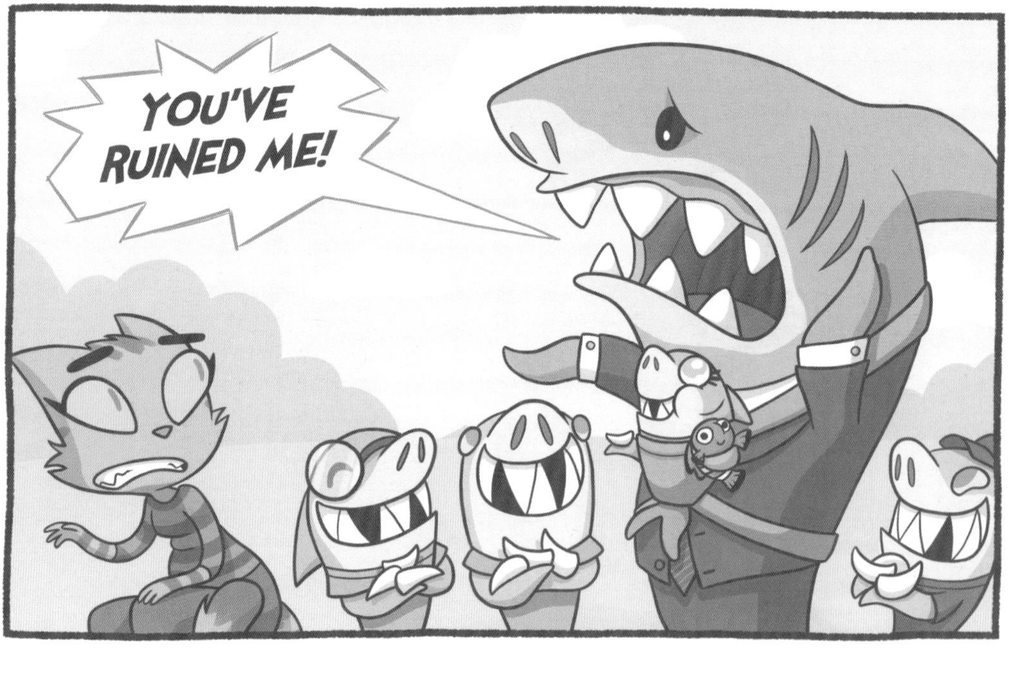
YOU'VE RUINED ME!

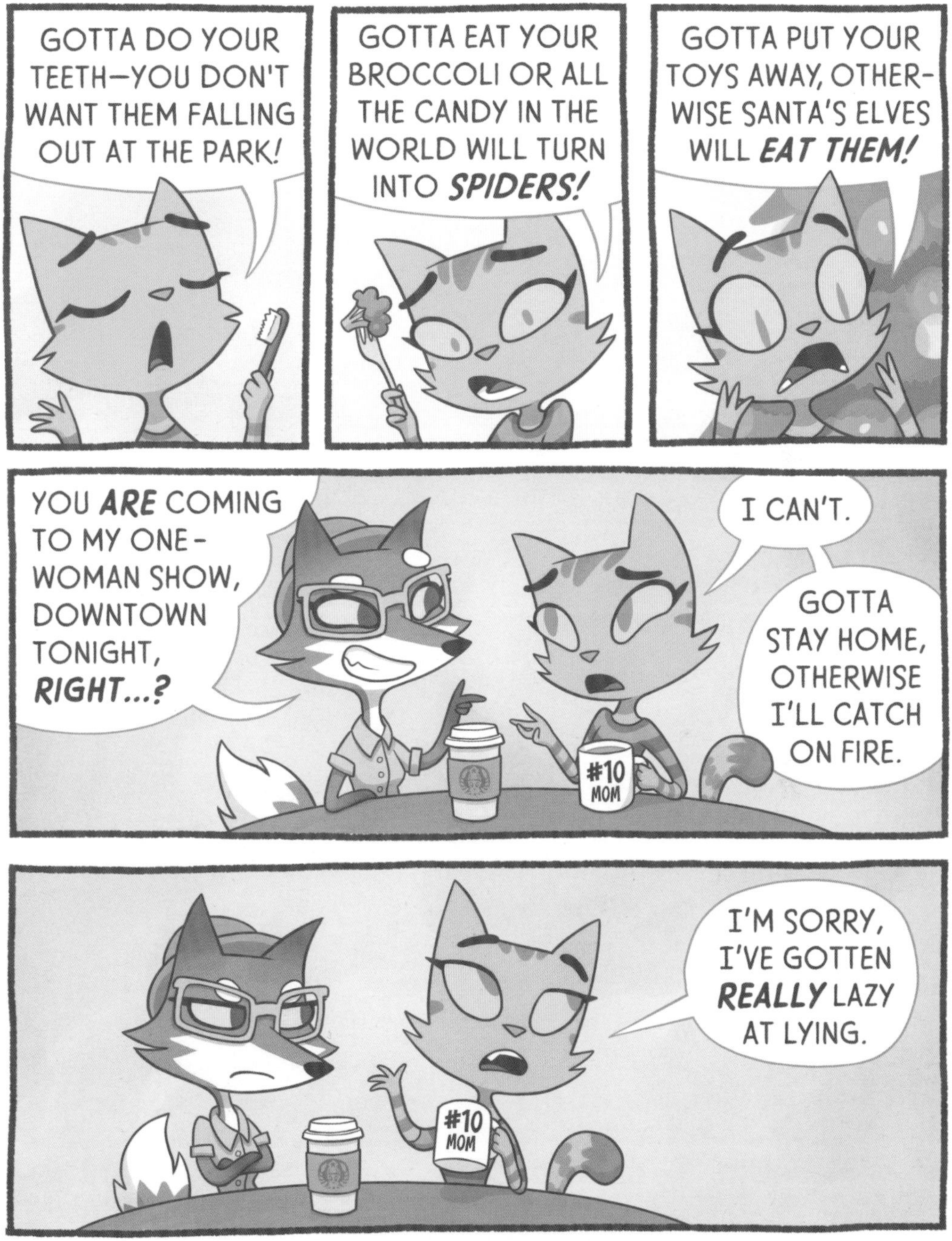
GOTTA DO YOUR TEETH—YOU DON'T WANT THEM FALLING OUT AT THE PARK!
GOTTA EAT YOUR BROCCOLI OR ALL THE CANDY IN THE WORLD WILL TURN INTO **SPIDERS!**
GOTTA PUT YOUR TOYS AWAY, OTHER-WISE SANTA'S ELVES WILL **EAT THEM!**
YOU **ARE** COMING TO MY ONE-WOMAN SHOW, DOWNTOWN TONIGHT, **RIGHT...?**
I CAN'T.
GOTTA STAY HOME, OTHERWISE I'LL CATCH ON FIRE.
#10 MOM
I'M SORRY, I'VE GOTTEN **REALLY** LAZY AT LYING.
#10 MOM

BEDTIME!

IT'S THE SAME EVERY NIGHT. THE BEDTIME CALL GOES OUT AND ALL PRIOR BARGAINS ABOUT BEING GOOD ARE IMMEDIATELY RENEGED ON. THE WAR HAS BEGUN. A SALVO OF NEGOTIATION, THREATS, AND BRIBES WILL EVENTUALLY DRIVE THE CHILDREN UPSTAIRS. THEY ARE THEN FILLED WITH AN UNHOLY STRENGTH AND FURIOUS VIGOR AS THEY SET ABOUT THEIR NIGHTLY WRESTLING MATCH, THE ONLY GUARANTEED PRIZE BEING TEARS. AFTER BOOBOOS ARE RUBBED BETTER AND "I TOLD YOU SO'S" ADMINISTERED, IT'S ON TO THE PJ'S AND TEETH-BRUSHING ROUND.

AND YET, SOMEHOW, WE MAKE IT THROUGH. KIDS ARE IN THEIR BEDS. SOME TIME TO WIND DOWN WITH A BOOK, AND CERTAINLY THEY'LL BE SLEEPING PEACEFULLY, RIGHT? NOPE. ALL OF THEIR MOST URGENT QUESTIONS COME BUBBLING TO THE SURFACE OF THEIR MINDS: BLACK HOLES, ABSOLUTE ZERO, DEATH, REINCARNATION, *THE MATRIX*, AND CANNIBALISM, AND THE EDGE OF THE UNIVERSE, AND DOLPHINS, AND . . . AND . . . AND! AND THEN I REALIZE THEY GOT ME AGAIN AND IT'S *MY* BEDTIME!

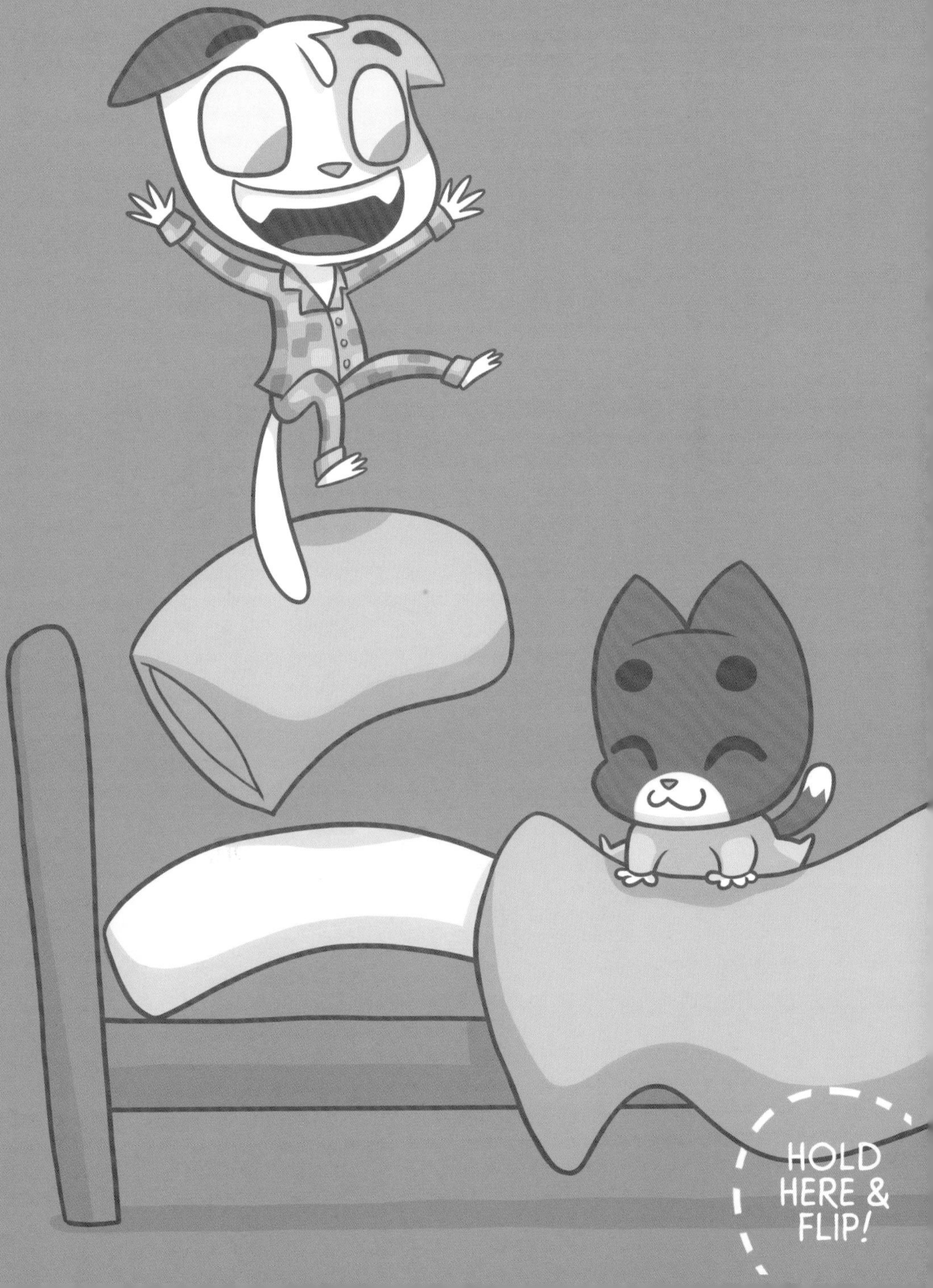
HOLD HERE & FLIP!

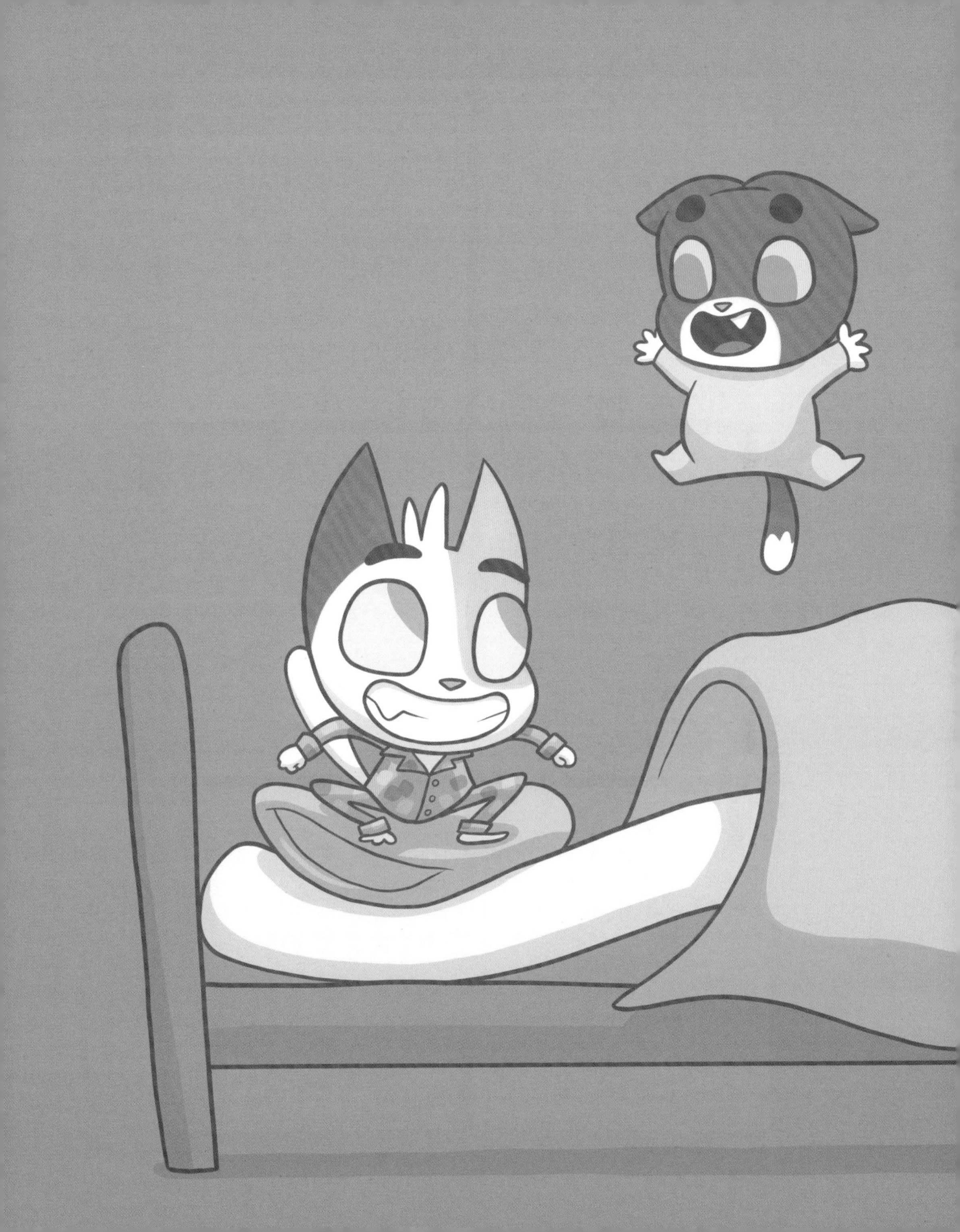

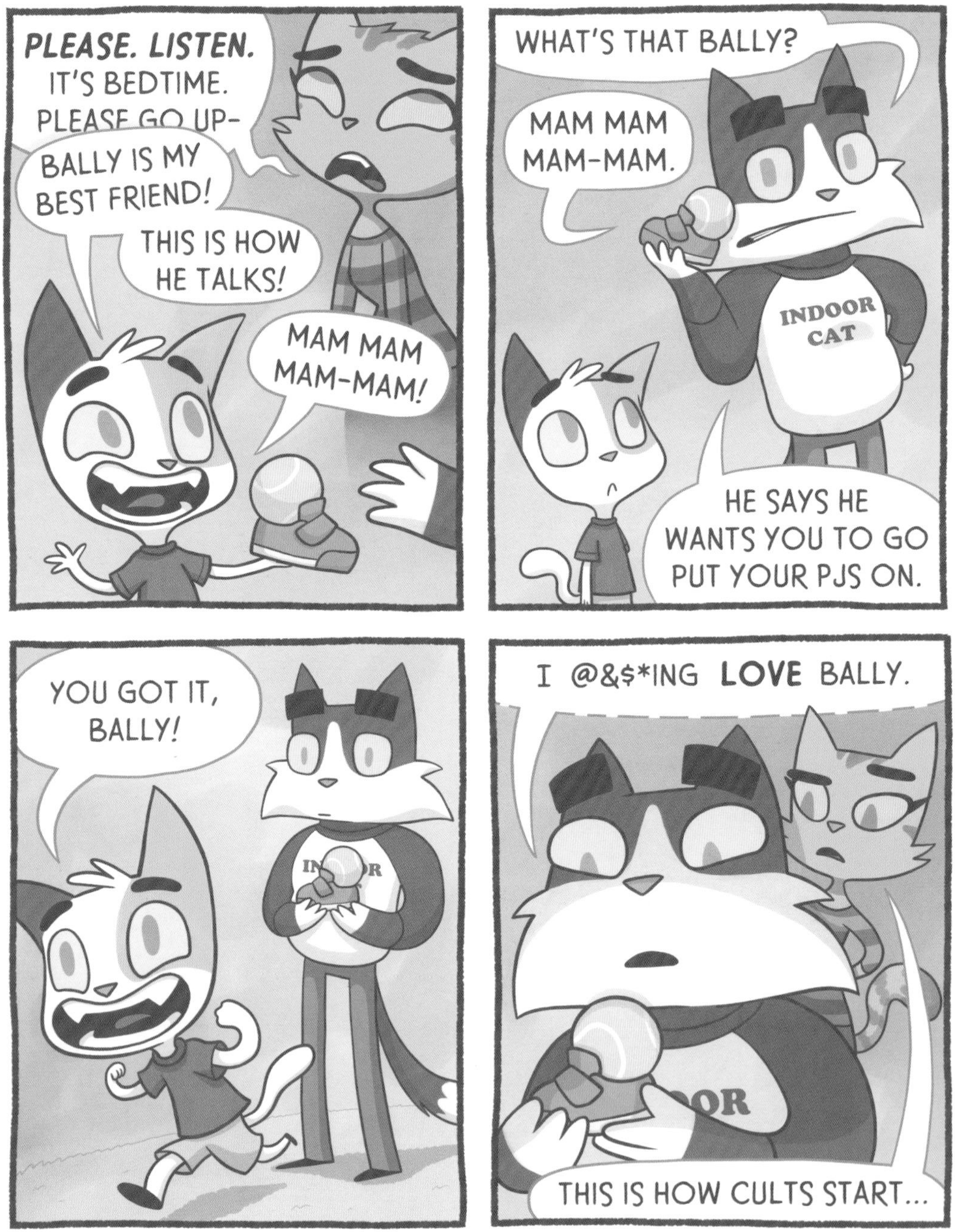
PLEASE. LISTEN. IT'S BEDTIME. PLEASE GO UP-
BALLY IS MY BEST FRIEND!
THIS IS HOW HE TALKS!
MAM MAM MAM-MAM!
WHAT'S THAT BALLY?
MAM MAM MAM-MAM.
INDOOR CAT
HE SAYS HE WANTS YOU TO GO PUT YOUR PJS ON.
YOU GOT IT, BALLY!
I @&$*ING **LOVE** BALLY.
THIS IS HOW CULTS START...

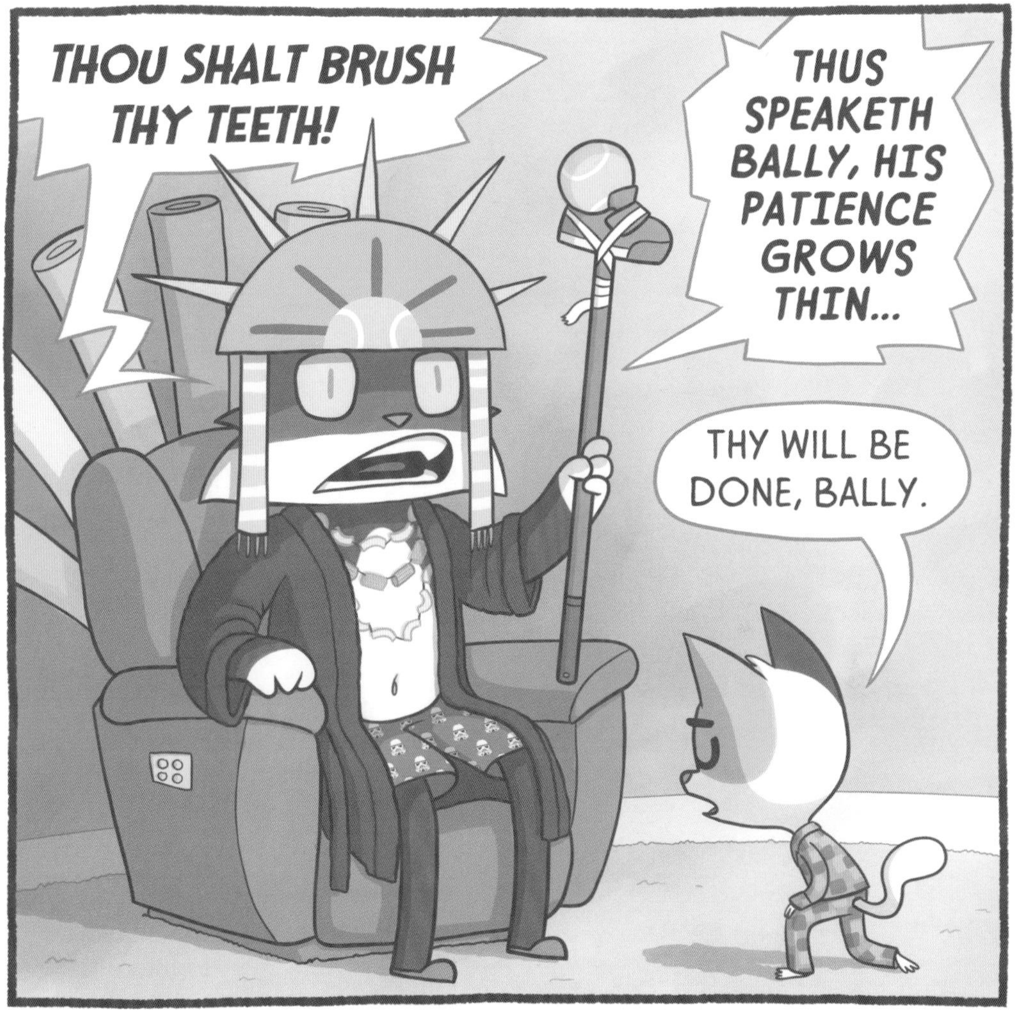
THOU SHALT BRUSH THY TEETH!
THUS SPEAKETH BALLY, HIS PATIENCE GROWS THIN...
THY WILL BE DONE, BALLY.

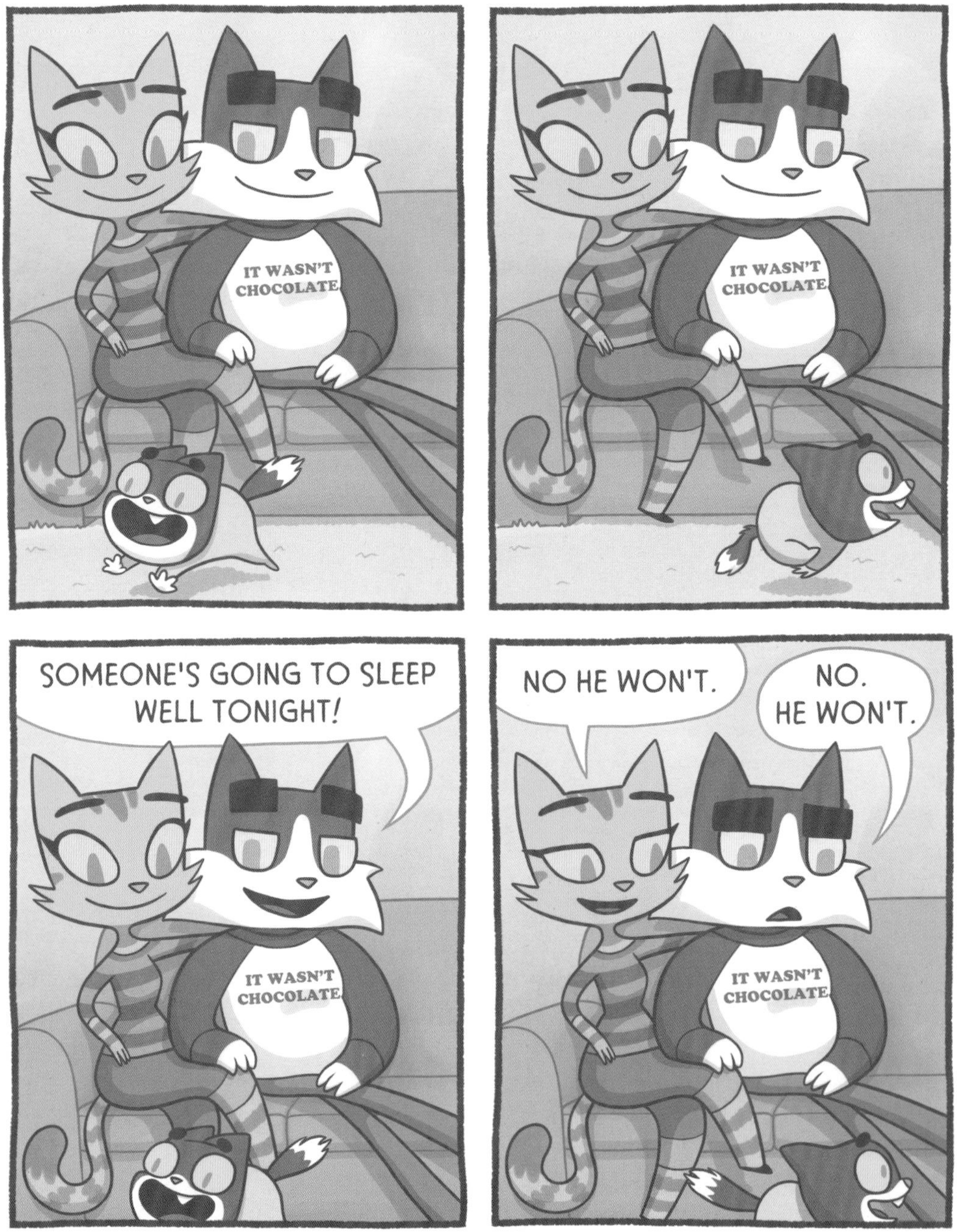
IT WASN'T CHOCOLATE
IT WASN'T CHOCOLATE
SOMEONE'S GOING TO SLEEP WELL TONIGHT!
IT WASN'T CHOCOLATE
NO HE WON'T.
NO. HE WON'T.
IT WASN'T CHOCOLATE

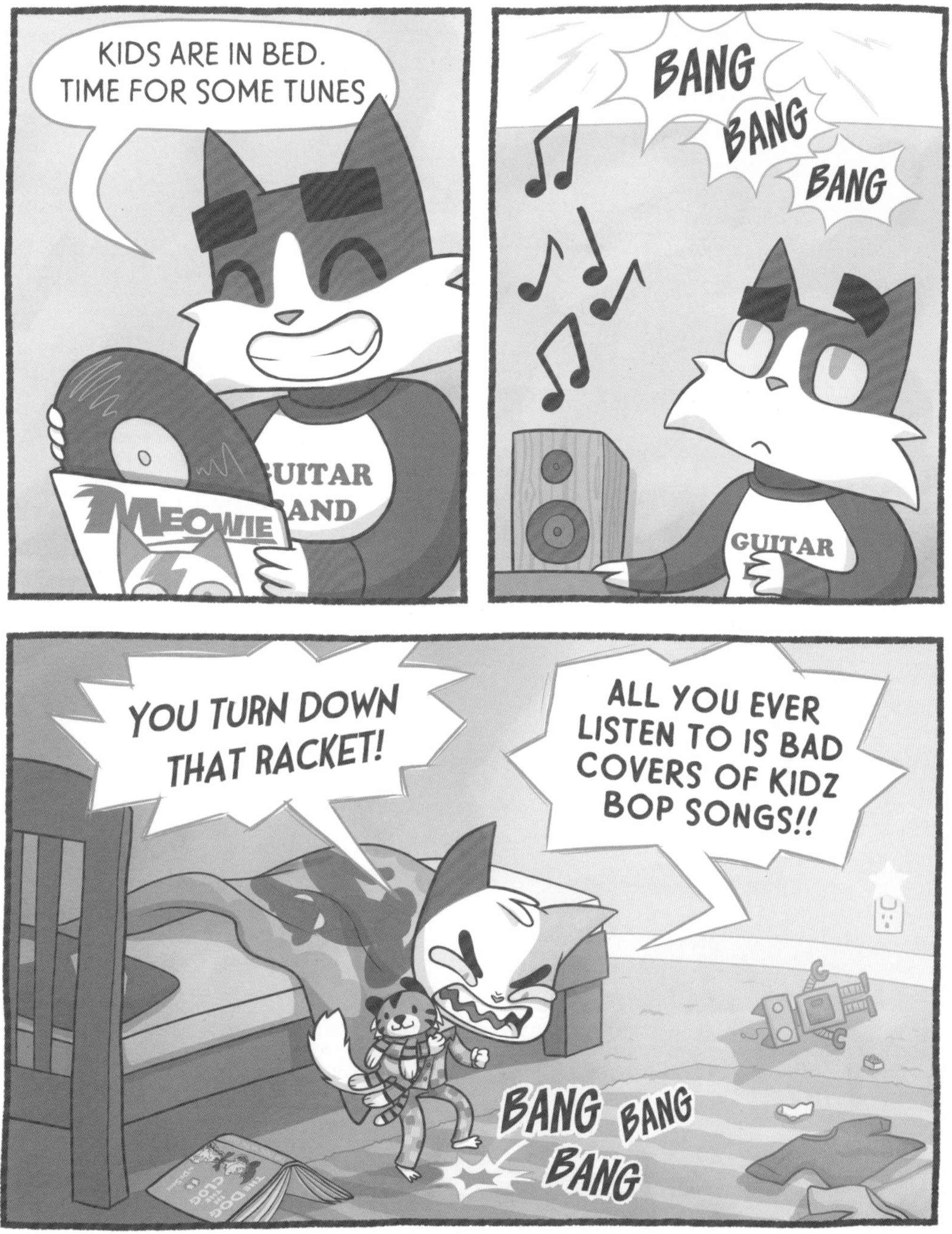
KIDS ARE IN BED. TIME FOR SOME TUNES
MEOWIE
BANG
BANG
BANG
GUITAR
YOU TURN DOWN THAT RACKET!
ALL YOU EVER LISTEN TO IS BAD COVERS OF KIDZ BOP SONGS!!
BANG BANG
BANG

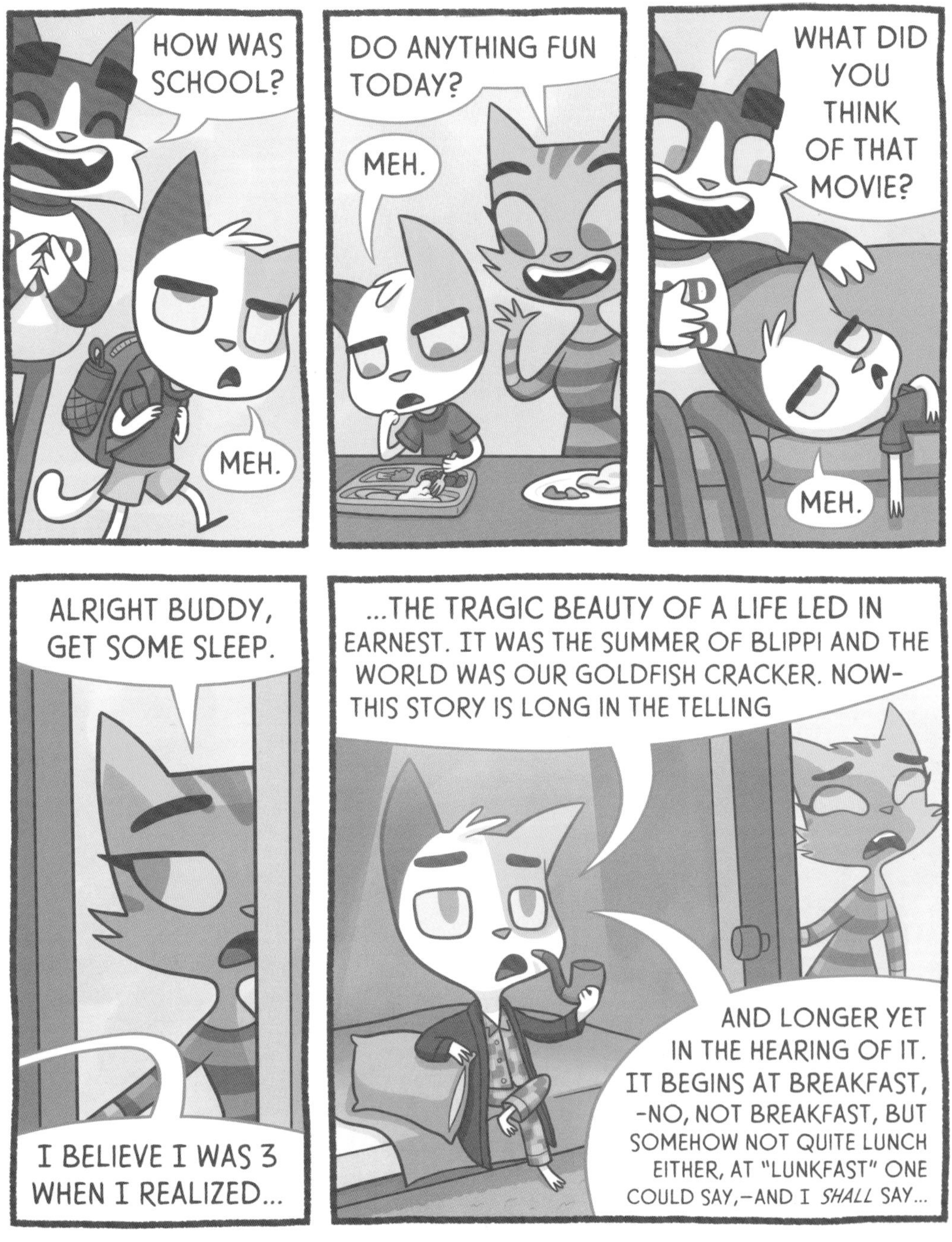
HOW WAS SCHOOL?
MEH.
DO ANYTHING FUN TODAY?
MEH.
WHAT DID YOU THINK OF THAT MOVIE?
MEH.
ALRIGHT BUDDY, GET SOME SLEEP.
I BELIEVE I WAS 3 WHEN I REALIZED...
...THE TRAGIC BEAUTY OF A LIFE LED IN EARNEST. IT WAS THE SUMMER OF BLIPPI AND THE WORLD WAS OUR GOLDFISH CRACKER. NOW- THIS STORY IS LONG IN THE TELLING
AND LONGER YET IN THE HEARING OF IT. IT BEGINS AT BREAKFAST, -NO, NOT BREAKFAST, BUT SOMEHOW NOT QUITE LUNCH EITHER, AT "LUNKFAST" ONE COULD SAY,—AND I *SHALL* SAY...

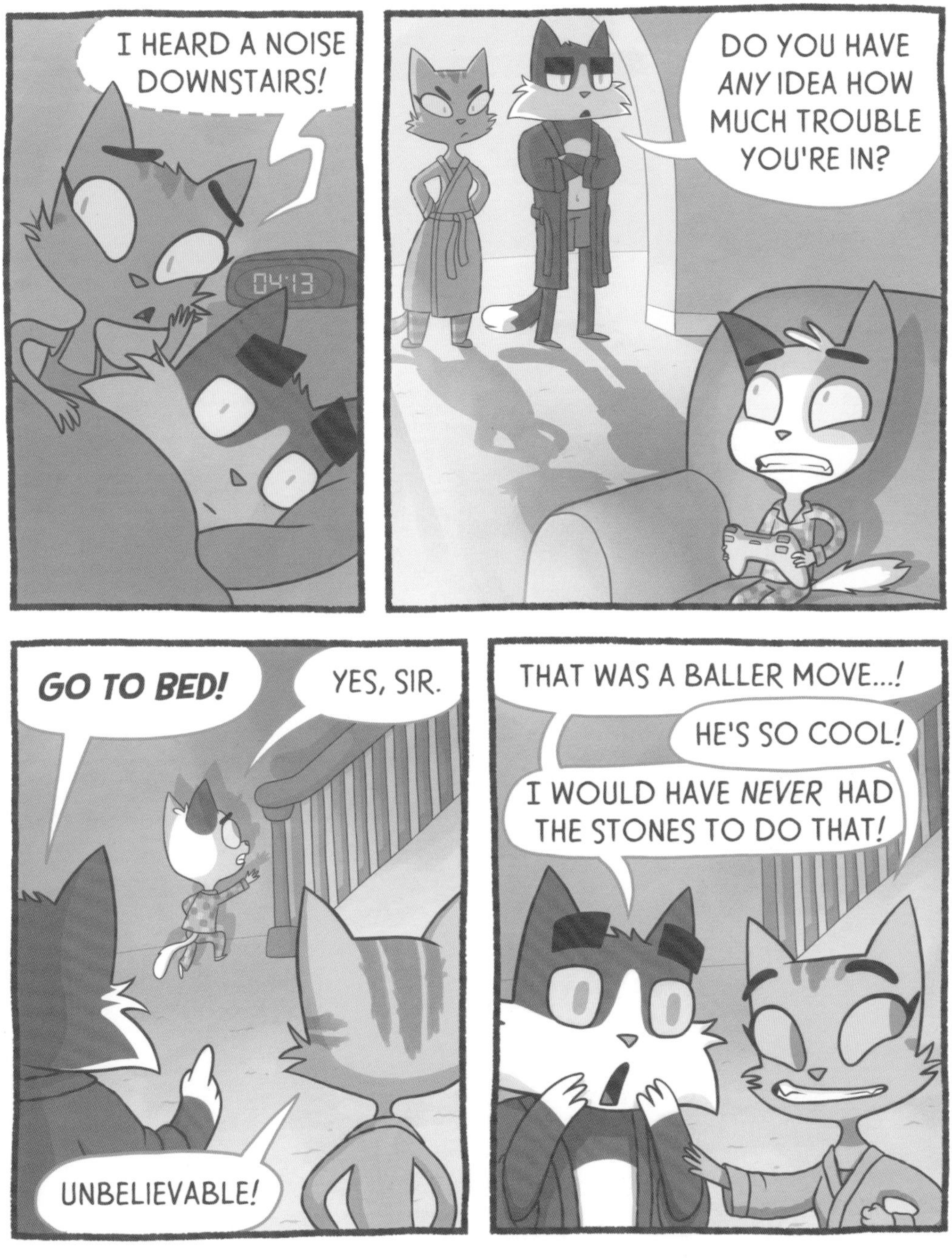
I HEARD A NOISE DOWNSTAIRS!
04:13
DO YOU HAVE *ANY* IDEA HOW MUCH TROUBLE YOU'RE IN?
GO TO BED!
YES, SIR.
UNBELIEVABLE!
THAT WAS A BALLER MOVE...!
HE'S SO COOL!
I WOULD HAVE *NEVER* HAD THE STONES TO DO THAT!

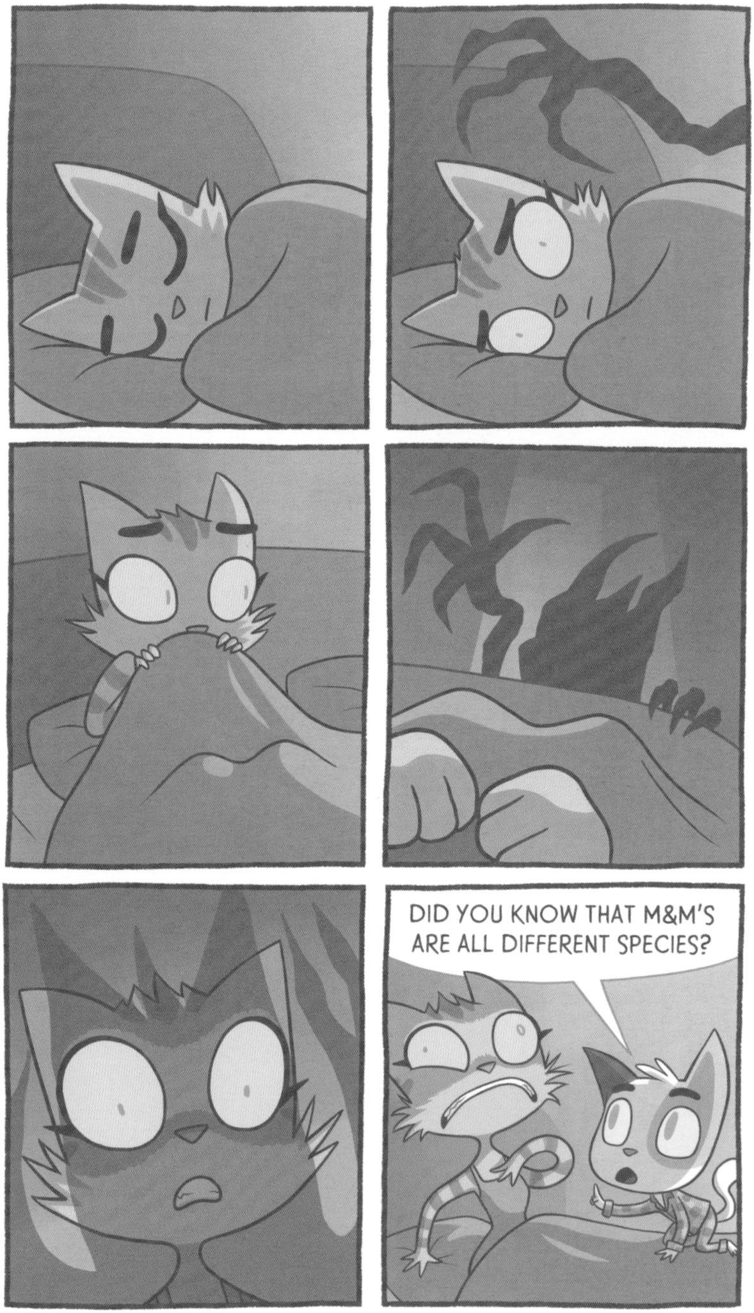
DID YOU KNOW THAT M&M'S
ARE ALL DIFFERENT SPECIES?

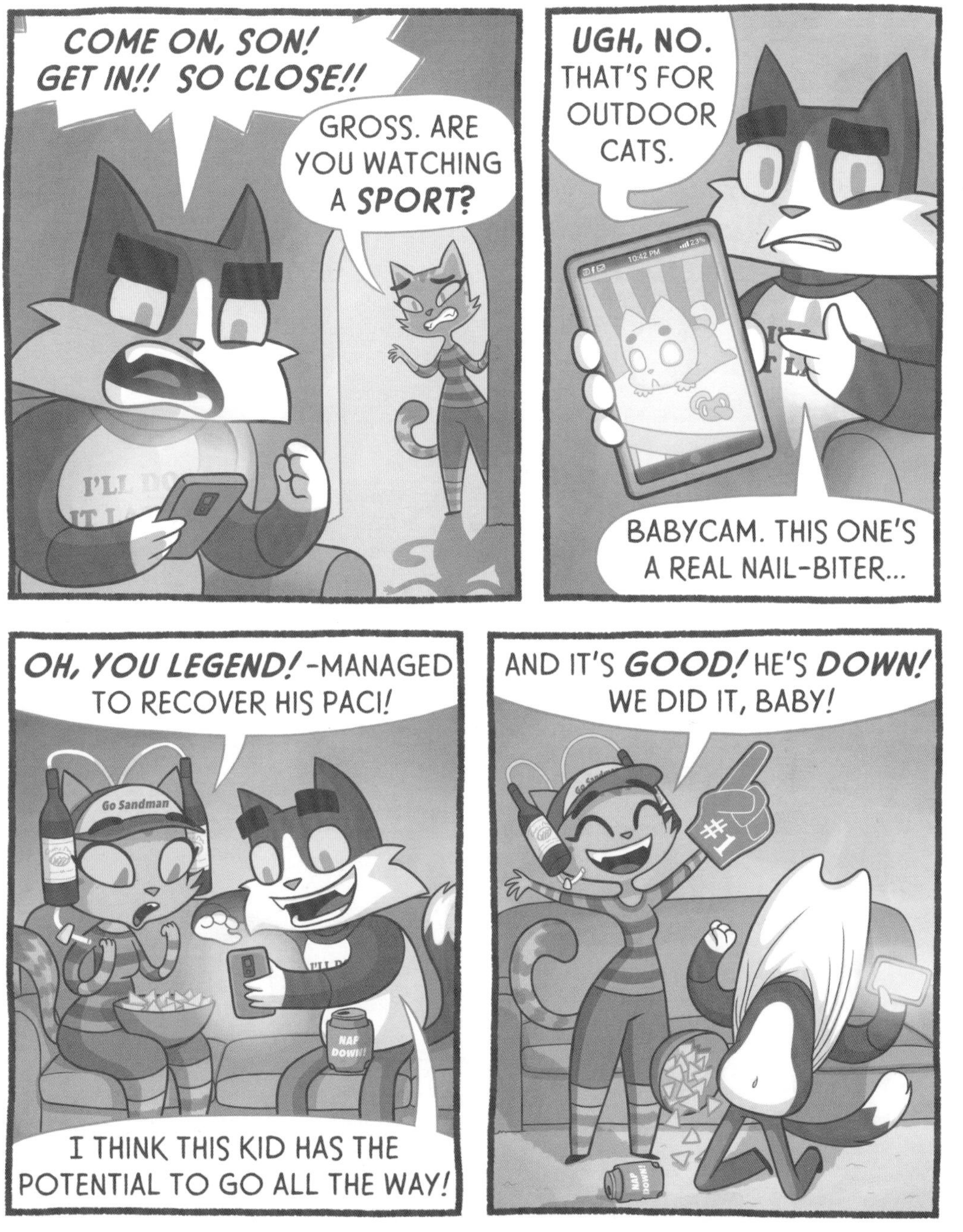
COME ON, SON! GET IN!! SO CLOSE!!
GROSS. ARE YOU WATCHING A SPORT?
UGH, NO. THAT'S FOR OUTDOOR CATS.
BABYCAM. THIS ONE'S A REAL NAIL-BITER...
OH, YOU LEGEND! -MANAGED TO RECOVER HIS PACI!
I THINK THIS KID HAS THE POTENTIAL TO GO ALL THE WAY!
AND IT'S GOOD! HE'S DOWN! WE DID IT, BABY!
Go Sandman
NAP DOWN!
#1

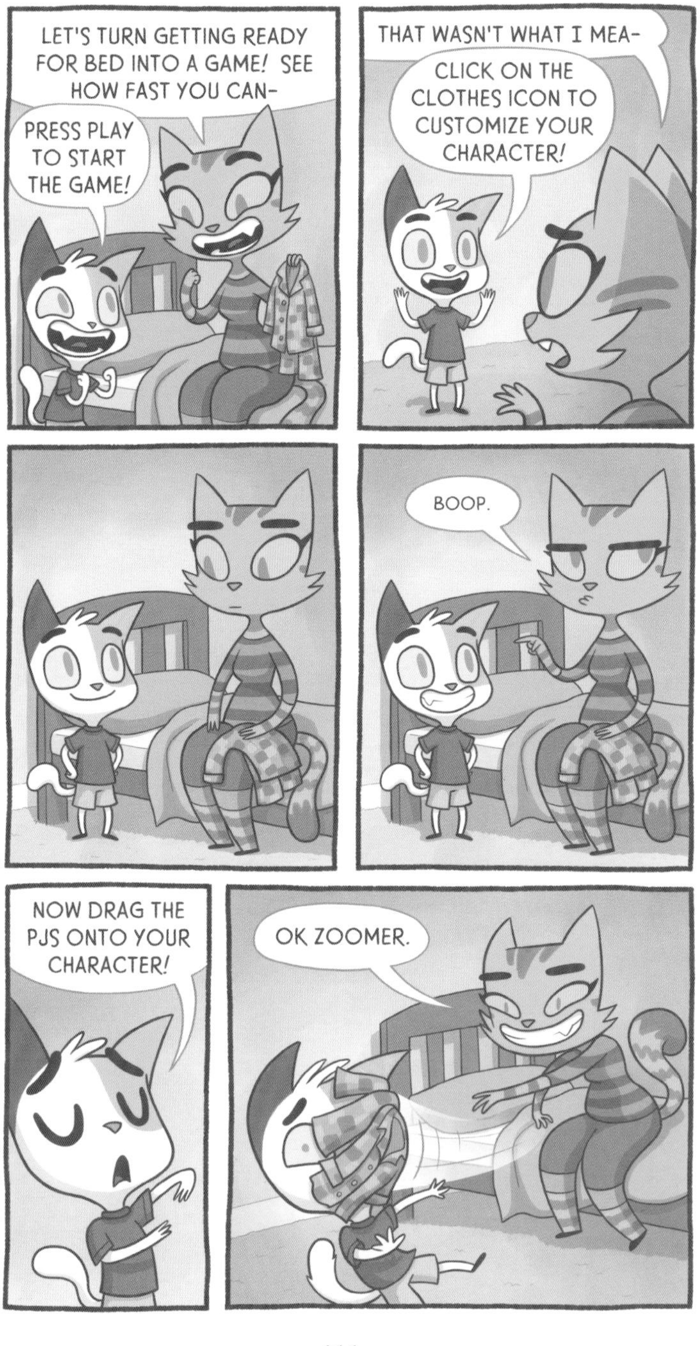
LET'S TURN GETTING READY FOR BED INTO A GAME! SEE HOW FAST YOU CAN-
PRESS PLAY TO START THE GAME!
THAT WASN'T WHAT I MEA-
CLICK ON THE CLOTHES ICON TO CUSTOMIZE YOUR CHARACTER!
BOOP.
NOW DRAG THE PJS ONTO YOUR CHARACTER!
OK ZOOMER.

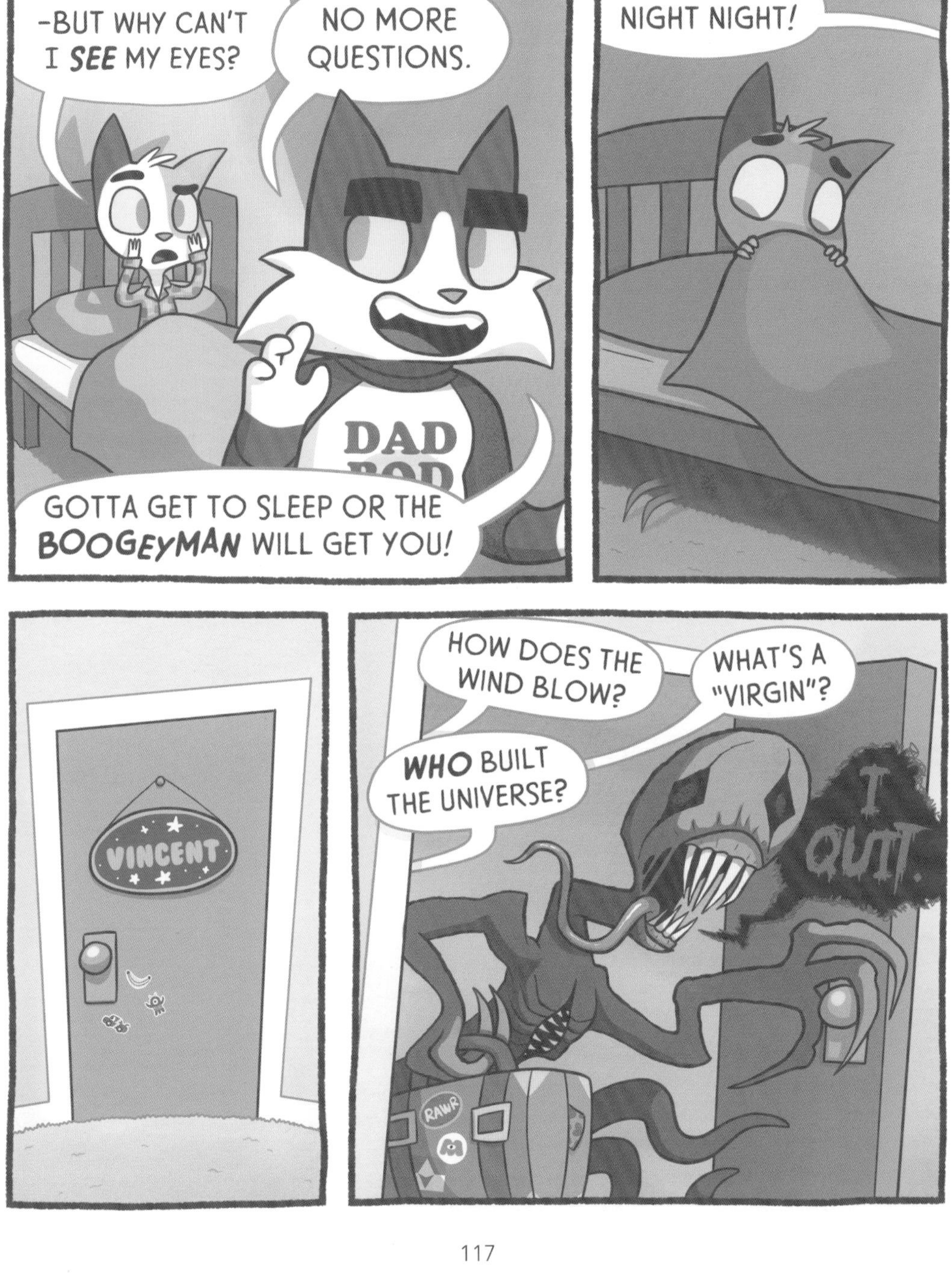
–BUT WHY CAN'T I **SEE** MY EYES?
NO MORE QUESTIONS.
GOTTA GET TO SLEEP OR THE **BOOGEYMAN** WILL GET YOU!
DAD
NIGHT NIGHT!
VINCENT
HOW DOES THE WIND BLOW?
WHAT'S A "VIRGIN"?
WHO BUILT THE UNIVERSE?
I QUIT.
RAWR

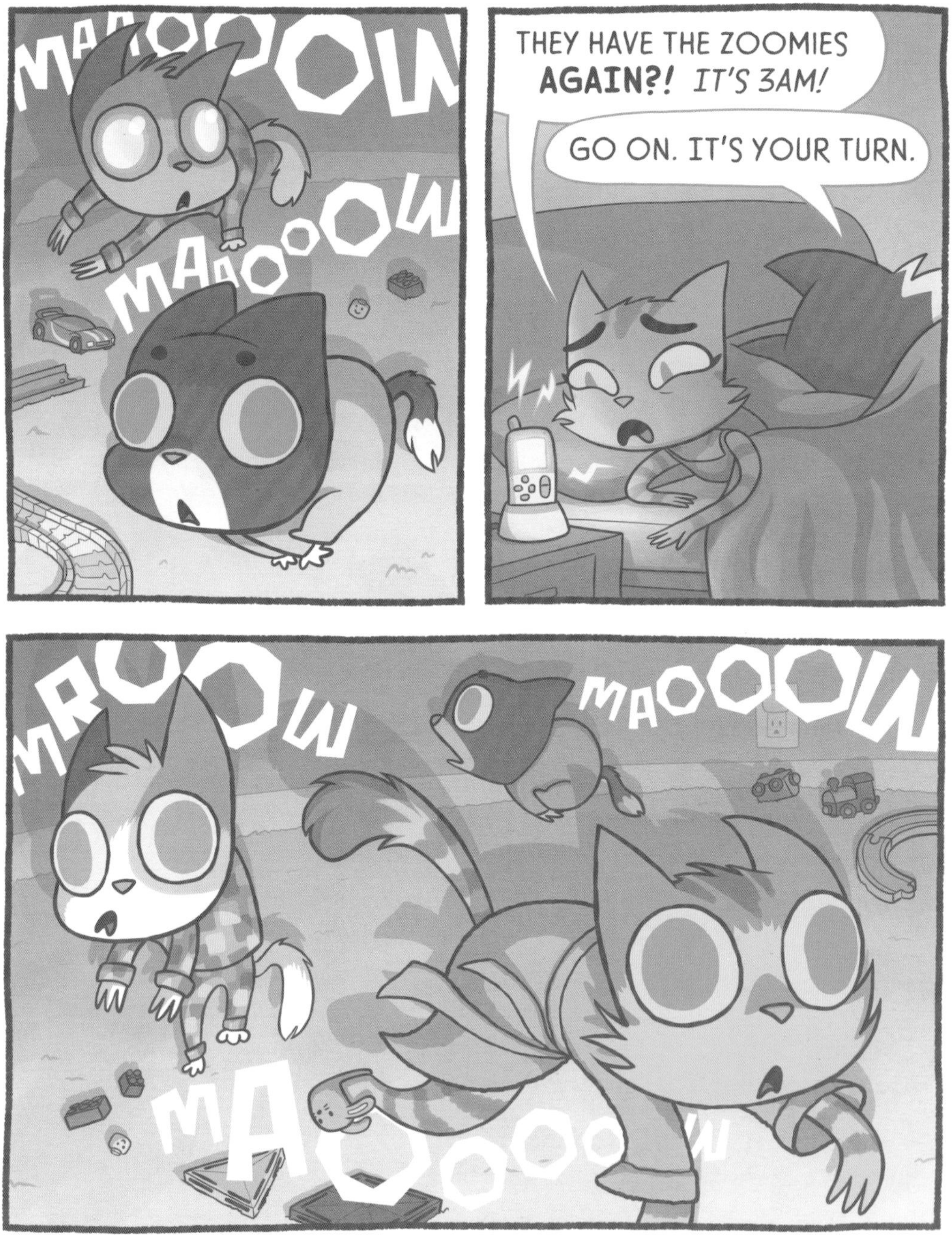
MAOOOOW
MAOOOW
THEY HAVE THE ZOOMIES **AGAIN?!** *IT'S 3AM!*
GO ON. IT'S YOUR TURN.
MROOW
MAOOOOW
MAOOOOOW

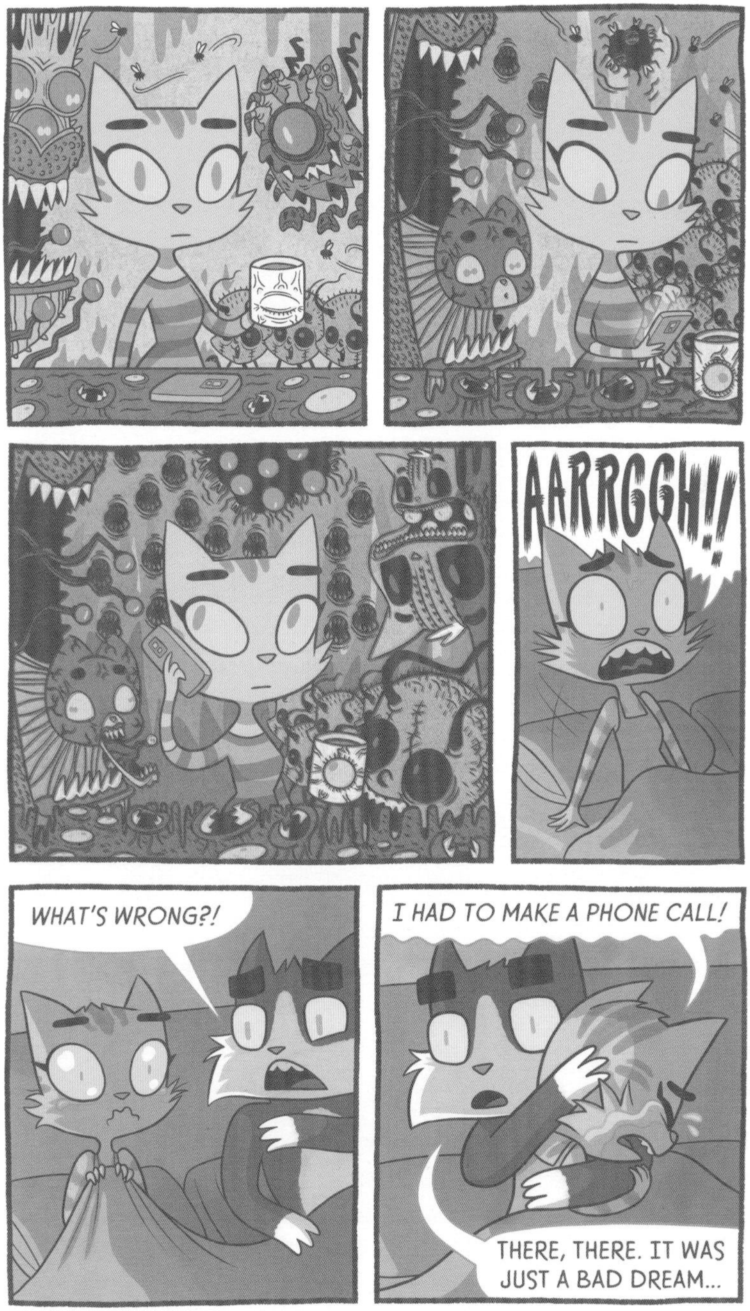
AARRGGH!!
WHAT'S WRONG?!
I HAD TO MAKE A PHONE CALL!
THERE, THERE. IT WAS JUST A BAD DREAM...

MONSTER ART BY @JEREMYTHEARTIST

COUPLES GOALS

I MET J IN 2000. HE STRODE INTO THE ROOM, LOOKING LIKE A BAD BOY WITH A LEATHER JACKET AND GUITAR, AND PLOPPED DOWN A PINK *POWERPUFF GIRLS* CD CASE ON THE TABLE. THIS GUY HAD LAYERS AND I WAS INTRIGUED!

AFTER A SUMMER OF TEXTING, I ACCEPTED AN INVITE TO BE HIS DATE TO THE FRESHMAN BALL. I WENT AS JESSICA RABBIT, AND HE WAS HUNTER S. THOMPSON—I SHOULD PROBABLY MENTION AT THIS POINT THAT THE BALL WAS *NOT* A COSTUME AFFAIR! I DON'T REMEMBER TOO MUCH OF THE EVENING, BUT I *DO* REMEMBER ASKING HIM TO BE MY BOYFRIEND. WE MOVED IN TOGETHER WEEKS LATER AND HAVE BEEN INSEPARABLE EVER SINCE.

THINGS GET WEIRD WHEN YOU'VE BEEN TOGETHER SO LONG. CATCHPHRASES WITH ORIGIN STORIES NEITHER OF YOU REMEMBER AND MEMES BUILT UPON MEMES RESULT IN A MUTUAL SHORTHAND, KIND OF LIKE THE NONSENSE LANGUAGES THAT YOU HEAR ABOUT PARTICULARLY CREEPY TWINS INVENTING.

LOOKING BACK ON THESE TWENTY-ODD YEARS, I STILL DON'T KNOW HOW WE KNEW WE WERE RIGHT FOR EACH OTHER, BUT I SURE AM HAPPY THAT JESSICA RABBIT MADE THE CHOICE SHE DID.

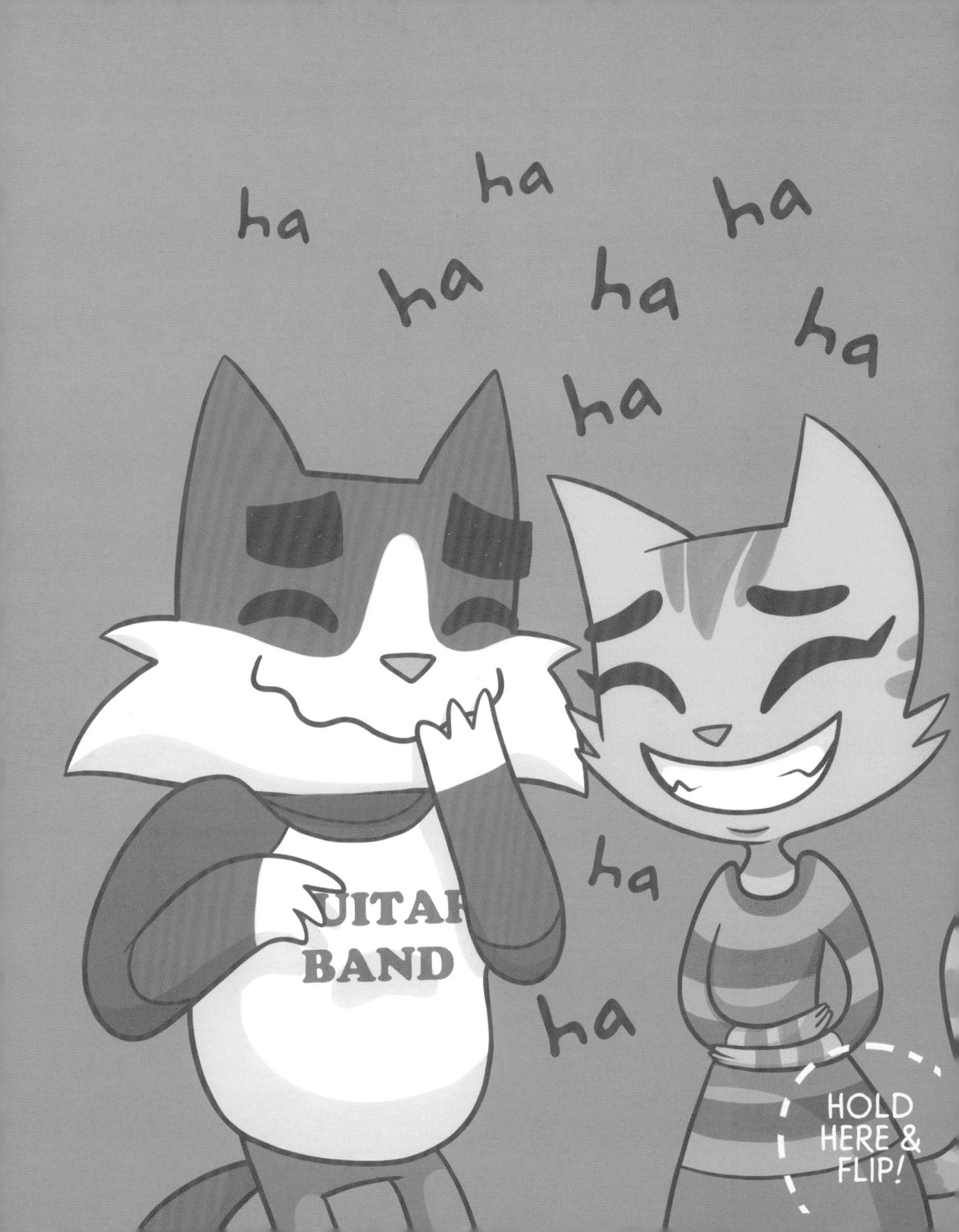
ha
ha
ha
ha
ha
ha
ha
ha
ha
UITAR
BAND
HOLD HERE & FLIP!

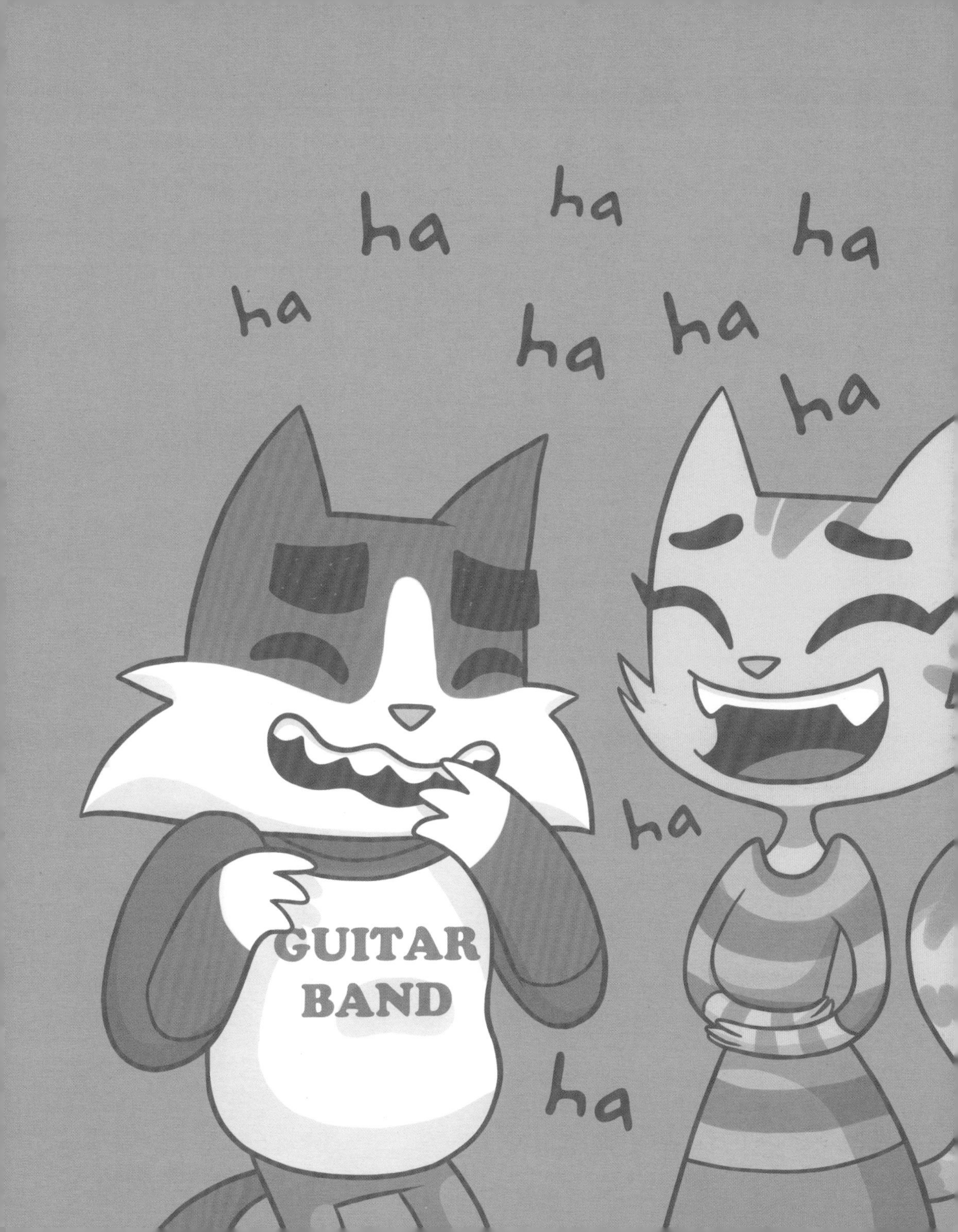
ha
ha
ha
ha
ha
ha
ha
GUITAR BAND
ha
ha

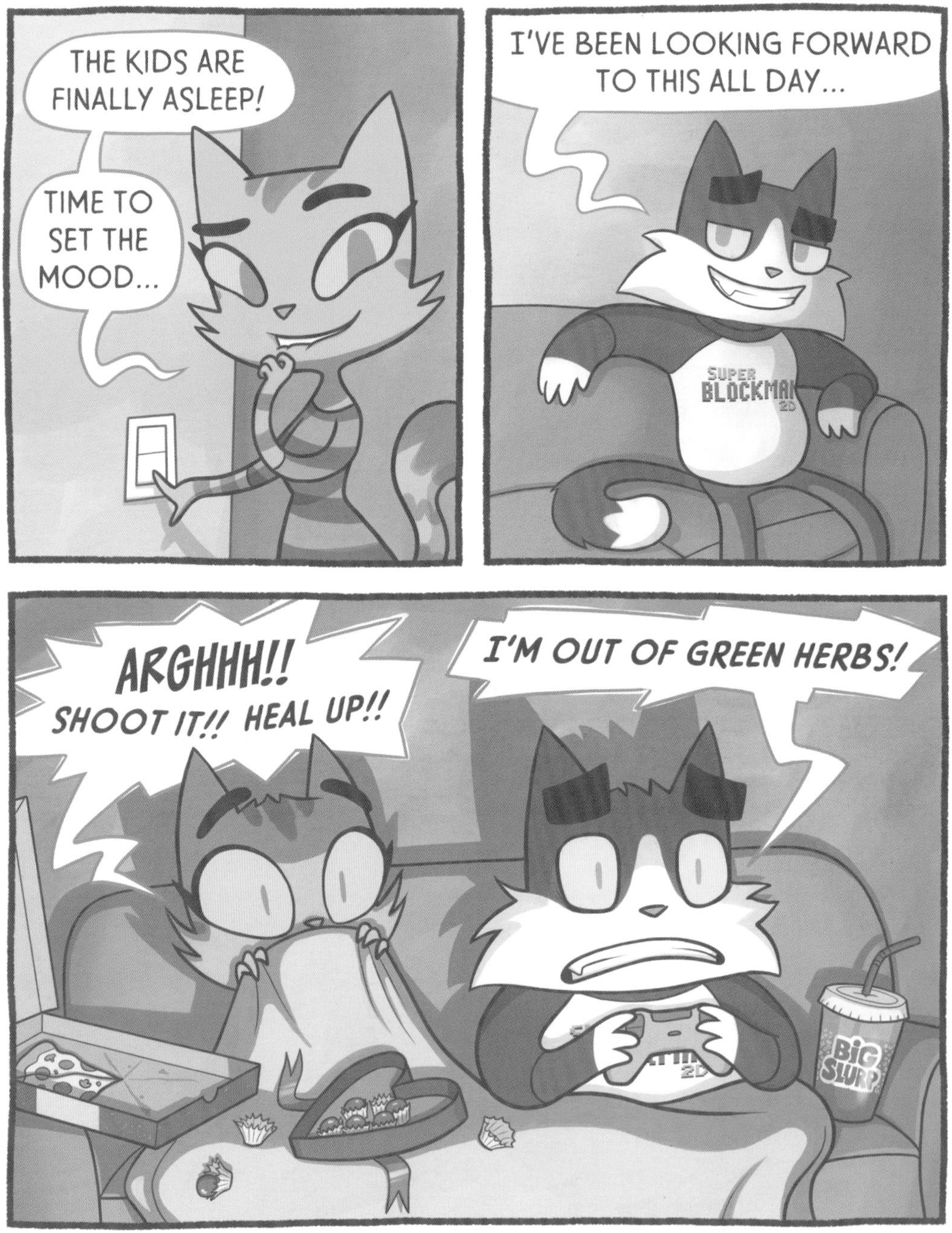
THE KIDS ARE FINALLY ASLEEP!
TIME TO SET THE MOOD...
I'VE BEEN LOOKING FORWARD TO THIS ALL DAY...
ARGHHH!! SHOOT IT!! HEAL UP!!
I'M OUT OF GREEN HERBS!
BIG SLURP

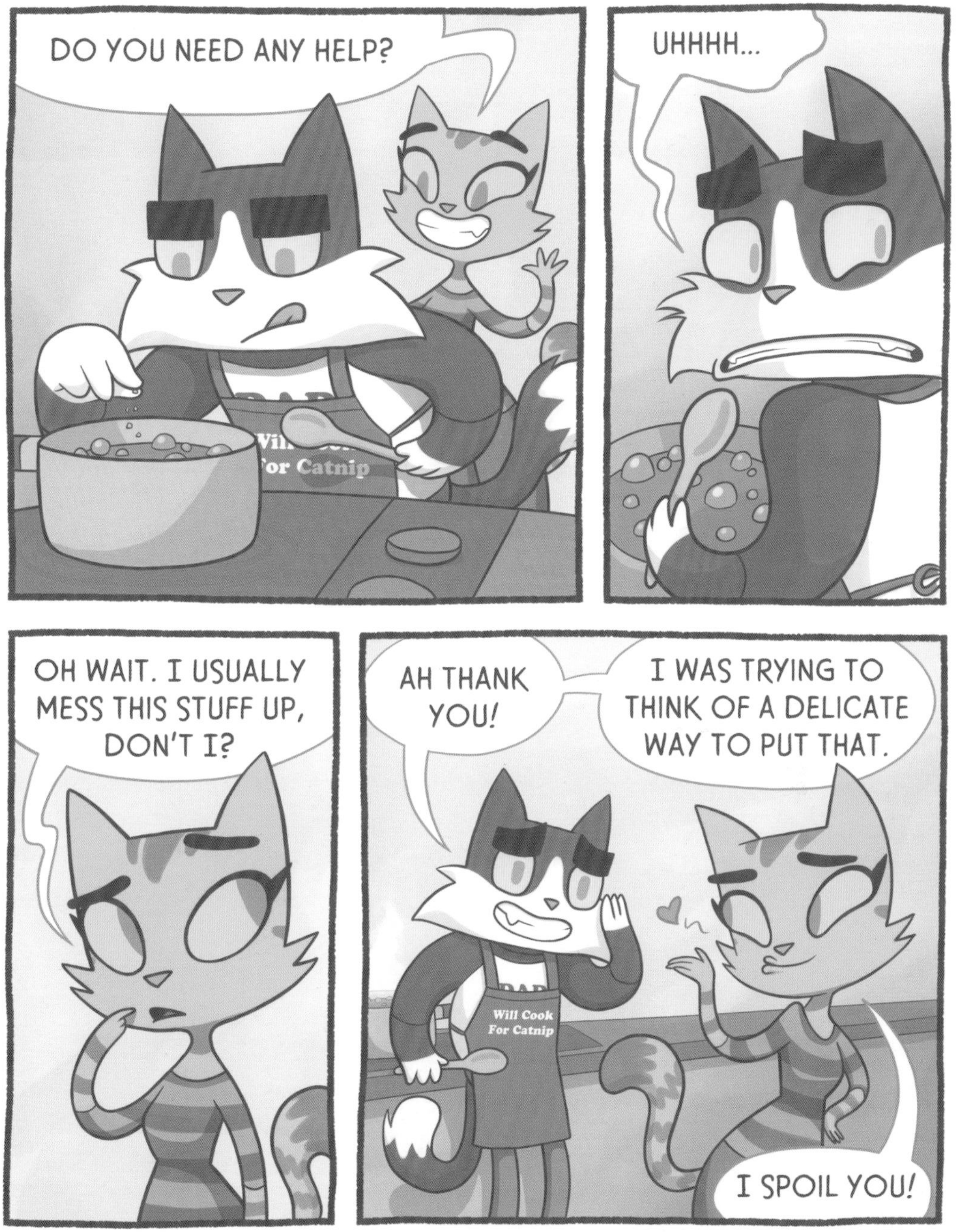
DO YOU NEED ANY HELP?
DAD
Will Cook For Catnip
UHHHH...
OH WAIT. I USUALLY MESS THIS STUFF UP, DON'T I?
AH THANK YOU!
I WAS TRYING TO THINK OF A DELICATE WAY TO PUT THAT.
DAD
Will Cook For Catnip
I SPOIL YOU!

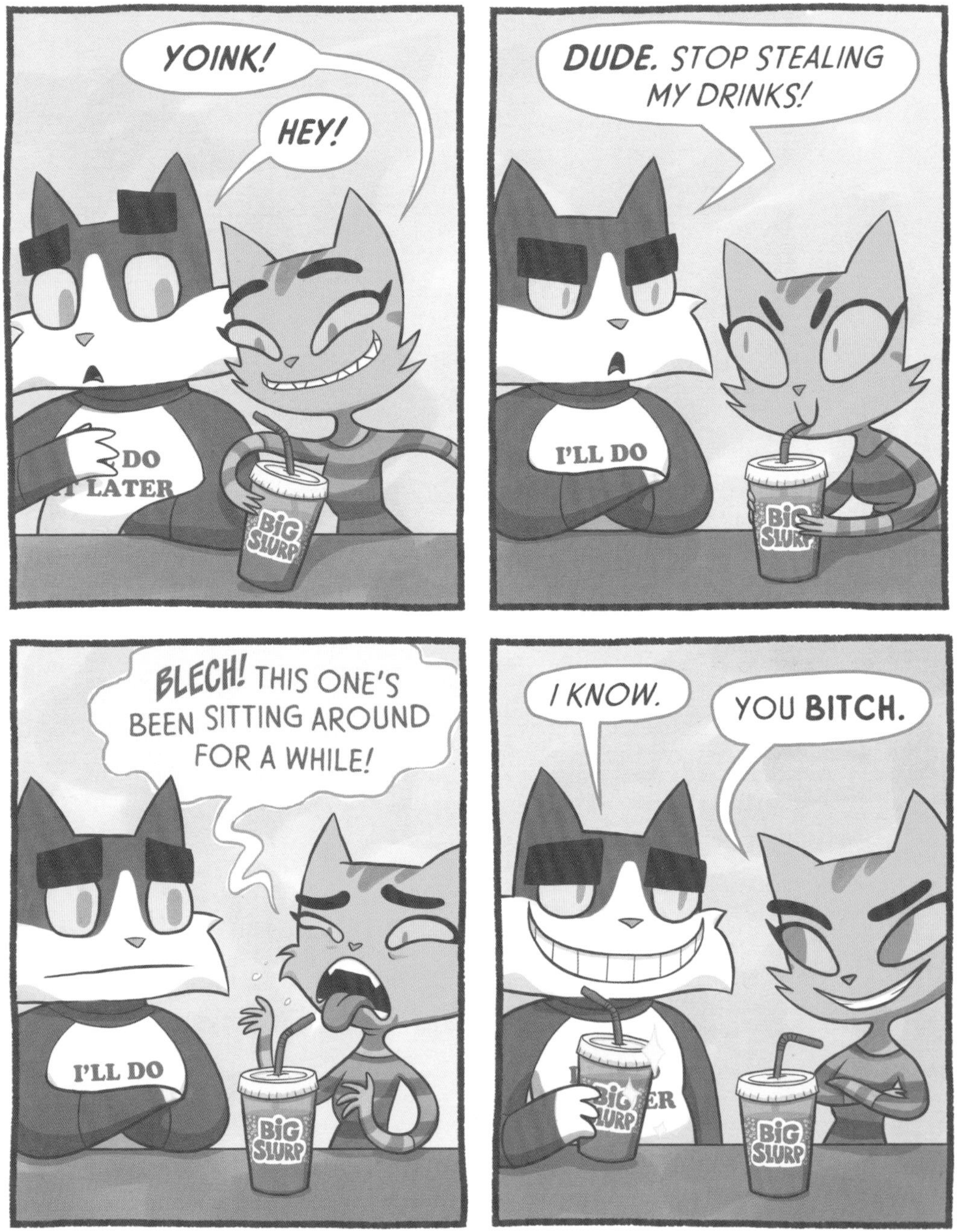
YOINK!
HEY!
DO
LATER
BIG SLURP
DUDE. STOP STEALING MY DRINKS!
I'LL DO
BIG SLURP
BLECH! THIS ONE'S BEEN SITTING AROUND FOR A WHILE!
I'LL DO
BIG SLURP
I KNOW.
YOU BITCH.
BIG SLURP
BIG SLURP

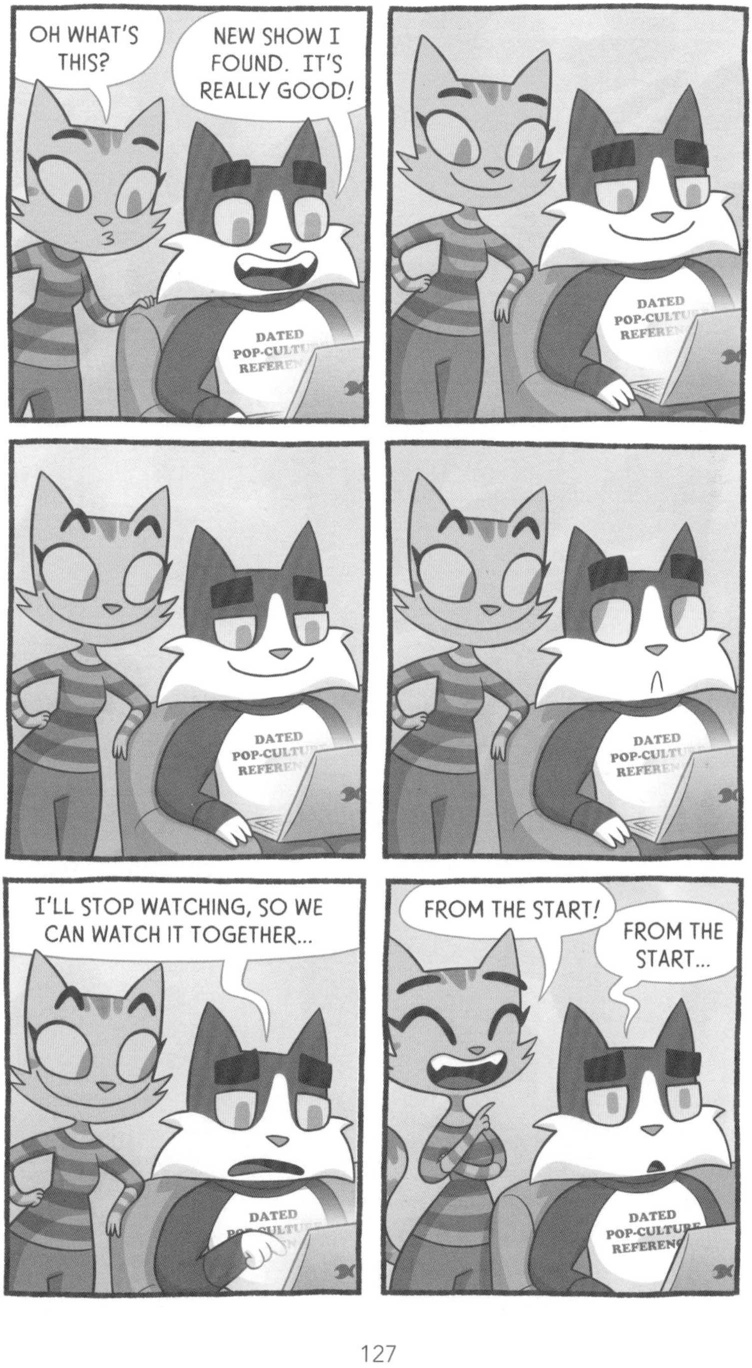
OH WHAT'S THIS?
NEW SHOW I FOUND. IT'S REALLY GOOD!
I'LL STOP WATCHING, SO WE CAN WATCH IT TOGETHER...
FROM THE START!
FROM THE START...

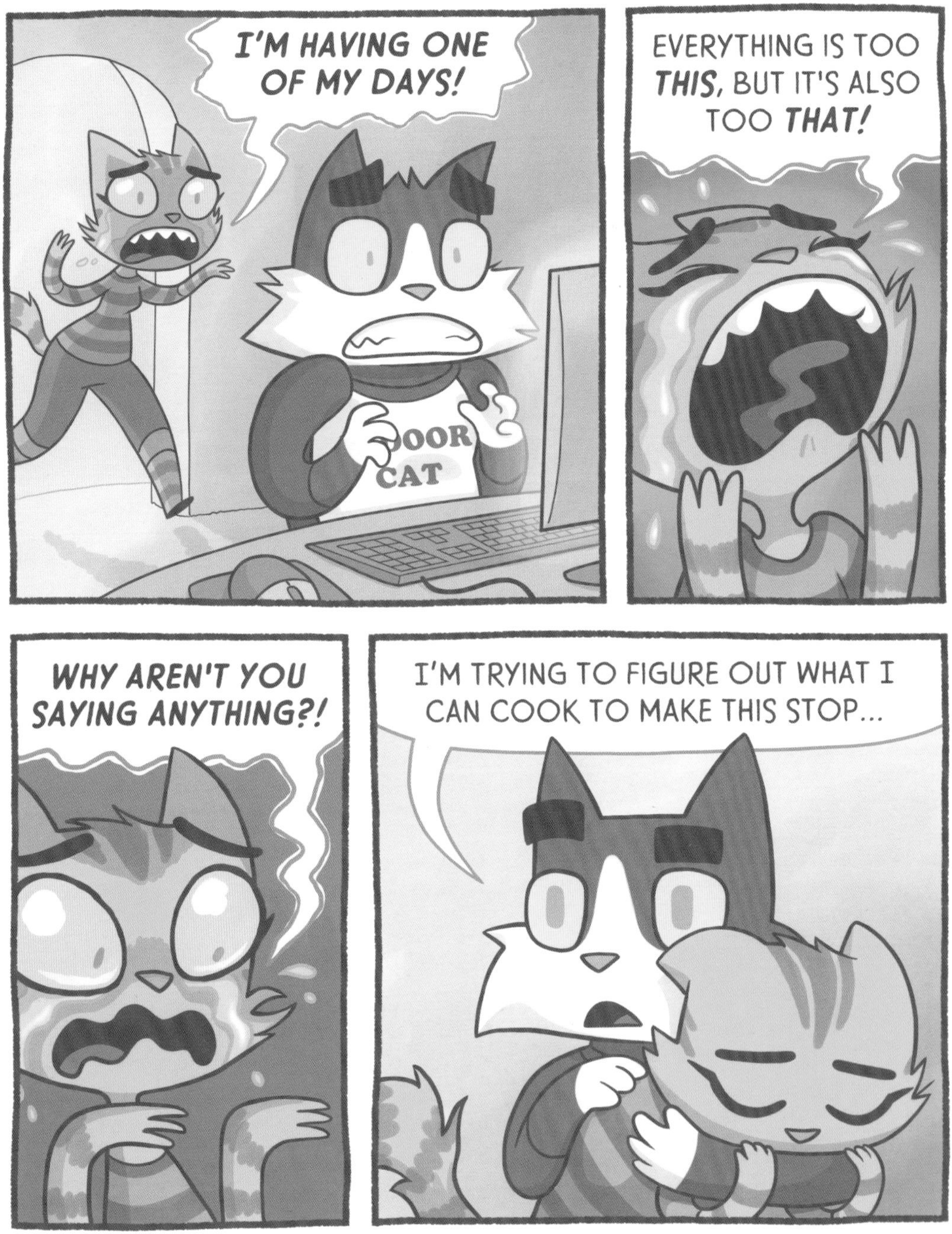
I'M HAVING ONE OF MY DAYS!
OOR
CAT
EVERYTHING IS TOO THIS, BUT IT'S ALSO TOO THAT!
WHY AREN'T YOU SAYING ANYTHING?!
I'M TRYING TO FIGURE OUT WHAT I CAN COOK TO MAKE THIS STOP...

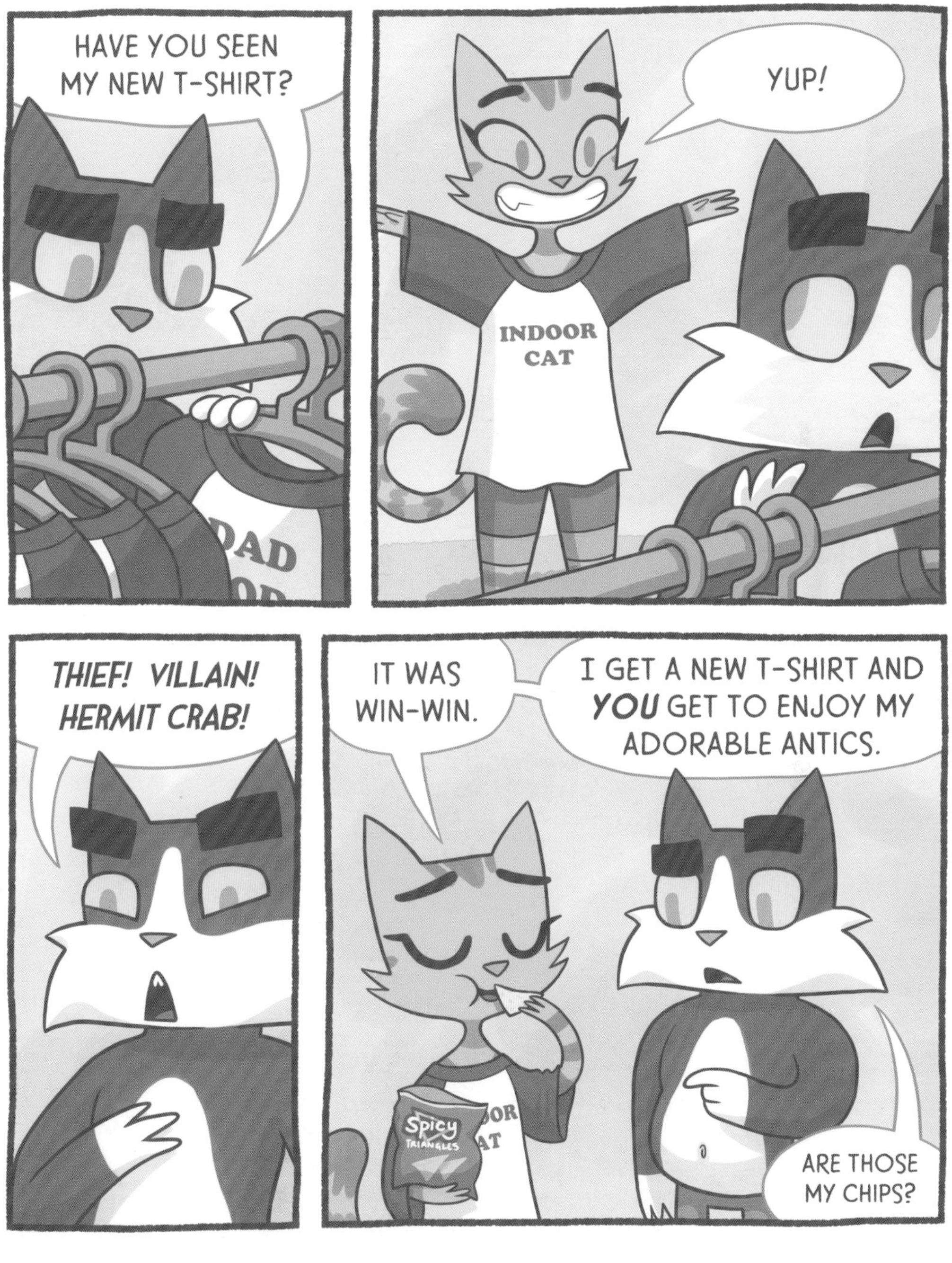
HAVE YOU SEEN MY NEW T-SHIRT?
DAD
YUP!
INDOOR CAT
THIEF! VILLAIN! HERMIT CRAB!
IT WAS WIN-WIN.
I GET A NEW T-SHIRT AND *YOU* GET TO ENJOY MY ADORABLE ANTICS.
Spicy TRIANGLES
ARE THOSE MY CHIPS?

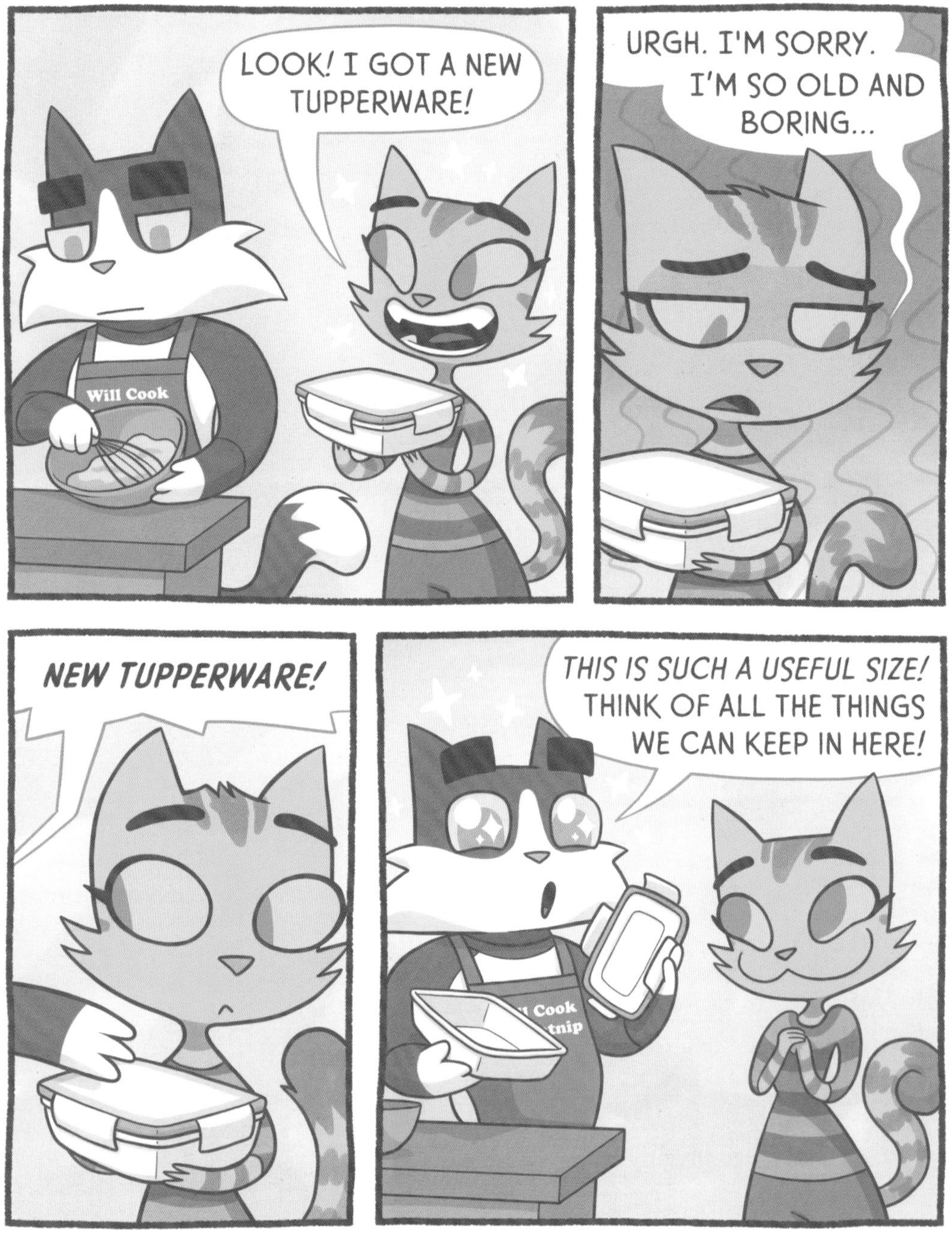
LOOK! I GOT A NEW TUPPERWARE!
Will Cook
URGH. I'M SORRY.
I'M SO OLD AND BORING...
NEW TUPPERWARE!
THIS IS SUCH A USEFUL SIZE! THINK OF ALL THE THINGS WE CAN KEEP IN HERE!

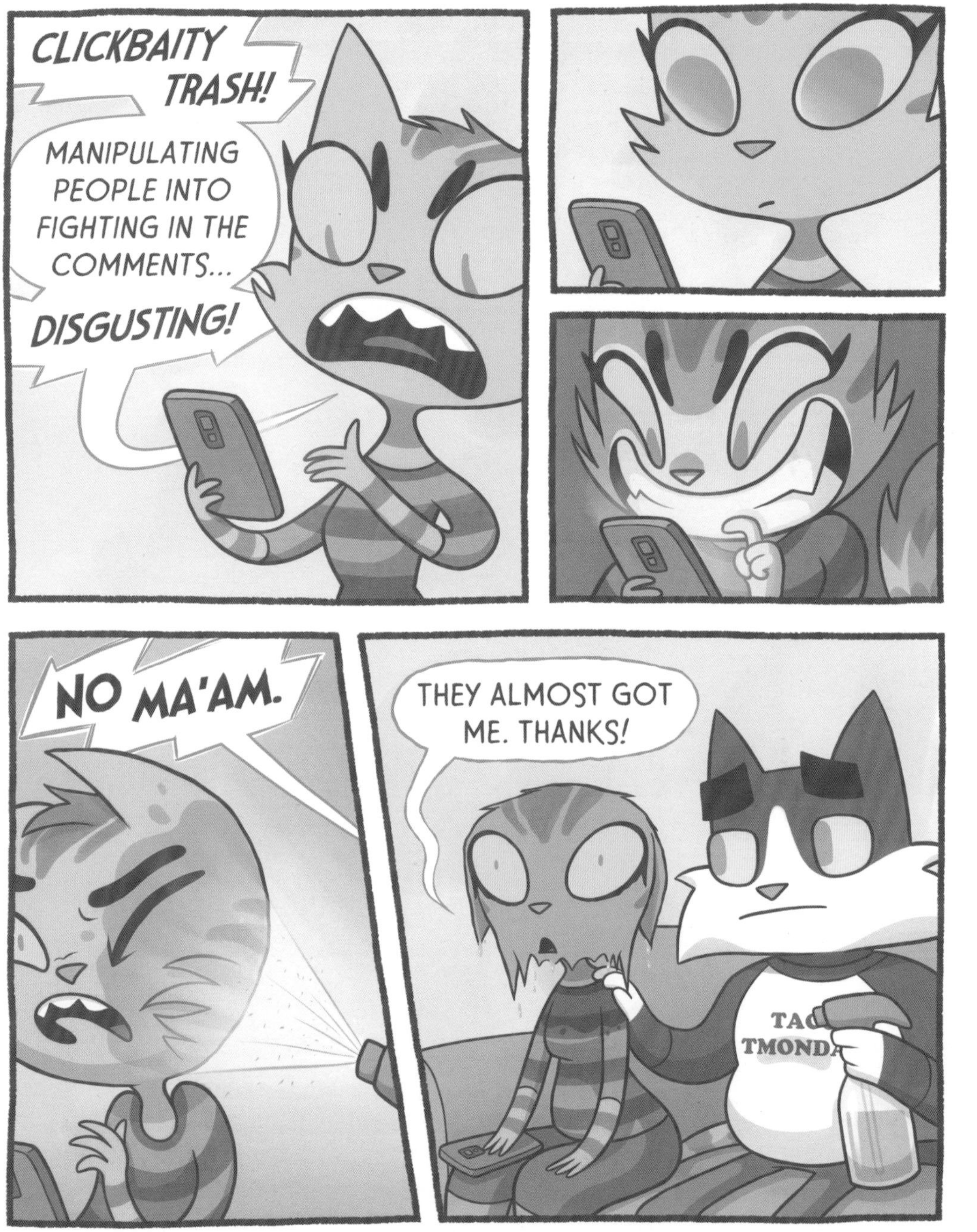
CLICKBAITY TRASH!
MANIPULATING PEOPLE INTO FIGHTING IN THE COMMENTS...
DISGUSTING!
NO MA'AM.
THEY ALMOST GOT ME. THANKS!
TAC
TMONDA

SCREEN TIME

WHEN I WAS 6, A DOCTOR SAT MY PARENTS DOWN AND CATALOGED THE MYRIAD OF ISSUES WITH MY EYES. HIS RECOMMENDATION? COMPUTER GAMES FOR HAND-EYE COORDINATION. WELL, WOULD YOU BELIEVE IT? THAT CHRISTMAS, SANTA BROUGHT ME A NINTENDO!

SO MUCH OF MY PERSONALITY IS WRAPPED UP IN GAMES AND TV, I FIND MY NEW ROLE AS "GATEKEEPER OF SCREENS" VERY UNCOMFORTABLE. ON ONE HAND, I DON'T WANT MY KIDS TO BE DROOLING TECH-ZOMBIES, BUT ON THE OTHER, I NEED TO PUMP THEM FULL OF THE SAME POP-CULTURE INFLUENCES THAT MADE ME *ME!*

IT'S A DELICATE BALANCE. PULL THE TRIGGER ON A BELOVED MOVIE TOO SOON AND THEY'LL WANDER OFF AND WATCH UNBOXING VIDEOS ON YOUTUBE. TOO LATE, AND YOU MISS THE CHANCE OF IT BECOMING A CORE MEMORY. BUT WHEN YOU GET IT RIGHT—OH BOY! THOSE ARE THE GOLDEN MOMENTS OF PARENTING!

HOLD HERE & FLIP!

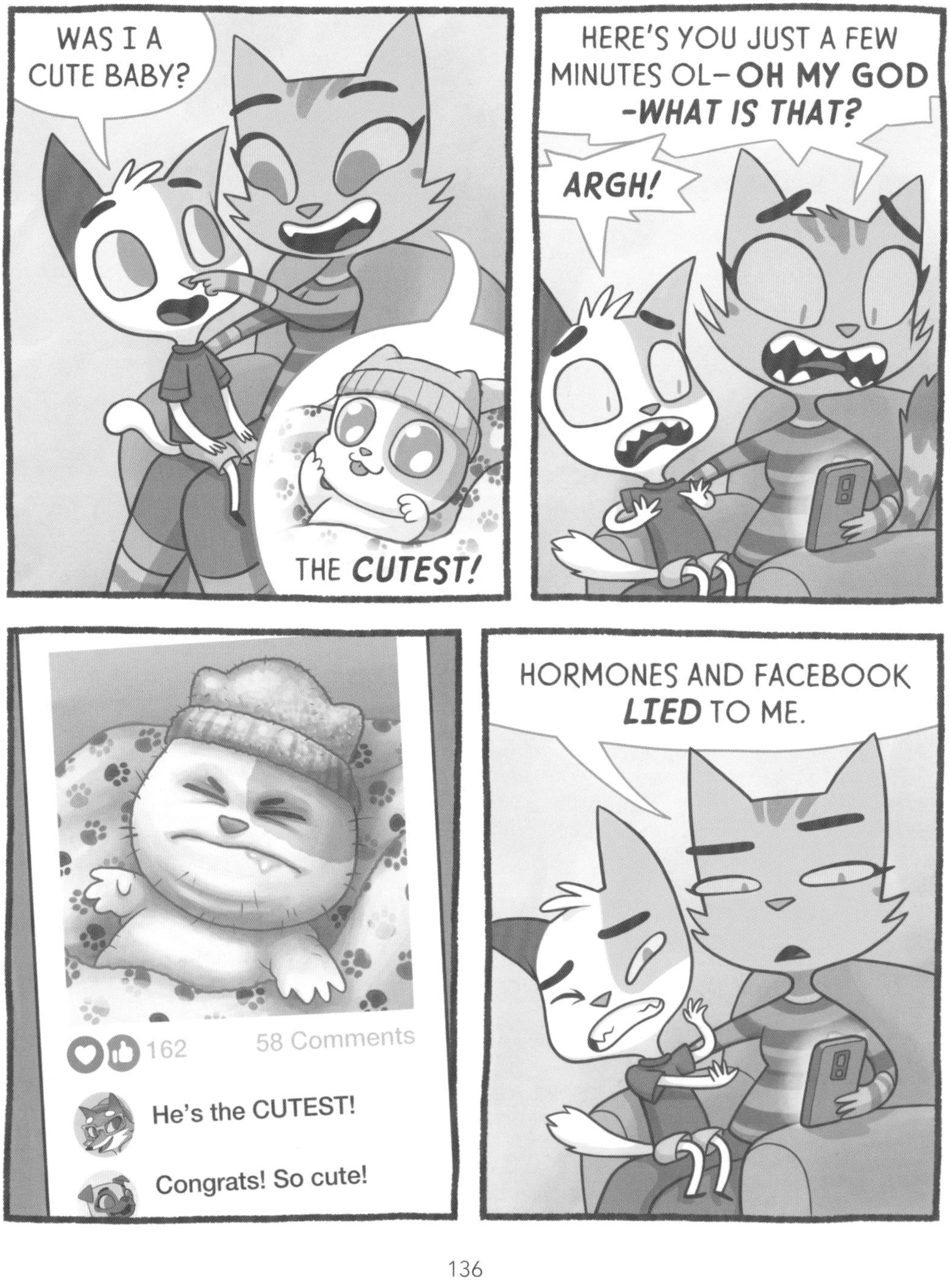
WAS I A CUTE BABY?
THE CUTEST!
HERE'S YOU JUST A FEW MINUTES OL—OH MY GOD -WHAT IS THAT?
ARGH!
162
58 Comments
He's the CUTEST!
Congrats! So cute!
HORMONES AND FACEBOOK LIED TO ME.

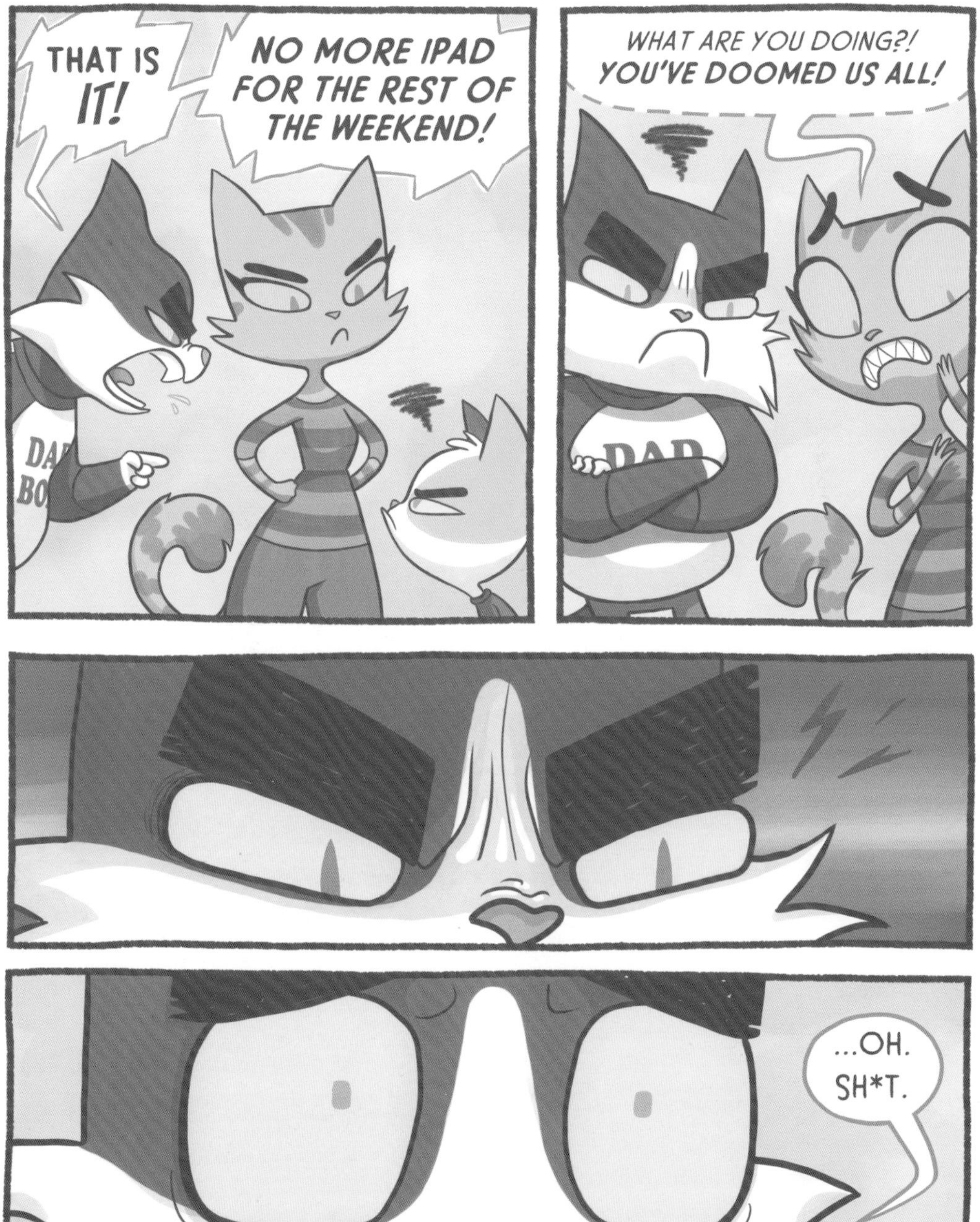
THAT IS IT!
NO MORE IPAD FOR THE REST OF THE WEEKEND!
WHAT ARE YOU DOING?! YOU'VE DOOMED US ALL!
...OH. SH*T.

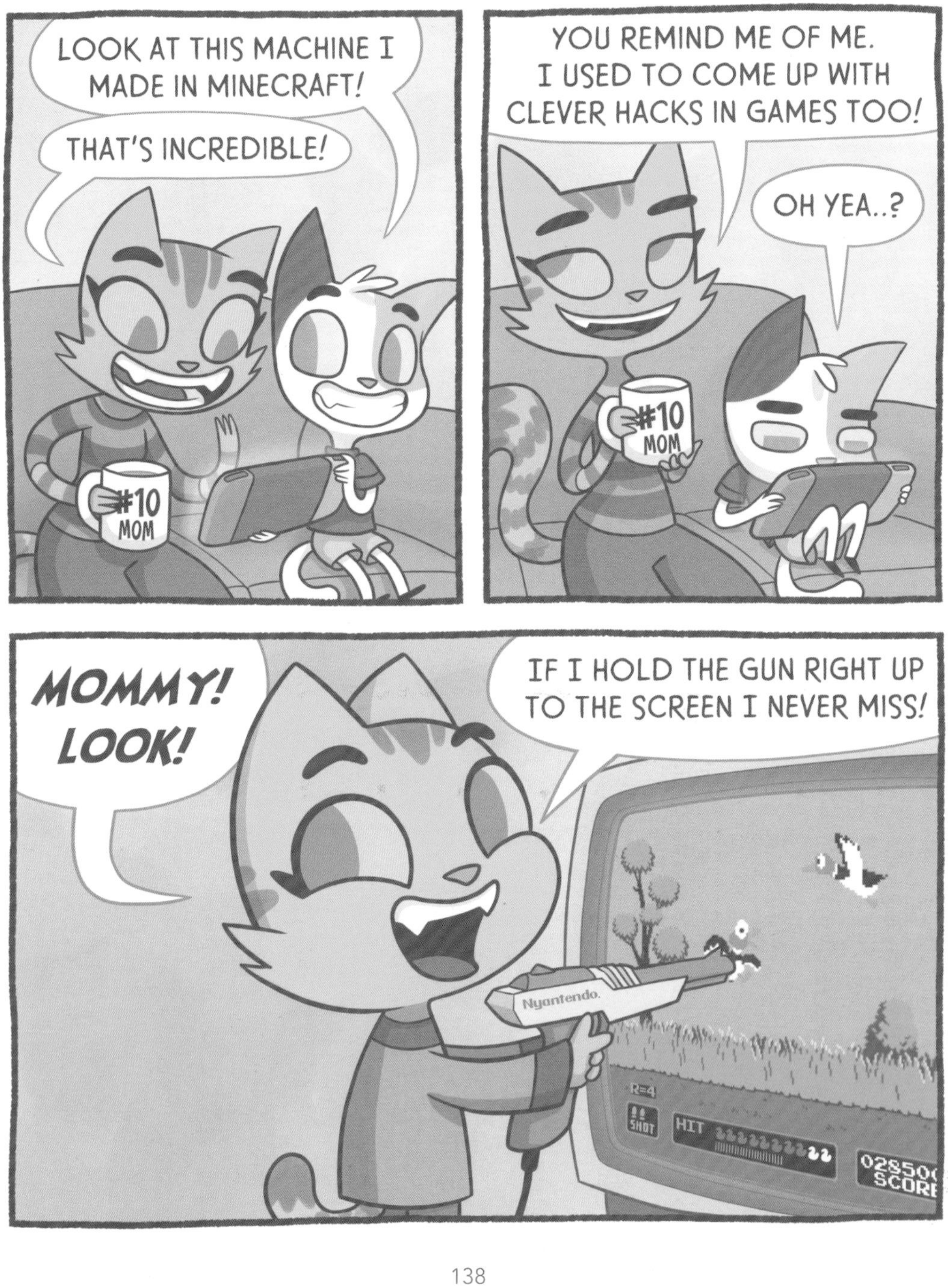
LOOK AT THIS MACHINE I MADE IN MINECRAFT!
THAT'S INCREDIBLE!
#10 MOM
YOU REMIND ME OF ME. I USED TO COME UP WITH CLEVER HACKS IN GAMES TOO!
OH YEA..?
#10 MOM
MOMMY! LOOK!
IF I HOLD THE GUN RIGHT UP TO THE SCREEN I NEVER MISS!
Nyantendo.
R=4
SHOT
HIT

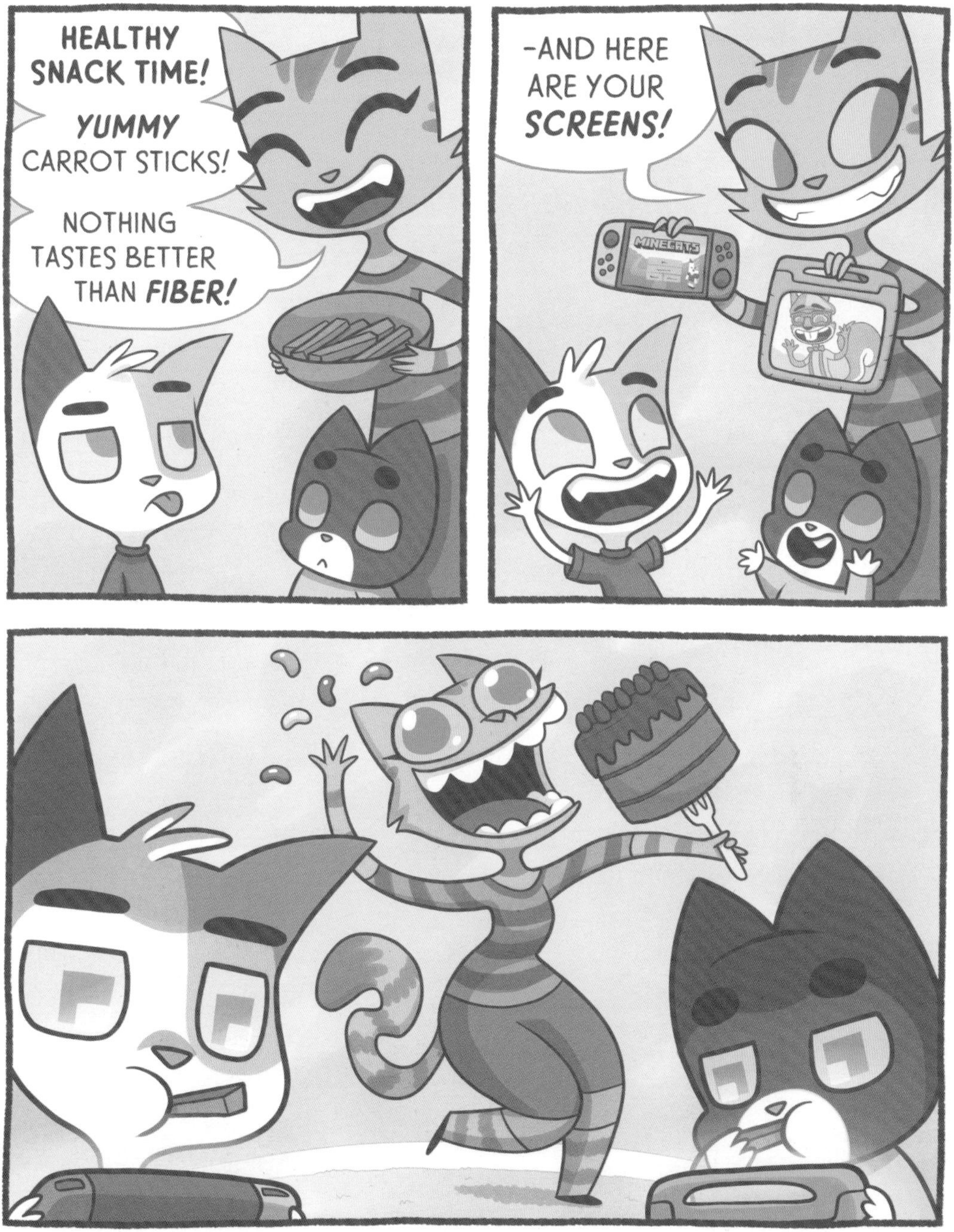
HEALTHY SNACK TIME!
YUMMY CARROT STICKS!
NOTHING TASTES BETTER THAN *FIBER!*
-AND HERE ARE YOUR *SCREENS!*
MINECATS

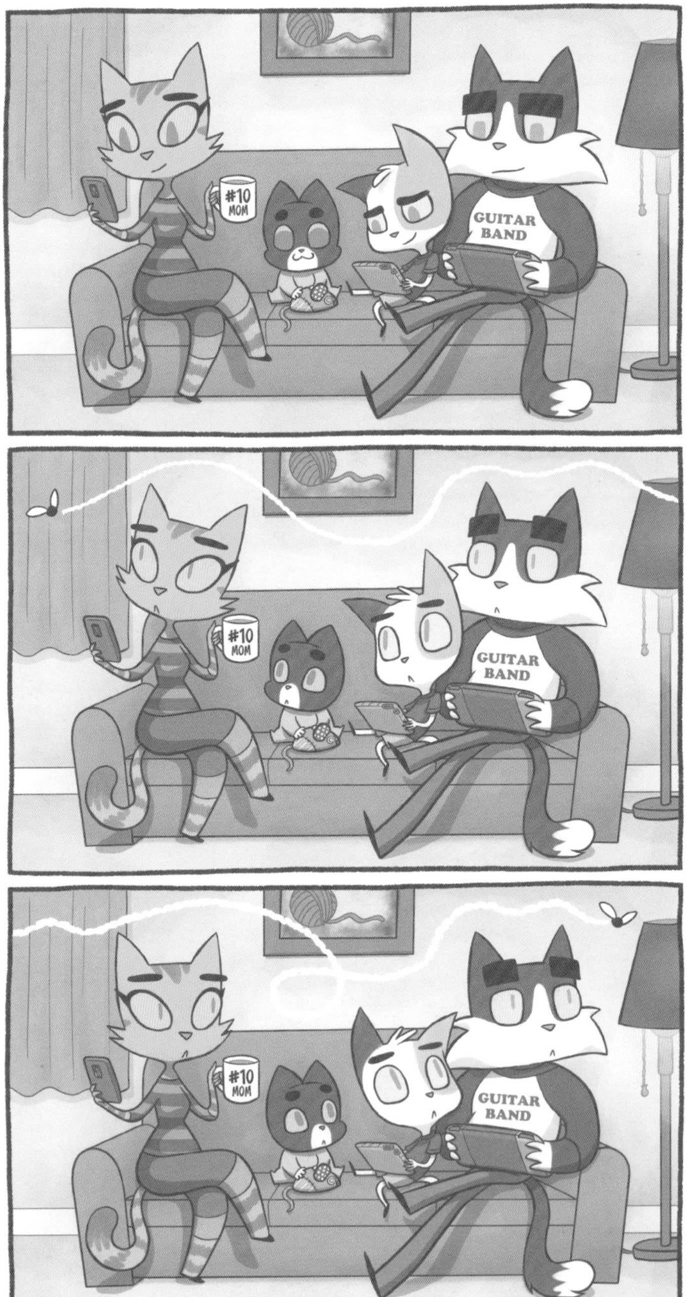
#10
MOM
GUITAR
BAND
#10
MOM
GUITAR
BAND
#10
MOM
GUITAR
BAND

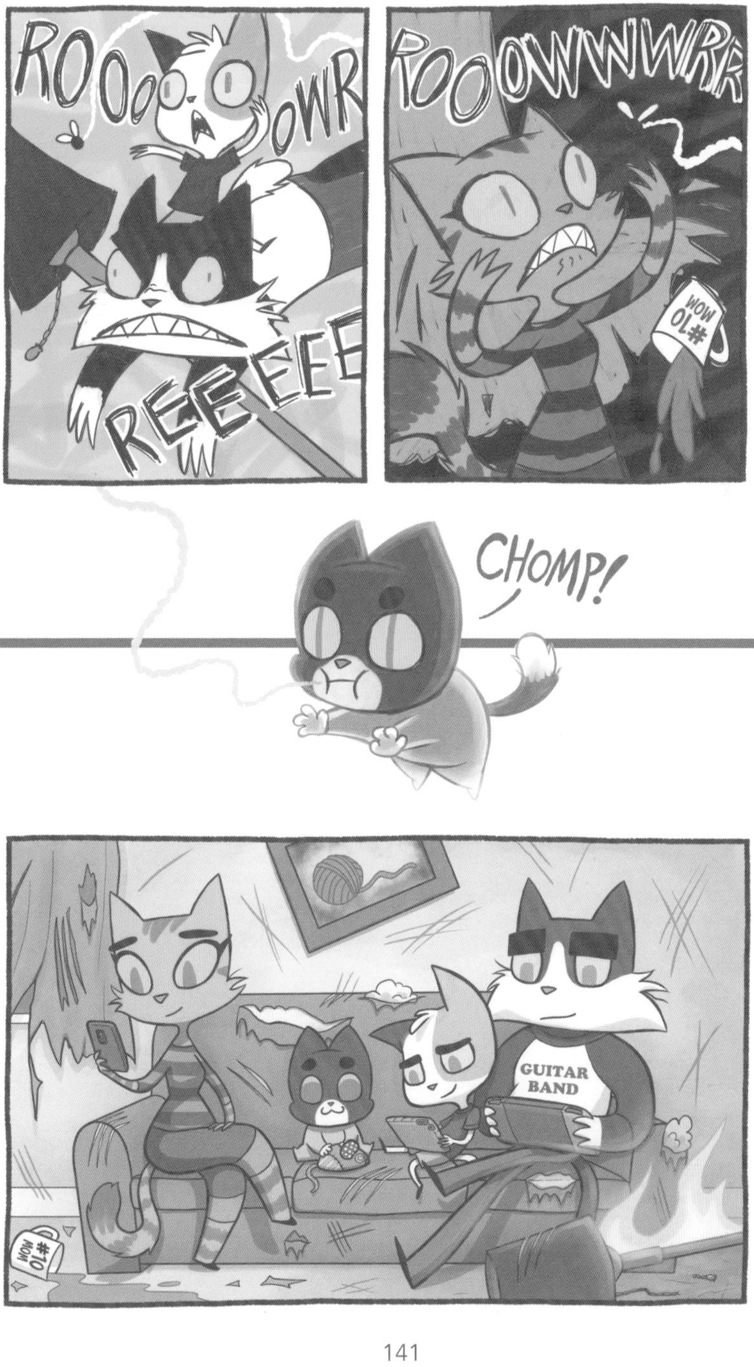
ROOOOOWR
REEEEEE
ROOOOWWWRR
#10 MOM
CHOMP!
GUITAR BAND
#10 MOM

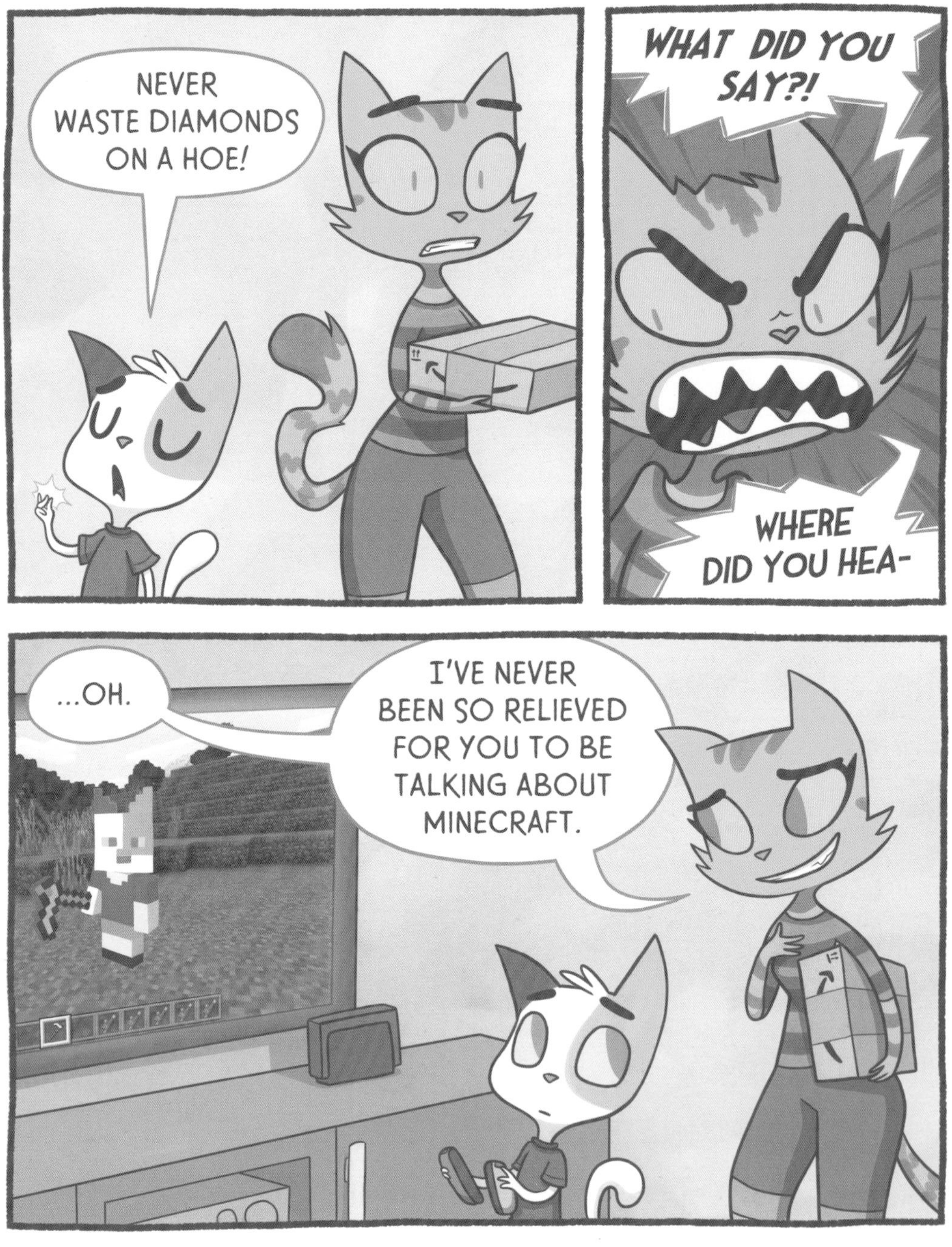
NEVER WASTE DIAMONDS ON A HOE!
WHAT DID YOU SAY?!
WHERE DID YOU HEA-
...OH.
I'VE NEVER BEEN SO RELIEVED FOR YOU TO BE TALKING ABOUT MINECRAFT.

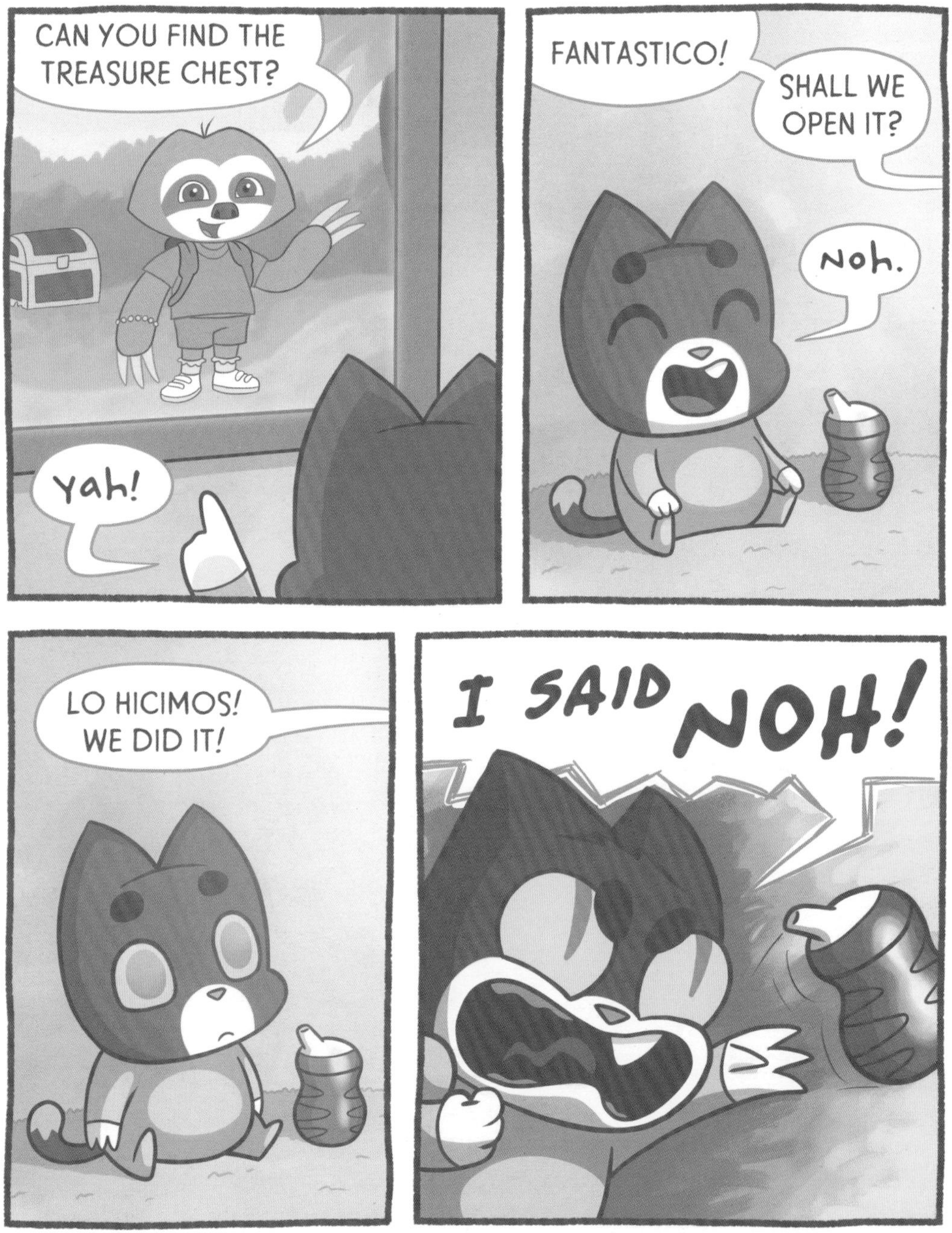
CAN YOU FIND THE TREASURE CHEST?
Yah!
FANTASTICO!
SHALL WE OPEN IT?
Noh.
LO HICIMOS! WE DID IT!
I SAID NOH!

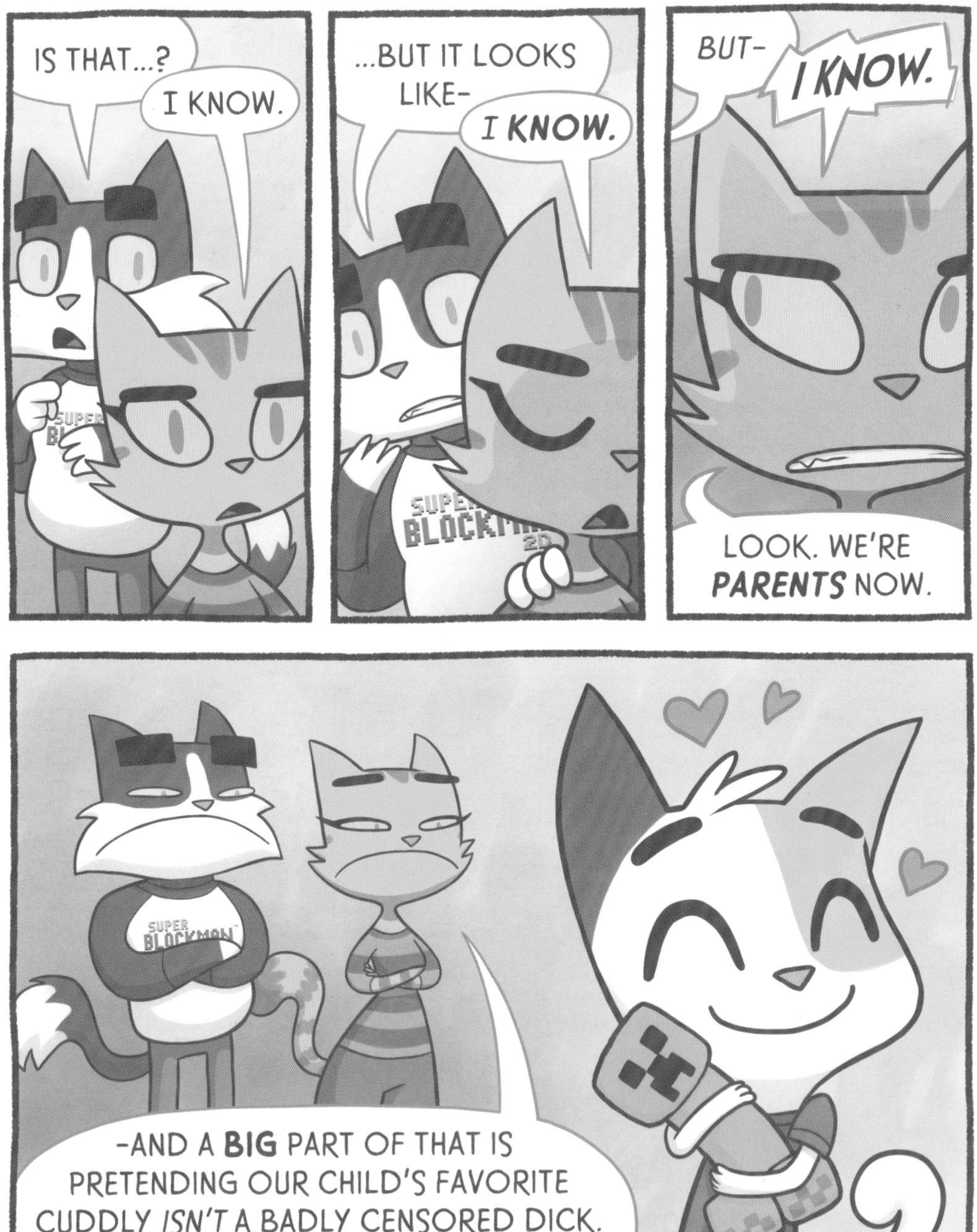
IS THAT...?
I KNOW.
...BUT IT LOOKS LIKE-
I **KNOW.**
BUT-
I KNOW.
LOOK. WE'RE **PARENTS** NOW.
-AND A **BIG** PART OF THAT IS PRETENDING OUR CHILD'S FAVORITE CUDDLY *ISN'T* A BADLY CENSORED DICK.

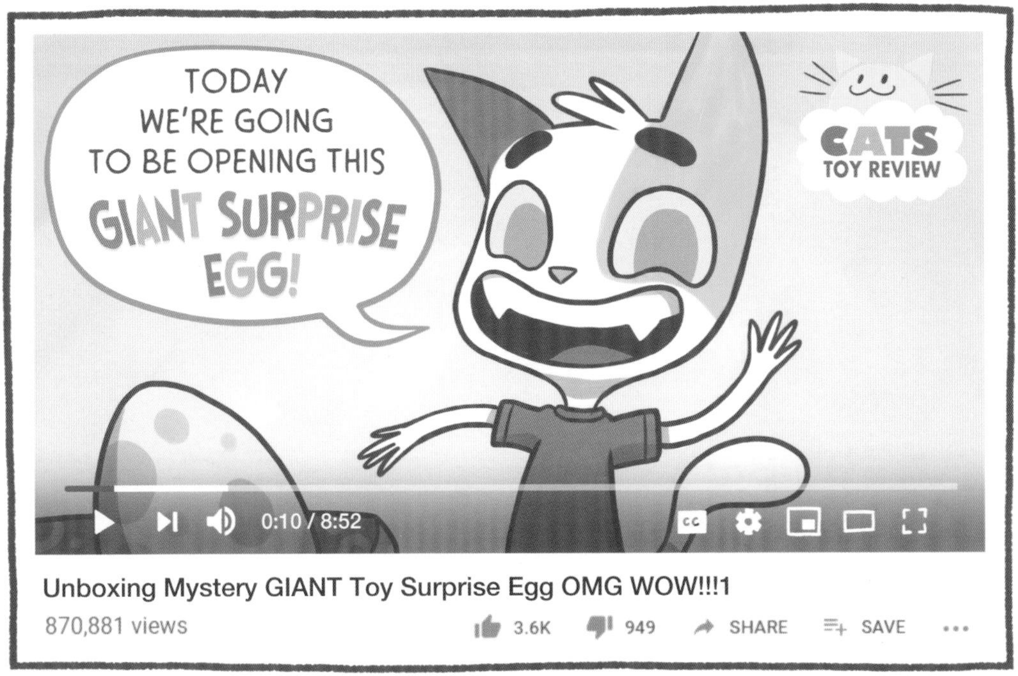
TODAY WE'RE GOING TO BE OPENING THIS GIANT SURPRISE EGG!
CATS TOY REVIEW
0:10 / 8:52
Unboxing Mystery GIANT Toy Surprise Egg OMG WOW!!!1
870,881 views
3.6K
949
SHARE
SAVE

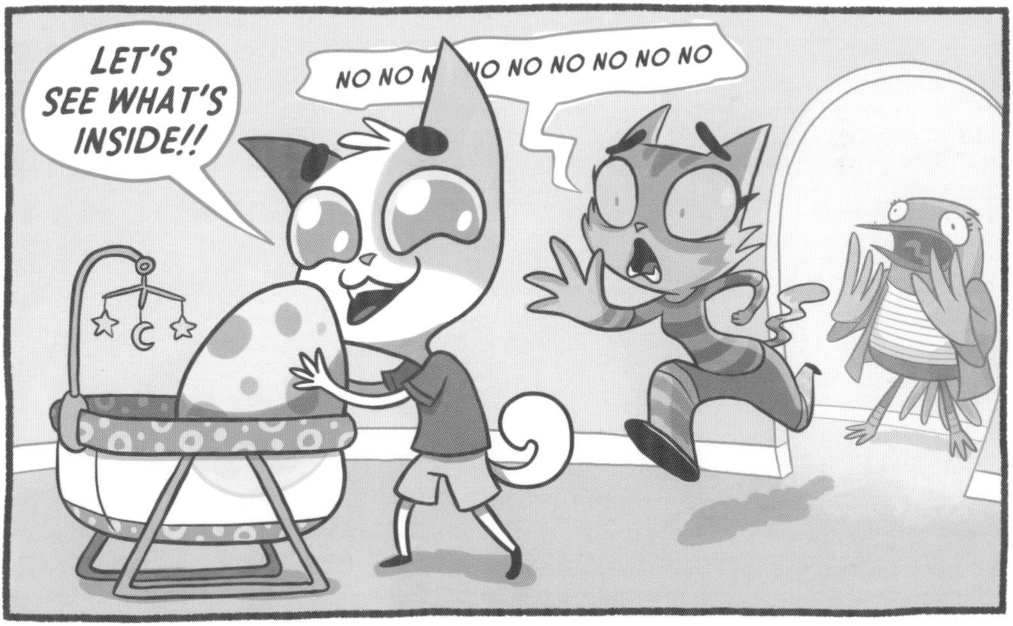
LET'S SEE WHAT'S INSIDE!!
NO NO NO NO NO NO NO NO NO

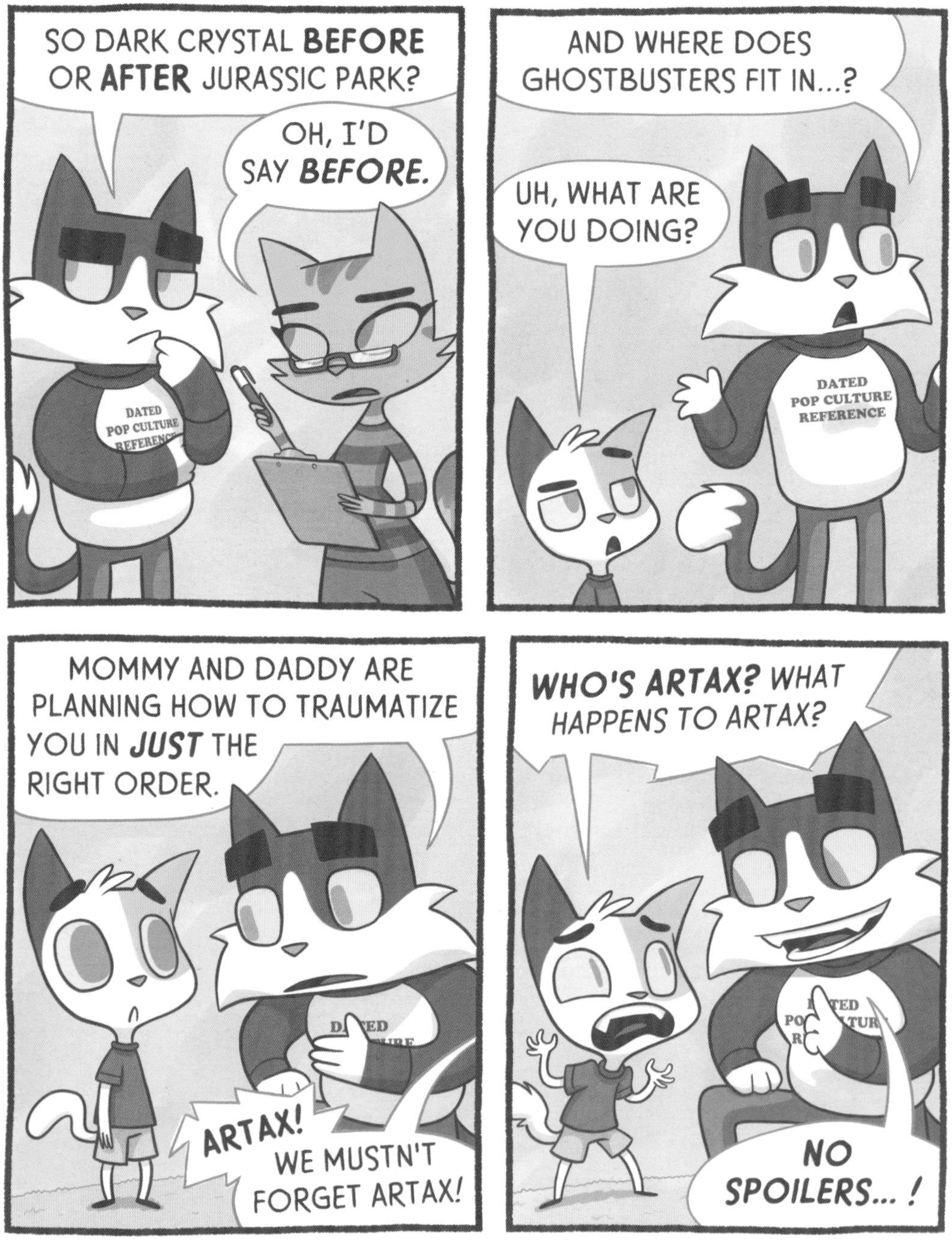
SO DARK CRYSTAL BEFORE OR AFTER JURASSIC PARK?
OH, I'D SAY BEFORE.
DATED POP CULTURE REFERENCE
AND WHERE DOES GHOSTBUSTERS FIT IN...?
UH, WHAT ARE YOU DOING?
DATED POP CULTURE REFERENCE
MOMMY AND DADDY ARE PLANNING HOW TO TRAUMATIZE YOU IN JUST THE RIGHT ORDER.
ARTAX! WE MUSTN'T FORGET ARTAX!
WHO'S ARTAX? WHAT HAPPENS TO ARTAX?
NO SPOILERS... !

WHAT IS VINCENT TALKING ABOUT?

M	I	N	E	C	R	A	F	T	C	M	T	F	I
I	N	M	T	F	A	R	C	E	N	I	M	N	C
N	M	I	N	E	C	R	A	F	T	N	I	M	F
E	F	I	M	C	T	F	A	R	C	E	N	I	M
C	M	I	N	E	C	R	A	F	T	C	E	N	I
R	C	E	T	E	R	F	C	R	I	R	C	E	N
A	T	F	A	R	C	E	N	I	M	A	R	C	E
F	M	I	N	E	C	R	A	F	T	F	A	R	C
T	F	N	C	R	T	F	A	M	C	T	F	A	R
F	M	I	N	E	C	R	A	F	T	I	T	F	A
T	F	A	R	C	E	N	I	M	T	F	C	T	F
C	N	T	F	T	M	I	N	E	C	R	A	F	T

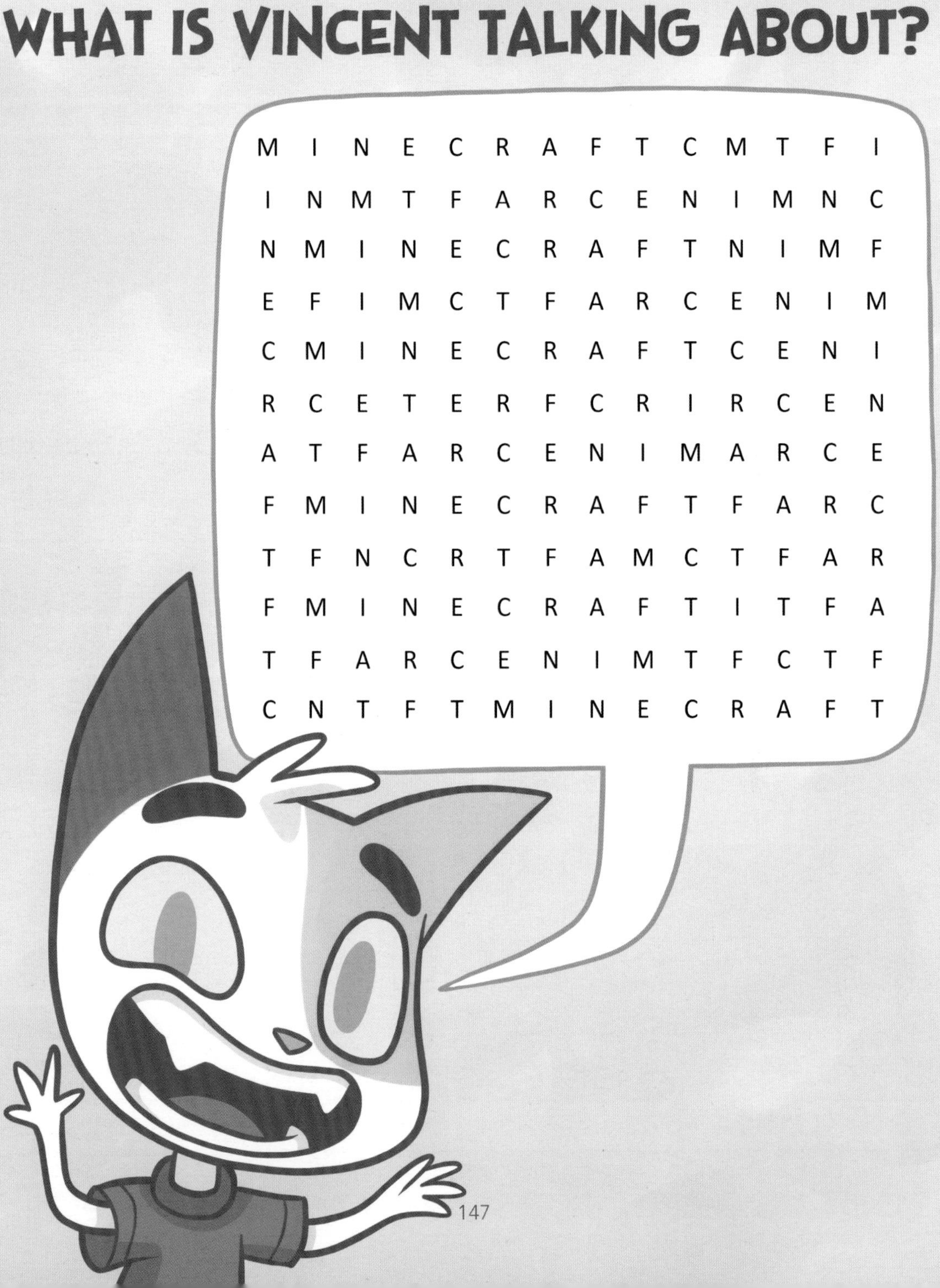

SCHOOL'S CALLING

OUR KIDS ARE DIFFICULT QUESTION FACTORIES, AND WE OFTEN HAVE TO DISAPPEAR DOWN SOME VERY WEIRD INTERNET RABBIT HOLES TO ANSWER THEM. THIS IS ALL VERY FINE AND SCIENTIFIC UNTIL THEY TROT INTO SCHOOL WITH A HALF-BAKED RECOLLECTION OF WHAT WE'VE TOLD THEM AND DECIDE TO DELIVER A GRIZZLY TED TALK ON MIKE THE CHICKEN, WHO LIVED EIGHTEEN MONTHS WITH NO HEAD, OR THE MORE EXCRUCIATING DETAILS OF THE BUBONIC PLAGUE (WE'VE BEEN TRYING TO EXPLAIN WHAT "READ THE ROOM" MEANS TO THEM, WITH LIMITED SUCCESS).

THEIR ART IS ALSO CRIMINALLY UNDERAPPRECIATED IN THEIR OWN TIME. WE HAVE A PAPER STACK AS TALL AS OUR YOUNGEST OF ASSIGNED ART AND COLORING PAGES THAT HAVE TAKEN A SHARP TURN FROM CHEERFUL SEASONAL TABLEAU TOWARD NIGHTMARISH HIERONYMUS BOSCH HELLSCAPE IN CRAYON. OR BUTTS.

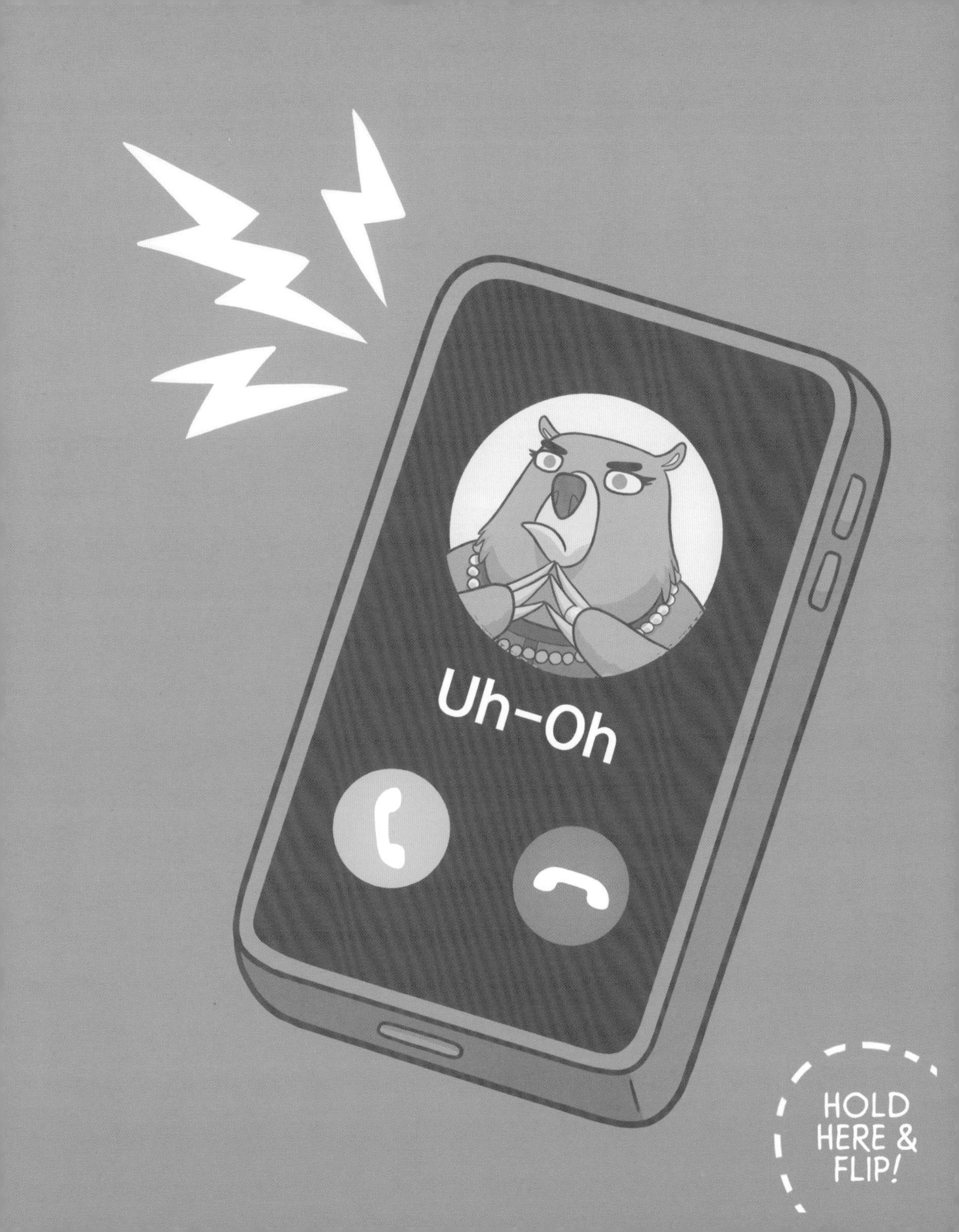
Uh-Oh
HOLD HERE & FLIP!

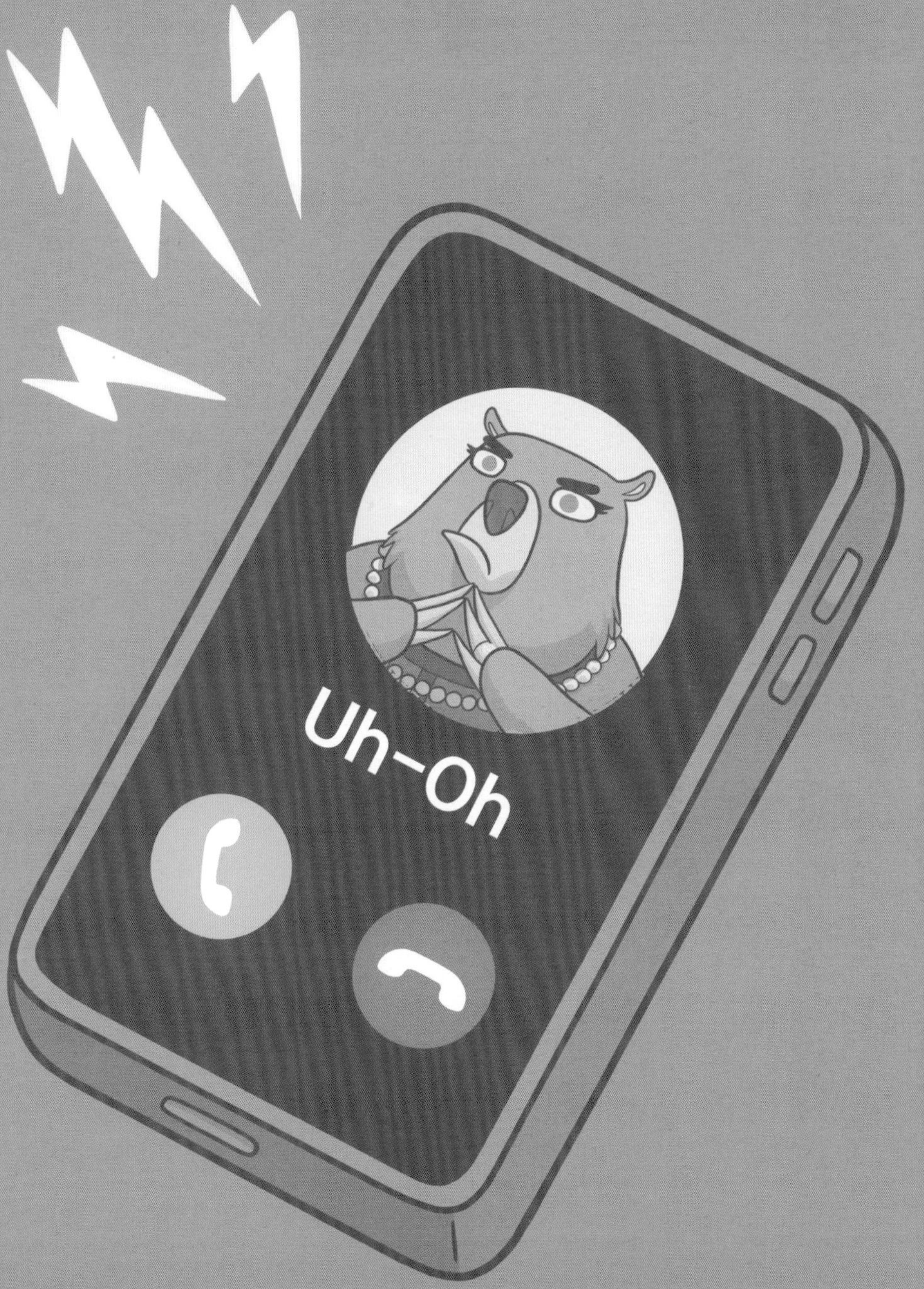
Uh-Oh

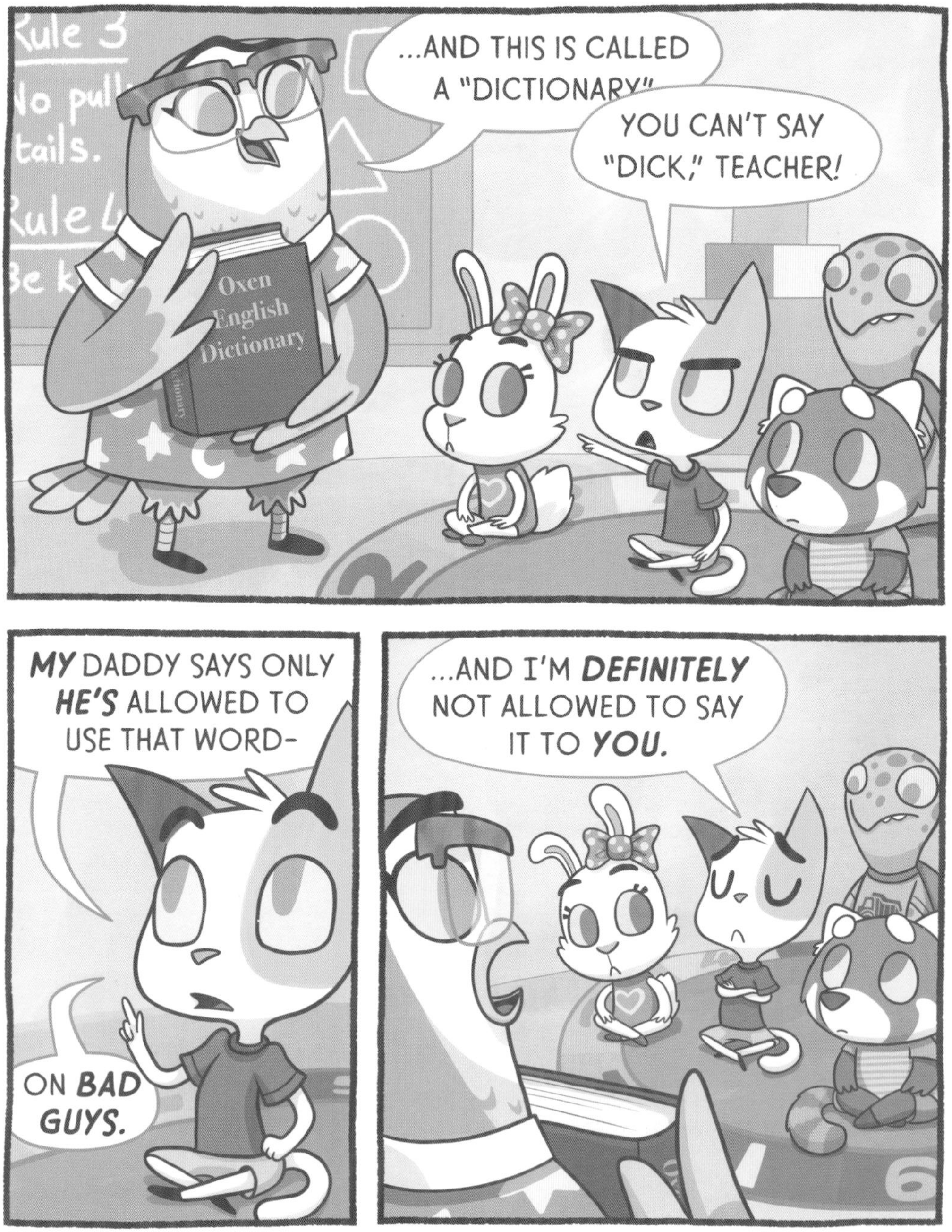
...AND THIS IS CALLED A "DICTIONARY"
Oxen English Dictionary
YOU CAN'T SAY "DICK," TEACHER!
MY DADDY SAYS ONLY HE'S ALLOWED TO USE THAT WORD-
ON BAD GUYS.
...AND I'M DEFINITELY NOT ALLOWED TO SAY IT TO YOU.

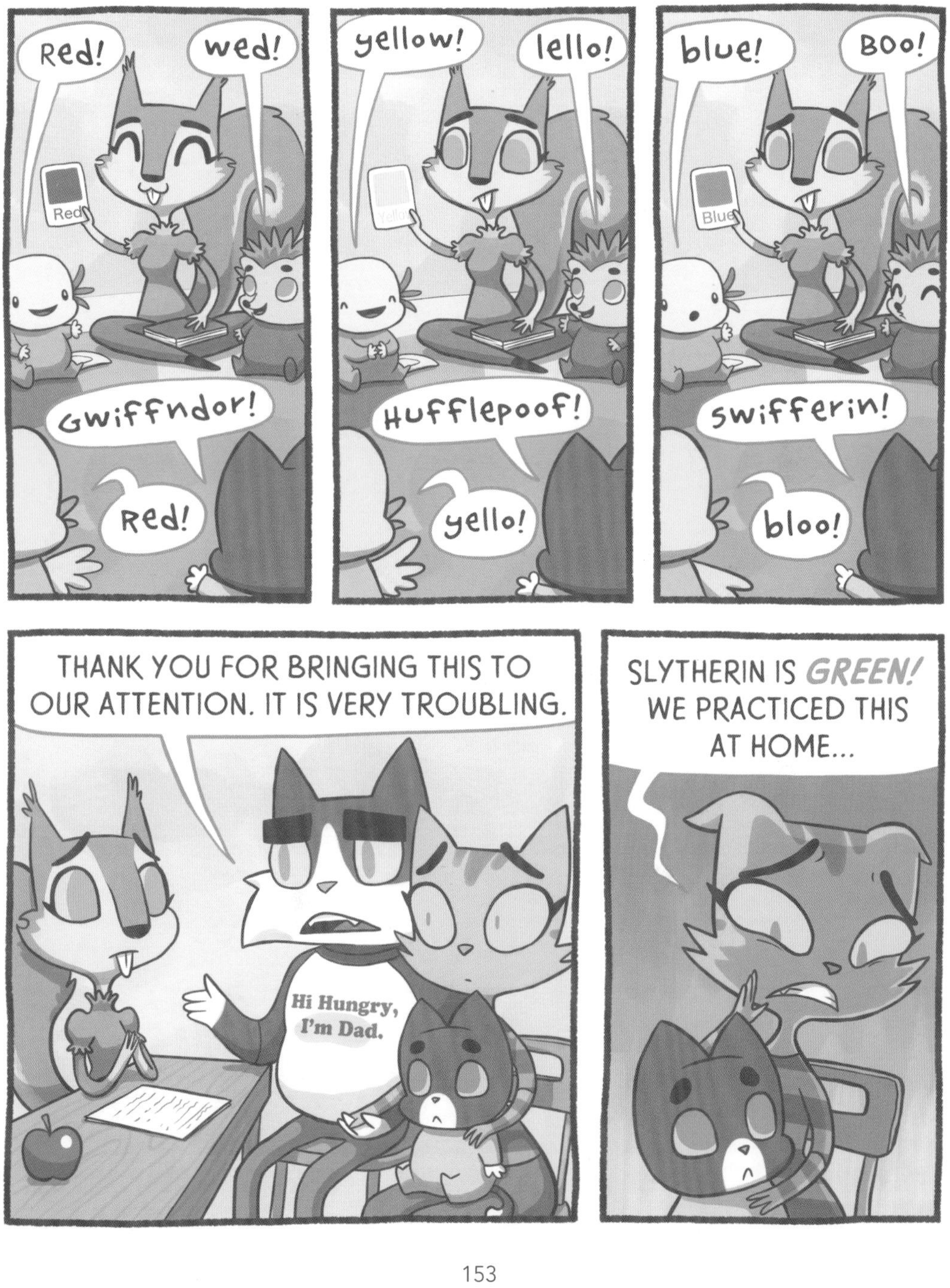
Red!
wed!
Red
Gwiffndor!
Red!
yellow!
lello!
Yellow
Hufflepoof!
yello!
blue!
BOO!
Blue
swifferin!
bloo!
THANK YOU FOR BRINGING THIS TO OUR ATTENTION. IT IS VERY TROUBLING.
Hi Hungry, I'm Dad.
SLYTHERIN IS GREEN! WE PRACTICED THIS AT HOME...

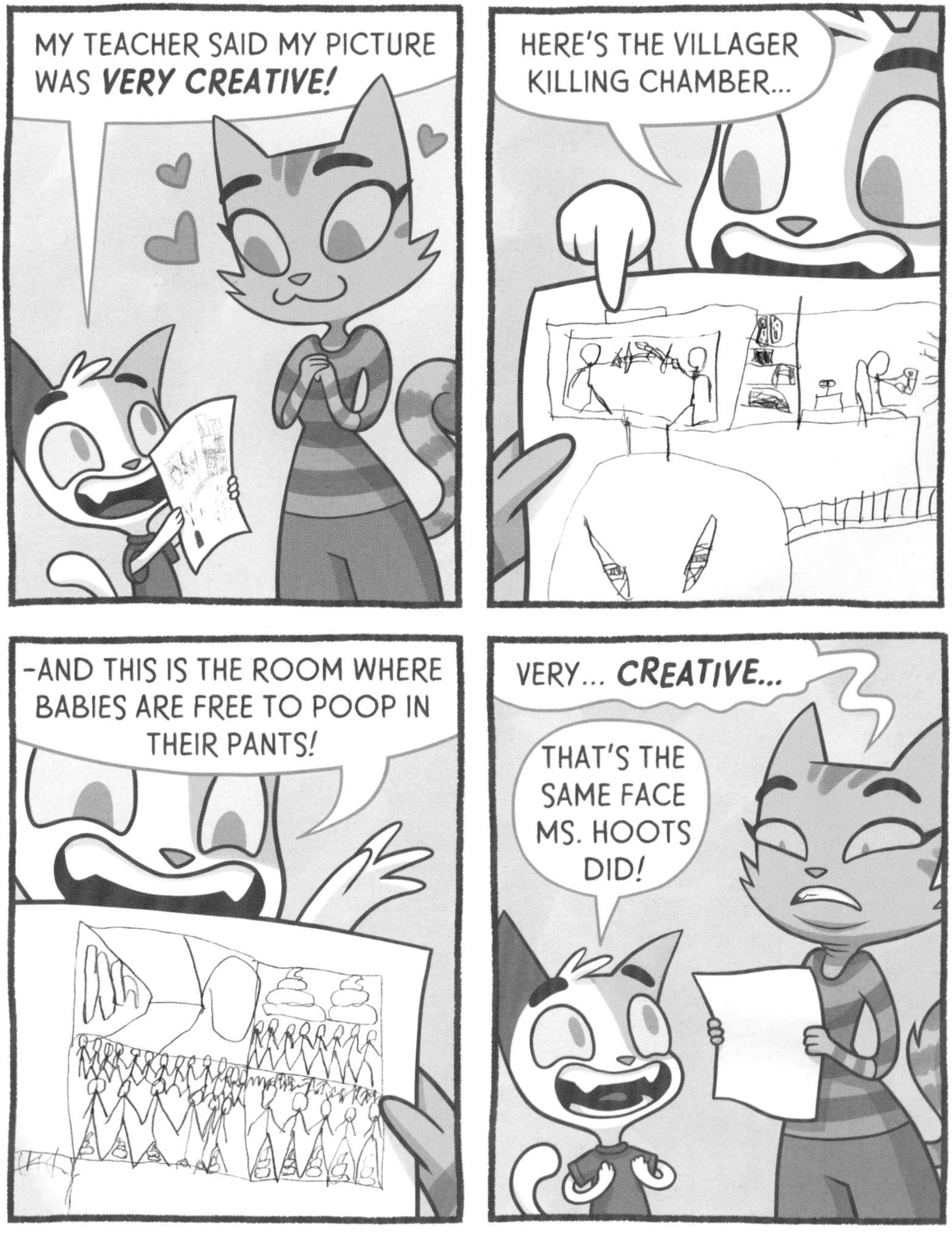
MY TEACHER SAID MY PICTURE WAS VERY CREATIVE!
HERE'S THE VILLAGER KILLING CHAMBER...
-AND THIS IS THE ROOM WHERE BABIES ARE FREE TO POOP IN THEIR PANTS!
VERY... CREATIVE...
THAT'S THE SAME FACE MS. HOOTS DID!

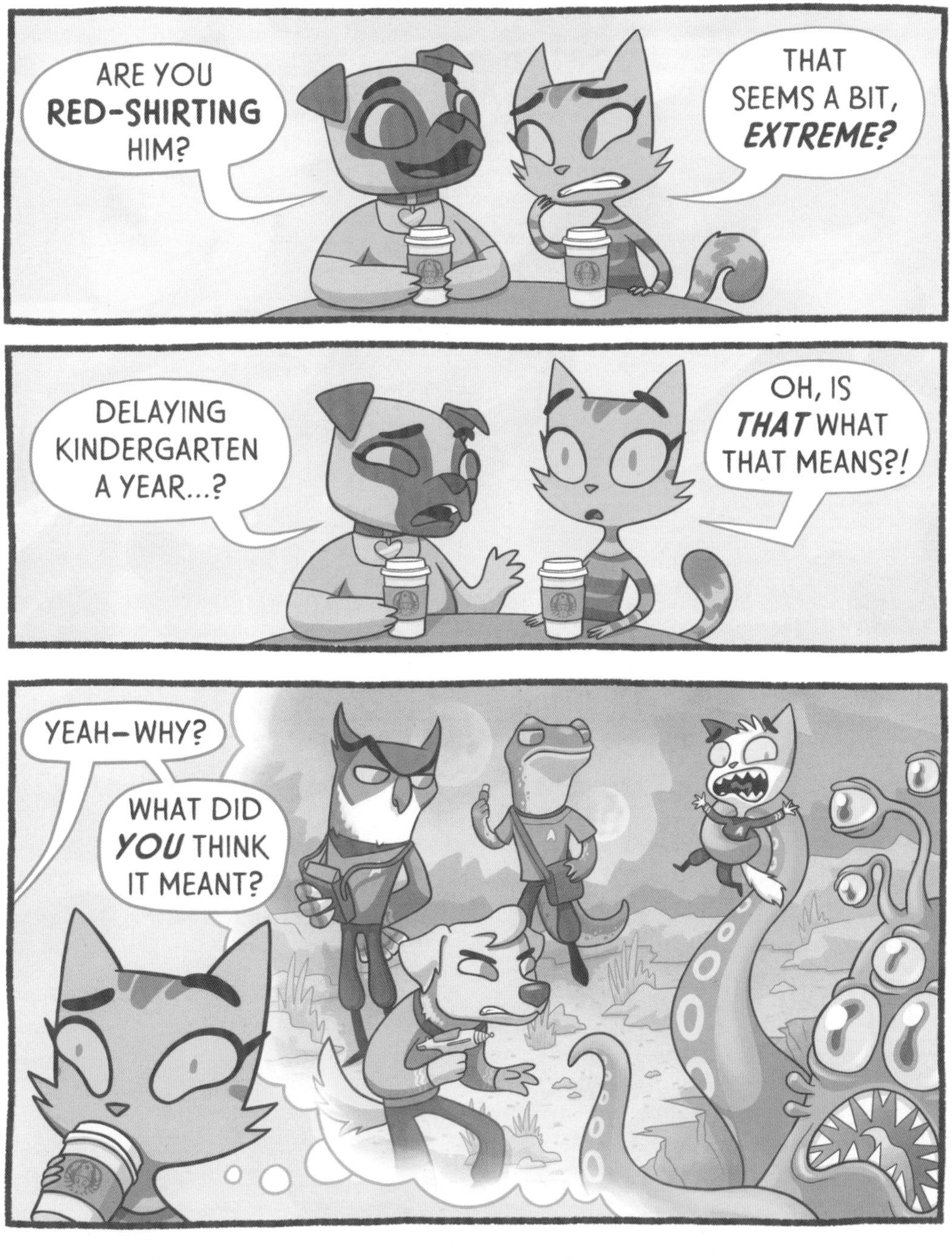
ARE YOU **RED-SHIRTING** HIM?
THAT SEEMS A BIT, ***EXTREME?***
DELAYING KINDERGARTEN A YEAR...?
OH, IS ***THAT*** WHAT THAT MEANS?!
YEAH—WHY?
WHAT DID ***YOU*** THINK IT MEANT?

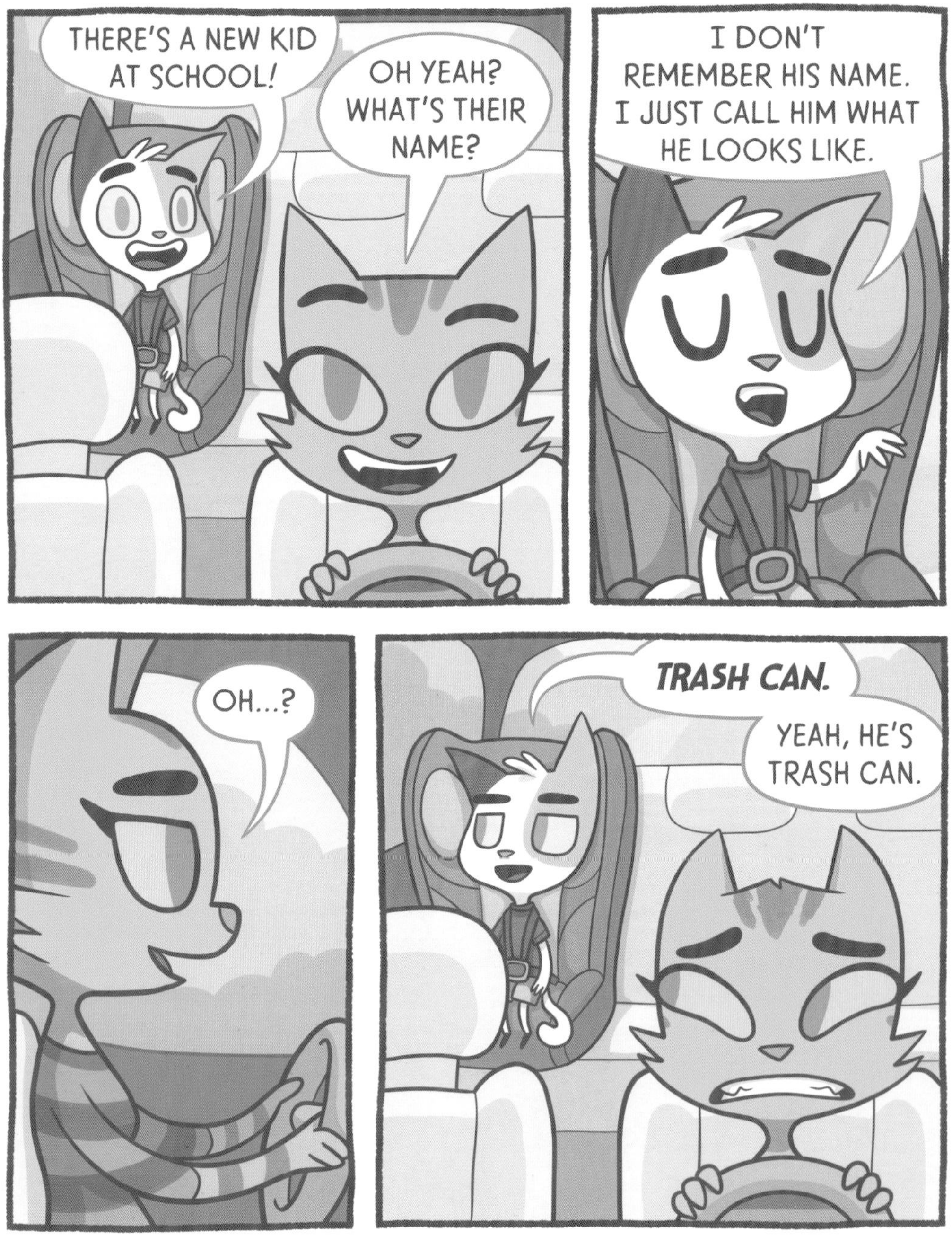
THERE'S A NEW KID AT SCHOOL!
OH YEAH? WHAT'S THEIR NAME?
I DON'T REMEMBER HIS NAME. I JUST CALL HIM WHAT HE LOOKS LIKE.
OH...?
TRASH CAN.
YEAH, HE'S TRASH CAN.

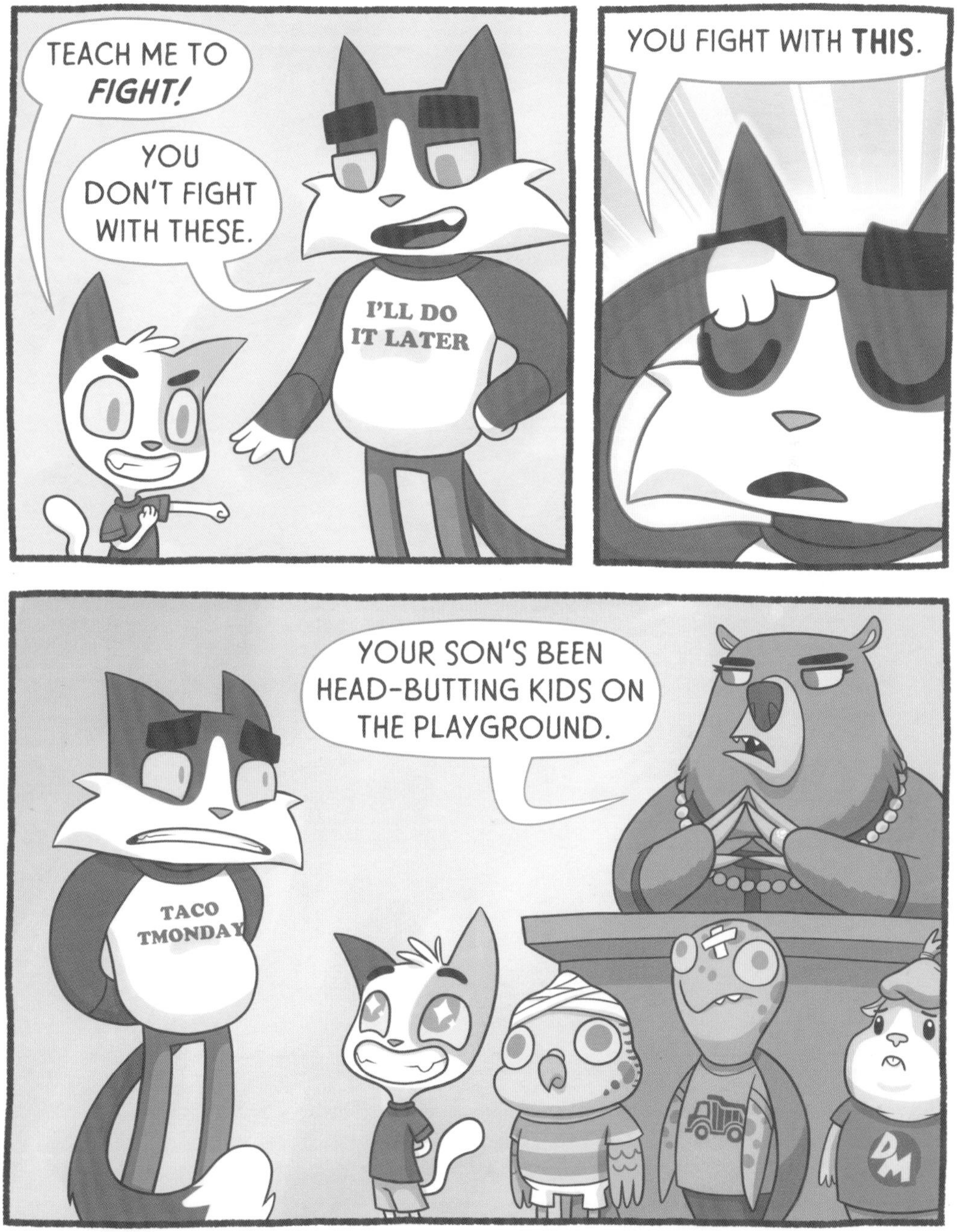
TEACH ME TO *FIGHT!*
YOU DON'T FIGHT WITH THESE.
I'LL DO IT LATER
YOU FIGHT WITH **THIS**.
YOUR SON'S BEEN HEAD-BUTTING KIDS ON THE PLAYGROUND.
TACO TMONDAY
DM

BASED ON A TWEET BY @THEDADVOCATE01

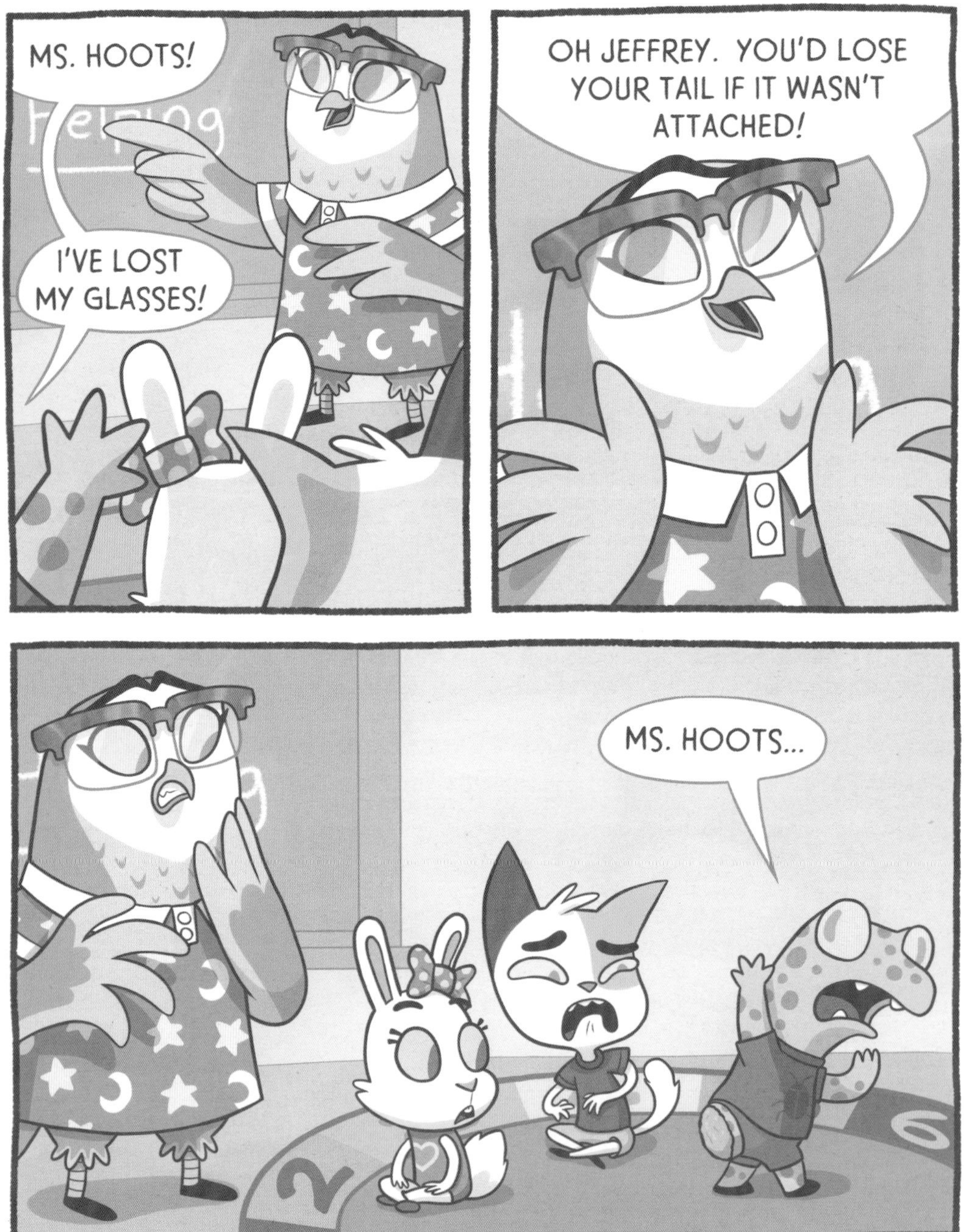
MS. HOOTS!
I'VE LOST MY GLASSES!
OH JEFFREY. YOU'D LOSE YOUR TAIL IF IT WASN'T ATTACHED!
MS. HOOTS...

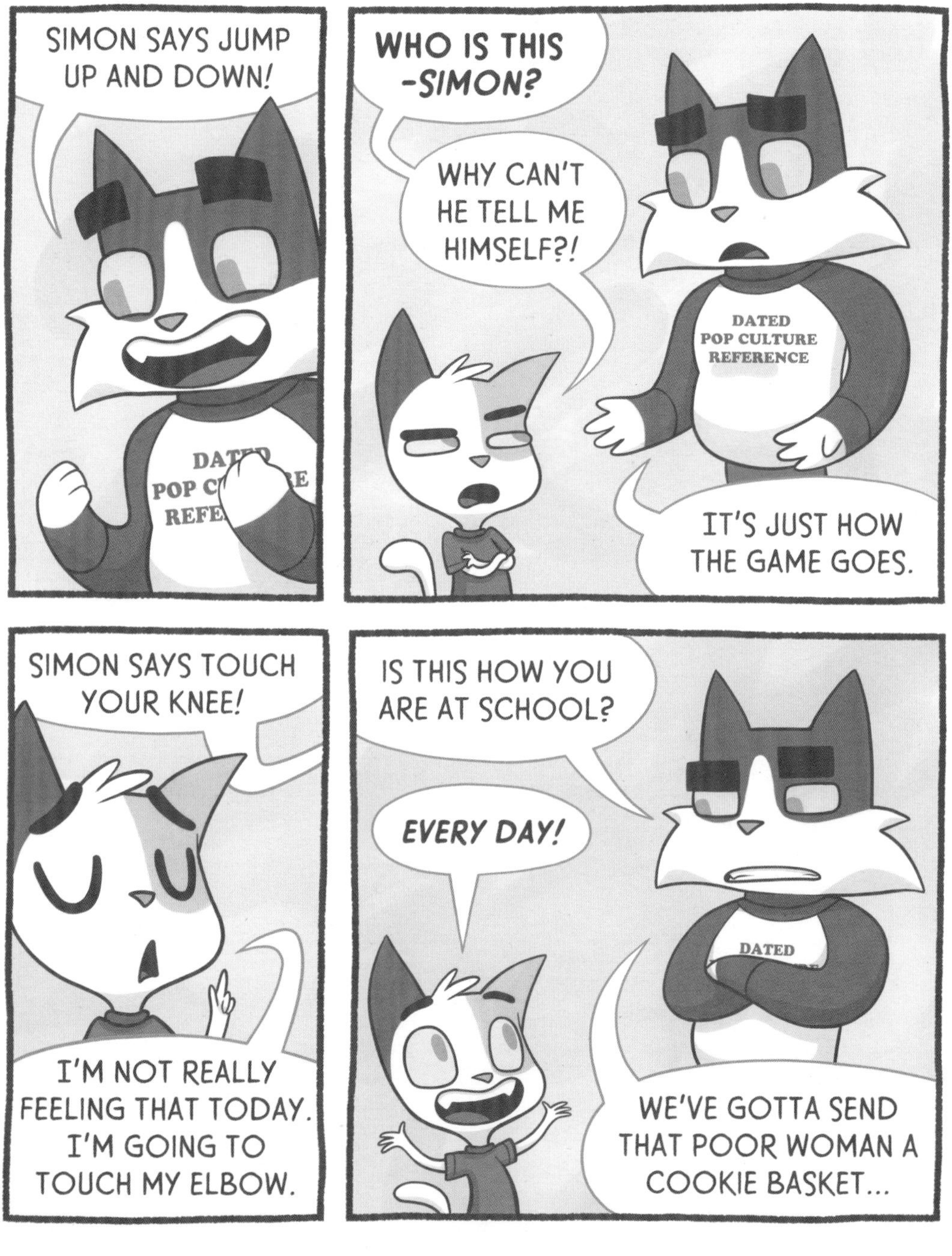
SIMON SAYS JUMP UP AND DOWN!
DATED POP CULTURE REFERENCE
WHO IS THIS -SIMON?
WHY CAN'T HE TELL ME HIMSELF?!
DATED POP CULTURE REFERENCE
IT'S JUST HOW THE GAME GOES.
SIMON SAYS TOUCH YOUR KNEE!
I'M NOT REALLY FEELING THAT TODAY. I'M GOING TO TOUCH MY ELBOW.
IS THIS HOW YOU ARE AT SCHOOL?
EVERY DAY!
DATED
WE'VE GOTTA SEND THAT POOR WOMAN A COOKIE BASKET...

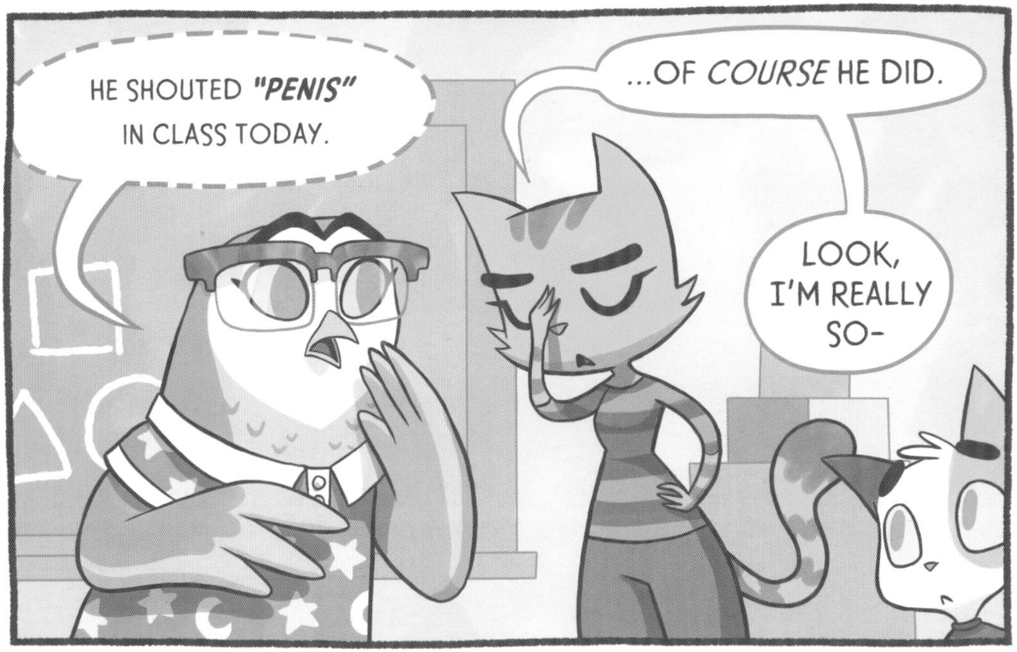
HE SHOUTED **"PENIS"** IN CLASS TODAY.
...OF *COURSE* HE DID.
LOOK, I'M REALLY SO-

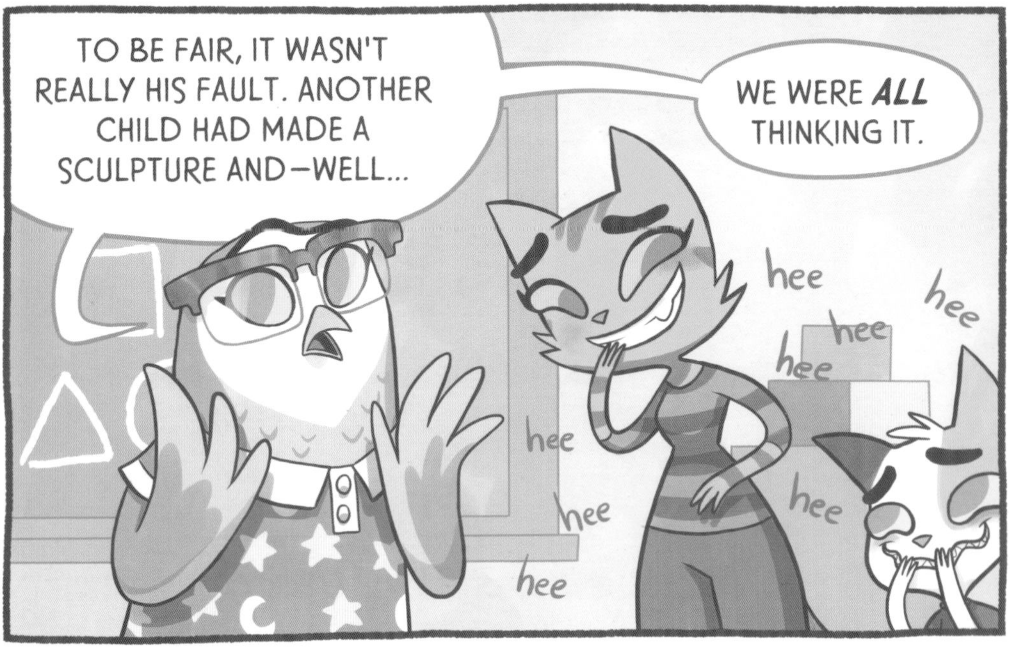
TO BE FAIR, IT WASN'T REALLY HIS FAULT. ANOTHER CHILD HAD MADE A SCULPTURE AND—WELL...
WE WERE ***ALL*** THINKING IT.
hee
hee
hee
hee
hee
hee
hee
hee

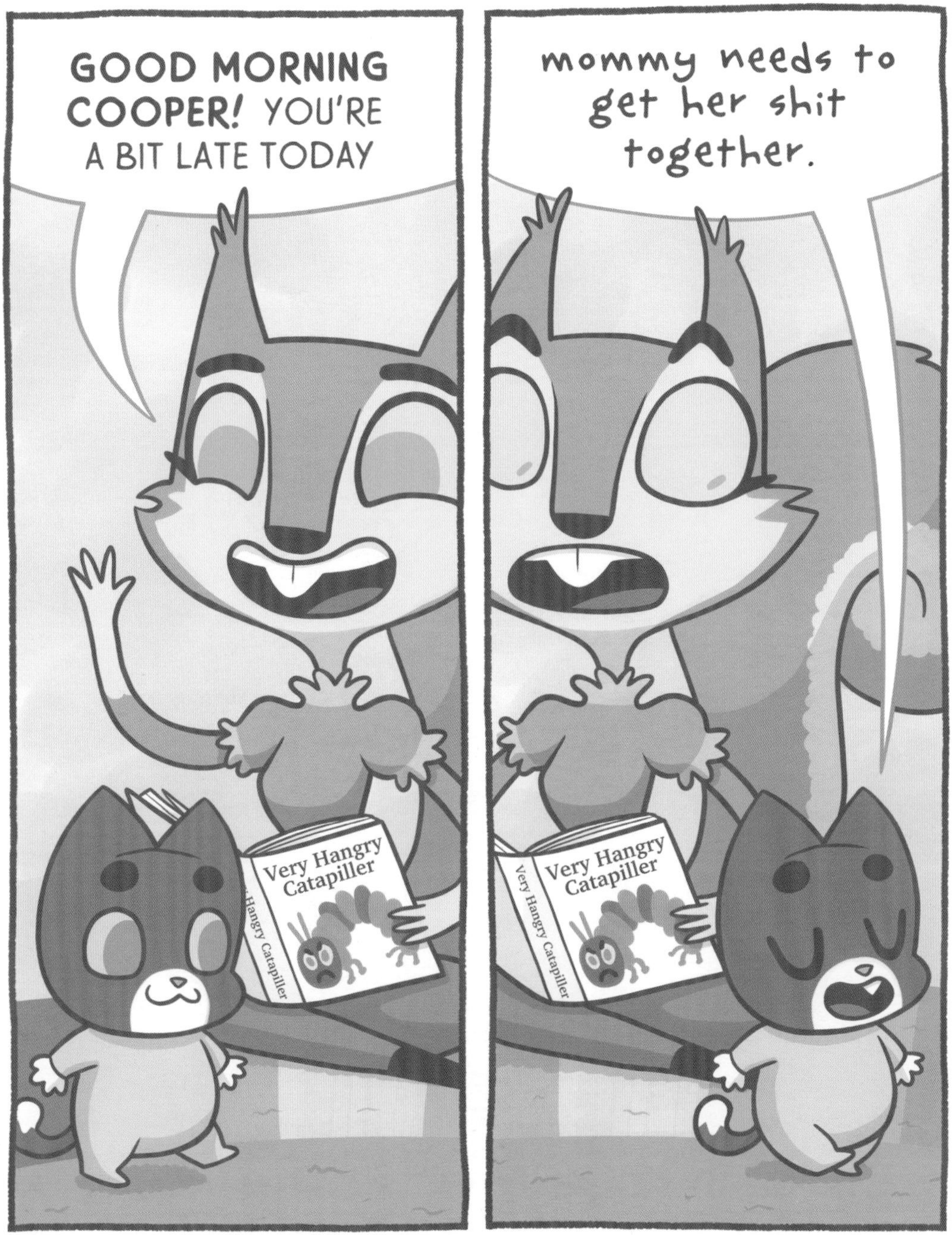
GOOD MORNING COOPER! YOU'RE A BIT LATE TODAY
Very Hangry Catapiller
mommy needs to get her shit together.
Very Hangry Catapiller

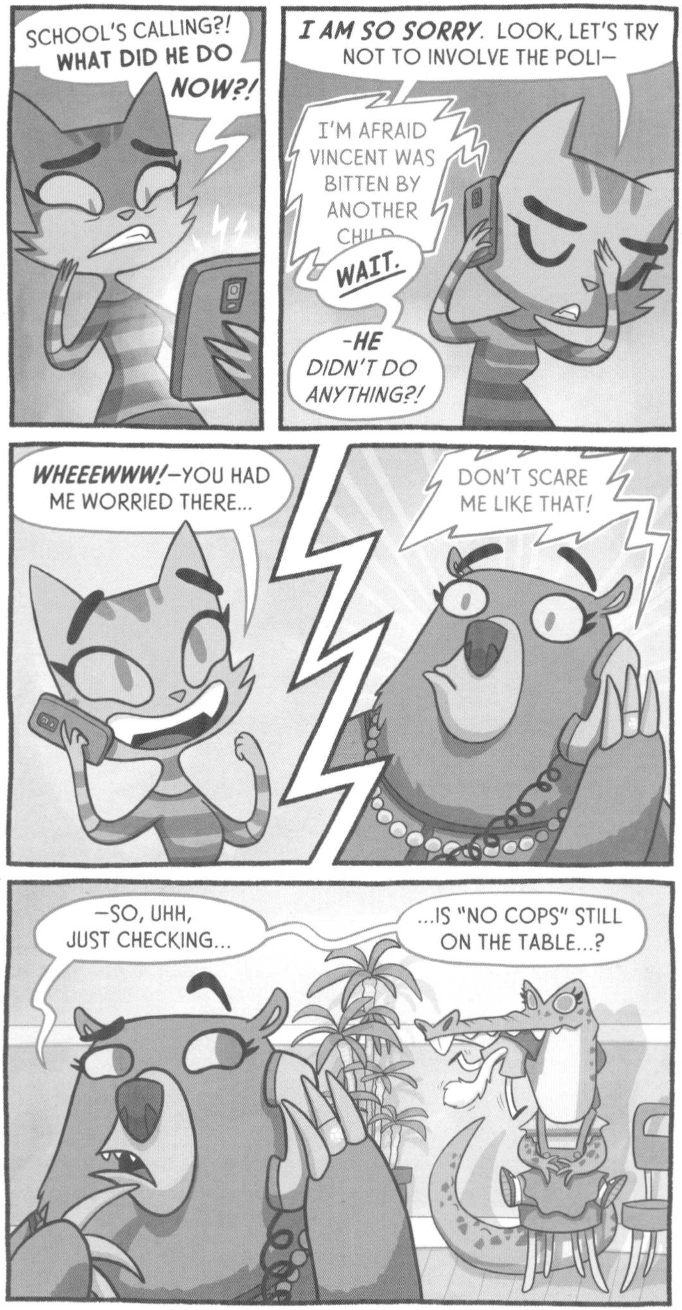
SCHOOL'S CALLING?! WHAT DID HE DO NOW?!
I AM SO SORRY. LOOK, LET'S TRY NOT TO INVOLVE THE POLI—
I'M AFRAID VINCENT WAS BITTEN BY ANOTHER CHILD.
WAIT.
-HE DIDN'T DO ANYTHING?!
WHEEEWWW!—YOU HAD ME WORRIED THERE...
DON'T SCARE ME LIKE THAT!
—SO, UHH, JUST CHECKING...
...IS "NO COPS" STILL ON THE TABLE...?

WHAT HAS COOPER PAINTED?

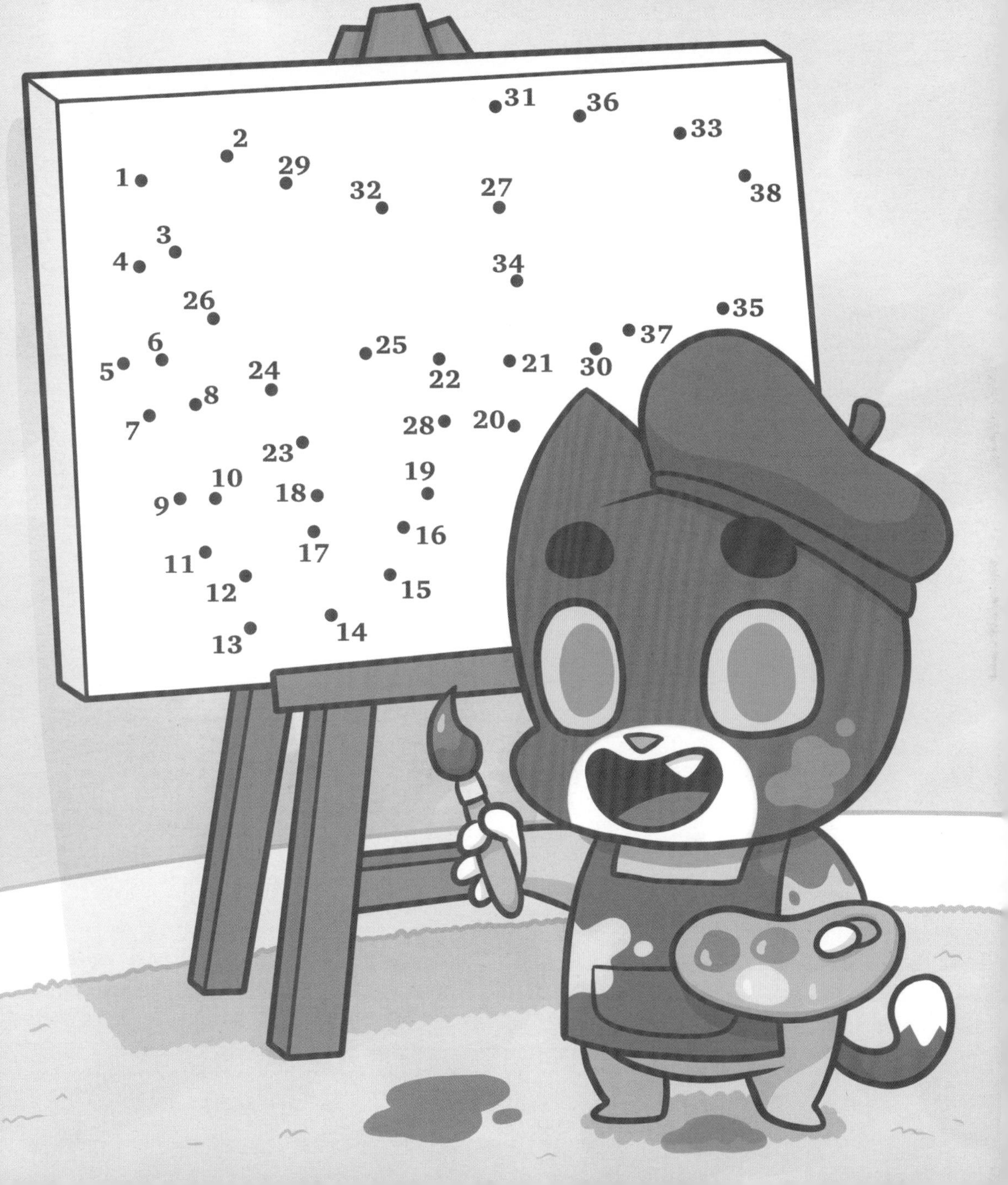
1
2
3
4
5
6
7
8
9
10
11
12
13
14
15
16
17
18
19
20
21
22
23
24
25
26
27
28
29
30
31
32
33
34
35
36
37
38

"QUALITY" TIME

DISNEY WORLD AS A PARENT IS A VERY DIFFERENT EXPERIENCE THAN AS A CHILD. GAWKING AT THE HUSTLE AND BUSTLE OF MAIN STREET, IT FELL TO ME TO FIGURE OUT WHERE TO GO, SO I HERDED MY ~~CATS~~ KIDS TO THE RIDE WITH THE SHORTEST LINE. IT WAS A ROCKET SHIP/MERRY-GO-ROUND CONTRAPTION THAT WENT UP IN THE AIR FOR A SPECTACULAR VIEW OF THE MAGIC KINGDOM. OUR OLDEST TOOK ONE LOOK AND NOPED OUT *WITH PREJUDICE*. WE FIGURED HE'D CHANGE HIS TUNE BY THE TIME WE REACHED THE FRONT OF THE HALF-HOUR LINE. HE DID NOT. THE DAY CONTINUED ALONG THIS UNMAGICAL COURSE (WITH THE EXCEPTION OF HAUNTED MANSION AND PIRATES, WHICH WE ALL AGREED WERE *BADASS*).

AFTER ALL THE MONEY AND EFFORT, QUALITY TIME ENDS UP BEING FOUND IN THE LITTLE THINGS. AND YOU LEARN THAT THE WORST MOMENTS TEND TO MAKE THE BEST STORIES. MY KIDS ARE NOW DELIGHTED BY PHOTOS OF THEM AS BABIES—THROWING TANTRUMS OR GETTING INTO PREDICAMENTS. I'M PROUD THAT WE'VE PASSED DOWN TO THEM THE SKILL OF LAUGHING AT THEMSELVES—IT IS, AFTER ALL, THE FAMILY BUSINESS.

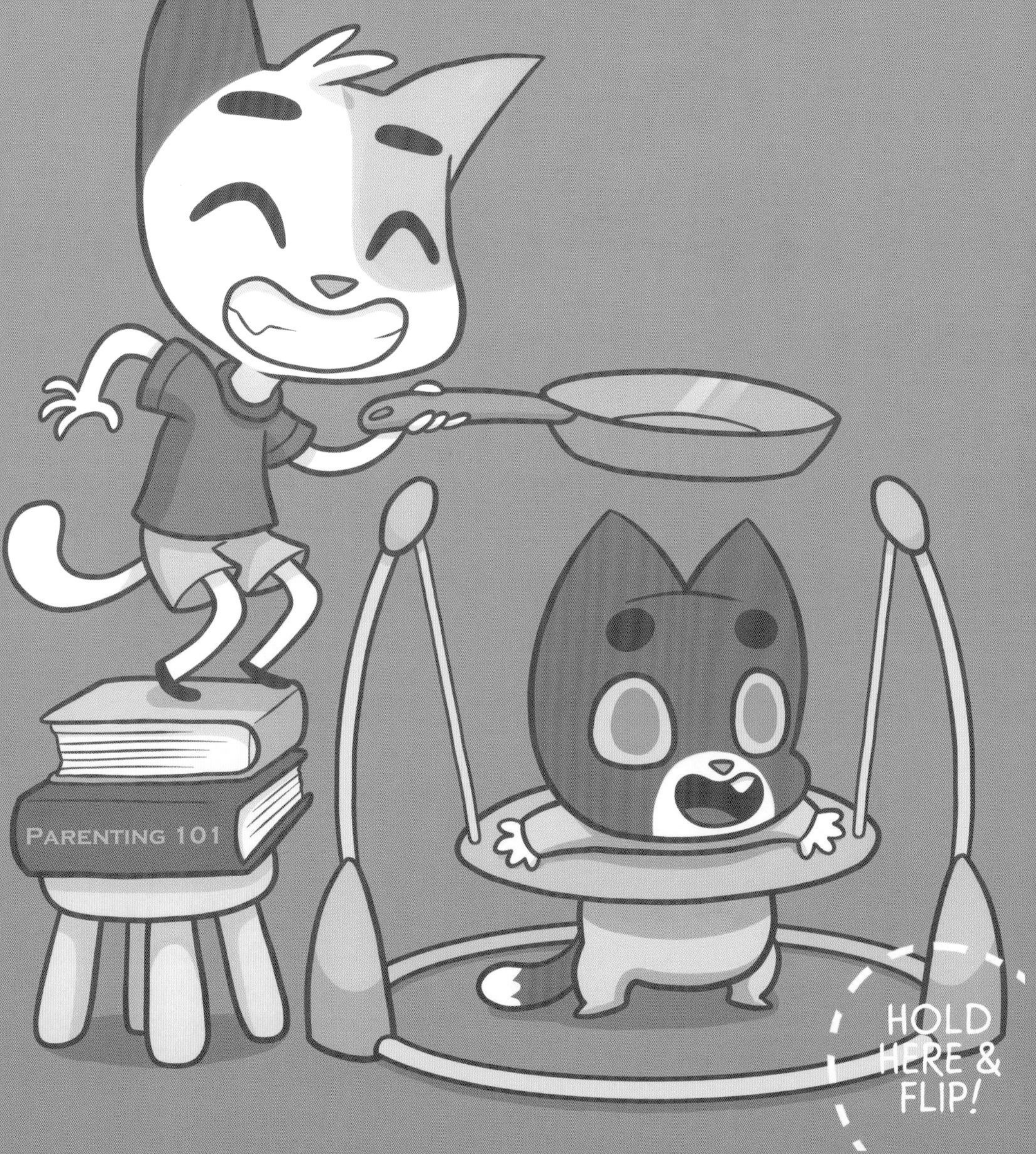
PARENTING 101
HOLD HERE & FLIP!

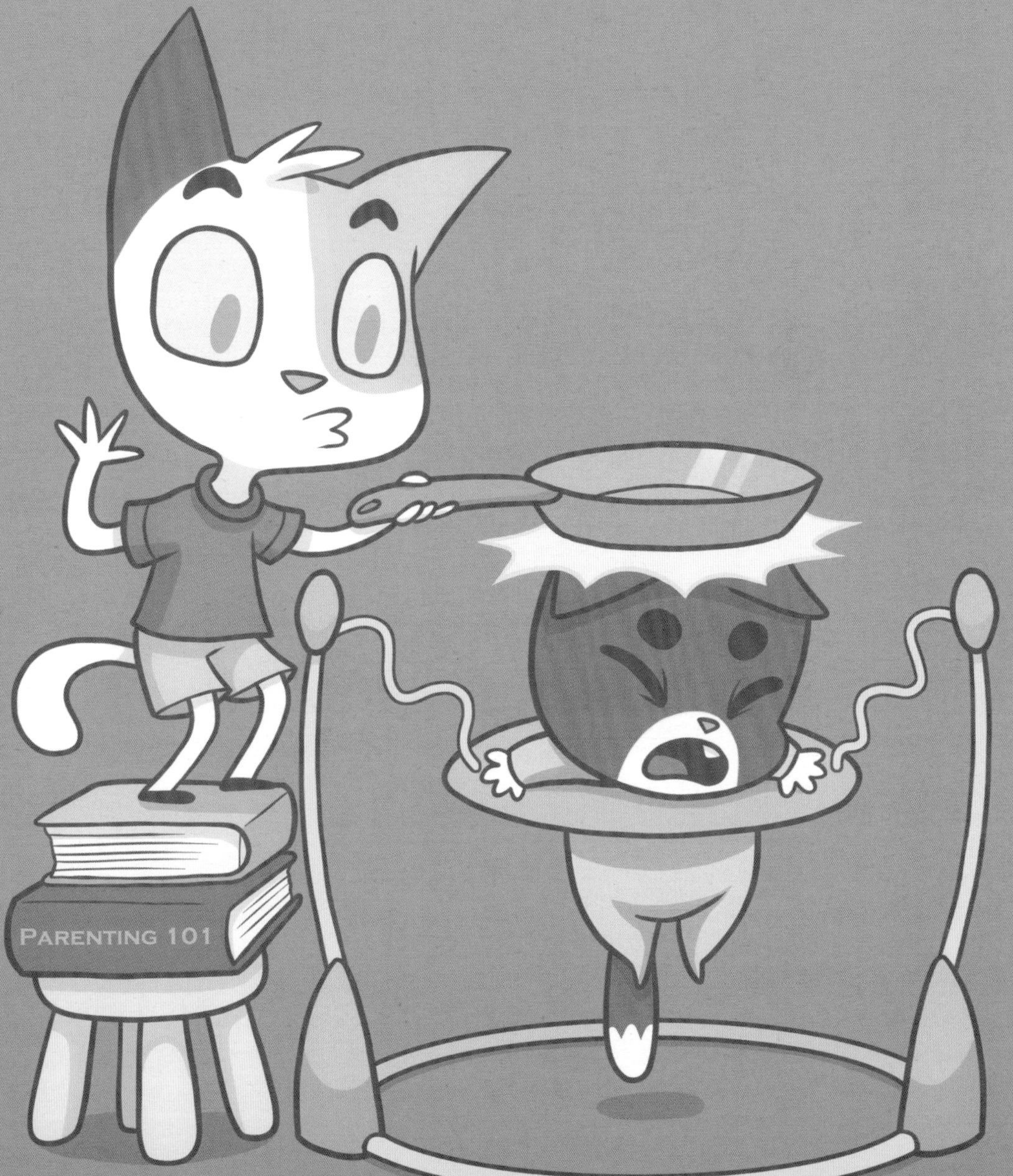
PARENTING 101

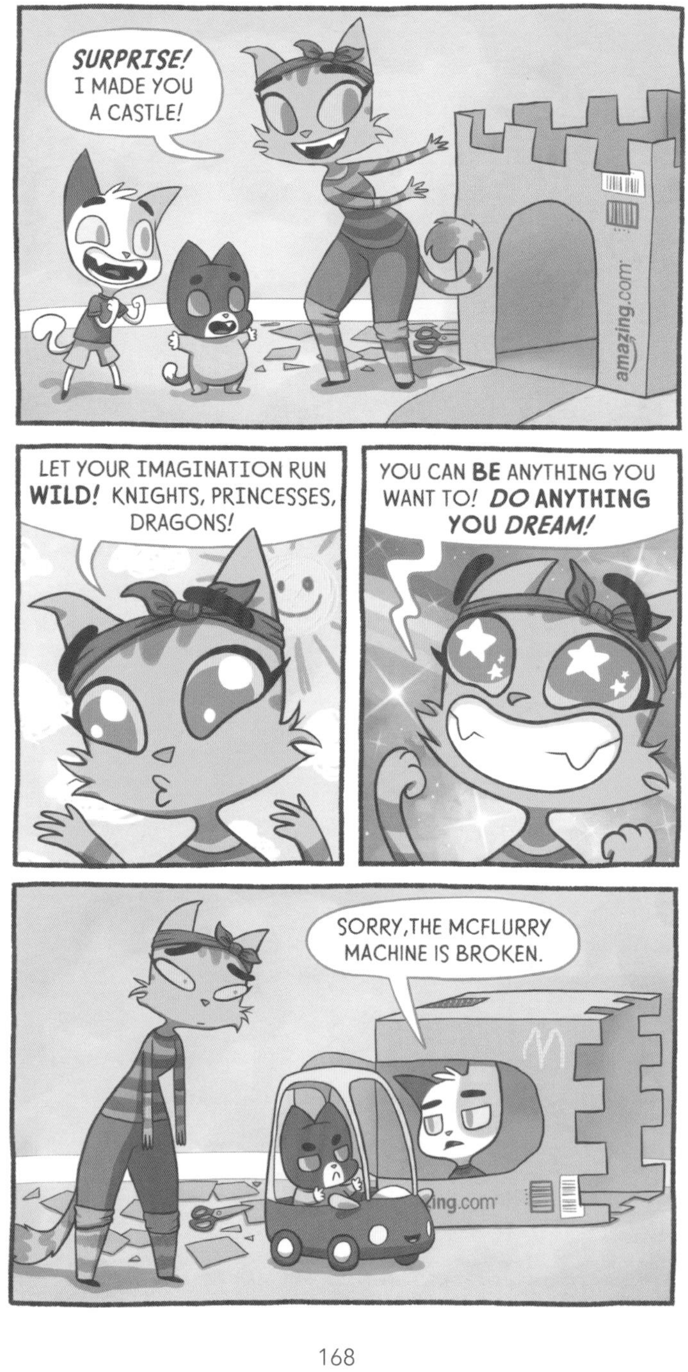
SURPRISE! I MADE YOU A CASTLE!
amazing.com
LET YOUR IMAGINATION RUN WILD! KNIGHTS, PRINCESSES, DRAGONS!
YOU CAN BE ANYTHING YOU WANT TO! DO ANYTHING YOU DREAM!
SORRY, THE MCFLURRY MACHINE IS BROKEN.

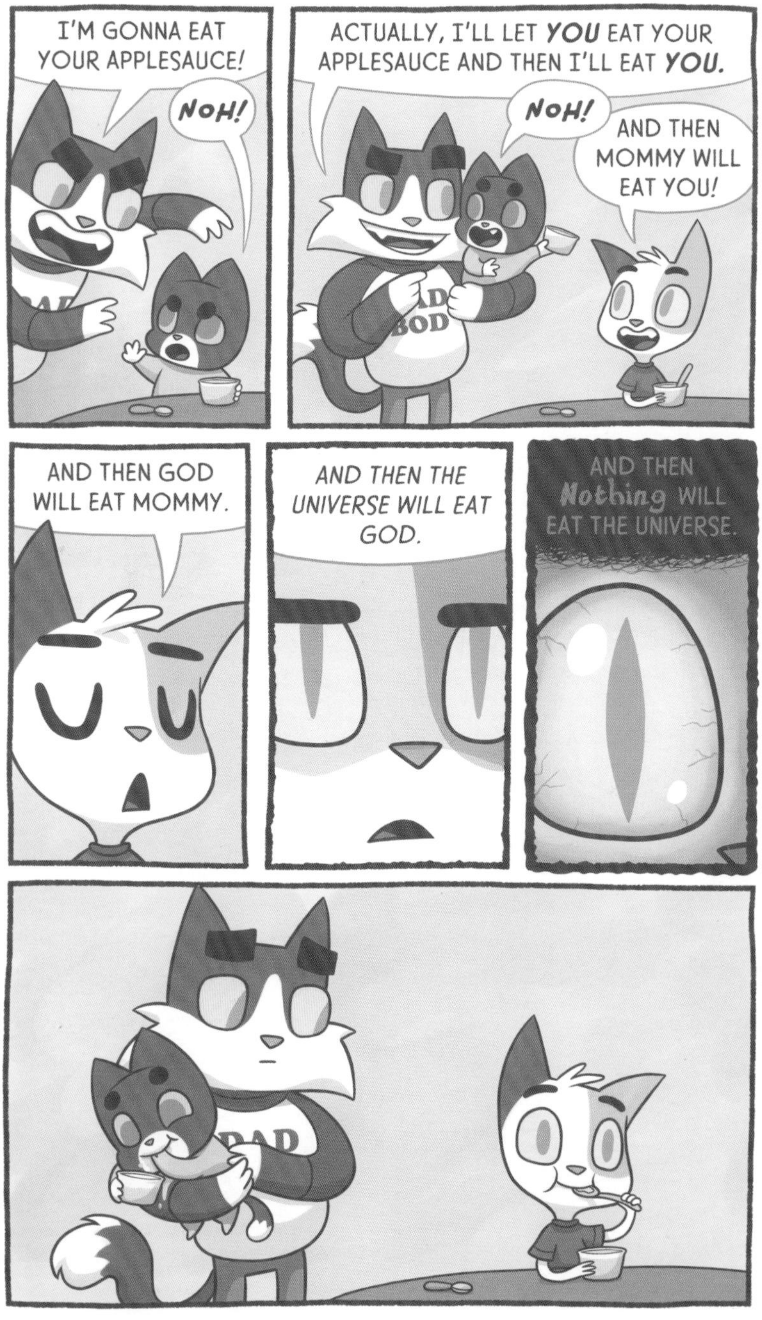
I'M GONNA EAT YOUR APPLESAUCE!
NOH!
ACTUALLY, I'LL LET YOU EAT YOUR APPLESAUCE AND THEN I'LL EAT YOU.
NOH!
AND THEN MOMMY WILL EAT YOU!
AND THEN GOD WILL EAT MOMMY.
AND THEN THE UNIVERSE WILL EAT GOD.
AND THEN Nothing WILL EAT THE UNIVERSE.

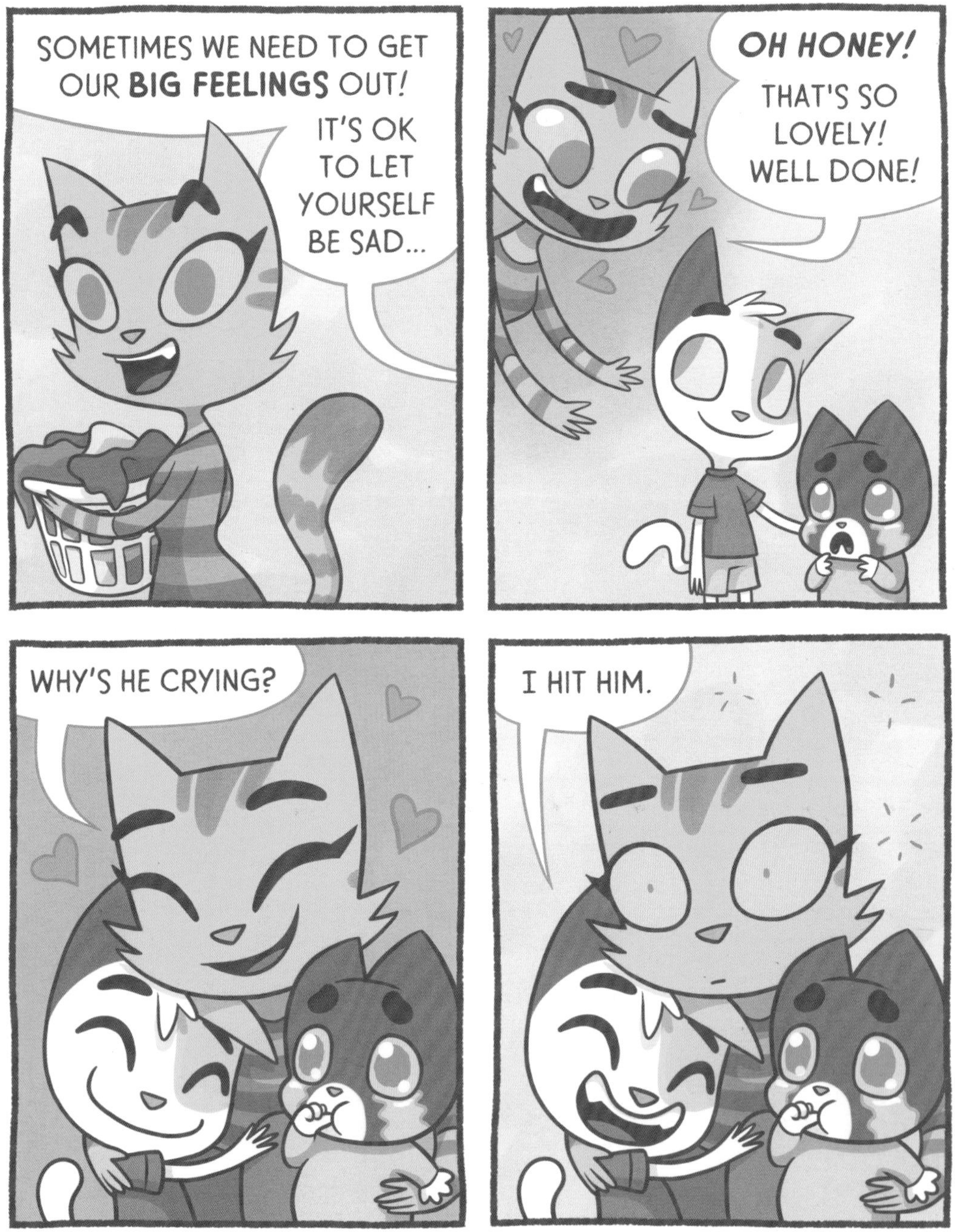
SOMETIMES WE NEED TO GET OUR **BIG FEELINGS** OUT!
IT'S OK TO LET YOURSELF BE SAD...
OH HONEY!
THAT'S SO LOVELY! WELL DONE!
WHY'S HE CRYING?
I HIT HIM.

BASED ON A TWEET BY @ELSPELLS13

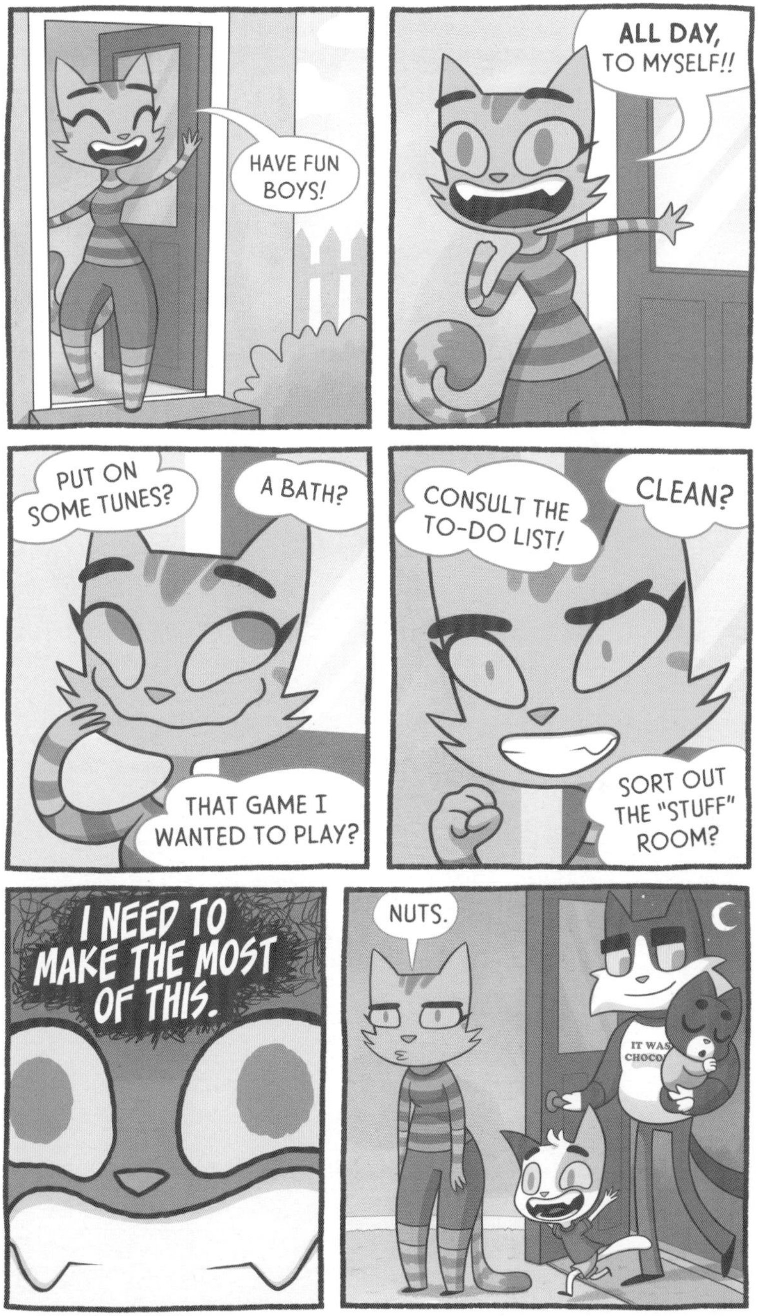
HAVE FUN BOYS!
ALL DAY, TO MYSELF!!
PUT ON SOME TUNES?
A BATH?
THAT GAME I WANTED TO PLAY?
CONSULT THE TO-DO LIST!
CLEAN?
SORT OUT THE "STUFF" ROOM?
I NEED TO MAKE THE MOST OF THIS.
NUTS.

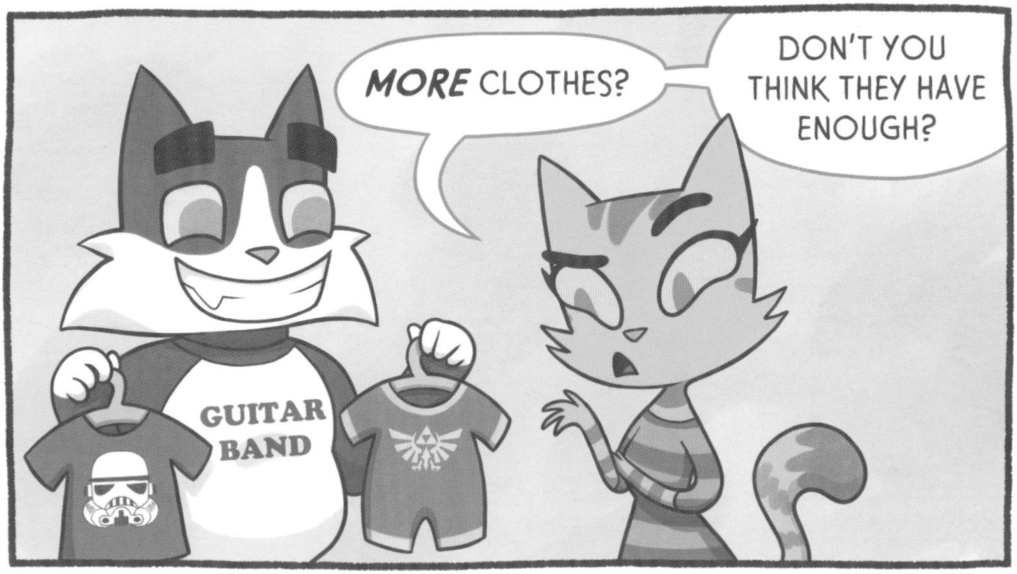
MORE CLOTHES?
DON'T YOU THINK THEY HAVE ENOUGH?
GUITAR BAND

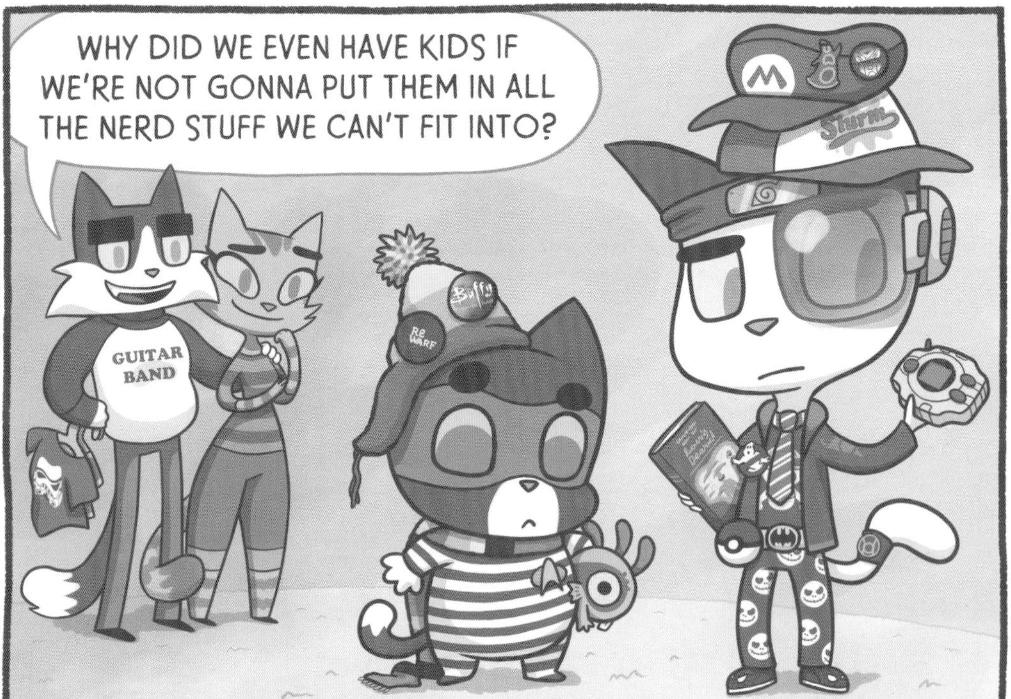
WHY DID WE EVEN HAVE KIDS IF WE'RE NOT GONNA PUT THEM IN ALL THE NERD STUFF WE CAN'T FIT INTO?
GUITAR BAND
Buffy
RE WARF
Sturm

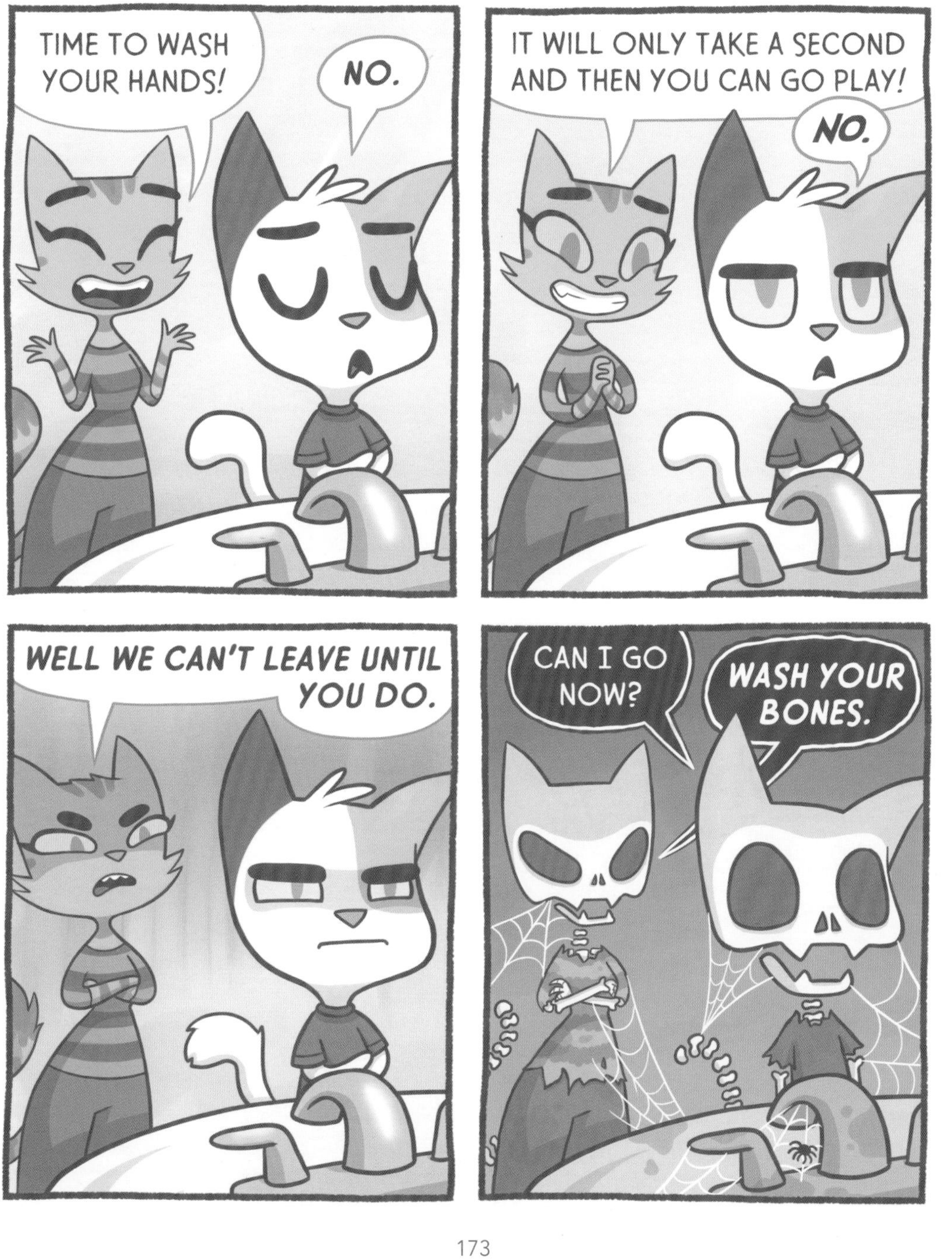
TIME TO WASH YOUR HANDS!
NO.
IT WILL ONLY TAKE A SECOND AND THEN YOU CAN GO PLAY!
NO.
WELL WE CAN'T LEAVE UNTIL YOU DO.
CAN I GO NOW?
WASH YOUR BONES.

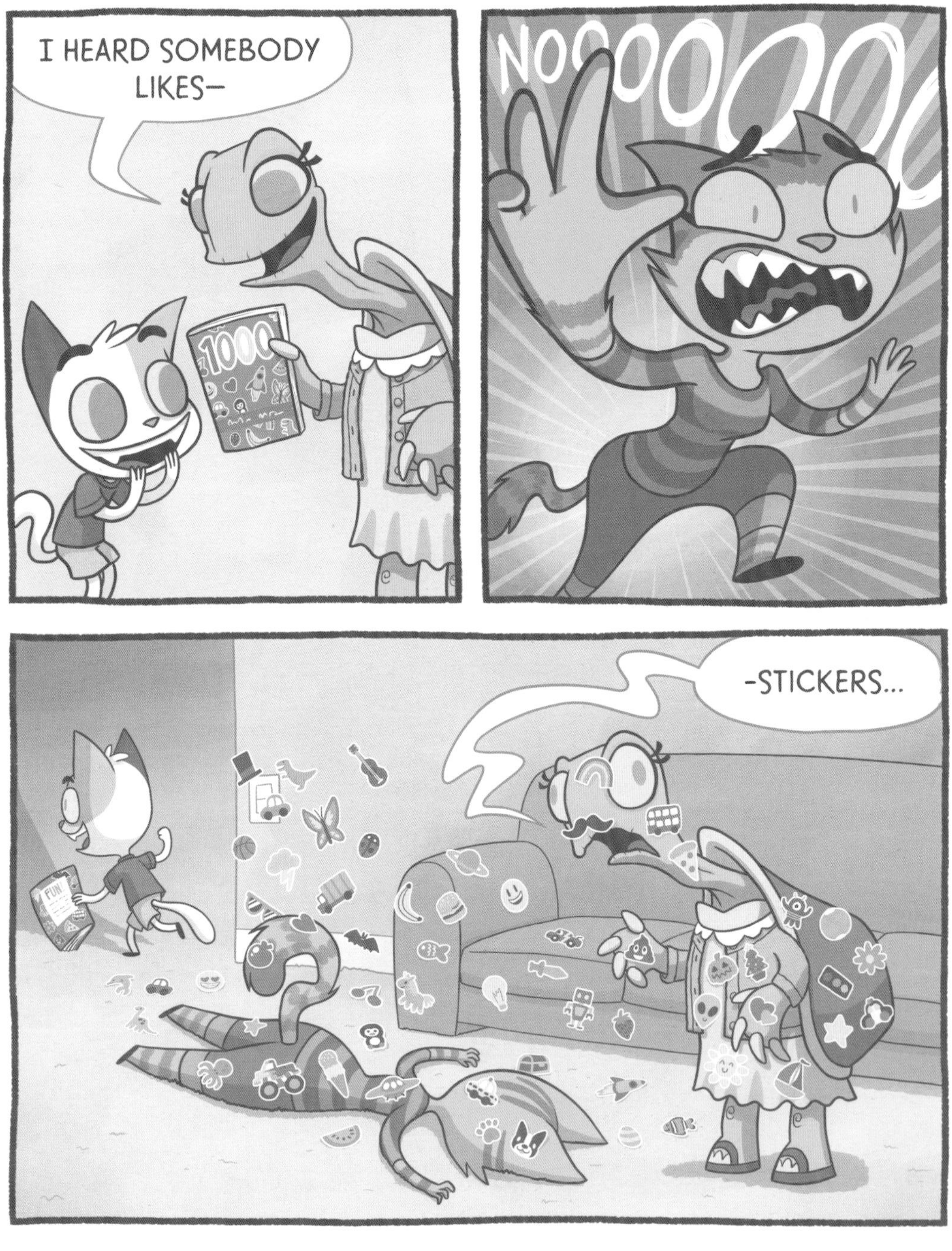
I HEARD SOMEBODY LIKES—
NOOOOOOOO
-STICKERS...

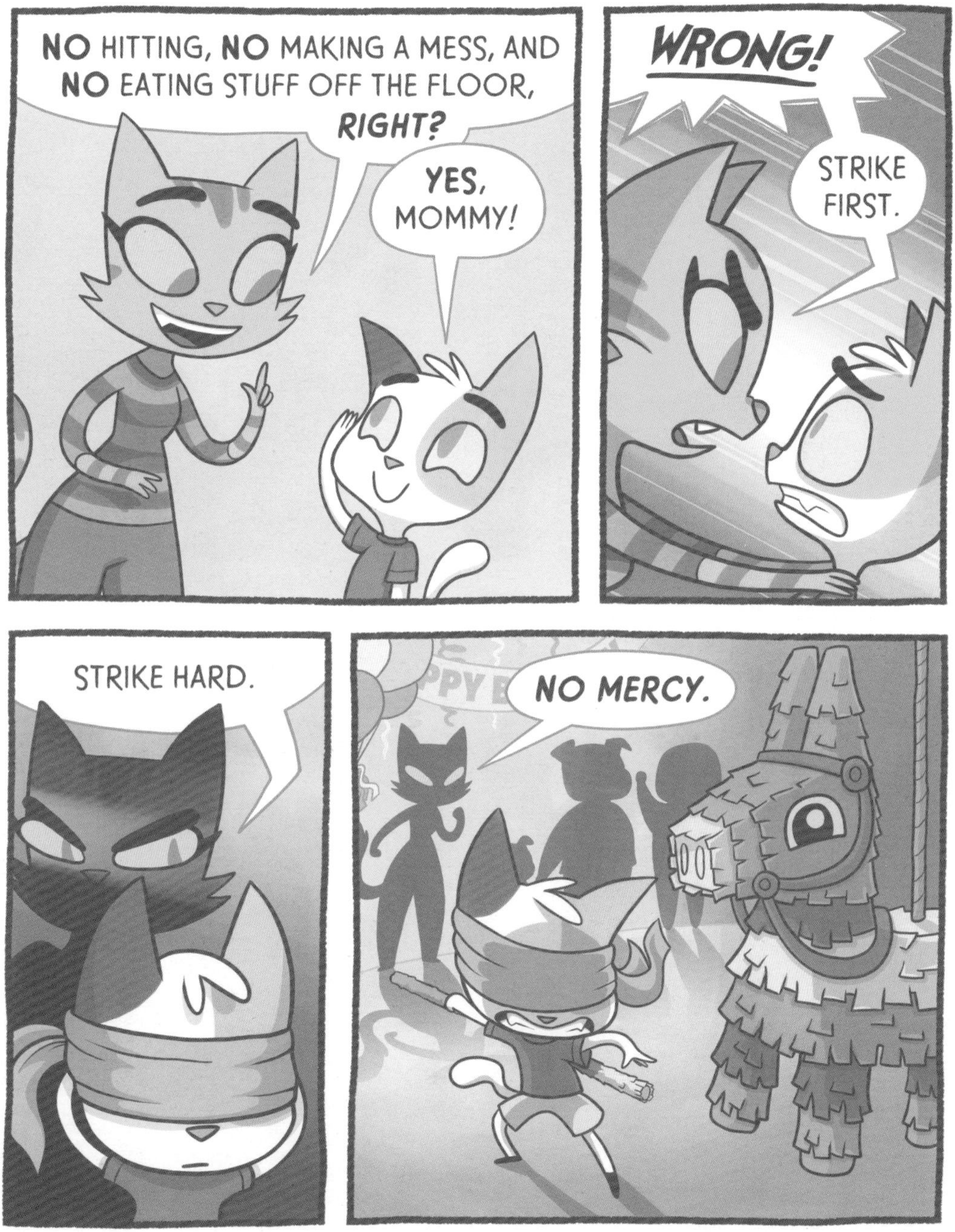
NO HITTING, NO MAKING A MESS, AND NO EATING STUFF OFF THE FLOOR, RIGHT?
YES, MOMMY!
WRONG!
STRIKE FIRST.
STRIKE HARD.
NO MERCY.

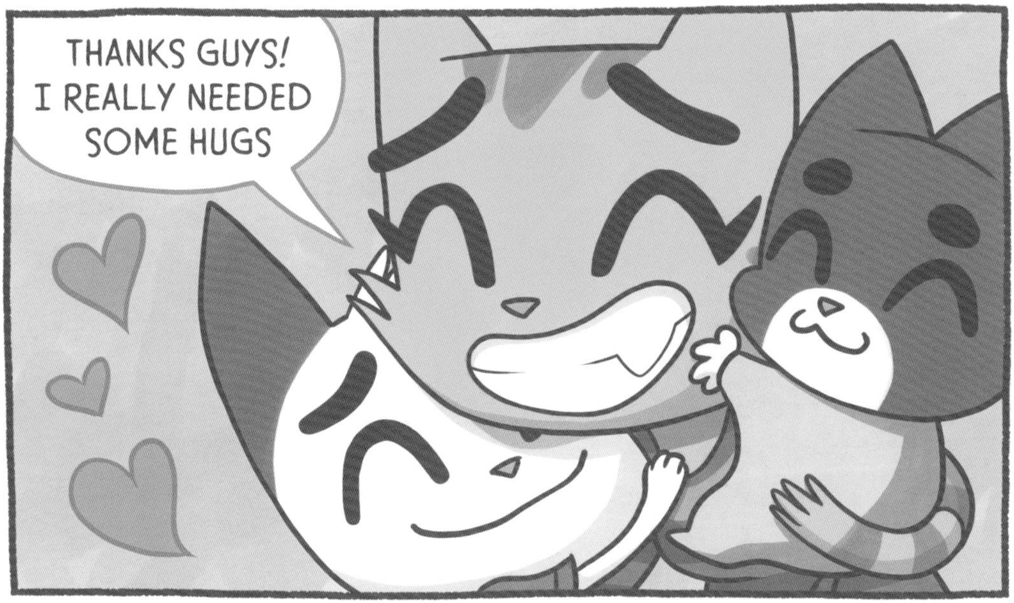
THANKS GUYS! I REALLY NEEDED SOME HUGS

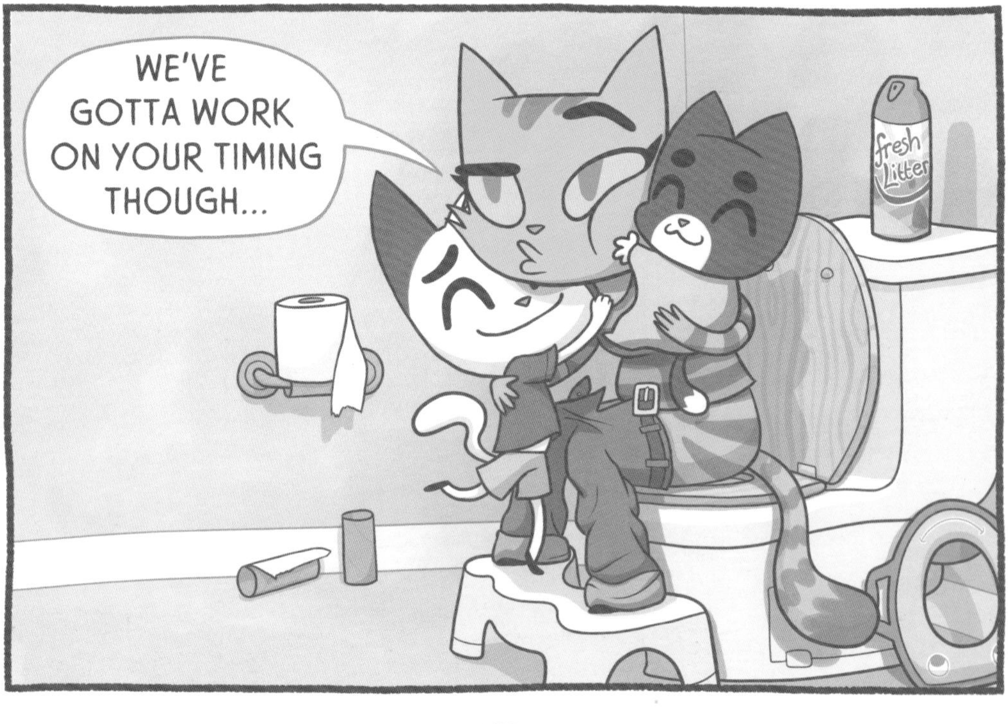
WE'VE GOTTA WORK ON YOUR TIMING THOUGH...
fresh Litter

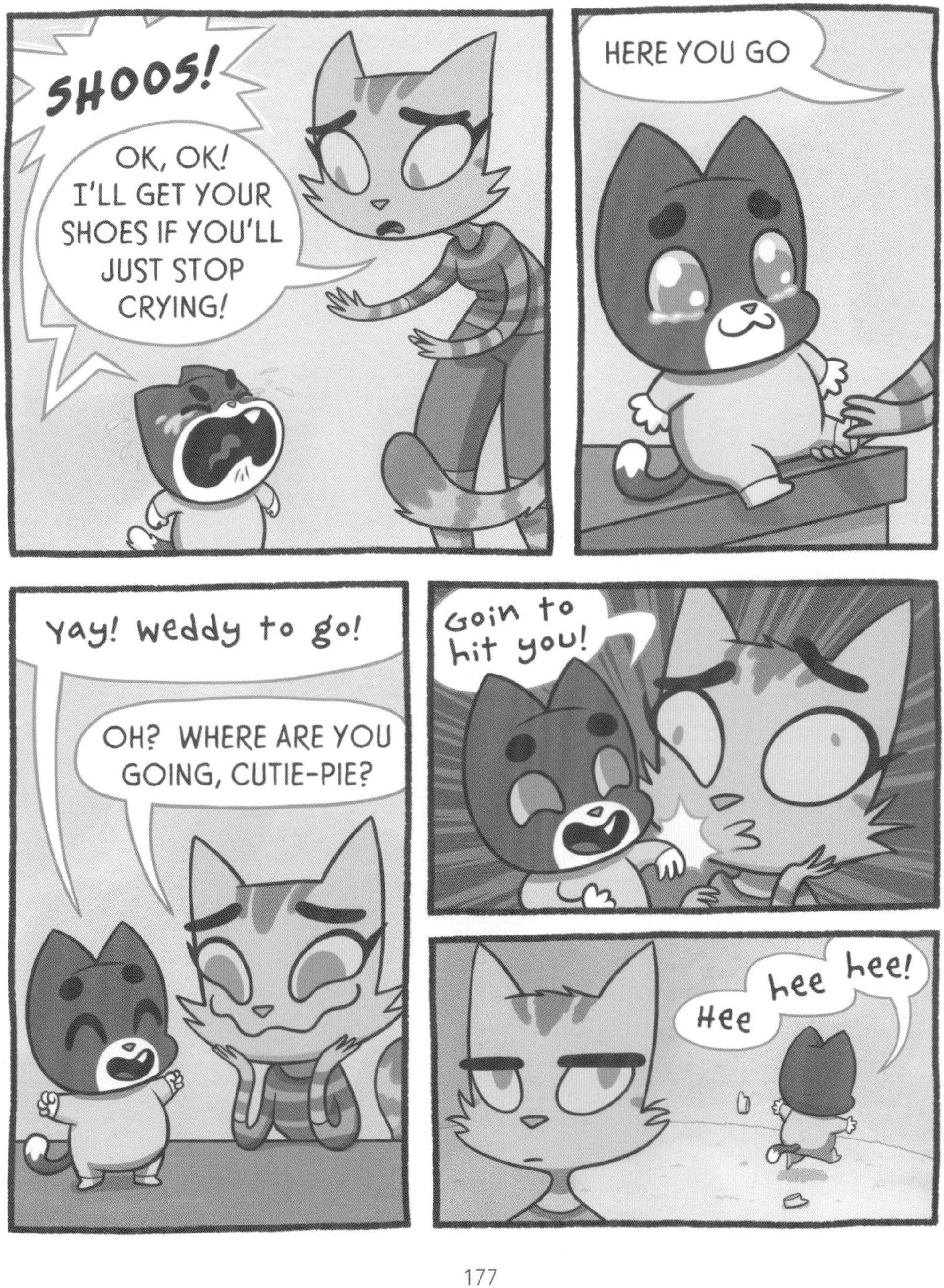
SHOOS!
OK, OK! I'LL GET YOUR SHOES IF YOU'LL JUST STOP CRYING!
HERE YOU GO
Yay! weddy to go!
OH? WHERE ARE YOU GOING, CUTIE-PIE?
Goin to hit you!
Hee hee hee!

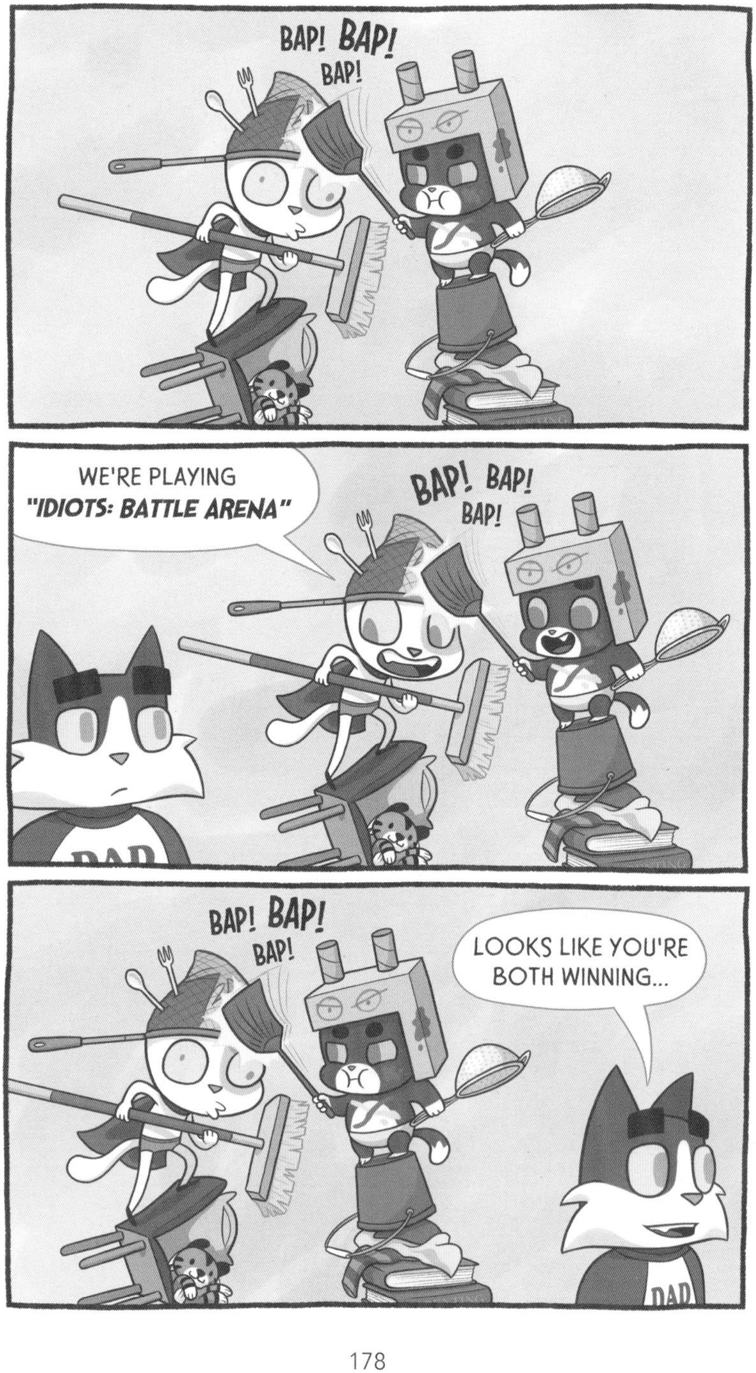
BAP! BAP!
BAP!
WE'RE PLAYING
"IDIOTS: BATTLE ARENA"
BAP! BAP!
BAP!
DAD
BAP! BAP!
BAP!
LOOKS LIKE YOU'RE
BOTH WINNING...
DAD

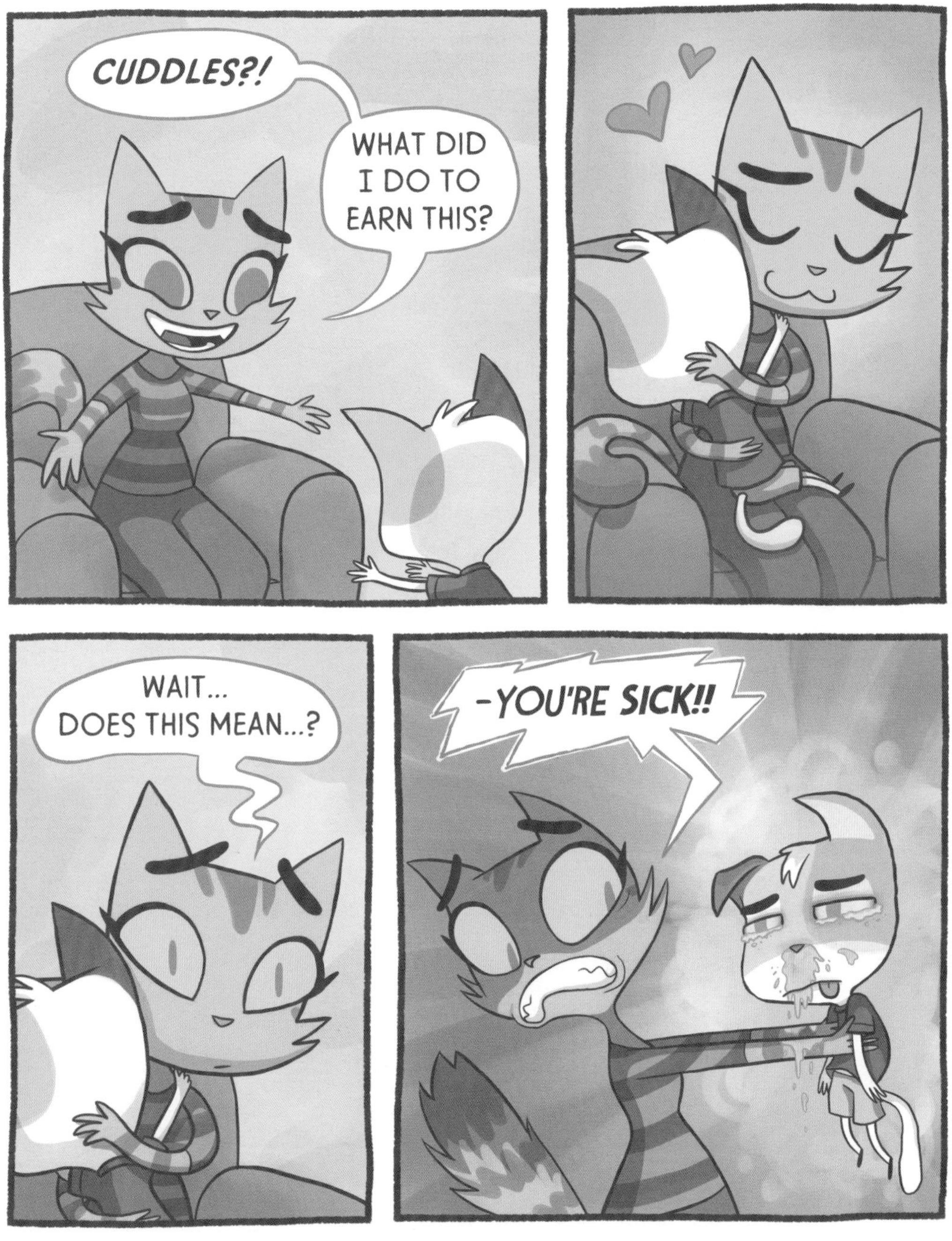
CUDDLES?!
WHAT DID I DO TO EARN THIS?
WAIT... DOES THIS MEAN...?
-YOU'RE SICK!!

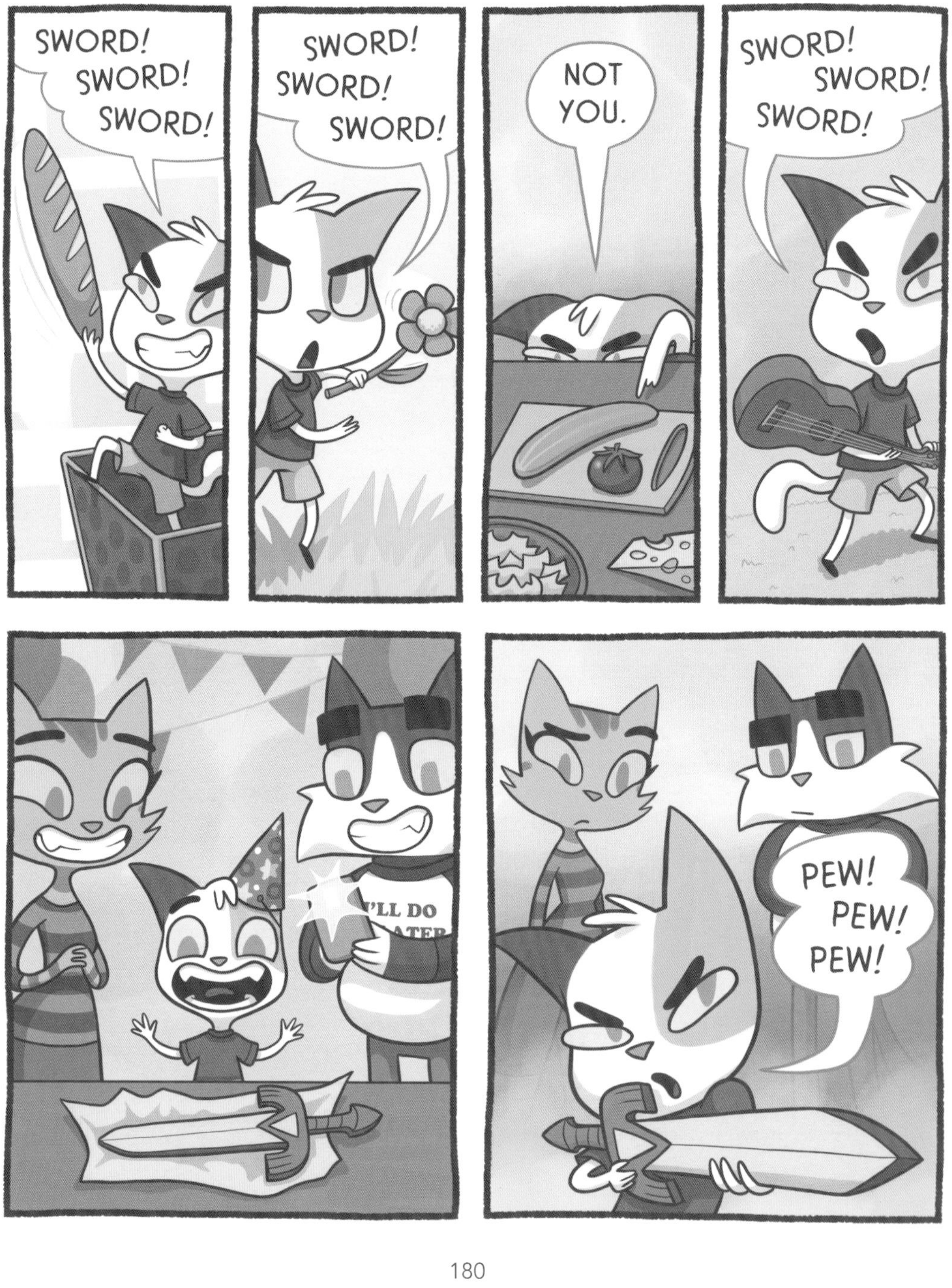
SWORD! SWORD! SWORD!
SWORD! SWORD! SWORD!
NOT YOU.
SWORD! SWORD! SWORD!
PEW! PEW! PEW!

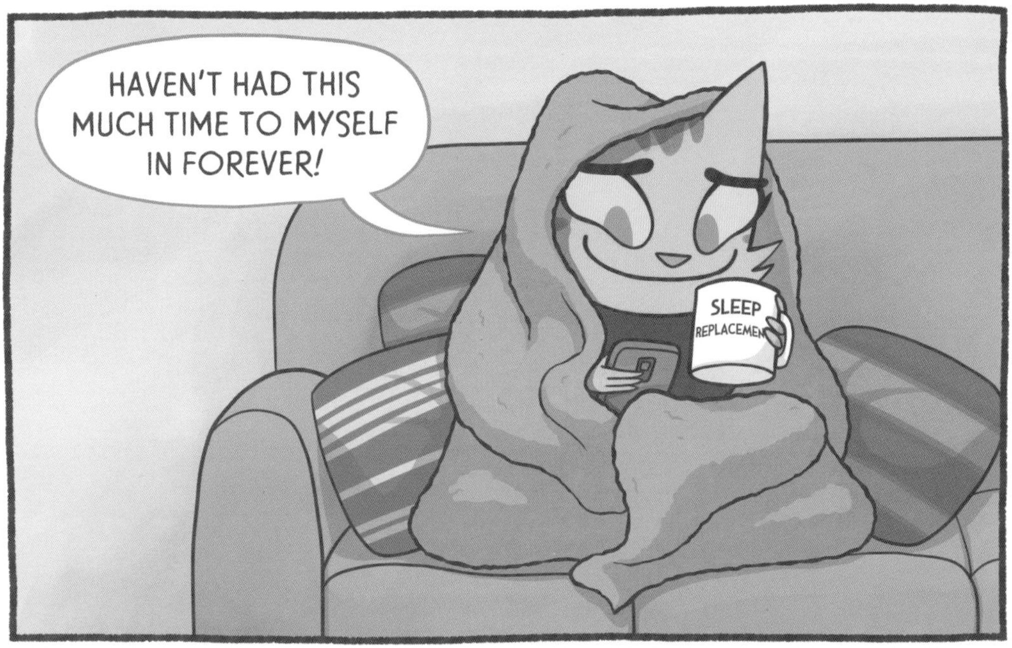
HAVEN'T HAD THIS MUCH TIME TO MYSELF IN FOREVER!
SLEEP REPLACEMEN

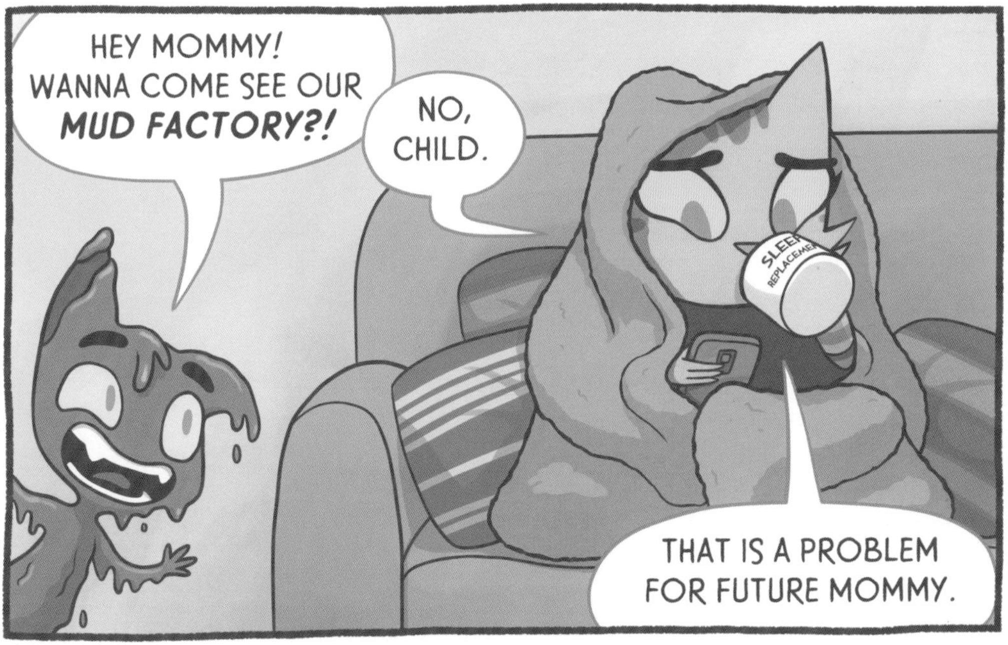
HEY MOMMY! WANNA COME SEE OUR **MUD FACTORY?!**
NO, CHILD.
THAT IS A PROBLEM FOR FUTURE MOMMY.

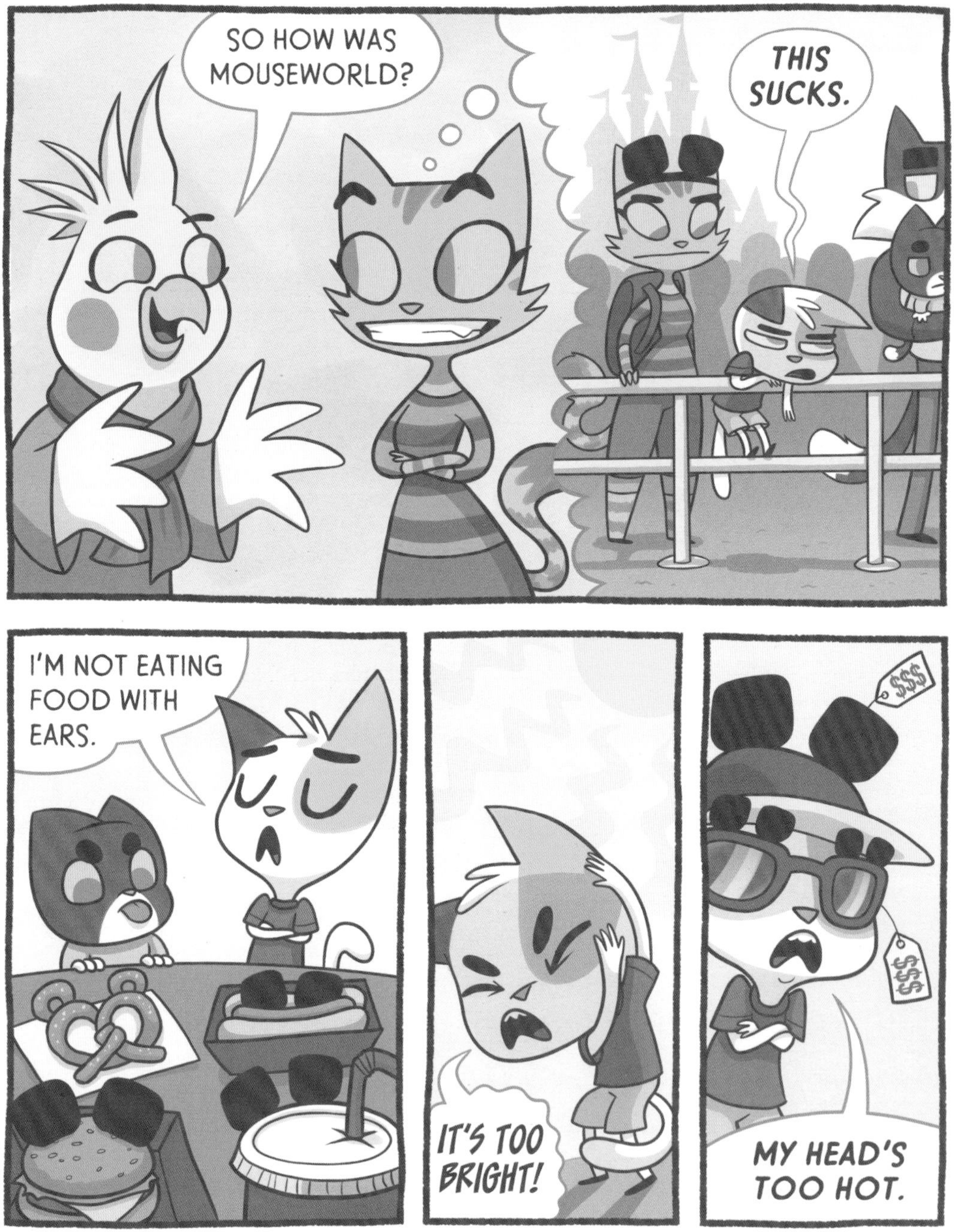
SO HOW WAS MOUSEWORLD?
THIS SUCKS.
I'M NOT EATING FOOD WITH EARS.
IT'S TOO BRIGHT!
$$$
$$$
MY HEAD'S TOO HOT.

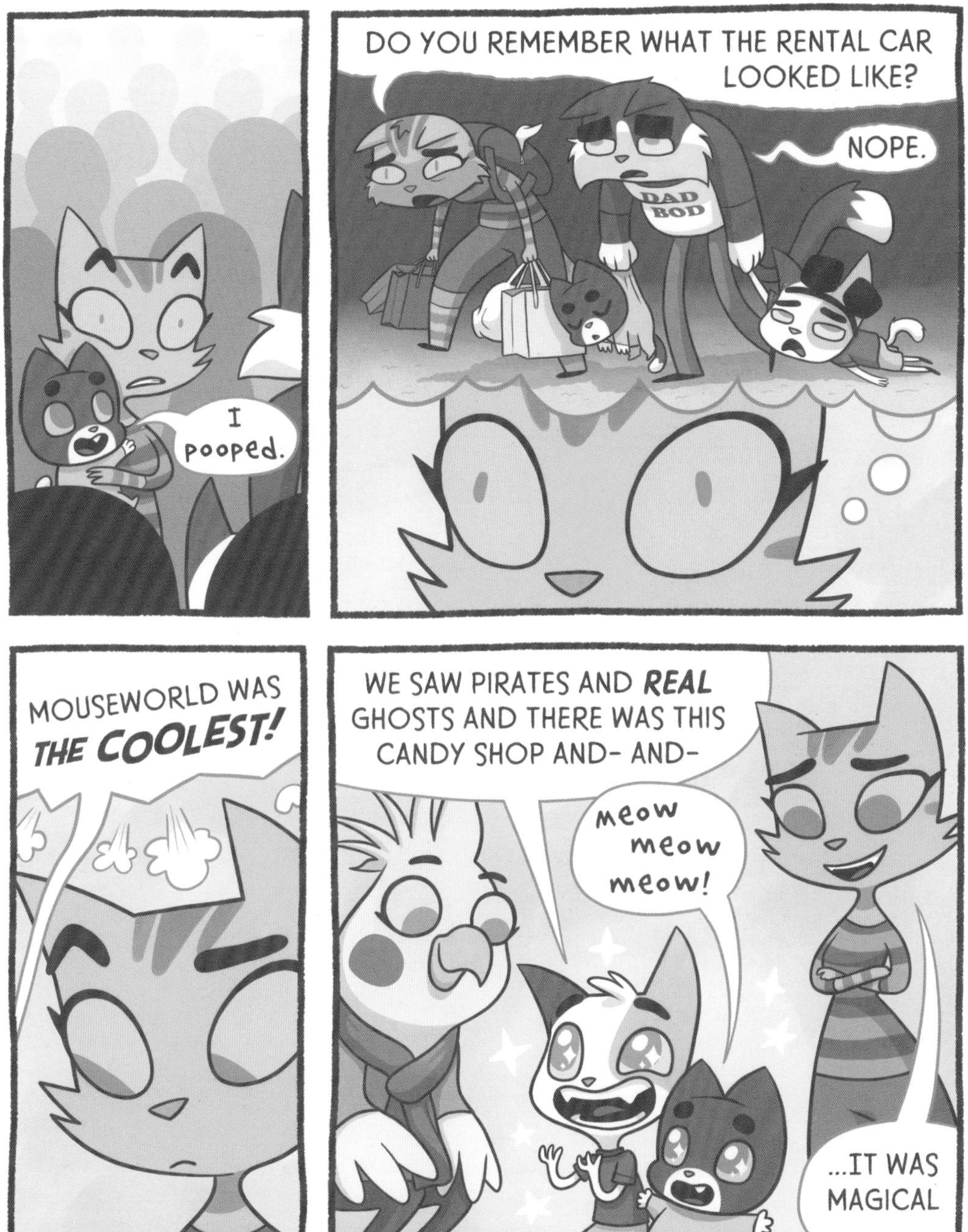
I pooped.
DO YOU REMEMBER WHAT THE RENTAL CAR LOOKED LIKE?
NOPE.
DAD BOD
MOUSEWORLD WAS THE COOLEST!
WE SAW PIRATES AND REAL GHOSTS AND THERE WAS THIS CANDY SHOP AND- AND-
meow meow meow!
...IT WAS MAGICAL

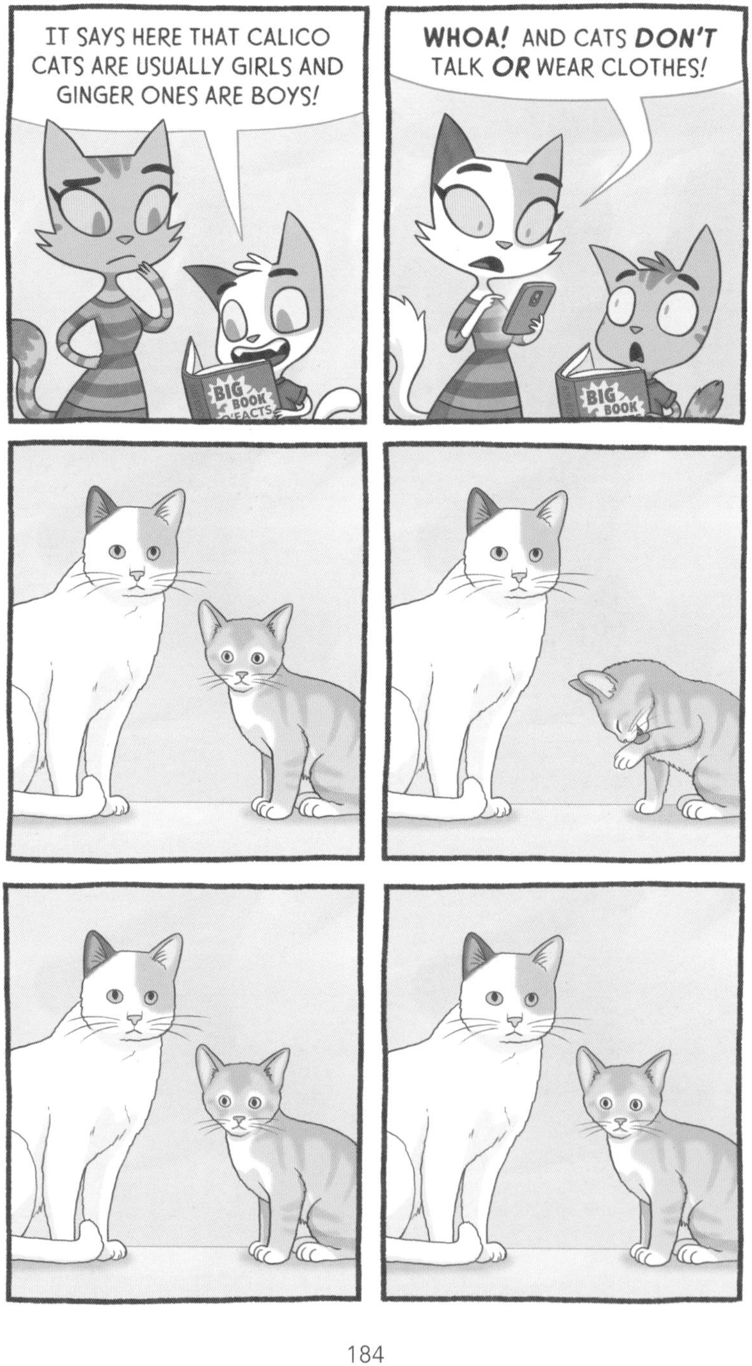
IT SAYS HERE THAT CALICO CATS ARE USUALLY GIRLS AND GINGER ONES ARE BOYS!
BIG BOOK O' FACTS
WHOA! AND CATS DON'T TALK OR WEAR CLOTHES!
BIG BOOK

Precious
Memories

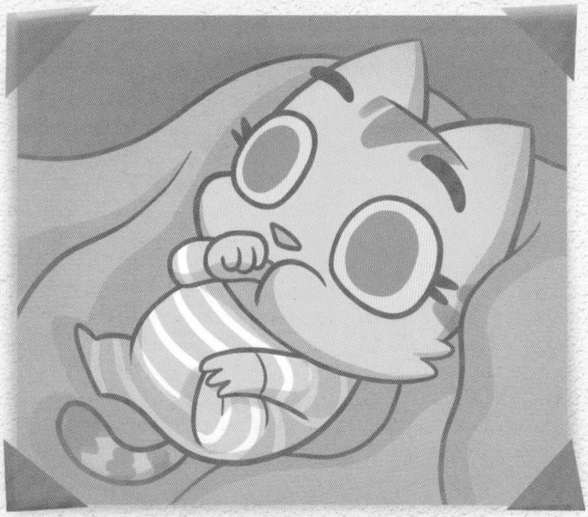

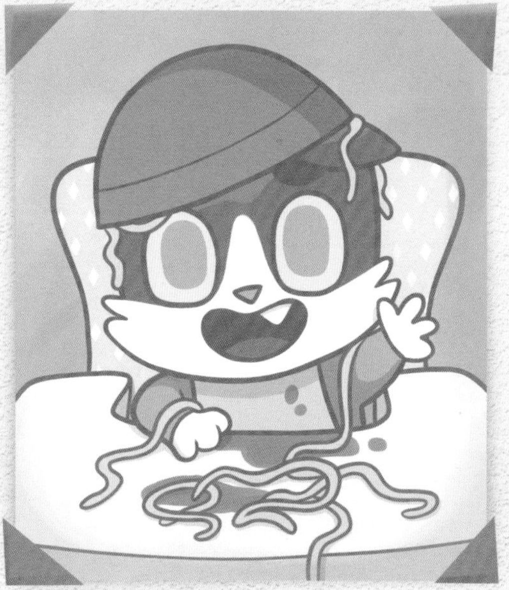

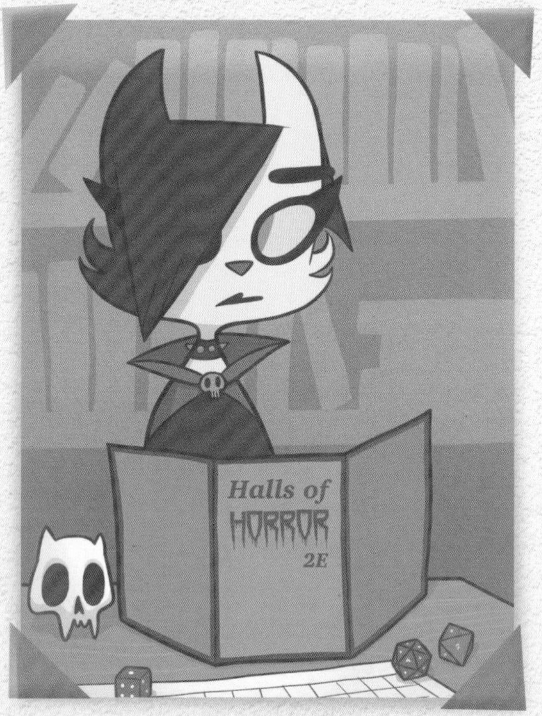
Halls of
HORROR
2E

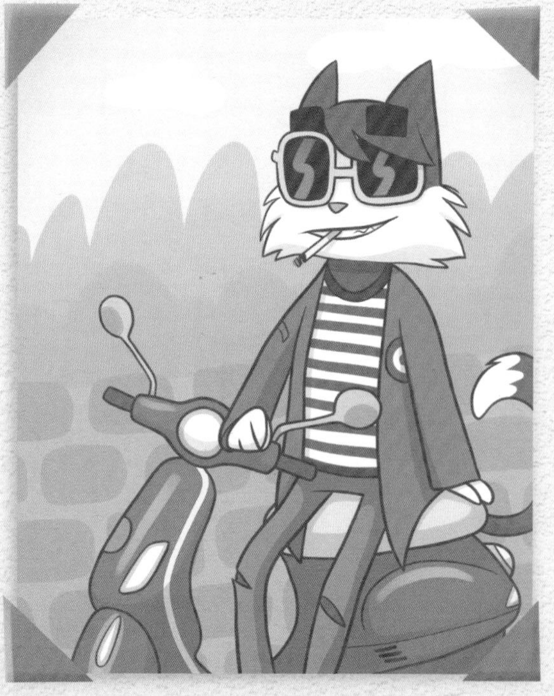

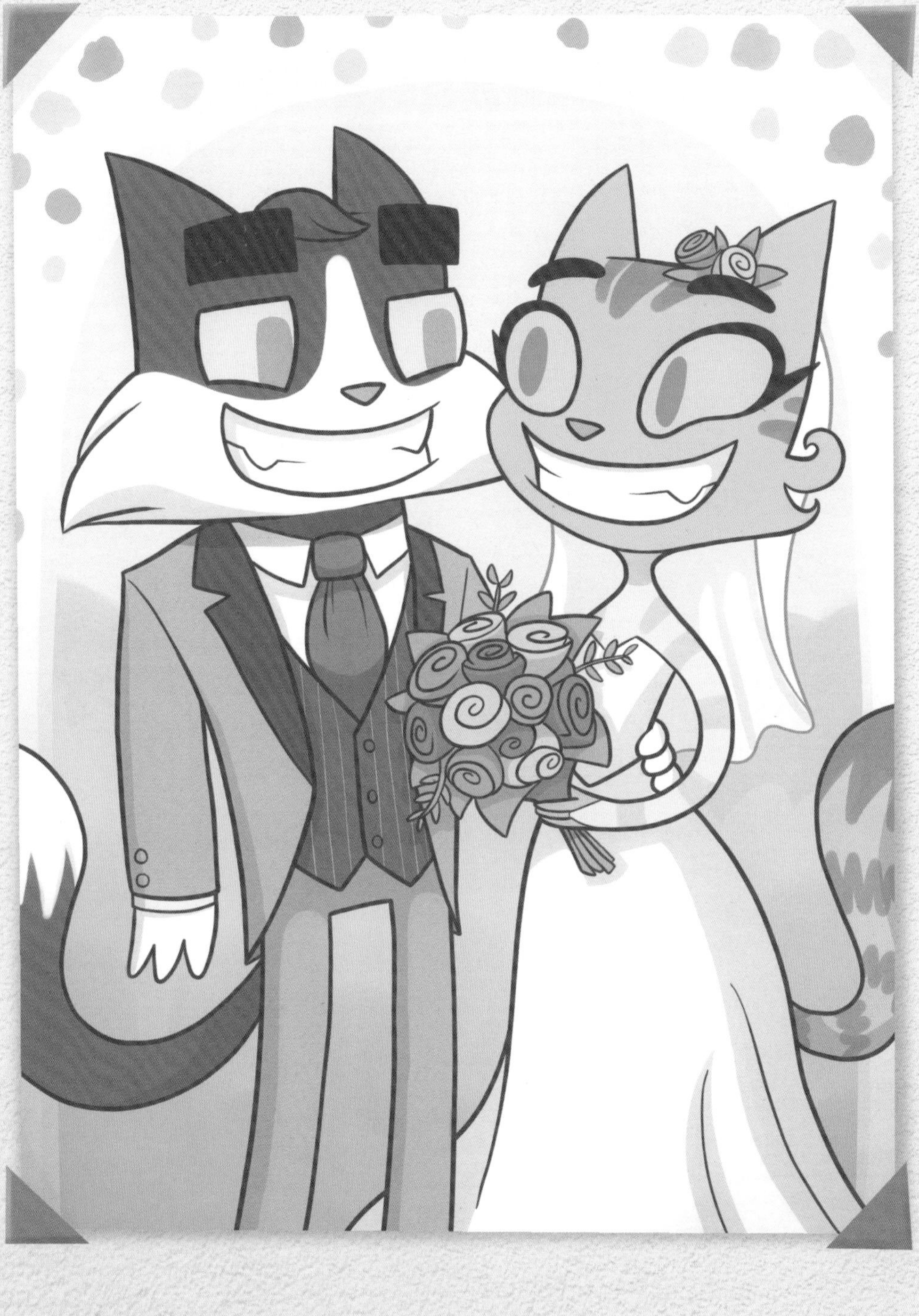

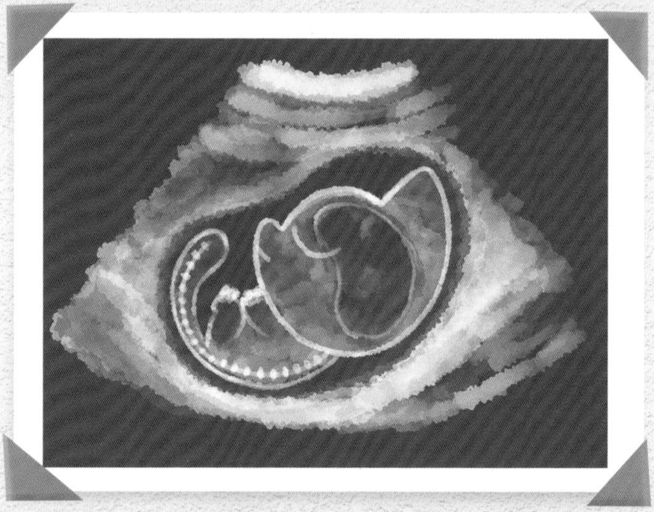

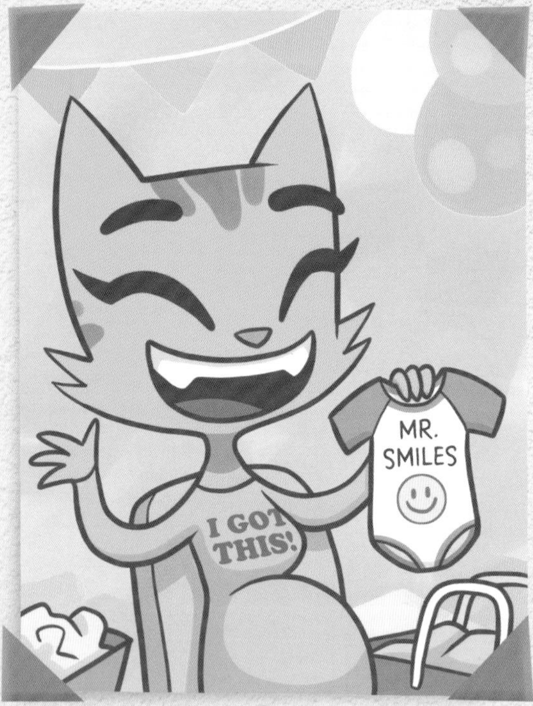
MR. SMILES
I GOT THIS!

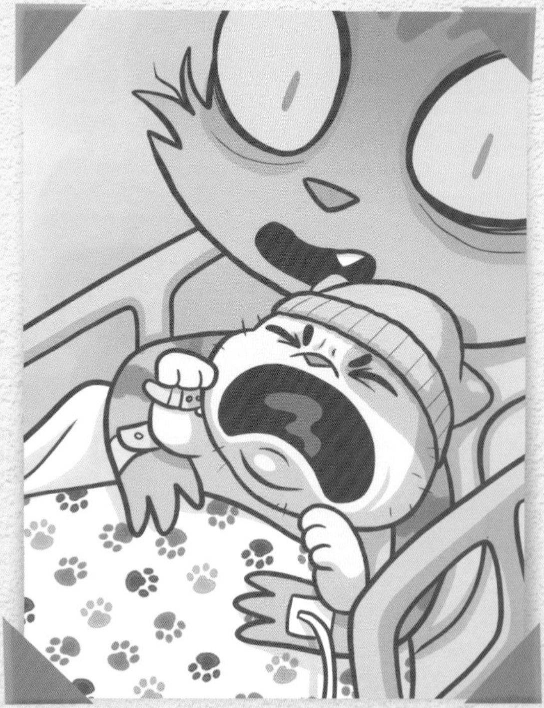

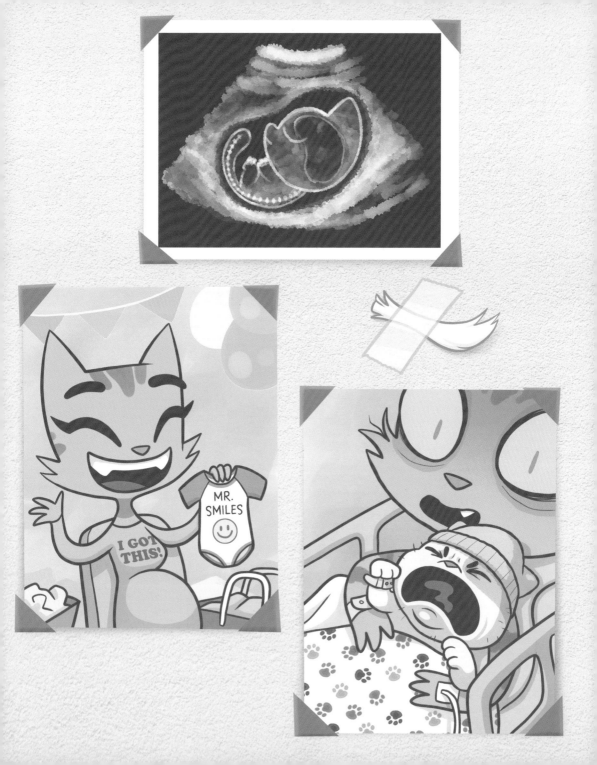

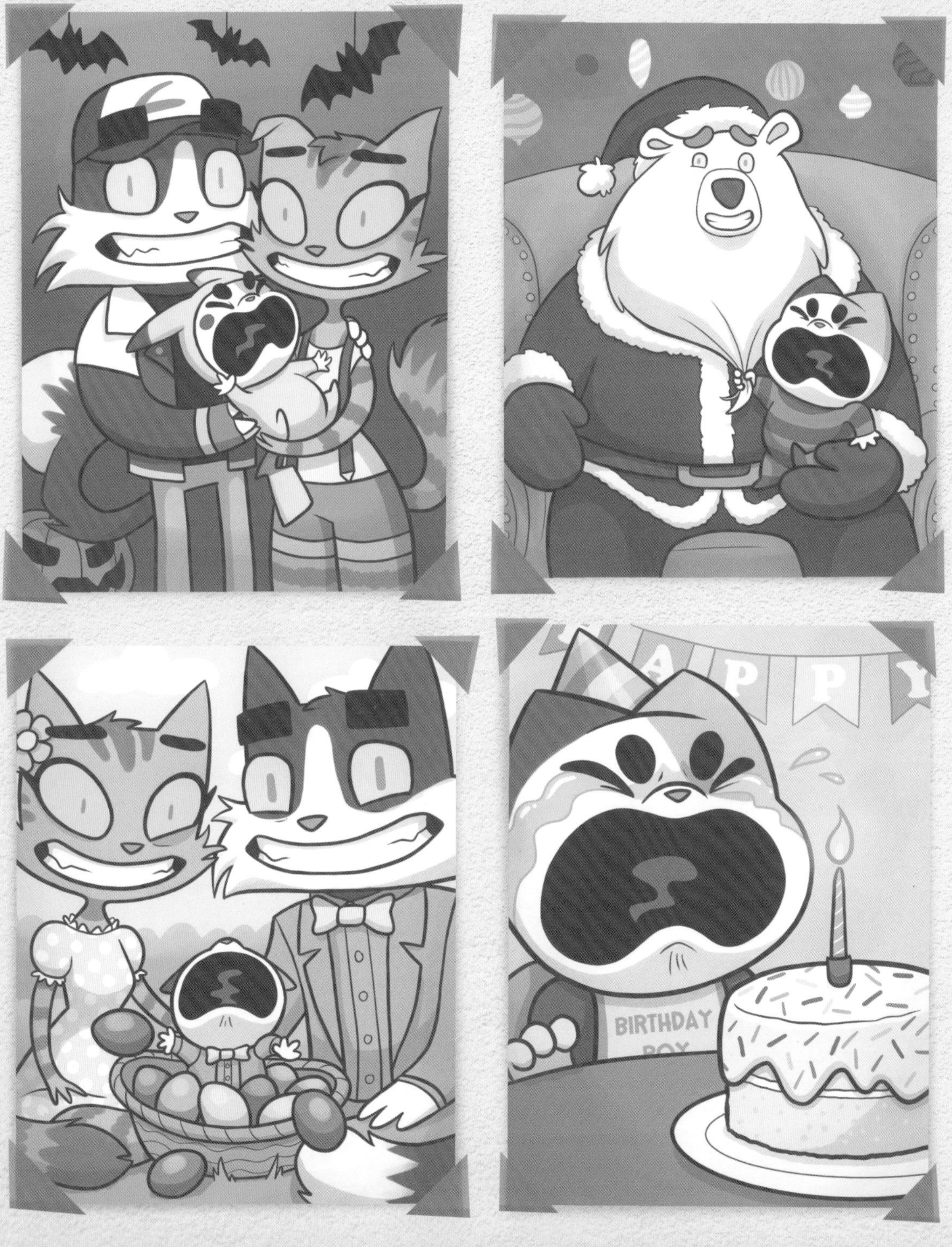
A P P
BIRTHDAY

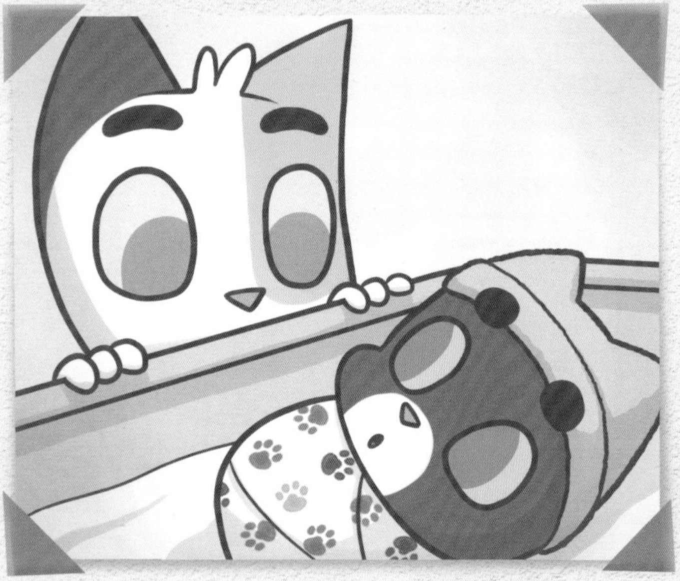

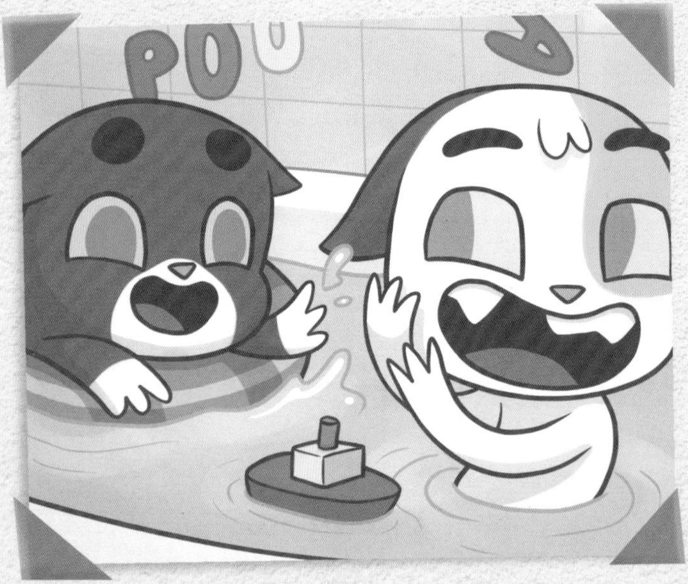

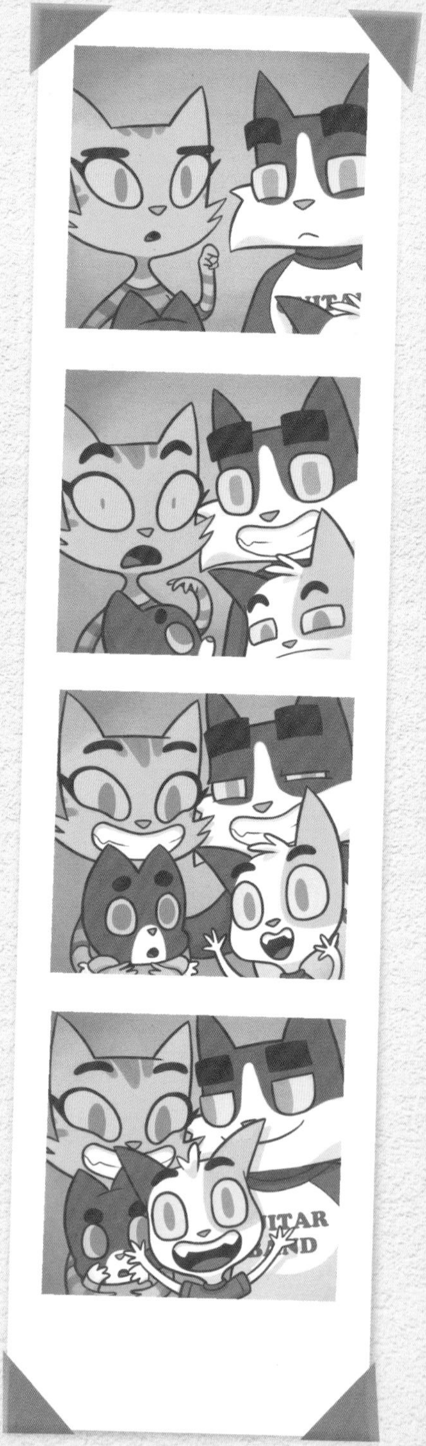

Name: Vincent

I am thankful for

MY family.

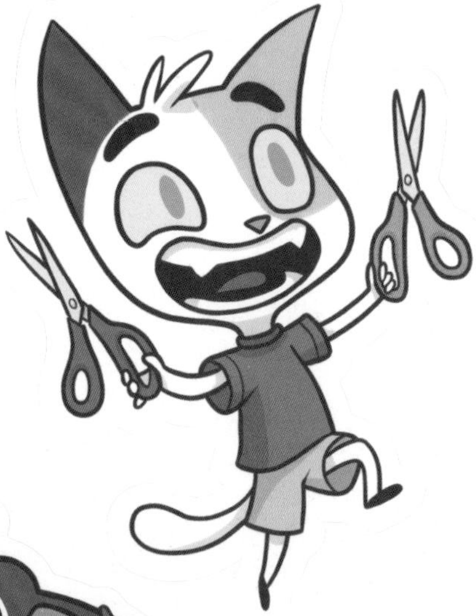

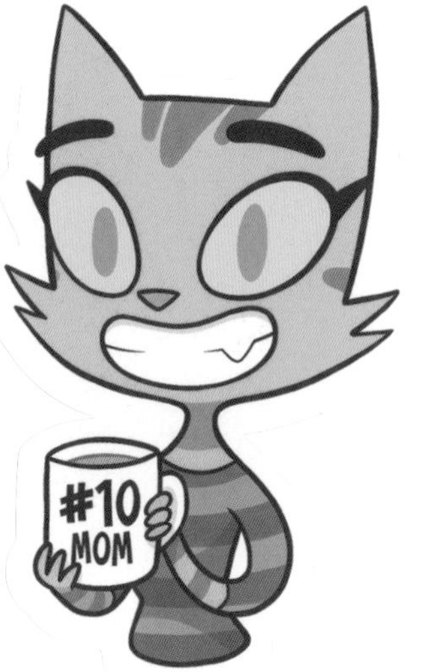
#10
MOM

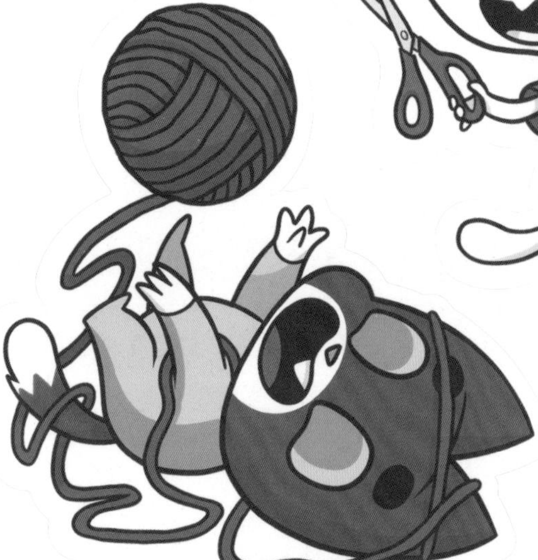

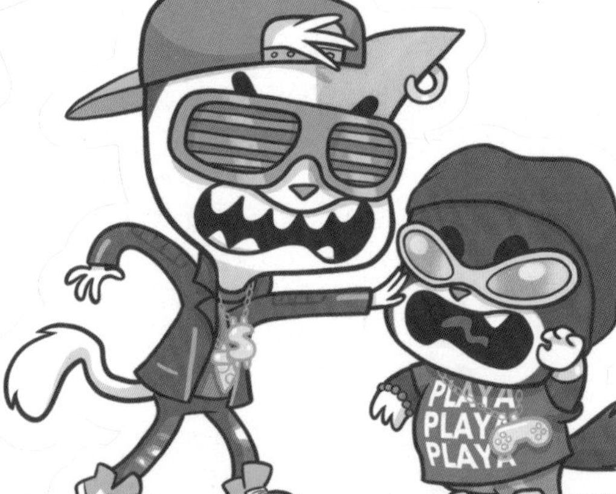
PLAYA
PLAYA
PLAYA

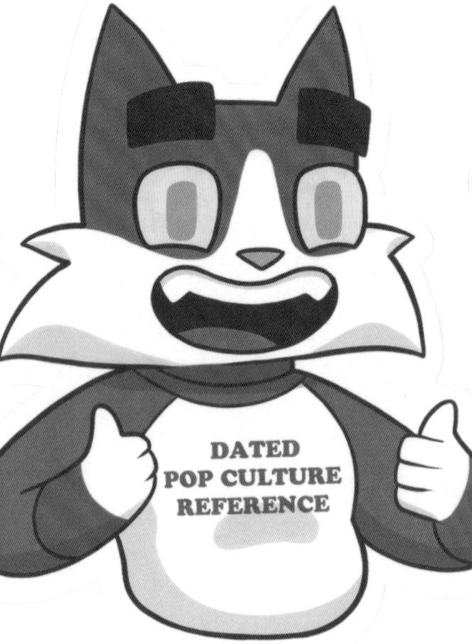
DATED
POP CULTURE
REFERENCE

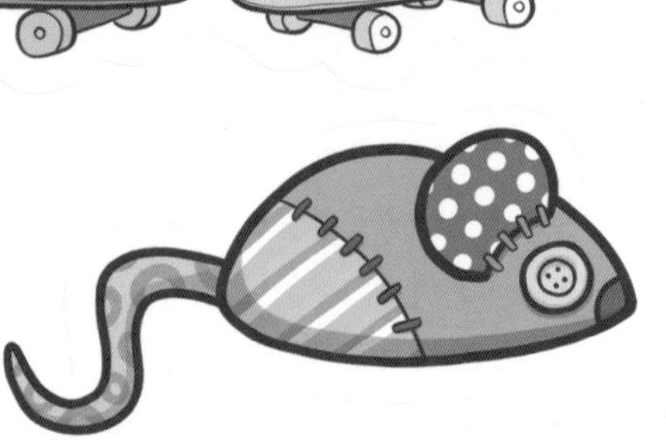